James Chapman is Professor of Film Studies at the University of Leicester. His previous books for I.B.Tauris include the bestsellers *Licence To Thrill: A Cultural History of the James Bond Films* and *Inside the Tardis: The Worlds of Doctor Who*, as well as (with Nicholas J. Cull) *Projecting Empire: Imperialism and Popular Cinema* and *Projecting Tomorrow: Science Fiction and Popular Cinema*. He is editor of the *Historical Journal of Film, Radio and Television*.

'In this judicious, authoritative, and fluent book, film historian James Chapman deftly plots the fertile marriage between the master of suspense and the espionage thriller. In doing so he achieves far more: a deeply researched and richly nuanced perspective upon the trajectory of Hitchcock's entire career after the coming of sound.'

Richard Allen, author of *Hitchcock's Romantic Irony*

'James Chapman is an authentic historian, and his expertise fully pays off in this important addition to the Hitchcock literature. His book achieves a pleasing balance between film and politics, between Hitchcock's own authorship and his multiple influences, and – especially welcome – between the British and American sections of his long career.'

Charles Barr, author of *Ealing Studios* and *The English Hitchcock*

HITCHCOCK AND THE SPY FILM

JAMES CHAPMAN

I.B. TAURIS
LONDON · NEW YORK

For my Llewella … forever

Published in 2018 by
I.B.Tauris & Co. Ltd
London • New York
www.ibtauris.com

ISBN: 978 1 78076 844 1
eISBN: 978 1 78672 307 9
ePDF: 978 1 78673 307 8

A full CIP record for this book is available from the British Library
A full CIP record is available from the Library of Congress

Library of Congress Catalog Card Number: available

Typeset in Stone Serif by OKS Prepress Services, Chennai, India
Printed and bound in Sweden by ScandBook AB

CONTENTS

ILLUSTRATIONS

Note: All the images in this book are DVD grabs which are included here under the fair dealing guidelines relating to criticism and review published by the Intellectual Property Office (June 2014).

ACKNOWLEDGEMENTS

Every film scholar should write a book on Hitchcock: this is mine. Hitchcock is a key figure not only in the history of cinema but also for film studies as an academic discipline: every major critical and theoretical perspective that has shaped the field over the last half century – from formalism and the *auteur* theory to structuralism and semiotics, from psychoanalysis and gender studies to historical reception and adaptation studies – has focused on Hitchcock at some point. To read the critical literature on Hitchcock is to learn about the intellectual history of our discipline. For that reason it seems to me that everyone interested in film probably has something to say about Hitchcock. The trick is to find something new to say: and while I believe that my focus on Hitchcock and the spy film does offer something new to the field, ultimately it is up to readers to decide how well I have achieved this.

The origins of this book extend back to my days as an undergraduate student at the University of East Anglia (1988–91) when I wrote an essay on *The 39 Steps* arguing – contrary to the received wisdom – that Hitchcock's film owed rather more to John Buchan's novel *The Thirty-Nine Steps* than had generally been allowed in the critical literature at the time. I owe a tremendous intellectual debt to Charles Barr, Emeritus Professor of Film Studies at UEA and a distinguished Hitchcock scholar, who introduced a generation of future film historians to the neglected world of British (or, as Charles would have it, English) Hitchcock. If it were not for an event of great significance in my personal life I would have dedicated this book to him: nevertheless it provides me with a welcome opportunity to acknowledge his influence in helping a passionate film enthusiast become a professional film historian.

Anyone writing on Hitchcock must acknowledge the work of previous scholars in the field while finding their own niche within it. While my bibliography lists the wide range of secondary sources that have informed this work, I should like here to place on record my appreciation of the undisputed pioneers in the field of Hitchcock scholarship: Eric Rohmer and Claude Chabrol, Robin Wood, Raymond Durgnat, Donald Spoto and William Rothman. Among the 'key texts' on which I have drawn for this study – and from which at times it has been difficult to maintain a respectable critical distance – are Tom Ryall's *Alfred Hitchcock and the British Cinema*, Robert E. Kapsis's *Hitchcock: The Making of a Reputation*, Charles Barr's *English Hitchcock*, and Patrick McGilligan's excellent biography *Alfred Hitchcock: A Life in Darkness and Light*. Many colleagues and fellow scholars have been generous with their knowledge and time but I should like to record in particular my thanks to Guy Barefoot, Alan Burton, Nick Cull, Sheldon Hall, Tobias Hochscherf, Phyllis Lassner, Paul Lesch, Laurence Napper, Jeffrey Richards and Sarah Street for sharing their thoughts and ideas over the many years in which this book has been in gestation. I am especially grateful to Richard Allen and Sid Gottlieb who invited me to contribute an essay on 'Hitchcock and Bond' to the *Hitchcock Annual* – a revised version of which appears in Chapter 13 – and to Mark Glancy, both for his excellent study of *The 39 Steps* for the 'British Film Guides' series and for kindly reading the first draft of the manuscript for this book. It is needless to say that any errors and all flights of interpretational fancy that may follow are entirely my own responsibility.

All scholars who privilege archival research, as I do, are indebted to those unsung heroes working in libraries and archives who make our research possible in the first place. This book simply could not have been written the way I wanted to write it without access to a wide range of both unpublished and published primary source materials. So stand up and take a bow, please, Jonny Davies (Special Collections Unit, British Film Institute Reuben Library, BFI Southbank, London), Harold L. Miller (Center for Film and Theater Research, Wisconsin Historical Society, University of Wisconsin – Madison), and Barbara Hall and Jenny Romero (Special Collections Department, Margaret Herrick Library, Academy of Motion Picture Arts and Sciences, Los Angeles).

Philippa Brewster, my commissioning editor at I.B.Tauris, has been supportive of this project from the outset, and like all the best publishers has been tactfully solicitous in enquiring of its progress and unfailingly patient as the original submission date was repeatedly pushed back. It seems a long time since our first emails were exchanged about *Hitchcock and the Spy Film* in 2011 and the fact that it has taken longer than expected to reach completion is due entirely to my own tardiness in getting down to writing it!

Finally, this is the first book that my wife, Llewella, has seen through the entirety of its writing. She has endured my moods and frustrations with greater tolerance than I deserve, and has accepted my long 'writing days' without complaint. She has also indulged my cricket metaphors, from the dog days when I could barely work the ball off the square to the glorious days when I was playing scoring shots freely all around the wicket. I cannot adequately express how much I love her or how richer my life is with her in it. This book is dedicated to her, as is its author.

ABBREVIATIONS

ABPC	Associated British Picture Corporation
AMPAS	Academy of Motion Picture Arts and Sciences
BBFC	British Board of Film Censors
BFI	British Film Institute
BIP	British International Pictures
CIA	Central Intelligence Agency
FBI	Federal Bureau of Investigation
GBPC	Gaumont-British Picture Corporation
MGM	Metro-Goldwyn-Mayer
MOI	Ministry of Information
OWI	Office of War Information
PCA	Production Code Administration

INTRODUCTION: AUTHORSHIP, GENRE, NATIONAL CINEMA

Alfred Hitchcock directed 53 feature films during a career that lasted half a century: twelve of those were spy films. Hitchcock's popular reputation as the 'master of suspense' was built on the back of the five spy pictures he directed in Britain in the 1930s – *The Man Who Knew Too Much* (1934), *The 39 Steps* (1935), *Secret Agent* (1936), *Sabotage* (1936) and *The Lady Vanishes* (1938) – and he returned periodically to the genre throughout his Hollywood career: *Foreign Correspondent* (1940), *Saboteur* (1942), *Notorious* (1946), *The Man Who Knew Too Much* (1956), *North by Northwest* (1959), *Torn Curtain* (1966) and *Topaz* (1969). Hitchcock was the first major film-maker to specialise in the genre: Eric Rohmer and Claude Chabrol, whose original auteurist study is one of the milestones of Hitchcock scholarship, averred that Hitchcock's spy films of the 1930s marked the emergence of a new cinematic genre which they dubbed 'le feuilleton d'espionage intelligent' ('the intelligent espionage thriller').[1] Indeed the spy film is more representative of Hitchcock's work than other thriller variants such as the murder mystery or the horror film: its prominence in Hitchcock's *œuvre* is such that these dozen films constitute a distinct group in their own right.

Hitchcock and the Spy Film sets out to position Hitchcock's work in relation to the history of the spy film in popular cinema. It differs from most Hitchcock scholarship in so far as it is not primarily an auteurist analysis – though inevitably the idea of Hitchcock as *auteur* features prominently – but rather an attempt to locate his spy films in their wider cultural and institutional contexts. It will explore Hitchcock's contribution to the evolution of the spy film in British and American cinema, but it will also consider the extent to which Hitchcock's authorial identity was shaped by the genre in which he became the pre-eminent specialist. The relationship between authorship and genre was the focus of much early genre criticism: Jim Kitses, for example, subtitled *Horizons West*, his classic study of the definitive American film genre, 'studies of Authorship within the Western'.[2] Just as the Western provided fertile ground for directors such as John Ford, Anthony Mann and Sam Peckinpah to explore their fascination with American national identity and the American past, Hitchcock found in the spy film a particularly suitable vehicle for his interest in stories of suspense and paranoia. As Lindsay Anderson – writing in 1949 about the British thrillers – observed: 'All these films are melodramas – stories of violence and adventure in which the emphasis is on incident rather than on characters or ideas. Hitchcock had himself come to realise that this was the form ideally suited to his talent and his temperament.'[3]

Any new study of Hitchcock has to contend with the massive volume of scholarship already devoted to cinema's best-known *auteur*. [4] There are very few Hitchcock films that can genuinely be described as unknown or neglected. Some of the films included herein, especially *The 39 Steps* and *North by Northwest*, are already very familiar texts in Hitchcock scholarship. Even so there is a tendency to regard them as Hitchcock films first and foremost and as spy films only secondarily if at all. (Two notable exceptions to this generalisation are Mark Glancy's 'British Film Guide' on *The 39 Steps* and James Naremore's introduction to the published screenplay of *North by Northwest* for the 'Rutgers Films in Print' series which both explore the films' origins in the tradition of British spy fiction.)[5] Other films are either typically regarded as minor Hitchcock works, such as the wartime American films *Foreign Correspondent* and *Saboteur*, or as flawed efforts, such as *Secret Agent* and *Sabotage*, neither of which proved as successful with critics or audiences as the consummately realised classic *The 39 Steps*, or the brace of 1960s Cold War thrillers, *Torn Curtain* and *Topaz*, both little regarded and often seen as exemplary of Hitchcock's declining years. The relative neglect of Hitchcock's spy films in comparison to some of his other work might be explained in part by their status as genre films: the preference of many *auteur* critics has been for Hitchcock's more personal films such as *Shadow of a Doubt* (1943), *Vertigo* (1958) and *Psycho* (1960). Indeed Hitchcock himself seems to have endorsed this view when he told two interviewers that '*North by Northwest* is an adventure film, treated with a certain levity of spirit. *Vertigo* is much more important to me than *North by Northwest*.'[6]

It is easy to understand why Hitchcock was championed by the early *auteur* critics – exemplified by the *Cahiers du Cinéma* group in France in the 1950s and by Anglophone critics such as Andrew Sarris and Robin Wood in the 1960s. Hitchcock was the *auteur* director *par excellence*: a film-maker whose work revealed consistent patterns and recurring motifs throughout the course of a long career (Hitchcock's active career as a director lasted from the mid-1920s until his last film *Family Plot* was released in 1976). In fact film critics had recognised Hitchcock's unique directorial style long before the emergence of the *auteur* theory. For example, Dilys Powell, the long-serving critic of the *Sunday Times,* remarked in her review of *Foreign Correspondent*: 'This is genuine Hitchcock, the kind of chiaroscuro of sinister and jolly which Hitchcock handles better than any other living director.'[7] What distinguished the *auteur* critics, however, was the assertion that Hitchcock deserved to be taken seriously as an artist – hitherto he had tended to be seen as a technically proficient but not particularly important film-maker – and that his films reflected a distinctive and coherent worldview. Rohmer and Chabrol, for example, see Hitchcock as a moralist whose interest in the themes of guilt, innocence and paranoia was a means of exploring existential and psychological conditions. They argue that his films always feature some form of 'exchange': 'The idea of the "exchange", which we find everywhere in his work, may be given either a moral expression (the transfer of guilt), a psychological expression (suspicion), a dramatic expression (blackmail – or even pure "suspense"), or a concrete expression (a to-and-fro movement).'[8] For Robin Wood, whose 1965 study *Hitchcock's Films* is another seminal auteurist text, the evidence for Hitchcock's artistry was to be found in the 'unity' of his films. Wood's preference was for Hitchcock's 'mature' films of the 1950s and 1960s – from *Strangers on a Train* (1951) to *Marnie* (1964) – as they revealed 'a consistent development, deepening and clarification' which 'seems to me the mark of an important artist – essentially, that which distinguishes the significant from the worthless'.[9]

Hitchcock's spy films fit easily into the critical framework of *auteur* theory as they mobilise the same recurring narrative patterns and thematic motifs. They usually feature an ordinary hero plunged by chance into a 'chaos world' of international espionage and political intrigue (professional spies are much less common in Hitchcock's films than the 'amateur' protagonist) and narratively they are constructed around a succession of suspense set pieces in which the hero is placed in situations of extreme jeopardy. Peter Wollen (writing under the pseudonym Lee Russell) saw 'the theme of chaos narrowly underlying order' as a recurring motif of Hitchcock's films: Hitchcock's protagonists 'are plunged into an anti-world of chaos and disorder'.[10] Hence a casual encounter in a music hall (*The 39 Steps*) or a simple case of mistaken identity (*North by Northwest*) propels the protagonist into extraordinary and life-threatening situations. Apparently normal locations turn out to be sites of danger and intrigue: a non-conformist chapel is the cover for a gang of anarchists (*The Man Who Knew Too Much*), a chocolate factory is a spy post office (*Secret Agent*) and a suburban cinema turns out to be a terrorist's hide-out (*Sabotage*). Other recurring motifs of Hitchcock's spy films include the suave and outwardly respectable chief villain (*The 39 Steps, Foreign Correspondent, Saboteur, Notorious, North by Northwest*) and the suspense climax set in or around a famous landmark (the Albert Hall in *The Man Who Knew Too Much*, the Statue of Liberty in *Saboteur*, Mount Rushmore in *North by Northwest*). Perhaps the most famous 'Hitchcockian' device is what he referred to as the 'MacGuffin': the object that sets the plot in motion such as a stolen aeroplane engine design (*The 39 Steps*), the secret clause of an international treaty (*The Lady Vanishes*), the uranium for an atomic bomb (*Notorious*) or the plans for a missile system (*Torn Curtain*). Hitchcock explained the role of the 'MacGuffin' thus: '"MacGuffin" is the term we use to cover all that sort of thing: to steal plans or documents, or discover a secret, it doesn't matter what it is … The only thing that really matters is that in the picture the plans, documents, or secrets must seem to be of vital importance to the characters. To me, the narrator, they're of no importance whatever.'[11]

There are of course many flaws with the *auteur* theory. In its purest form it becomes reductive: everything in the film is seen as the outcome of the director's creative agency and as an expression of his 'worldview'. It can also become excessively hermetic: the *auteur* and his films are seen to exist as if in a vacuum sealed off from the industrial and economic conditions in which the films were produced. And its emphasis on the individuality and uniqueness of the *auteur* neglects any comparative framework that considers what their films might have in common with, as well as how they are different from, those of other film-makers working in the same institutional and cultural contexts. As Tom Ryall puts it in the introduction to his book *Alfred Hitchcock and the British Cinema*:

> *Auteur* criticism has wrenched films and their directors from the historical circumstances of production and has defined the expression of the author's consciousness as responsible for the shape, form and meaning of a text. The individuality and uniqueness of the authorial *oeuvre* has often been an assumption based upon a self-contained study of a director's work rather than a quality requiring demonstration through comparison with, for example, the norms and conventions of film making during the period of the author. If Hitchcock's British work does display such qualities of individuality, the activity of returning the films to their historical context will reveal this more certainly.[12]

Of course there is an argument that Hitchcock was something of a special case: he was always closely involved in the writing of his films even if he rarely took a screen credit, and in the later stages of his career he enjoyed greater autonomy over most aspects of the production of his films than most of his contemporaries. Yet even so Hitchcock did not work in a vacuum: his films should be understood in the economic and ideological contexts of the film industries in which he worked.

A welcome trend of recent Hitchcock scholarship has been to consider Hitchcock the *auteur* in a less hermetic context. Charles Barr's *English Hitchcock*, for example, shows how the narrative and thematic patterns of Hitchcock's films of the 1920s and 1930s took shape through his collaborations with particular writers, notably Eliot Stannard and Charles Bennett. The latter is particularly important for a study of Hitchcock's spy films: Bennett – a prolific playwright and screenwriter whose work included *Blackmail*, a play which Hitchcock adapted for his, and Britain's, first talking picture in 1929 – was involved in the scripting of five of Hitchcock's spy pictures between 1934 and 1940: *The Man Who Knew Too Much*, *The 39 Steps*, *Secret Agent*, *Sabotage* and *Foreign Correspondent*. This is not to set up Bennett as an alternative *auteur* to Hitchcock but rather to consider how Bennett's contribution to the structure of the films helped to crystallise the 'distinctive and dynamic narrative frameworks for the kinds of theme and effect that were already consistently recognisable in Hitchcock's output'.[13] Similarly the recent critical interest in the relationship between Hitchcock's films and their source texts – exemplified in collections edited by R. Barton Palmer and David Boyd (*Hitchcock at the Source*) and Mark Osteen (*Hitchcock and Adaptation*) – 'breaks new ground by restoring to critical focus the shaping power of the director's literary sources, which constitute an important element of his cinematic authorship'.[14] Hitchcock was not only the master of suspense but also a master of adaptation: 41 of his 53 feature films were based on literary or theatrical properties.[15]

The fact that several of Hitchcock's spy films are based on novels – including *The 39 Steps*, *Secret Agent*, *Sabotage*, *The Lady Vanishes* and *Topaz* – locates them in a tradition of popular fiction that has particular cultural and ideological roots. The spy story emerged in British popular fiction around the turn of the twentieth century – exemplified by William Le Queux's *The Great War in England* (1893), E. Phillips Oppenheim's *The Mysterious Mr Sabin* (1898), Erskine Childers's *The Riddle of the Sands* (1903), Edgar Wallace's *The Four Just Men* (1905), Joseph Conrad's *The Secret Agent* (1907) and G. K. Chesterton's *The Man Who Was Thursday* (1908) – when it has been seen as a reflection of increasing international tension in the decade or so before the First World War: *The Riddle of the Sands*, for example, drew upon British anxiety over the rise of German naval power. From there the history of the spy thriller is usually mapped through the work of key authors whose work has either defined the genre or has represented a significant shift within it: the adventure stories of John Buchan (whose most famous protagonist, Richard Hannay, first appeared in *The Thirty-Nine Steps* in 1915) and 'Sapper' (whose Bulldog Drummond made his debut in 1919) during the interwar period, the greater realism of W. Somerset Maugham's *Ashenden* (1928), the early novels of Graham Greene and Eric Ambler in the 1930s, the snobbery-with-violence thrillers of Ian Fleming (whose 'secret agent' James Bond first appeared in *Casino Royale* in 1953) and the cynical 'anti-Bond' novels of John le Carré, Len Deighton and others in the 1960s.

Spy fiction – whether in literature or in film and television – shares common features with other related genres such as the detective story, but it is defined by its narrative focus on the subject matter of spying and espionage. Some of Sir Arthur Conan Doyle's Sherlock Holmes stories and Agatha Christie's mysteries, for example, feature spying in a secondary capacity but are best understood as detective stories. On one level spy fiction reflects – albeit usually in an exaggerated and distorted way – the world of 'real' espionage and counter-espionage: it is no coincidence that several prominent authors of spy fiction have worked for the intelligence services, whether on the periphery, such as Somerset Maugham and Graham Greene, or more directly, such as Ian Fleming, assistant to the Director of Naval Intelligence during the Second World War, and John le Carré, an officer of the Secret Intelligence Service, popularly known as MI6, before he become a full-time writer.[16] On another level the spy story has been understood as a vehicle for exploring wider social and political anxieties: the dominant way of 'reading' spy fiction has been as a reflection of the historical and ideological landscape against which the fiction is set. As Michael Denning writes in the introduction to his book *Cover Stories*:

> Since the turn of the century, spy thrillers have been 'cover stories' for our culture, collective fantasies in the imagination of the English-speaking world, paralleling reality, expressing what they wish to conceal, and telling the 'History of Contemporary Society'. Thrillers use cover stories about assumed identities and double agents, and take their plots from the cover stories of the daily news; and their tales of spies, moles, and the secret service have become a cover story, translating the political and cultural transformations of the twentieth century into the intrigues of a shadow world of secret agents.[17]

It is no coincidence that the key moments in the development of spy fiction have been during periods of ideological tension in global politics. The spy story emerged during the period of imperial rivalries before the First World War; it was transformed during the interwar period when it reflected the uncertainty of a world challenged by the competing ideological systems of Fascism and Communism; and it reached its height of popularity during the Cold War where the global division into two opposing geopolitical and ideological power blocs provided ideal subject matter for the genre. In Britain, especially, spy fiction has been read as a narrative of the decline of British power: Denning avers that 'the spy thriller narrates the crises and contradictions in ideologies of nation and Empire and of class and gender'.[18]

The critical literature on the spy thriller has focused mostly on its literary form, and typically maps its history through two parallel lineages or taxonomies. Denning, for example, distinguishes 'between those that we might call magical thrillers, where there is a clear contest between Good and Evil with a virtuous hero defeating an alien and evil villain, and those that we might call existential thrillers, which play on a dialectic of good and evil overdetermined by moral dilemmas'.[19] These lineages might also be described as the sensational and realist modes of the thriller. On the one hand the magical or sensational thriller is characterised by an emphasis on adventure and action, by fast-moving narratives of chase and pursuit, and by a public-school ethos of spying as a game or sport. It is exemplified on either side of the First World War by the stories of William Le Queux and E. Phillips Oppenheim, with their tales of intrigue in the courts and governments of Europe, and during and after the war by the fiction of John Buchan and 'Sapper', with their upstanding, patriotic heroes protecting the British Empire from the ambitions of antagonistic foreign powers and international anarchists. The sensational thriller reached its height with Ian Fleming's James Bond, who was pitted against dastardly espionage organisations SMERSH (a contraction of the Russian *Smiert Spionam* – 'Death to Spies') and SPECTRE (the Special Executive for Counter-Intelligence, Terrorism, Revenge and Extortion) and diabolical master criminals such as Le Chiffre, Mr Big, Dr No, Goldfinger and Ernst Stavro Blofeld. On the other hand the existential or realist thriller is more concerned with characterisation and psychology than with action, and tends to use the activity of spying as a means of exploring social and existential anxieties. It is exemplified by Joseph Conrad's *The Secret Agent* and W. Somerset Maugham's *Ashenden* and by the novels of Eric Ambler and Graham Greene with their innocent protagonists accidentally and reluctantly caught up in the world of espionage and international skulduggery. It also reached its height during the Cold War when the novels of John le Carré and Len Deighton portrayed espionage as a seedy activity that was the antithesis of the glamorous and sophisticated world of James Bond. The 'mole-hunt' narratives of le Carré and Deighton also responded to the revelation of Soviet penetration of Britain's security services following the exposure and defections of intelligence officers Guy Burgess and Donald Maclean (1951) and Harold 'Kim' Philby (1963).

The history of the spy thriller in cinema has been less fully documented and analysed than its literary counterpart but even a brief overview of the genre indicates that similar taxonomies emerge: perhaps this is not surprising given that many spy films have been adapted from literary sources. The first films focusing on the activities of spies and secret agents were produced on the eve of the First World War: films such as *Lieutenant Rose and the Secret Code* (1911) and *Lieutenant Daring and the Mine Fields* (1912) reflected increasing international tensions with their foreign agents threatening Britain's naval security. Fritz Lang's *Spione* (*Spies*, 1928) in Germany marked 'the first true espionage feature, as opposed to adventures, romances or comedies on the spy motif'.[20] While its melodramatic devices and master criminal reminiscent of Lang's Dr Mabuse locate it firmly within the sensational lineage of the thriller, *Spione* also reflects something of the political unrest and uncertainty of the period immediately before the rise of National Socialism. However, it was in British cinema during the 1930s that the spy film really emerged as a genre in its own right: Hitchcock's films for the Gaumont-British Picture Corporation were part of a production trend across the industry as a whole that peaked in the years leading up to the Second World War. Peter John Dyer argues that 'there was a school of British thrillers as effective as Hollywood's Chans and Motos and as national as Duvivier's *Tête d'Un Homme*': Hitchcock was its foremost practitioner but there were others including Walter Forde, who made a triptych of lively spy thrillers – *Rome Express* (1932), *Bulldog Jack* (1935) and *The Four Just Men* (1939) – and Carol Reed, whose *Night Train to Munich* (1940) was a sequel of sorts to Hitchcock's *The Lady Vanishes*.[21] Hitchcock's British spy films included examples of both the sensational (*The Man Who Knew Too Much*, *The 39 Steps*, *The Lady Vanishes*) and the existential (*Secret Agent*, *Sabotage*) thriller: this to-ing and fro-ing between the two modes would continue into his American films. Otherwise the sensational spy thriller is exemplified by the various screen incarnations of Bulldog Drummond produced in Britain and Hollywood during the 1930s and by the series of James Bond films beginning with *Dr No* in 1962, while the existential lineage is represented by films such as Carol Reed's *The Fallen Idol* (1948) and *The Third Man* (1949), by John Frankenheimer's exemplary paranoid conspiracy thriller *The Manchurian Candidate* (1962), and by the cycle of 'anti-Bond' films headed by *The Spy Who Came in from the Cold* (1965) and *The Ipcress File* (1965).

It is not difficult to see why Hitchcock was drawn to the thriller, and to the spy thriller in particular. The thriller was the ideal genre for a film-maker interested in the mechanics of story-telling and the manipulation of audiences. Steve Neale suggests that the defining characteristic of the thriller in cinema is not so much its content as its mode of address: 'Whatever the structure, whatever the specificity of the diegesis in any particular thriller, the genre as a whole, unlike that of the gangster film or the detective story, is specified in the first instance by its address, by the fact that it always, though in different ways, must have the generation of suspense as its core activity.'[22] Hitchcock always maintained that he was interested in suspense rather than surprise and therefore preferred the thriller to the detective or mystery story because 'mystery is seldom suspenseful. In a whodunit, for instance, there is no suspense, but a sort of intellectual puzzle. The whodunit generates a kind of curiosity that is void of emotion and emotion is an essential ingredient of suspense.'[23] And it is hardly surprising that a director whose films are so often constructed around the act of looking (or spying) should have come to specialise in the spy film. Indeed Hitchcock's films are often about spying even when they are not actually about spies as such: *Rear Window* (1954) – where James Stewart's character Jeff becomes an unseen voyeur spying on his neighbours with the aid of binoculars and a telephoto lens – is the best-known example.

To consider Hitchcock's spy films as spy films rather than solely as Hitchcock films is to open up a different perspective on their narrative conventions and genre motifs. For example, the motif of the 'chaos world' of anarchy and subversion is as much an aspect of the thriller genre as a whole as it is of Hitchcock's films specifically. In fact many supposedly 'Hitchcockian' characteristics – including the innocent protagonist caught up in mystery and intrigue, the narrative of chase and pursuit, and the abstract plot object that Hitchcock called the 'MacGuffin' – were already well established in spy fiction by the 1930s. It is significant in this regard that all bar one of Hitchcock's British spy thrillers were adapted from novels: and even the one original screenplay (*The Man Who Knew Too Much*) had started out as a Bulldog Drummond film. The work of John Buchan was undoubtedly an important influence on the development of the 'Hitchcockian' thriller. Hitchcock acknowledged that 'Buchan was a strong influence a long time before I undertook *The Thirty-nine Steps*, and some of it is reflected in *The Man Who Knew Too Much* ... What I find appealing in Buchan's work is his understatement of highly dramatic ideas.'[24] From Buchan, for example, comes the motif of the 'thin protection of civilisation' that some commentators have attributed to Hitchcock. As Sir Edward Leithen reflects in Buchan's novel *The Power-House* (1913): 'Now I saw how thin is the protection of civilisation. An accident and a bogus ambulance – a false charge and a bogus arrest – there were a dozen ways of spiriting me out of this gay, bustling world.'[25]

Hitchcock's spy films span a period of 35 years – from *The Man Who Knew Too Much* in 1934 to *Topaz* in 1969 – and encompass both British and American cinema: therefore to examine them historically allows us to map the development of Hitchcock's film-making not only over time but also across two different national cinemas. A common feature of much *auteur* criticism is that it privileges Hitchcock's later American films which are often seen as richer and more complex than his earlier work in Britain in terms of both their themes and their formal characteristics. Few today would accept Robin Wood's sweeping dismissal (in 1965) of the British films as being 'so overshadowed by his recent development as to seem, in retrospect, little more than 'prentice work, interesting chiefly because they are Hitchcock's ... The notion that the British films are better than, or as good as, or comparable with the later Hollywood ones seems to me not worth discussion'.[26] Indeed, Wood would later retract his 'embarrassingly ignorant and supercilious dismissal of the first half of Hitchcock's career'.[27] Ironically it was an American academic, Maurice Yacowar, who was the first to argue that Hitchcock's British films were more than apprentice works: 'One can watch Hitchcock's British films in order to come to a better understanding of his American ones. But also because they are so good in themselves, so moving, so thoughtful and so much fun.'[28] Nevertheless it would still be fair to say that even after the reappraisal of British (or English) Hitchcock by film historians such as Tom Ryall and Charles Barr, the British years usually tend to be seen as a formative period for Hitchcock's film-making which only reached its full maturity in America in the 1950s and 1960s.

Hitchcock was not unique in working in different national cinemas – René Clair, Fritz Lang, Max Ophüls and Douglas Sirk were among his contemporaries who worked in Europe and in Hollywood – but few other directors have ever been as able to adjust to the different institutional and industrial conditions as successfully as Hitchcock did. Hitchcock emerged as Britain's leading film director in the 1920s and 1930s largely on account of his technical abilities – in this context it should always be remembered that he learned his craft during a spell at the UFA studios in Germany – but until 1934 he did not specialise in any particular genre. It was the success of *The Man Who Knew Too Much* which led him to specialise in the spy film for most of the remainder of his time in Britain. Hitchcock moved to Hollywood in 1939 and quickly adapted to the studio mode of production. He was initially under contract to David O. Selznick but he made more films on loan to other studios. Hitchcock's experience of working independently meant that he was better equipped than many of his contemporaries to adjust to the changing conditions in the US film industry following the decline of the studio system. His ability to navigate structural changes in the film industry helps to explain the thematic and stylistic consistency of his work and reinforces the idea of Hitchcock as an *auteur*. At the same time, however, the Hitchcock of 1959 or 1969 was not the same Hitchcock as in the 1930s. While *auteur* critics naturally emphasise the similarities between, say, *The 39 Steps* and *North by Northwest*, attributing those similarities to Hitchcock's authorship, at the same time there are also significant differences between the two films in terms of scale and scope which reflect the production contexts of the British film industry (specifically the Gaumont-British Picture Corporation) in the 1930s and the US film industry (specifically MGM) in the late 1950s. In order to understand how the different production contexts influenced the content and form of Hitchcock's films it is therefore necessary to look beyond the *auteur* theory.

Hitchcock and the Spy Film sets out to locate Hitchcock's spy films in three overlapping contexts: authorship (as films reflecting the film-making practice and the formal and thematic preoccupations of their director Alfred Hitchcock), genre (as examples of the spy film in popular cinema) and national cinema (as products of the film industries and film cultures of Britain and the United States at different moments between the 1930s and 1960s). Hitchcock's films are the focus of the book, which is structured around case studies of each of his spy films in chronological sequence but there are also contextualising chapters which explore the place of the spy genre in British and American cinema. It differs from much Hitchcock scholarship in that my focus is as much on the contexts of production and reception as it is on narrative or formal analysis of the films themselves. To this end I have drawn upon a range of primary sources to document the production and reception histories of the films: these include studio archives, personal papers, scripts, censors' reports, publicity materials, the film trade press and contemporary reviews. The Alfred Hitchcock Collection held by the Margaret Herrick Library (Academy of Motion Picture Arts and Sciences) provides an invaluable repository of archival materials: it is much more extensive for the later period of Hitchcock's career than for the British films where the archival sources are rather more patchy. Memoirs and autobiographies – provided they are treated with the caution and scepticism due to all such sources – help to fill in some of the gaps. The British producers Michael Balcon and Walter Mycroft, for example, each offered slightly different accounts of the circumstances that brought Hitchcock to Gaumont-British to direct *The Man Who Knew Too Much* in 1934. Hitchcock never penned his own memoirs, though there are abundant interview sources from the 1930s through to the book-length interview by François Truffaut in 1968 in which he discusses his working methods and the sources and techniques of his films.

My analysis of the films themselves is concerned primarily with their status as genre films: to this end I have focused on their mobilisation of the narrative conventions and motifs of the spy genre. For those films adapted from literary source texts I have compared the film with the original to assess how much of the film was imported from the source and how much was Hitchcock's own invention, while for films based on original screenplays I have documented the development of the scripts through their various drafts and the interventions of different writers. My textual analysis focuses on the films' representational politics – particularly in relation to nationhood, class and gender – as well as their relationship to the political contexts and ideological conditions in which they were made. It has been argued, for example by Robin Wood, that Hitchcock's spy films are not really about international politics except on the most superficial level: he suggests that the spy plot of *The 39 Steps*, for instance, is merely 'a cover for the film's real concerns with gender relations and sexuality'.[29] Of course the films are about more than just espionage: one of the reasons for the enduring appeal of Hitchcock's films is that their thematic depth and formal complexity mandates multiple readings from a range of perspectives. Yet it seems to me that the espionage components are more than mere plot devices and that they are integral to the politics of the films. Hitchcock's British spy films of the 1930s, for example, were produced against the background of the rise of European Fascism, whereas his post-war American spy thrillers were products of the ideological context of the Cold War: hence the identity of the enemy and the nature of the conspiracy changes in those films. And this also influences their social politics: the representation of gender and sexuality in the American films, for example, is informed to some extent by the politics of the Cold War.

Hitchcock and the Spy Film will not be the last word on these films and nor should it be: indeed it is unlikely that anyone will ever have the last word on a director whose films have been so central to the intellectual history of film studies as a discipline and which will no doubt continue to reward re-viewing and reassessment as long as film remains a subject of critical and historical inquiry. What I hope to achieve, however, is to provide a different perspective on this group of films by considering them as genre films rather than just as *auteur* films. And in the process I hope to rehabilitate some of Hitchcock's under-appreciated films as well as shedding new light on several of his canonical works.

PART I

BRITAIN

1

HITCHCOCK AND BRITISH CINEMA

Although Alfred Hitchcock directed 23 British films between *The Pleasure Garden* in 1926 and *Jamaica Inn* in 1939, his reputation rests largely on the cycle of six thrillers he made for the Gaumont-British Picture Corporation between 1934 and 1938: *The Man Who Knew Too Much, The 39 Steps, Secret Agent, Sabotage, Young and Innocent* and *The Lady Vanishes*.[1] It was through this cycle of films – which Raymond Durgnat labelled 'the classic thriller sextet' – that Hitchcock affirmed his reputation as Britain's foremost movie director and came to the attention of Hollywood.[2] These films established many of the characteristic 'Hitchcockian' motifs that were to recur throughout his work, including the fast-paced narrative of pursuit and suspense, the innocent protagonist plunged headlong into a world of chaos and anarchy, and the heterosexual couple whose relationship develops from initial antagonism to romantic union. As well as consolidating key elements of Hitchcock the *auteur*, however, the classic thriller sextet also laid the foundations of the spy film in popular cinema. David Freeman, a future Hitchcock collaborator as writer of his final, unrealised film, *The Short Night*, averred that *The 39 Steps* and *The Lady Vanishes* 'are surely the glory of Hitch's and England's thirties. So great is their forming influence on all the subsequent international intrigue pictures – including his own *North by Northwest* (1959) – that no one can see, let alone make, a spy picture without, knowingly or not, building on Hitch's foundation.'[3]

Hitchcock's 'classic thriller sextet' is by any measure a remarkable corpus that fully deserves the reputation it has garnered. At the same time, however, these films were not in themselves representative of Hitchcock's British career: only in hindsight have they been seen as marking the emergence of the 'Hitchcockian' thriller. Indeed Hitchcock was not regarded primarily as a thriller director before making *The Man Who Knew Too Much*. Only two of the sixteen films he directed before 1934, *The Lodger* and *Blackmail*, fit easily into the retrospective critical construction of Hitchcock as an *auteur*, while another two, *Murder!* and *Number Seventeen*, although both containing 'Hitchcockian' elements, have generally been regarded as minor works. If Hitchcock was associated with a particular type of film before *The Man Who Knew Too Much* it was the theatrical or literary adaptation. Yet these films – including adaptations of plays by Noël Coward (*Easy Virtue*), Eden Phillpots (*The Farmer's Wife*), Sean O'Casey (*Juno and the Paycock*) and John Galsworthy (*The Skin Game*) – remain marginal texts in Hitchcock scholarship because they do not conform to the later pattern. As Tom Ryall observes, 'the run of middlebrow theatrical adaptations that Hitchcock directed for Gainsborough and British International Pictures seem out of character and difficult to relate to the authorial profile of subsequent criticism'.[4]

Hitchcock's initiation into film-making had been at Gainsborough Pictures in the mid-1920s where he worked in various capacities, including as screenwriter and assistant director, before directing his first films, *The Pleasure Garden* (1926) and *The Mountain Eagle* (1926) – the latter now the only 'lost' Hitchcock film – at the UFA studios in Munich under a co-production arrangement between Gainsborough and the German producer Erich Pommer.[5] Hitchcock was greatly influenced by the visual style of German silent cinema with its fluid camera movement and expressionist *mise-en-scène*: he would always maintain that 'silent pictures were the purest form of cinema'.[6] His breakthrough came with his third film, and first in Britain, *The Lodger* (1926), a psychological crime drama notable for its expressionist style which came to be seen (in his own words) as 'the first true "Hitchcock movie"'.[7] At a time when many British films were static theatrical or literary adaptations, *The Lodger*, while based on a novel (by Marie Belloc Lowndes), stood out for its expressionist visual style and bold, artistic flourishes. Indeed *The Lodger* was deemed 'too highbrow' by distributor C. M. Woolf and Hitchcock was obliged to recut it before release.[8] Following *The Lodger*, Hitchcock directed two theatrical adaptations, *Downhill* (1927) and *Easy Virtue* (1927), before leaving Gainsborough for the larger British International Pictures.

British International Pictures (BIP) was one of two vertically integrated combines that emerged in the late 1920s (the other was the Gaumont-British Picture Corporation) when a congruence of factors – including the Cinematograph Films Act of 1927 and the advent of talking pictures – created the conditions for the structural reorganisation of the British film industry. The Cinematograph Films Act (popularly known as the Quota Act) was a response to the decline of the British production sector in the 1920s and the fact that American movies dominated British screens. It was a protectionist measure that mandated a minimum quota of British films for both distributors (initially set at 7.5 per cent rising to 20 per cent by 1936) and exhibitors (5 per cent rising to 20 per cent).[9] The institution of the quota was a factor in the process of vertical integration as small and medium-sized companies with interests in one of the three sectors of the film industry – production, distribution, exhibition – merged. Another driver in this process was the cost of converting studios and cinemas to sound: larger companies were better able to attract capital investment from the City of London. Under its managing-director John Maxwell, a former solicitor who entered the industry as an exhibitor, and its head of production Walter Mycroft, BIP was a conservative studio both economically and culturally. It squeezed production costs in order that its films might return a profit from the home market alone and its strategy was based on the adaptation of theatrical and literary properties that were already familiar to audiences. In her definitive study of the British film industry in the 1930s, Rachael Low observes that BIP 'operated a policy of cut-price window dressing, trying to make cheap films which looked like expensive ones'.[10]

Hitchcock's five years at BIP have been described as his period of 'Elstree blues'.[11] Although there were some highlights, notably directing the first British full-talking picture in 1929 (*Blackmail*), Hitchcock found that BIP was rather less receptive to his ambitions than the more creative environment he had experienced at the smaller Gainsborough Pictures. His own retrospective assessment of this period was that it marked the 'lowest ebb' of his career. Other than *The Ring* (1927) – a boxing drama which he directed from his own screenplay – and *Blackmail*, Hitchcock was disparaging in the extreme of his films for BIP. He told François Truffaut that *Champagne* (1928) 'was probably the lowest ebb in my output', while *The Manxman* (1929) 'was a very banal picture'.[12] He evidently disliked BIP's strategy of theatrical adaptation and averred that he did not choose these films. He claimed that he did not want to make *Juno and the Paycock* (1929): 'I must say that I didn't feel like making the picture because, although I read the play over and over again, I could see no way of narrating it in cinematic form'. He even confessed that he was 'ashamed' of the finished film 'because it had nothing to do with cinema'.[13] All he would say of *The Skin Game* (1931) was: 'I didn't make it by choice, and there isn't much to be said about it.'[14] It was an indication of Hitchcock's declining fortunes at BIP in the early 1930s that his last film for the studio was a low-budget affair. *Number Seventeen* (1932) has sometimes been labelled a 'quota quickie' – one of the cheaply made films churned out to exploit the guaranteed market for British product that was an unintended consequence of the Cinematograph Films Act. 'A disaster!' was Hitchcock's verdict: he later sought to distance himself from the film, saying that the property 'was bought by the studio and they assigned me to the picture'.[15]

Hitchcock's critical reputation at this time was best summed up in John Grierson's description of him as 'no more than the world's best director of unimportant pictures'.[16] On the one hand his films were admired for their technical skill and for the stylistic flourishes that – even at this early stage of his career – marked out Hitchcock's directorial signature. He was one of only two British directors – the other was his near-contemporary Anthony Asquith – whom critics felt understood film as a medium in its own right rather than as an adjunct to the novel or the stage. On the other hand Hitchcock was thought to have wasted his talent on trivial subject matter: his films were characterised by a level of surface realism and detail in their *mise-en-scène* but he was not interested in representing the lives and experiences of ordinary people on the screen. This was what Grierson meant when he expressed the hope that one day Hitchcock would 'give us a film of the Potteries or of Manchester or of Middlesborough – with the personals in their proper places and the life of a community rather than a benighted lady at stake'.[17] Hitchcock, however, professed not to be interested in filming a 'slice of life': 'I don't want to film a "slice of life" because people can get that at home, in the street, or even in front of the movie theatre. They don't have to pay money to see a slice of life.'[18] This view was consistent with the prevailing attitude in the British film industry at the time that audiences preferred escapism to social realism. As Michael Balcon – the co-founder of Gainsborough Pictures who, following its merger into the Gaumont-British combine, served the parent company as head of production between 1931 and 1936 – later remarked: 'We were in the business of giving the public what it seemed to want in entertainment. We did not talk about art or social significance.'[19]

Hitchcock always acknowledged Balcon's influence on his early career. It was Balcon who had facilitated Hitchcock's entry into direction at Gainsborough in the mid-1920s and Balcon who helped to revive his career following the period of 'Elstree blues'. Hitchcock's biographers have typically presented this as being due to an entirely serendipitous moment.[20] Following the end of his BIP contract, Hitchcock made one film as a freelance director: *Waltzes from Vienna* (1933) for independent producer Tom Arnold. *Waltzes from Vienna* was a vehicle for music hall star Jessie Matthews: Hitchcock called it 'a musical without music, made very cheaply. It had no relation to my usual work.'[21] However, *Waltzes from Vienna* was shot at the Gaumont-British studios at Lime Grove, Shepherd's Bush, where Hitchcock renewed his friendship with Balcon, who happened to be visiting the set one day. Apparently Balcon asked Hitchcock what he was doing next and Hitchcock mentioned a thriller he had started working on for BIP. Balcon agreed to buy the property from BIP: this was the origin of the film that became *The Man Who Knew Too Much*.

It is a good story that conforms to the 'happy accident' narrative of film history. Yet even without this fortuitous meeting on set there is good reason to believe that Hitchcock and Balcon would sooner or later have come back into each other's orbits in any event. There were clear advantages for both parties. For Hitchcock, Gaumont-British represented a more ambitious studio than BIP which allowed him access to higher budgets and bigger stars. He would work with some of the major British stars of the day, including Leslie Banks (*The Man Who Knew Too Much*), Robert Donat (*The 39 Steps*) and Madeleine Carroll (*The 39 Steps, Secret Agent*), as well as Hollywood stars Robert Young (*Secret Agent*) and Sylvia Sidney (*Sabotage*). And from the studio's perspective, Hitchcock was a 'name' director who, despite some recent misfires, brought a well-earned reputation for technical excellence and popular appeal. In particular Balcon had set his sights on establishing a presence in the American market. Hitchcock's films would be an important part of this international strategy: the US trade press recognised him as 'a director with an American sense of box-office values'.[22] To this extent Hitchcock's move to Gaumont-British was perhaps less an instance of serendipity and more an outcome of converging trajectories in the mid-1930s.

Gaumont-British was the largest British producer-distributor-exhibitor of the 1930s: its holdings included two film studios (Lime Grove and Islington), over 300 cinemas, film printing works and subsidary companies producing newsreels (Gaumont-British News) and documentary films (GB Instructional). Its production strategy was based around popular genres and stars. Hitchcock's thrillers were one strand of a balanced production programme that also included the musicals of Jessie Matthews (*Evergreen, First A Girl, It's Love Again, Gangway*), star vehicles for George Arliss (*The Iron Duke, East Meets West, His Lordship*), a triptych of British Empire adventures (*Rhodes of Africa, The Great Barrier, King Solomon's Mines*), the comedies of Jack Hulbert and Cicely Courtneidge (*The Ghost Train, Jack's the Boy, Happy Ever After, Falling for You*), and a series of films based on the Aldwych farces of Ben Travers (*A Night Like This, Turkey Time, Cuckoo in the Nest*). The studio aimed to produce around 20 medium-budget films a year: it left 'quota quickies' to others but nor did it go in for the expensively budgeted extravaganzas of a producer such as Alexander Korda. Its strategy was evidently successful: it has been estimated that Gaumont-British's films had a share of around 7 per cent of the domestic market, which made it the leading British producer with only Hollywood giants such as MGM and Paramount ahead of it.[23]

It is clear that Hitchcock found the working environment at Gaumont-British more to his liking than at BIP. Balcon's regime was evidently quite liberal: he encouraged initiative and allowed directors to develop their own projects. According to Ivor Montagu, who worked in various capacities at Gaumont-British as a writer and associate producer:

> Mick would be inclined to make pictures that his contract directors wanted to make. They would ask to do a thing and he would say no or yes but they would be expected to make suggestions … Hitch could choose his own picture and we were choosing these sort of pictures to go back to.[24]

Hitchcock's status at Gaumont-British was probably *primus inter pares* alongside the likes of Walter Forde and Victor Saville: Low describes them as an 'impressive trio of directors'.[25] Hitchcock testified at the time that Balcon 'allowed me to follow my celluloid whims and I am grateful to him'.[26]

It is important to place Hitchcock's Gaumont-British films in their institutional contexts of production not to discredit the *auteur* theory as such but rather to understand how the production strategies and working practices of the studio contributed to the making of Hitchcock's reputation: the fact that the emergence of the 'Hitchcockian' thriller is so closely associated with his period as a contract director at GBPC would suggest that the institutional context was a factor in shaping that authorial identity. Robert E. Kapsis, among others, has suggested that 'the high degree of continuity and consistency among the films of Hitchcock's thriller sextet' was due to a large extent to the production environment.[27] Evidence of the privileged status that Hitchcock enjoyed at Gaumont-British is that his films were produced by what amounted to a dedicated production unit. This was a model of studio management adopted by the Hollywood studios in the mid-1930s but was less usual in Britain where the studio system was less fully institutionalised.[28] There was a quite remarkable stability in key production personnel throughout the 'classic thriller sextet'. Ivor Montagu was the associate producer of *The Man Who Knew Too Much*, *The 39 Steps*, *Secret Agent* and *Sabotage*, while Charles Bennett was involved in the scripting of all bar *The Lady Vanishes*. Bernard Knowles was the director of photography on *The 39 Steps*, *Secret Agent*, *Sabotage* and *Young and Innocent*, Charles Frend was the editor of *Secret Agent*, *Sabotage* and *Young and Innocent*, and Penrose Tennyson was assistant director on five films in succession from *The Man Who Knew Too Much* to *Young and Innocent*. Louis Levy, credited as 'musical director', was a constant presence on all six films. It was only on *The Lady Vanishes* – the last of the sextet – where most of the regular production team were not present.

Hitchcock's Gaumont-British films can also be seen in relation to the studio's strategy of employing European émigré film-makers in key roles. Many of these were exiles from Nazi Germany whose politics and conscience had obliged them to leave their native industry in order to find work elsewhere. Kevin Gough-Yates has argued forcefully that 'the history of British cinema of the period is inextricably linked with that of the exiled European film-makers' and that the influx of émigrés, especially in areas such as art direction and costume design, 'introduced a combination of technical skill and aesthetic confidence to Britain and its backward industry'.[29] It is hardly surprising that Hitchcock, whose formative film-making experiences had been at UFA, would have found an affinity with German artists. Hitchcock's early films, especially *The Lodger*, were influenced strongly by the 'German style', and while the stylisation of his films was less extreme by the 1930s, the thrillers were particularly suited to the sort of expressive *mise-en-scène* associated with German cinema. His Gaumont-British films employed the talents of German art directors Alfred Junge (*The Man Who Knew Too Much*, *Young and Innocent*) and Oscar Wendorff (*The 39 Steps*, *Secret Agent*, *Sabotage*). German cinematographer Curt Courant photographed *The Man Who Knew Too Much*, and costume designer Joe Strassner is credited with 'dresses' for *The 39 Steps*, *Secret Agent* and *Sabotage*. Other émigrés who played important roles in Hitchcock's Gaumont-British films included actors Peter Lorre – born in Hungary but working in German cinema from the late 1920s – in *The Man Who Knew Too Much* and *Secret Agent*, Lucie Mannheim in *The 39 Steps* and Oscar Homolka in *Sabotage*.

The presence of émigré artistes was itself an indication of the cosmopolitan outlook of Gaumont-British in the 1930s. Like the major Hollywood studios, Gaumont-British often reflected an ideological standpoint in its films. It is surely significant to understanding the politics of Hitchcock's spy films that they were produced for the most staunchly anti-fascist of British studios. Balcon and the three Ostrer brothers, Isidore, Mark and Maurice, merchant bankers who were majority shareholders in the corporation, were all Jewish. Ivor Montagu, son of a life peer, was a communist and a leading figure in the alternative film culture of the interwar period exemplified by the Film Society (founded in London in 1925 for the purpose of showing foreign and non-mainstream films) and the Progressive Film Institute (founded in 1935 for the purpose of producing and distributing non-theatrical political films). Gaumont-British produced the first explicitly anti-Nazi British film, *Jew Süss* (1934), an adaptation of the novel by Leon Feuchtwanger by a German director (Lothar Mendes) and with a German art director (Alfred Junge). Balcon's autobiography certainly sought to cast the studio's films in an anti-fascist context: he recalled a visit from a representative of the German ambassador to complain about the portrayal of a German officer in Gaumont's *I Was A Spy* (1933) which ended with Balcon sending the diplomat packing.[30]

Quite aside from its politics, however, the overriding imperative of Gaumont-British was commercial. In this context it is significant that Hitchcock's arrival at the studio in 1934 coincided with Balcon's decision to orient production more towards the US market. This was partly a response to the success of Alexander Korda's *The Private Life of Henry VIII* (1933) which had been the first British talking picture to become a major popular success in the United States. Balcon explained the studio's international strategy thus:

> The growth of the film industry in this country during the past few years, and the welcome extended to British pictures, not only in our own Dominions but in the vast American market, have proved beyond doubt that in order to progress still further we must pursue a production policy ever less and less parochial and more and more international in appeal. 'Internationalism' sums up G.B. policy.[31]

The lucrative US market has always been something of a Holy Grail for British producers, though it would be fair to say that consistent success at the American box office has proved elusive. There were two factors influencing Gaumont-British's strategy of 'internationalism' in the 1930s. One, it seems, was envy: there was evidently some resentment of the perception that Korda was the only British producer with big ambitions. Balcon felt the need to rebut the suggestion that 'the public here think there are two classes of films only: quota quickies and good British pictures all of which are made by Korda'.[32] The other factor – and probably the most important one – was a simple matter of economics. The British market alone was not large enough to return a profit for any but the most modestly budgeted films: this helps to explain why BIP concentrated on relatively low-cost films. In contrast Gaumont-British made a concerted effort to break into the American market: it sent Arthur Lee to New York to head its American distribution arm, Balcon regularly visited Hollywood to meet leading producers and observe working practices in the studios, and it recruited American talent such as actor Robert Young (who appeared in Hitchcock's *Secret Agent* and opposite Jessie Matthews in *It's Love*

Again) and director Raoul Walsh (who came to Britain to make the adventure film *O.H.M.S.* in 1936). And in 1935 the studio announced 'sixteen star-spangled specials' to the US trade press: films that it felt had particular appeal for America.[33]

The success of Gaumont-British's international strategy needs to be carefully nuanced. On the one hand British films were always at a competitive disadvantage in the US market where they were squeezed out by the economic might of the Hollywood majors who controlled most of the first-run cinemas: hence British films tended to be shown in smaller independent cinemas and did not enjoy widespread national release. And even when British films did well in particular locations – for example *Chu Chin Chow* (1934) and *The 39 Steps* were both held over for a second week at the Roxy Theatre in New York – their box-office performance often did not match American movies showing in the preceding or following weeks.[34] On the other hand their success was not negligible: they were favourably reviewed in the American press and undoubtedly raised the profile of British films in America where the received wisdom was that audiences were deterred by British accents.[35] The appeal of the Hitchcock films in the United States seems to have been primarily for cineastes in larger metropolitan centres. According to *Time* magazine: 'More popular in England than in the U.S., Hitchcock pictures like *The 39 Steps, Secret Agent* are often too intricately built and written to appeal to mass audiences. To connoisseurs of spy melodrama, they rate as classics, and play steady revival engagements in Manhattan and London.'[36]

As well as the studio context of Gaumont-British, Hitchcock's 'classic thriller sextet' must be placed within the genre profile of British entertainment cinema of the 1930s. British cinema was a cinema of genres: musicals, comedies, melodramas, costume films, detective films and thrillers were the staple products of the British studios. It would be fair to say that for the most part British films were not viewed with much critical favour – they were often considered technically inferior and as lacking the populist appeal of their Hollywood competitors – though recent historical research into the tastes of British audiences has increasingly challenged the view that British films were not popular with cinema-goers.[37] Nevertheless a view still persists that the only British films of any note in the 1930s were the films of the documentary movement: the progressive sector of the British film industry that clustered around John Grierson and the Empire Marketing Board (later General Post Office) Film Unit. Documentary films were admired for their sense of social purpose and for their realistic representation of ordinary people. Otherwise British feature films of the 1930s were often derided for their melodramatic content and lack of social import. The progressive critic Russell Ferguson wrote scornfully in the journal *World Film News* in 1937:

> Our national life, as reflected in British films, is full of interesting features. We are a nation of retired business men, millowners, radio singers, actors, detectives, newspapermen, leading ladies, soldiers, secret servicemen, crooks, smugglers, and international jewel thieves ... Happily we are not bothered with unemployment, malnutrition, depressed areas, disease or poverty, but the number of chemical formulae, state documents and bonds that are stolen every year is most distressing ... Our greatest trouble is spies and fanatics, who threaten from time to time to blow up London, or to bring down all the machines at Hendon with death rays. There has been a great deal of this in recent months. Where the emissaries and agents come from is not always very clear, but it is certain that they are active enough ... [and] what with armaments rings, assassins and political madmen, it is a mercy that a good proportion of our population are in the secret service.[38]

John Grierson – the leading advocate of a more socially purposeful cinema –- was similarly dismissive of the triviality of British films: 'We need something better to build with than racing scandals and the campaigns of silly asses against impossible Bolsheviks.'[39]

Yet how prominent were spies, saboteurs and secret service agents in British films of the 1930s? Any attempt to provide a comprehensive list of all spy films produced during the decade will inevitably be flawed. For one thing genre terminology was different: trade papers such as *Kinematograph Weekly* tended not to differentiate contemporary spy or espionage films from the broader categories of 'melodrama' or 'crime'. Crime was undoubtedly a major genre: around 350 British feature films between 1930 and 1939 – representing one-fifth of all features produced in Britain during the decade – were crime subjects of one sort or another.[40] The distinction between the spy film and the crime film more generally is not always clear: there is a grey area between those films in which the activity of spying or espionage is the main focus of the narrative and others where spying or espionage is an incidental aspect of a detective or murder mystery. For example, *Lloyd of the CID* (1932) – a twelve-episode serial produced in Britain by Universal Pictures – was a hybrid of the 'Scotland Yard' detective story and the sensational thriller in the Sexton Blake-Bulldog Drummond tradition. A further complicating factor is that the activity of spying or espionage sometimes features in other genres such as comedy – examples include BIP's *Josser Joins the Navy* (1932), *I Spy* (1933) and *Freedom of the Seas* (1934) – and even musicals, for example, *Café Colette* (1937). If we include only 'straight' examples of the genre where spying or espionage is the main focus of the narrative then the annual production of spy films in the 1930s was as shown:.[41]

Year	Films
1930	*The W Plan, The Last Hour*
1931	*Midnight, The Lame Duck, The Flying Fool*
1932	*The Chinese Puzzle, The Silver Greyhound, Rome Express*
1933	*I Was A Spy, On Secret Service*
1934	*The Return of Bulldog Drummond, The Man Who Knew Too Much*
1935	*Bulldog Jack, The 39 Steps, Flame in the Heather, Expert's Opinion, The Crouching Beast*
1936	*Troubled Waters, The Secret Voice, The Prison Breaker, Secret Agent, Spy of Napoleon, The Secret of Stamboul, Second Bureau, Sabotage*
1937	*Dark Journey, The Windmill, Bulldog Drummond at Bay, Secret Lives, The Fatal Hour, Passenger to Land, Midnight Menace, Mademoiselle Docteur*
1938	*The Last Barricade, Strange Boarders, The Lady Vanishes, Luck of the Navy, Anything to Declare?*
1939	*Q-Planes, The Spy in Black, Spies of the Air, Secret Journey, The Four Just Men, An Englishman's Home, Ten Days in Paris, Meet Maxwell Archer, Traitor Spy, Sons of the Sea*

There are several points to be made about this list before we examine the reasons for the emergence of the spy film. The first is that the total number of spy films was quite small as a percentage of British film production overall: there were probably no more than 50 films (I have identifed 47) in which spying or espionage was the main focus of the narrative out of the approximately 1,750 features produced in Britain during the decade. This constitutes less than 3 per cent of total output: to this extent the spy film is probably better understood as a production cycle or trend rather than as a genre with a consistent and continuous presence such as the musical or comedy. The second point is that the production of spy films was very sporadic during the first half of the decade with only a handful of films a year, but increased significantly in the second half of the decade with peaks of eight in 1936 and 1937 and ten in 1939. And a third point is that the production of spy films was undertaken both by the major studios and by quota producers. BIP (which from 1933 became the Associated British Picture Corporation) produced seven spy films (*The W Plan, The Lame Duck, The Flying Fool, On Secret Service, The Return of Bulldog Drummond, Bulldog Drummond at Bay, Luck of the Navy*) and Gaumont-British produced eight (*Rome Express, I Was A Spy, The Man Who Knew Too Much, The 39 Steps, Bulldog Jack, Secret Agent, Sabotage, Strange Boarders, The Lady Vanishes*). The lower end of the genre was represented by quota producers such as Nettlefold (*The Last Hour*) and Twickenham

Studios (*The Chinese Puzzle*) as well as by films sponsored by American distributors in order to meet their British quota obligations: these included Paramount (*Flame in the Heather, Expert's Opinion, The Secret Voice, The Fatal Hour*), RKO (*The Crouching Beast, Second Bureau, Meet Maxwell Archer*) and Fox British (*Troubled Waters, Passenger to Land, The Last Barricade*).

A number of trends can be identified. There was a distinct cycle of period spy dramas set during the First World War that ran throughout the decade including *The W Plan, I Was A Spy, Secret Agent, Second Bureau, Dark Journey, The Windmill* and *The Spy in Black*. The sense that these films constituted a sub-group in their own right is supported by the presence of the same stars in several films of the cycle including Madeleine Carroll (*The W Plan, I Was A Spy, Secret Agent*) and German émigré Conrad Veidt (*I Was A Spy, Dark Journey, The Spy in Black*). *Second Bureau* was a remake of a French film (*Deuxième Bureau*), as was the period spy drama *Mademoiselle Docteur*. However, it was the success of Gaumont-British's *Rome Express* (1932) that really marked the arrival of the contemporary spy film in British cinema. Directed by Walter Forde, *Rome Express* was a combination of international crime, political intrigue and romantic melodrama. It was the first film shot at Gaumont's recently refurbished Lime Grove Studios and was admired for its high level of technical proficiency as well as for Forde's skilful direction of a complex storyline with multiple sub-plots. It also drew upon the talents of émigré artistes in the form of its German star Conrad Veidt and Austrian cinematographer Günther Krampf. *Rome Express* preceded Hitchcock's spy cycle by a full two years: it demonstrates that the genre was already established in the production portfolio of Gaumont-British before *The Man Who Knew Too Much*.

The emergence of the spy film as a production cycle needs to be understood in the economic and ideological contexts of the British film industry of the 1930s. Crime – broadly defined to include detective and gangster films as well as spy films – was a prolific genre. While there had been crime films during the 1920s, notably the Stoll Film Company's successful adaptations of the Sherlock Holmes stories of Sir Arthur Conan Doyle, it was in the wake of the Cinematograph Films Act that crime became a significant production trend. The crime film was ideally suited to the economic conditions of quota production as it was one of the less expensive genres: crime subjects did not require the elaborate sets of the musical or the period trappings of the historical film. Indeed the Hitchcock films represented the high end of a genre that was associated in the main with quota films – including Hitchcock's own *Number Seventeen* for BIP.[42] In its way the crime film can also be seen as representative of the British film industry's strategy of literary and theatrical adaptation. The films listed above included adaptations of novels by popular authors including John Buchan (*The 39 Steps*), E. Phillips Oppenheim (*Strange Boarders*), 'Sapper' (the Bulldog Drummond films), Edgar Wallace (*Prison Breaker, The Four Just Men*) and Denis Wheatley (*The Secret of Stamboul*), and plays by Charles Bennett (*The Last Hour*), Jeffrey Dell (*Spies of the Air*), Guy du Maurier (*An Englishman's Home*) and Arnold Ridley (*The Flying Fool*). To this extent crime and spy subjects represent an alternative tradition of literary adaptation to films based on the work of more 'respectable' writers. It is a singular fact that the most-filmed author of the 1930s was not J. B. Priestley or A. J. Cronin but Edgar Wallace, the prolific thriller writer whose novels and plays provided source material for 33 British feature films.[43]

The spy film should also be placed within the ideological framework of censorship in Britain. The British Board of Film Censors (BBFC) was the organisation responsible for the regulation of film content: it operated a rigorous policy of moral and political censorship whose underlying principle was to keep all controversial subject matter off the screen.[44] The BBFC operated a policy of pre-production scrutiny of scripts and scenarios to advise producers on their suitability for filming: the process was voluntary but most producers availed themselves of the opportunity so as not to invest time and money in subjects likely to be deemed prohibitive. The BBFC had been particularly alarmed by the cycle of American gangster films in the early 1930s such as *The Public Enemy* (1931) and *Scarface* (1932): it was not only the violence of these films that was problematic but also the fact that they focused on organised criminal gangs.[45] The censor resolved not to allow any British films of the 'American Gangster type' and repeatedly rejected such scenarios when they were put forward by producers. The censor's internal report on Edgar Wallace's novel *When the Gangs Came to London* – put forward as a possible film by a British quota producer in 1932 – summed up the policy thus:

> The British Board of Film Censors have had a good deal of trouble with 'gangster' films in recent years, and it was only because they were so obviously American that they finally passed… We do not recognise 'Third Degree' methods nor do we permit the suggestion that our Police force would arrange for the murder of a criminal if they thought the evidence was too weak to secure a conviction. Wholesale Machine-gun murders in the streets of Chicago possibly are deemed to come under the head of 'Topicals', but, in London, would be quite prohibitive.[46]

On this matter the BBFC's position was consistent. In 1935 it rejected a book titled *Soho Racket* because it 'is told in lurid American fashion, and has nothing to commend it except its violence and improbability'.[47] Indeed the prohibition of gangster subjects may have been a factor influencing the production of spy films which did not feature organised crime and where violent incidents such as murder and robbery were not the primary concern.

Nevertheless there were restrictions on what could and could not be shown in the spy film. The reason why the identity of foreign agents and emissaries was usually quite vague (as noted by Russell Ferguson) was that the BBFC actively discouraged films making direct reference to foreign countries. In particular the censor consistently rejected any topics that smacked of what it called 'political propaganda'. In 1933, for example, Gaumont-British received short shrift when it submitted a play titled *The Rumour* for consideration by the BBFC: 'This is a play with a strong flavour of political propaganda. I consider it would be quite prohibitive to show England or any other recognisable Great Power in the light of a stirrer-up of strife for mercenary ends.'[48] The studio was also rebuffed when it submitted a scenario titled *Sabotage* – unrelated to the Hitchcock film of the same title – concerning the Moscow show trial of six British engineers working for the Metropolitan-Vickers Electrical Company accused of espionage in Russia: 'Political propaganda, brought very much up to date. We consider the subject unsuitable.'[49] And when an American producer (RKO) solicited the BBFC's advice on the suitability of Sir Robert Bruce Lockhart's *Memoirs of a British Agent*, which chronicled his adventures during the Russian Revolution, the censor advised 'that it would be quite impossible to film this book. The main interest is the hitherto untold secrets of our Foreign Office diplomacy ... Our FO would never consent to such revelations on the screen'.[50] (A film titled *British Agent* was produced in Hollywood by Warner Bros. in 1934: it was notionally based on Lockhart's book but in reality bore little resemblance to the source material.) In contrast spy subjects that were recognisably fictional were generally much less problematic for the censor. The scenario for *Rome Express*, for example, was deemed 'quite free from objection'.[51] *The 39 Steps* was a 'harmless melodrama, with various very improbable adventures'.[52] And the producer who submitted Dennis Wheatley's novel *The Eunuch of Stamboul* ('A thrilling Spy story of modern Constantinople') was advised that 'the main plot is permissible providing the politics are left out as much as possible and Austapha Kemal is not shown'.[53]

Yet despite the constraints imposed by censorship, the British spy film of the 1930s was nevertheless informed by the political climate in which the films were produced. The decade provided fertile ground for the genre. In particular the rise of Fascism at home and abroad was the ideological background for the thriller in film and fiction. The British Union of Fascists was formed by Sir Oswald Mosley in 1932 and attracted 50,000 members over the next two years until its support faded following the violence that attended its rallies such as the infamous 'Battle of Cable Street' (6 October 1936). And the election of Hitler and the Nazis in Germany in 1933 prompted a marked increase in international tensions and raised the spectre of another world war. It is surely no coincidence that the production of spy films increased between the German reoccupation of the Rhineland (1936) and the Munich Crisis (1938). In December 1939 a report on film trends compiled by the social survey organisation Mass-Observation noted the proliferation of spy films in 1938 and suggested that they 'give a good picture of the mentality of the sort of people producing films at that time and of the general atmosphere of inferiority and paranoia which the American [sic] democracies were unconsciously feeling towards aggressive Germany'.[54]

The spy film became a vehicle for exploring the ideological tensions of the time. The genre was able to circumvent the restrictions of censorship through a strategy of ideological displacement: political ideologies such as Communism and Fascism were displaced onto general all-purpose villains such as anarchists and arms manufacturers. BIP's *The Return of Bulldog Drummond* (1934) – an adaptation of *The Black Gang* and not to be confused with the novel of the same title – is a good case in point: in place of Sapper's Jewish-Bolshevik conspirators the film substitutes 'an international armament ring... endeavouring to create distrust and if possible war between the nations of the world'. Drummond – played by Ralph Richardson – is the leader of a secret society known here as the 'Black Clan' dedicated to running undesirables out of Britain. The film acknowledges the ideologically problematic nature of such activity when the police commissioner advises Drummond that 'black clans, pink shirts, green jerseys don't fit in this grey country of ours': in 1934 this would surely be understood as a reference to the British Union of Fascists who were known as 'Blackshirts'. And in *Bulldog Drummond at Bay* (1937) the villains are thinly disguised Russian émigrés with names such as Gregoroff and Kalinsky who hide behind the front of an organisation known as the Key Club which ostensibly is committed to promoting peace but in reality seeks to foment conflict in order to sell arms ('Lucky for us there are so many fools willing to give money in the sacred cause of peace'). The villain's reference to 'peace in our time' was too early to be understood ironically: the film was released eighteen months before Neville Chamberlain's pronouncement after returning from his meeting with Hitler at Munich. Hitchcock would also use the device of a peace organisation as the front for a spy ring in his first Hollywood spy thriller

Foreign Correspondent: evidence that this was a convention of the genre rather than being a specifically 'Hitchcockian' motif.

British film-makers may have been prevented by censorship from making any direct reference to Germany but some of the films leave little doubt as to the identity of the enemy power who remains so conspicuously unnamed. The *mise-en-scène* of the spy film – often influenced by émigré artistes – was replete with visual codes that spelled out 'Germany': Tobias Hochscherf observes that 'the combination of claustrophic sets and the villains' SS or Gestapo-like leather coats and uniforms, created by German-speaking designers, became an inherent part of the iconography of 1930s British spy thrillers'.[55] The presence of so many German émigré actors in the genre was another way of coding the films: it is ironic in the extreme that a generation of actors who fled Nazi Germany found employment playing thinly disguised Nazi villains in spy movies in Britain and Hollywood. By the end of the decade the identity of the unnamed foreign power in films such as Alexander Korda's *Q Planes* (1939) was barely disguised. *Q Planes* starred Laurence Olivier as a daring test pilot and Ralph Richardson as an urbane secret service agent who thwart a conspiracy to sabotage a new British bomber: the enemy uses a disguised salvage ship to intercept the plane with a radio beam. The US trade paper *Variety* detected 'a hint or two of anti-German propaganda ... All of the crew speak with German accents and little doubt is left as to who the villains are.'[56]

Ealing Studios' *The Four Just Men* (1939) demonstrates the ideological strategies of the British spy film on the eve of the Second World War. It is significant in the context of Hitchcock's spy films as it was produced by Michael Balcon – who had taken up appointment as Head of Production at Ealing shortly before the outbreak of war – and one of the writers, Angus MacPhail, had made uncredited contributions to Hitchcock's Gaumont-British films. The film is an adaptation of Edgar Wallace's 1905 novel of the same title that reverses the politics of its source text. Wallace's Four Just Men were a pan-European secret society who conspired to assassinate the British Foreign Secretary when he introduced an 'Aliens Political Offences Bill' that makes it more difficult for foreign nationals to seek asylum in Britain: the assassination is justified on the grounds of protecting Britain's historic liberal tradition as a safe haven for refugees from political oppression. The 1939 film Anglicises the society who are now cast unambiguously as patriots and protectors of the British Empire. The opening sequence in which one of the Four is rescued from 'Regensberg' prison – complete with a Teutonic monocled commandant – leaves little to the imagination regarding the identity of the enemy. In 1939 the film's reference to a conspiracy that will leave 'world domination in one man's hands' can have been understood only as a reference to the territorial ambitions of the German Chancellor. The *Motion Picture Herald* remarked that *The Four Just Men* exemplified 'Britain's self-appointed characterization as defier of Dictators'.[57]

As directed by Walter Forde, *The Four Just Men* is a highly effective thriller in the sensational mould that includes some effective Hitchcock-type touches such as the set piece in which James Terry (Frank Lawton) is rescued from prison and a later scene in which Terry is poisoned by an enemy agent at Victoria Station: the semi-circular camera movement is a technique that Hitchcock also used on several occasions including in *Dial M for Murder* and *Rear Window*. *The Four Just Men* is also significant ideologically in that – rather like Hitchcock's last British spy film *The Lady Vanishes* – it contains what amounts to a critique of the British government's policy of appeasement towards Nazi Germany. It transpires that a British MP has been leaking defence secrets to the enemy in the name of peace: Sir Haymer Ryman is characterised as a misguided idealist ('I have devoted my entire political career to the cause of peace') who opposes rearmament ('England is committing suicide with her own armaments'). As in the novel Ryman is electrocuted in his bath: Humphrey Manfred (Hugh Sinclair) then disguises himself as Ryman to make a speech to the House of Commons retracting his previous position and calling for rearmament. Hence *The Four Just Men* shows how a British film could circumvent the censor to make a political statement: Charles Barr remarks that 'the film enforces, irresistibly, the inference that appeasement is treachery'.[58]

The cycle of British spy films in the 1930s was therefore shaped by a combination of industrial conditions, ideological determinants and popular culture. The genre may not have been prolific but it represented a significant production trend, especially in the latter half of the decade. It was also a genre ideologically attuned to the political and geopolitical climate of the decade: along with the costume film – whose politics were displaced into a historical or a fictional past – the spy film was a vehicle through which British film-makers were able to overcome censorial mandates and examine issues of topical interest. These were the contexts for Hitchcock's 'classic thriller sextet': now we may turn to the films themselves.

2

'GOOD, THICK-EAR MELODRAMA OF AN ODDLY ENGLISH TYPE': *THE MAN WHO KNEW TOO MUCH* (1934)

The origins of *The Man Who Knew Too Much* are to be found in the tail end of Hitchcock's time at British International Pictures when he and screenwriter Charles Bennett – author of the play *Blackmail* on which Hitchcock's 1929 film was based – had begun working on a scenario titled *Bulldog Drummond's Baby*. In February 1933 *The Times* reported that Hitchcock was 'making a film of Bulldog Drummond for British International Pictures'.[1] There are conflicting accounts of why *Bulldog Drummond's Baby* did not proceed beyond an initial scenario. Hitchcock later came to believe that Walter Mycroft, BIP's script editor and effectively second-in-command at the studio, 'was intriguing against me and the picture'.[2] Mycroft's own account, however, suggests that it was BIP chief John Maxwell who disliked the scenario.[3] Maxwell let Hitchcock buy the rights to the story – which Hitchcock in turn sold to Gaumont-British – though without the right to use the Bulldog Drummond character. BIP, under its new name the Associated British Picture Corporation, went on to produce *The Return of Bulldog Drummond* (1934) and *Bulldog Drummond at Bay* (1937).

Bulldog Drummond was the protagonist of a series of adventure thrillers by a former Royal Engineers officer, H. C. McNeile, who wrote under the pen name of 'Sapper'.[4] Unlike John Buchan's Richard Hannay, the Bulldog Drummond character has fallen from popular favour on account of his latent xenophobia and undisguised anti-Semitism: to modern eyes the protagonist seems more of an authoritarian vigilante with fascistic tendencies than 'a sportsman and a gentleman' as described in the first book. Yet he was an enormously popular character during the interwar period and had been adapted for both stage and screen. There had been two British silent pictures, but the definitive film was *Bulldog Drummond* (1929), an early talking picture produced in Hollywood by Sam Goldwyn starring Ronald Colman. It fell to Darryl F. Zanuck to produce a sequel, *Bulldog Drummond Strikes Back* (1934), again starring Colman, after which Paramount Pictures produced a series of supporting features between 1937 and 1939.[5] As well as the two ABPC Bulldog Drummond films of the 1930s – which, unlike the Paramount films, were based on specific Sapper stories – Gaumont-British also produced its own Bulldog Drummond film. *Bulldog Jack* (1935), directed by Walter Forde, was a pastiche starring the lantern-jawed comedian Jack Hulbert as a London playboy who assumes the identity of Bulldog Drummond when the real Drummond (Atholl Fleming) is injured in an ambush. *Bulldog Jack* was a lively comedy-thriller with some 'Hitchcockian' touches – including an atmospheric robbery sequence in the British Museum and a climax on board a speeding London Underground train – that *Film Weekly* felt deserved comparison with the real thing: 'Apart from the fact that the central character is burlesqued, the plot might easily be mistaken for a genuine Bulldog Drummond adventure.'[6] Alfred Junge, the German art director of *The Man Who Knew Too Much*, also designed *Bulldog Jack*.

The writing credits for *The Man Who Knew Too Much* are convoluted in the extreme: according to the film's titles it was 'by Charles Bennett and D. B. Wyndham Lewis' with the 'scenario' by Edwin Greenwood and A. R. Rawlinson and 'additional dialogue' by Emlyn Williams. As there are no pre-production screenplays of *The Man Who Knew Too Much* in either the Alfred Hitchcock Collection at the Margaret Herrick Library or the British Film Institute's Scripts Collection, the only sources regarding the scripting process are anecdotal.[7] Charles Bennett later claimed that *The Man Who Knew Too Much* 'has to be one of the best stories I think I ever wrote in my life – and I wrote it, let's face it, and nobody else'.[8] Bennett averred that D. B. Wyndham Lewis – no relation to the artist of same name – 'was brought in while we were working on "Bulldog Drummond's Baby" to write some dialogue, which was never used, but since he had been brought in, it was eventually decided to give him a story credit'. The other credits arose because 'they kept calling in people to alter scenes – not necessarily *construction* – but *scenes*'.[9] Edwin Greenwood and A. R. Rawlinson were both writers of plays, novels and screenplays – Greenwood also collaborated with Hitchcock on *Young and Innocent* – while Emlyn Williams was a playwright and actor best known for his play *The Corn is Green* who enjoyed a prolific career in British films.

In the absence of any surviving script materials, the only archival evidence regarding the development of *The Man Who Knew Too Much* is to be found in the scenario reports of the British Board of Film Censors. These reveal that when the original scenario, at the time titled *The Hidden Hand*, was submitted for pre-production scrutiny in February 1934 it was still cast as a Bulldog Drummond film:

> Captain Hugh Drummond, his wife and their small daughter Jane were staying at a Hotel in Switzerland for winter sports. The evening, at a hotel dance, Louis Bernard a hotel acquaintance was shot dancing with Mrs Drummond. Just before he died he whispered to Mrs Drummond to tell her husband to send his brushes to the Foreign Office. Capt D went at once to the room and found a piece of paper concealed in the handle of Bernard's shaving brush, which he put in his pocket. He was found in Bernard's room and detained on suspicion of being implicated in his death. Drummond gets a note to hand over the hidden paper to a man named Levine, but he denies that there is any paper. His daughter Jane is kidnapped, and in spite of active police investigations no trace of her can be found. Drummond is again warned that if he hands over the paper to the police or the FO his child will be killed. After three weeks' anxiety Drummond gets a faint clue which he follows up, to a mysterious house in the East End of London which he and his friend Algy enter.
>
> They recognise that they are up against their ancient enemy Dr Petersen, but they are also recognised and a desperate fight ensues. Drummond is overpowered and Algy escapes to warn the police. He returns with a single policeman and Dr Petersen successfully bluffs it out and gives Algy in charge [sic]. Drummond now discovers that the plot is to assassinate a foreign diplomat at the Albert Hall.
>
> In spite of being handcuffed and guarded by an armed gunman, Drummond effects his escape, gets to the Albert Hall in time to stop the murder, rescues his child, and all ends happily.[10]

It is clear from the scenario report that the basic structure of *The Man Who Knew Too Much* was present in this early draft: this would tend to substantiate Charles Bennett's claim that he was responsible for the narrative construction and that other writers contributed mostly to the dialogue. The characters of Drummond's sidekick Algy Longworth and his arch-enemy Carl Petersen are from Sapper's novels. The three main differences between the scenario and the finished film are that the film downplays the role of the police in the investigation, allows greater narrative agency for the wife, and includes an additional action sequence following the Albert Hall involving a shoot-out between the conspirators and the police.

There were evidently some changes before filming began in June 1934. All references to Bulldog Drummond were dropped. A copy of the script was sent to Sapper's confidant Gerald Fairlie, who replied that 'I personally cannot see any resemblance to Sapper's works which could lead to any sort of trouble'.[11] When a revised scenario – now titled *The Man Who Knew Too Much* – was submitted to the BBFC in May 1934 the censor raised concerns that it now 'ends with a sort of Sidney Street battle, an attack on the gang's headquarters in Wapping by armed police and two lorry loads of troops. Machine guns used on both sides. Many casualties shown.'[12] The siege of Sidney Street – also known as the 'Battle of Stepney' – was an incident before the First World War (3 January 1911) when a group of anarchists exchanged gunfire with the police: the incident became infamous due to the presence on site of the Home Secretary Winston Churchill. The censors' report deemed the sequence 'quite prohibitive' as it contravened their ban on the representation of American-style gangsterism in Britain. The matter was discussed at some length between the BBFC and Gaumont-British. The censors insisted that troops must not be shown involved in the battle: in the end it was agreed 'that a young policeman could remark to his sergeant that they ought to send for soldiers, and the sergeant could retort fiercely that the police were quite competent to deal with the situation themselves'.[13] The eventual solution was to omit the army but to include a scene where the police officer in charge sends for rifles to equip his men.[14]

It would seem that Gaumont-British saw *The Man Who Knew Too Much* as a routine production rather than a 'special'. Its budget of £38,094 (a figure that excludes payments to contract artistes) indicates an economical production, and even its final cost of £48,075 was towards the bottom end of the studio's budget range.[15] It was shot over six weeks at Lime Grove studios from 29 May 1934 with a further eight days of exteriors.[16] The imperative of keeping costs down is revealed by an internal memorandum regarding a special effects shot using the Schüfftan process (an optical effect named after its inventor Eugene Schüfftan that used an angled mirror to reflect miniature sets in the background) in preference to building a full set: 'In order to do this job the cheapest possible way, after very careful discussion, it was decided that the cheapest way to build this set would be in conjunction with the Shuffton [sic] process.'[17] Nor did the film feature any internationally recognised stars. Leslie Banks and Edna Best, starring as Bob and Jill Lawrence, as the Drummonds had become, were not known outside Britain – even though Banks had made his film debut in *The Most Dangerous Game* (1932) for RKO Radio Pictures in Hollywood – while of the supporting cast Pierre Fresnay as the murdered agent Louis Bernard was a star in France and Peter Lorre was known to cineastes for his role as the psycopathic child-murderer in Fritz Lang's *M* (1931).

There is some anecdotal evidence that the film trade was initially lukewarm about *The Man Who Knew Too Much*, though the sources are contradictory. On the one hand it has been alleged that Gaumont's head of distribution, C. M. Woolf, disliked the film and wanted another director (Maurice Elvey) to reshoot some of it.[18] The story has some credence in that Hitchcock and Woolf were old antagonists: eight years earlier at Gainsborough Pictures Woolf had insisted on re-editing *The Lodger* which he considered 'too highbrow'.[19] In the event Woolf relented over *The Man Who Knew Too Much* but supposedly took his revenge by distributing it as a supporting feature on a double bill. On the other hand, however, Michael Balcon testified in his autobiography that it was cinema exhibitors who were reluctant to book *The Man Who Knew Too Much* and that Woolf was instrumental in securing its release: 'It was only after the intervention of C. M. Woolf that they agreed to play the film, and then only at a modest fixed price instead of the standard participation in box-office receipts usually paid for what cinema men thought to be "good" films.'[20] These accounts are difficult to reconcile with the overwhelmingly positive reviews of *The Man Who Knew Too Much* in the British trade press and should therefore be treated with some caution. In the event the film seems to have been a middling popular success. John Sedgwick's research into popular film preferences – employing statistical methodology to calculate a film's 'popularity index' based on the length of its run at a sample of cinemas – places *The Man Who Knew Too Much* in forty-second place of all films released in Britain in 1934.[21]

In the United States, the release of *The Man Who Knew Too Much* faced an obstacle of a different kind. In 1930 the US trade body the Motion Picture Producers and Distributors of America had introduced the Production Code – popularly known as the Hays Code after former US Postmaster-General and MPPDA President Will H. Hays who devised it – in an attempt to 'clean up' the content of movies and in particular to police the representation of violence and sexuality. The establishment of the Production Code Administration (PCA) in 1934 meant that producers could no longer ignore the Code as the PCA's seal of approval was required before any film could be distributed or exhibited by MPPDA members. Like their counterparts at the BBFC, the PCA had been much concerned by the cycle of gangster films in the 1930s: accordingly it had obliged the studios to tone down the violence and had mandated that such films should focus on the efforts of law-enforcement agencies in fighting organised crime rather than making gangsters themselves the protagonists. When *The Man Who Knew Too Much* was submitted to the

PCA early in 1935 – Gaumont had not availed themselves of the opportunity to submit the script for pre-production scrutiny – it ran foul of PCA chief Joseph Breen who took exception to its climax which he felt violated the Code's guidelines regarding screen violence: 'There is too much slaughter; too much gunplay; too much murdering of policemen.'[22] Breen explicitly compared *The Man Who Knew Too Much* to US gangster films: he complained that 'the final two reels of the film presents a slaughter the like of which we have not seen since the days of *Scarface*'. He elaborated:

> The British picture follows the *formula* of our once popular gangster films. True, the heavies are not gangsters as we commonly tab such here in America. They are rather international madmen, or patriots, seeking to assassinate, in London, the representative of an unidentified European power. The kidnapping is merely incidental, but there is staged a battle between the London police and these four or five would-be assassins which follows quite closely the last two or three reels of *Scarface* in which Scarface barricaded himself in a building, and with the aid of his sister, held off the police in a bloody pistol battle.[23]

It is not clear whether the print of the film submitted to the PCA was the same as the one that had been approved for release in Britain by the BBFC: Breen's reference to the number of deaths ('twenty or thirty of the police are killed') does not tally with any extant print of *The Man Who Knew Too Much* but this may simply have been hyperbole on his part.[24] For Breen, evidently, the issue at stake was the possible accusation of double standards if the British film were allowed in its full gory detail: 'I am certain that none of our people here would even think of staging a slaughter such as is presented in this British film ... [If] we *approve* of something in this picture which we persistently *refuse to approve* in films made here, we are going to be exposed to serious criticism on all sides'.[25]

The PCA therefore exercised its authority to insist on deletions which, it explained, 'are concerned, first, with removing all indications of the slaughter of policemen by the criminals, and second, removing as much as possible of the gun play which converts the last two reels of the picture into a shambles'.[26] Gaumont-British had no real option other than to make the required deletions as the PCA would otherwise withhold its seal of approval for the film. Accordingly the gun battle was heavily edited: in particular the PCA insisted on the deletion of all 'scenes in which policemen are shown being cut down' and 'several scenes of street strewn with dead policemen'. Even so the first resubmitted print evidently did not meet the PCA's conditions as further deletions were required before the film was approved.[27] And there were further problems with some local censors' boards including Pennsylvania (where a print still containing several profanities – including 'Good Lord!' and 'for God's sake' – was submitted by mistake) and Chicago (where the nature of the problem is not clear).[28]

The Man Who Knew Too Much was Hitchcock's first fully fledged spy adventure film and his first excursion into the world of international intrigue and conspiracy that would provide such fertile material for so many of his later films including *The 39 Steps, The Lady Vanishes, Foreign Correspondent, Saboteur, North by Northwest, Torn Curtain* and *Topaz*. It belongs firmly within the sensational lineage of the thriller with its emphasis on fast-moving action (the film's running time is an economical 75 minutes) and its suspenseful set pieces (notably the sequence of the attempted assassination in the Albert Hall and the climactic gun battle around the villains' East End hide-out). Writing in 1961, Peter John Dyer suggested that *The Man Who Knew Too Much* marked the emergence of a new style of British film:

> *The Man Who Knew Too Much*, the first of his celebrated Gaumont-British talkies, was outright melodrama, deficient in structure and flawed in its logic. But its very recklessness gave it an excitement hitherto unknown in British cinema.
>
> Kidnapping, hypnosis, codes inside shaving brushes, brilliantined sharpshooters, scarred and smiling anarchists, sun-worshippers and sieges in Wapping – these were among the outlandish elements that went to make up Hitchcock's declaration of independence; and since it paid off, and was good cinema, it was by way of being a starter's pistol for other film-makers.[29]

This is a claim that needs to be qualified. *The Man Who Too Much* was neither the first contemporary spy thriller produced in Britain in the 1930s nor the first to include the sort of 'outlandish' plot devices that Dyer identifies: *The Return of Bulldog Drummond* – which, with its secret societies, international criminal syndicate, kidnapping and thick-ear violence, is every bit as sensational as *The Man Who Knew Too Much* – had preceded it into cinemas in 1934.[30] Instead Hitchcock's film should be seen as just one example of a shift towards the sensational thriller mode that occurred in British cinema from the mid-1930s: others included the Sexton Blake trilogy of 1936–8 (*Sexton Blake and the Bearded Doctor, Sexton Blake and the Mademoiselle, Sexton Blake and the Hooded Terror*), *Bulldog Jack, Bulldog Drummond at Bay, Spies of the Air, Q-Planes* and *The Four Just Men*. Therefore *The Man Who Knew Too Much* should be seen as a representative (if superior) example of the sensational thriller of the 1930s rather than as a unique or stand-out film in its own right.

As an original screenplay – it is the only one of the 'classic thriller sextet' not based on a literary source text – *The Man Who Knew Too Much* draws upon motifs from across the genre. In *The Return of Bulldog Drummond*, for example,

Drummond's wife is kidnapped by the villains and he has to rescue her: *The Man Who Knew Too Much* also combines its public narrative (the assassination plot) with a parallel private narrative (the Lawrences seeking to rescue their kidnapped daughter). The climactic shoot-out between villains and police had a cinematic predecessor in Howard Hawks's American gangster film *Scarface* (1932) as well as a real-life parallel in the Sidney Street siege. And in particular *The Man Who Knew Too Much* demonstrates the influence of John Buchan: Charles Barr even suggests that '*The Man Who Knew Too Much* carries the Buchan mark rather more clearly than *The 39 Steps* does'.[31] Thus Bob Lawrence's attempts to unravel the cryptic code he finds in Louis Bernard's shaving brush ('WAPPING G. BARBOR MAKE CONTACT A. HALL MARCH 21st.') recalls the message which Richard Hannay puzzles over in *Greenmantle* ('Kasredin. cancer. v.I.'), while child kidnapping is the plot device that drives *The Three Hostages*. The latter novel also features Hannay and his wife acting independently of each other – as Bob and Jill Lawrence do in *The Man Who Knew Too Much* – and employs hypnotism as a plot device, as does *The Man Who Knew Too Much* when Clive is hypnotised at the Tabernacle of the Sun. At different points in his career Hitchcock considered filming both *Greenmantle* and *The Three Hostages*.

At the same time, however, *The Man Who Knew Too Much* also stands apart from the genre in certain important respects. Bob Lawrence is no Bulldog Drummond: he seems to lack the competitive nature of Sapper's hero and related characters such as Richard Hannay. In the opening scenes in St Moritz, for example, Bob ignores his wife's flirtation with Louis (the 'real' Drummond would surely have punched the other man on the nose!) and acts with languid nonchalance in the face of Jill's humorous but near-the-bone banter ('I'm going off with another man … You go to bed early – with Betty'). (The Freudian overtones of this – and other – exchanges have been grist to the mill for Hitchcock scholars. It is a characteristically Hitchcockian representation of a marriage that is not quite stale but has settled into familiar domesticity: the Lawrences have sometimes been seen as an older version of the couple in Hitchcock's marital melodrama *Rich and Strange*.) Bob remains unflappable in a crisis: his friend Clive describes him as 'not the sort of chap to give things away and lose his head and all that sort of business'. Indeed his demeanour at times seems rather too laid-back for a man whose daughter has been kidnapped: this might be interpreted as Bob performing the expected 'stiff-upper-lip' character of the English gentleman hero. But he has only one real heroic moment in the film when he overcomes the sinister dentist Barbor whose surgery is a meeting place for the conspirators. For approximately the last third of the film –

1   The middle-class English family and the foreigner who 'wears too much brilliantine': Bob Lawrence (Leslie Banks, *left*), Jill Lawrence (Edna Best, *centre right*) and Betty (Nova Pilbeam, *right*) meet Ramon (Frank Vosper, *centre left*) in a studio in St Moritz in *The Man Who Knew Too Much* (Gaumont-British Picture Corporation, 1934).

following his and Clive's entry into the Tabernacle of the Sun – Bob is a prisoner: he is sidelined at the end of the film when he is shot in the arm and cannot effect his daughter's rescue.

In contrast it is Jill Lawrence who demonstrates more traditionally heroic – one might even say masculine – attributes. It is established near the beginning of the film that Jill is an expert rifle markswoman: on holiday in St Moritz she is engaged in a clay pigeon-shooting contest against a foreigner called Ramon (later revealed as the would-be assassin) which she loses when distracted at the crucial moment by her own daughter. Jill's comment in defeat ('We must have another battle one day, shall we?') and Ramon's reply ('I shall live for that moment') prefigures the film's climax: it is an instance of the classical narrative construction in which the end mirrors the beginning that is particularly characteristic of Hitchcock's films. It is Jill who assumes the conventional heroic role during the film's two climaxes: her actions are decisive in preventing the assassination (she distracts Ramon by screaming at

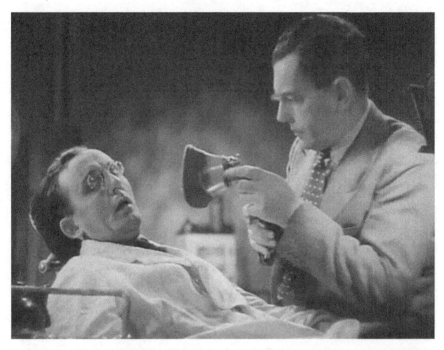

2   Bob Lawrence's heroic moment as he overcomes the sinister dentist in *The Man Who Knew Too Much* (Gaumont-British Picture Corporation, 1934).

the crucial moment) and in saving Betty's life (Jill takes the shot that kills Ramon – threatening Betty – on the roof of the villains' hide-out when a policeman cannot fire for fear of hitting the girl). This decisive intervention bestows upon Jill Lawrence in the British version of *The Man Who Knew Too Much* a degree of narrative agency not afforded to her equivalent in the American remake. It might be seen as another instance of the influence of John Buchan on *The Man Who Knew Too Much* in that Richard Hannay's wife Mary (who figures prominently in *Mr Standfast* and *The Three Hostages*) demonstrates her ability to act independently (she is a British agent when Hannay first meets her) and takes an active role in the narrative.

To highlight the place of *The Man Who Knew Too Much* in the thriller genre is not to deny Hitchcock's authorship. If *The Man Who Knew Too Much* is a superior example of the genre, indeed, this is due in large measure to Hitchcock's direction. *The Man Who Knew Too Much* exemplifies Hitchcock at his most economical: the narrative is stripped down to its essentials with no superfluous scenes or dialogue and few of the director's trademark stylistic

3   Jill Lawrence at the Albert Hall in *The Man Who Knew Too Much* (Gaumont-British Picture Corporation, 1934).

flourishes. It is a perfectly classical film in its structure: events are set in motion by a disruption (the murder of Louis Bernard and subsequent kidnapping of Betty, which breaks up the Lawrence family) and from that moment the film works through towards its resolution (in which Betty is rescued and the family is reunited). Hitchcock's one bravura directorial set piece is the Albert Hall sequence: this is the centrepiece – in dramatic, structural and formal terms – of the film. Jill has gone to the Albert Hall in the knowledge that an assassination has been planned but without knowing the details: the suspense arises in part from the audience's knowledge that the assassin will shoot the visiting statesman at the point when a clash of cymbals in the performance will disguise the noise of the shot. The sequence is a textbook demonstration of Hitchcock's use of montage: tension builds through the repetition of shots of the orchestra, the audience, Jill, and Ramon's pistol pointing from behind a curtain. It is tempting to ascribe to the music – a piece composed especially by Arthur Benjamin and known as the 'Storm Cloud Cantata' – some sort of ideological significance: the metaphor of 'storm clouds' became a familiar one for the increasing international tensions of the 1930s.

The Man Who Knew Too Much is characteristic of British spy films of the 1930s in so far as the identity of the conspirators is never revealed. There is a suggestion that the villains are a group of international anarchists rather than being aligned with a particular nation state: at one point Nurse Agnes refers to 'our cause' ('You took this on for our cause, and you've got to go through with it', she tells Ramon when he is about to get cold feet). This may be a legacy of the film's original source: Bulldog Drummond's antagonist Carl Petersen was the head of an international criminal syndicate whose aim was to foment revolution in Britain. The leaders of the conspiracy are foreign of course: it has long been a convention of the British spy thriller that 'you only had to scratch a foreigner to find a villain'.[32] We know that Ramon is a villain from the moment that Betty says she dislikes him because he wears 'too much brilliantine': evidently no pukka Englishman would do this. The vagueness around the identity of the villains is enhanced by the casting: the conspirator-in-chief is played by the decidedly foreign Peter Lorre but has a traditional British name (Abbott), while the assassin Ramon has a Spanish-sounding name but is played by a British actor (Frank Vosper).

Yet the vagueness of the conspiracy does not mean that *The Man Who Knew Too Much* is an apolitical film. For one thing it accrued – entirely coincidentally – a rare degree of topicality following the assassination of King Alexander of Yugoslavia shortly before its release: the king was shot by a Bulgarian nationalist in Marseilles on 9 October 1934 while on a state visit to France. Furthermore, the weapon used by the assassin Vlado Cemozemski was a German-made Mauser C96 pistol – coincidentally the same gun that Ramon has in *The Man Who Knew Too Much*. (Of the two dozen contemporary reviews of *The Man Who Knew Too Much* I have read, only one – in the *Yorkshire Post* – mentioned the assassination of King Alexander, though many of them related the film to the siege of Sidney Street.[33]) And for another thing, the film draws an explicit parallel between the fictional assassination plot and the origins of the First World War. In one scene Bob is confronted by Gibson of the Foreign Office, who informs him that the murdered Louis Bernard 'was one of our people – Special Service' and appeals to him to disclose what he knows. Bob, however, is more concerned for the safety of his daughter than the wider political implications:

Bob: Why should we care if some foreign statesman we've never heard of were assassinated?

Gibson: Tell me: in June 1914 had you ever heard of a place called Sarajevo? Of course you hadn't. I doubt if you'd ever heard of the Archduke Ferdinand.

> But in a month's time, because a man you've never heard of killed another man you've never heard of in a place you'd never heard of, this country was at war.

In the context of British cinema of the 1930s this was about as close as a film could get to addressing the contemporary international situation without incurring the wrath of the censor. At the same time it accrued – albeit again coincidentally – a degree of political significance that cannot have been anticipated at the time. Bob's comment about 'some foreign statesman we've never heard of' anticipates, quite uncannily, a remark four years later by the British Prime Minister Neville Chamberlain, who infamously referred to the Sudetenland Crisis as 'a quarrel in a faraway country, between people of whom we know nothing'.[34]

Raymond Durgnat offers a speculative reading of *The Man Who Knew Too Much* as an allegory of British foreign policy during the 1930s:

> It's easy to imagine a *tragic* version of *The Man Who Knew Too Much*. The couple, like Britain in the early '30s, put domestic matters before European involvements. They allow the spies to assassinate the statesman, just as Britain allowed Hitler to assassinate Czechoslovakia. And they lose their child anyway, because no man is an island. All in all, Hitchcock shies away from such grim possibilities ... The result is that the film never quite finds the theme for which, via an intense atmosphere, it none the less gropes: the theme of private involvement in an apparently remote politics, bringing civic anarchy in their train. But it is possible, after all, that the wife's cry of warning was meant as exemplary, and that Hitchcock, or his producers (one of whom was the Communist Ivor Montagu), sensing that Europe was sinking into dispirited appeasement, intended the film as a self-satisfying prophesy.[35]

It is an intriguing reading though also a problematic one. The idea that Hitchcock or Montagu set out to make a statement about the futility of appeasement in 1934 seems more than a little far-fetched (it would be a different matter with *The Lady Vanishes* in 1938, though Montagu was not involved with the later film). Appeasement had not yet become a dirty word: indeed there was a growing feeling that some of Germany's grievances were not entirely unjustified. At the same time as *The Man Who Knew Too Much*, for example, Gaumont-British released *The Iron Duke* (1934), a historical drama starring George Arliss as the Duke of Wellington which focused on its protagonist's role as a diplomat rather than as a soldier and drew quite explicit parallels between the fair-minded treatment of France at the end of the Napoleonic Wars and the harsh settlement imposed on Germany at the Treaty of Versailles.[36]

The critical reception of *The Man Who Knew Too Much* suggests that it was not seen as a political allegory at the time. In Britain the reviews focused on its qualities as entertainment and melodrama. The trade paper *Kinemato-graph Weekly*, which represented the views of cinema exhibitors, called it a 'glorious melodrama ... staged on a spectacular scale' and, contrary to the suggestion that exhibitors were reluctant to book it, predicted that it would 'prove a first class attraction'. It also suggested that Hitchcock had 'obviously learnt by past experience that real money lies only in mass appeal, and with this wise thought in mind he has given us a piece of first class melodrama'.[37] The mass-market magazine *Film Weekly* thought it 'a candid, unashamed melodrama which is as good as anything of its kind produced in the past four years'.[38] The British Film Institute's *Monthly Film Bulletin* – a sober publication less inclined to hyperbole than the trade or fan press – nevertheless admired the film and averred that its success was due largely to Hitchcock's accomplished direction: 'It is first-class cinema, and all its main virtues are essentially cinematic virtues ... [It] is the unifying hand of the director which to the observant eye is chiefly in evidence.'[39] Even the more progressive *Cinema Quarterly* felt that 'Alfred Hitchcock is much more comfortable and successful with this melodrama of a plot to assassinate a foreign statesman in London than he was with the romantic musical comedy of *Waltzes from Vienna*'.[40]

The national press also heaped praise upon *The Man Who Knew Too Much* both as a welcome relief from the literary and theatrical adaptations that characterised British cinema and as a return to form for Hitchcock himself. *The Times*, for example, felt that Hitchcock 'makes a striking "come-back"' and praised his 'rare gift for the macabre. With the aid of a few shadows, a dozen stairs or so, and a sinister-looking figure, he manages to keep his audience in a suspended state of expectation ...'[41] And C. A. Lejeune of the *Observer* – a consistent advocate of a genuinely British (or as she called it English) cinema – welcomed *The Man Who Knew Too Much* as 'good, thick-ear melodrama of an oddly English type' and 'the most promising that Hitchcock has produced since *Blackmail*, and quite possibly the best film he has ever made'. She echoed the trade press in welcoming Hitchcock's decision to abandon more intellectually ambitious film-making in favour of popular genre fare:

'Hitch' has been known too long as a 'critics' director'. This reputation has done him no good. His films have been largely attended by long-haired intellectuals sleuthing out subtleties ... Now at last he has thrown critics and intellectuals overboard with one of his incomparable rude gestures, and gone in for making pictures for the people. *The Man Who Knew Too Much* is sheer melodrama ... complete with murders, kidnapping, smiling villains, code messages and the rest.[42]

The idea that *The Man Who Knew Too Much* exemplified a robust British (or English) style of thriller also informed later critical assessments of the film. Reviewing it on the occasion of a Hitchcock retrospective at the National Film Theatre in April 1953, for instance, Richard Winnington suggested that its characters 'belong to the world of Sapper – a clearer, simpler world than that in which Hitchcock has since ventured more skilfully'.[43]

The American reception of *The Man Who Knew Too Much* differed from the British in two main respects: there was much more emphasis on its British origins and on its similarities to Hollywood's gangster films. All the US critics agreed that *The Man Who Knew Too Much* was anything but the anodyne fare that usually came out of British studios. 'The British cinema, never notable for its command of filmic pace, goes in for a blistering style of story-telling in *The Man Who Knew Too Much*,' remarked André Sennwald in the *New York Times*. 'Directed with a fascinating staccato violence by Alfred Hitchcock, it is the swiftest screen melodrama this column can recall.'[44] Gerald G. Gross of the *Washington Post* described it as 'a gangster picture made by Englishmen which in many important respects is better than most of the Tommy gun-Colt-police siren variety of motion picture that comes out of Hollywood-Astoria … *The Man Who Knew Too Much* is sufficient to stand alongside our better pictures of similar theme.'[45] And Roland Barton writing in the *Independent Exhibitors' Film Bulletin* considered it 'a gripping, blood-curdling melodrama that matches anything the American screen has ever seen'. '*The Man Who Knew Too Much*', he added, 'contains some of the most important elements which have brought world-wide popularity to American films'.[46] To this extent *The Man Who Knew Too Much* seems to have been understood as a British film in the American style: this was precisely what Hitchcock – who admired the American cinema above all others – had set out to do.

However, there were some caveats. *Harrison's Reports* – a publication for exhibitors – agreed that it was an 'exciting melodrama' but added: 'The one drawback as far as American audiences are concerned is the thick English accents of all the players.'[47] This was a familiar complaint about British films following the arrival of talking pictures: in particular American audiences seem to have been deterred by what were termed 'Oxford' accents – the sort of received pronunciation of Leslie Banks and Edna Best in *The Man Who Knew Too Much*.[48] *Variety* thought it was a good film ('An action film from England is unusual. This one has enough excitement and production values to stack up') but felt that its box-office potential was limited by its largely unknown (to American audiences at least) cast: 'It's not big time, largely because of paucity of names for US, but ought to please any audience that can be coaxed in and should do okay by itself in nabes [*sic* – i.e. neighbourhood theatres], and a cinch for double bills.' [49] Indeed the US publicity for *The Man Who Knew Too Much* billed Peter Lorre and Nova Pilbeam above Banks and Best. At the time Lorre was under contract to Columbia Pictures, though he had yet to make any films in Hollywood. Pilbeam had attracted good notices for her role in *Little Friend* (1934) and was seen by some critics as a British Shirley Temple (though Pilbeam, born in 1919, was nine years older than Temple). In the event *The Man Who Knew Too Much* had a limited release in America: it seems to have done well at metropolitan cinemas specialising in foreign films such as the Belasco in Washington, DC, and the Mayfair in New York (where it was held over for three weeks). [50]

Later critical assessments of *The Man Who Knew Too Much* have seen it not only as Hitchcock's 'comeback' film but also as representing the best qualities of his British work. It has become a matter of faith for British critics, especially, that the original version of *The Man Who Knew Too Much* is superior to Hitchcock's own Hollywood remake: hence it has become a key reference point in debates over the relative merits of British Hitchcock versus American Hitchcock. For Raymond Durgnat: 'The first is faster, more irrational, and sports a poetic flair for the bizarre, while the latter is more elaborate, not to say plodding, in its identifications and its tourist appeal ... I prefer the original, as more humorous, spontaneous, poetic and avant-garde.'[51] For John Pett, writing in 1959, the Albert Hall sequence of the British *The Man Who Knew Too Much* was 'less leisurely than the same scene in the recent disappointing remake: here every camera trick and cutting device is used, economically and with beautiful timing'.[52] Leslie Halliwell simply remarked that the British *The Man Who Knew Too Much* was 'two-thirds the length of Hitch's 1956 remake and twice as effective'.[53] In contrast the *Cahiers du Cinéma* school felt that *The Man Who Knew Too Much* was 'one of the least successful films of the English period'.[54] For Eric Rohmer and Claude Chabrol, 'in spite of its many good qualities, the first version of *The Man Who Knew Too Much* is somewhat irritating and unsatisfying, except perhaps for the final shoot-out (which is not repeated in the second version)'.[55] And for Robin Wood, 'the 1934 version seems to me a pleasant minor entertainment, one of the least interesting films of Hitchcock's first (British) maturity. The lingering belief that it is superior to the American version is incomprehensible outside the most flagrant chauvinism.'[56]

It seems to me that those who prefer the British version of *The Man Who Knew Too Much* exhibit not chauvinism but rather a different sense of formal and aesthetic priorities. The British film is shorter and more economical than the remake: if it seems slightly rough-edged at times this is both a consequence of the conditions under which it was made and part of its charm. The American version is longer and has higher production values: its virtues are those of the Hollywood studio system with its slick professionalism and box-office stars. But if the British film is shorter and less polished than the remake this does not mean that it is any less complex: and it certainly does not merit Wood's remark that '[the] thinness of the British version ... is the result of its not being about anything very much beyond its McGuffin [sic]'.[57] *Au contraire*: the British version of *The Man Who Knew Too Much* is about much more than its assassination plot. It is about the politics of class and nationhood; it is about the dislocation and restoration of the family; and it is fundamentally about the 'thin protection of civilisation' that is an important motif not only of Hitchcock's films but also of the thriller genre. *The Man Who Knew Too Much* was the first of Hitchcock's films to open up the 'chaos world' of anarchy and peril that lies beneath the surface of everyday normality: to this extent it became the template not only for the rest of the 'classic thriller sextet' but for all future films of political conspiracy and international intrigue.

3

HITCHCOCK AND BUCHAN: *THE 39 STEPS* (1935)

The influence of John Buchan on Hitchcock's films has frequently been acknowledged – not least by Hitchcock himself. As he told François Truffaut: 'Buchan was a strong influence a long time before I undertook *The Thirty-nine Steps*, and some of it is reflected in *The Man Who Knew Too Much*... What I find appealing in Buchan's work is his understatement of highly dramatic ideas.'[1] It is unsurprising that Hitchcock should be drawn to Buchan given the similarities in their work. Like Hitchcock, Buchan specialised in the adventure thriller in which an ordinary man is plunged into a world of mystery and danger. Buchan's dedication of his most famous story describes it as an example of 'that elementary type of tale which the Americans call the "dime novel" and which we know as the "shocker" – the romance where the incidents defy the probabilities, and march just inside the borders of the possible'.[2] This could equally well have been a description of Hitchcock's films.

Although John Buchan (1875–1940) had a remarkably varied public career – barrister, journalist, historian, diplomat, propagandist and politician – he is best known today for his fiction and in particular as the author of the classic adventure thriller *The Thirty-Nine Steps*. Buchan wrote *The Thirty-Nine Steps* during the early months of the First World War when he was recovering from a short illness (he suffered for much of his life from a duodenal ulcer) and the story is set in the summer of 1914 immediately before the outbreak of war. It was published as a novel in October 1915 following serialisation in *Blackwood's Magazine* and by the end of the year had sold close to 25,000 copies.[3] *The Thirty-Nine Steps* was the first of what would become a series of five novels featuring the protagonist Richard Hannay: it was followed by *Greenmantle* (1916), *Mr Standfast* (1919), *The Three Hostages* (1924) and *The Island of Sheep* (1936). Buchan's Hannay is often seen as being cut from the same cloth as Bulldog Drummond in popular accounts of the 'clubland heroes' of early twentieth-century British popular fiction, though he does not exhibit anything like the xenophobic extremes of his near-contemporary. The later Hannay adventures would see him undertaking undercover missions on behalf of British Intelligence but in the first novel he is an outsider suspected of murder and forced to go on the run in order to unravel the mystery through his own resources and so clear his name. *The Thirty-Nine Steps* may be seen as the origin of the double-hunt narrative in which the protagonist is pursued both by the police authorities and by the real perpetrators of the crime. This is seen as such a characteristically 'Hitchcockian' motif that is important to remember that it was fully in place in the source text.

The Thirty-Nine Steps belongs squarely to the lineage of the magical or sensational thriller. It is a narrative of movement and pursuit that allows little space for characterisation and has full resort to melodramatic plot devices. Richard Hannay is a South African mining engineer returning to London in 1914 who is shaken from his metropolitan *ennui* ('I had been three months in the Old Country, and was fed up with it') by the murder of his neighbour, an American called Scudder, a spy who claims to have uncovered a plot to assassinate the Greek prime minister and so precipitate a European war. Hannay deciphers the code in Scudder's notebook, which reveals a German conspiracy to steal British naval plans and so deliver a decisive blow against the Royal Navy upon the outbreak of the war. Hannay adopts a variety of identities and disguises on his journey to Scotland (reflecting Buchan's Scottish roots) where he has to keep one step ahead of both the police and the enemy agents pursuing him. Finally he returns south and, having persuaded the authorities of the truth, tracks down the German spymaster known as the 'Black Stone'. The book's title is literal: the thirty-nine steps are a staircase leading from the enemy spy's villa to the sea.

Buchan may have considered *The Thirty-Nine Steps* an 'elementary type of tale' but it is nevertheless an important milestone in the history of the thriller in English literature. Most of the spy stories in the decade or so before the First World War – represented pre-eminently by the work of E. Phillips Oppenheim and William Le Queux – had been tales of intrigue and conspiracy in the courts and governments of Continental Europe. Buchan evidently saw his own work in this tradition: he described *The Power-House* (1913) – his first true spy novel in which he had introduced another recurring protagonist in Sir Edward Leithen – as 'a tribute to my great master in fiction – E. Phillips Oppenheim'.[4] Yet *The Thirty-Nine Steps* represented a shift away from the cloak-and-dagger world of the Oppenheim-Le Queux tradition: instead its fast-paced narrative of action and pursuit drew upon the conventions of late nineteenth-century imperial adventure fiction such as Robert Louis Stevenson and H. Rider Haggard. A character in *The Thirty-Nine Steps* even remarks that 'it is all pure Rider Haggard and Conan Doyle'.[5] Some of the later Hannay stories, notably *Mr Standfast*, would be more reflective in tone, but in *The Thirty-Nine Steps* the emphasis is on pace and movement. 'What I like in *The Thirty-nine Steps* are the swift transitions', Hitchcock said: he was talking about the film, but, again, the description could apply equally well to both book and film.[6]

In a contemporary interview, Hitchcock claimed that he had wanted to make a film of *The Thirty-Nine Steps* since reading it 'about 1919 or 1920... I said that if I ever became a director I would make a picture of it. It was, therefore, on my suggestion that Gaumont-British decided to make the film so many years later.'[7] Indeed *The 39 Steps* seems such a quintessentially 'Hitchcockian' film that it comes as something of a surprise to discover in the archives a note from Michael Balcon that asks: 'Thirty Nine Steps [*sic*]. Is the script being written any good for a director other than A.J.H.?'[8] It is perfectly plausible to imagine one of Gaumont-British's other directors such as Walter Forde or Robert Stevenson making *The 39 Steps*: Forde, for example, had directed both *Rome Express* and *Bulldog Jack*, while Stevenson was a highly versatile director who made films across a range of genres including the historical film (*Tudor Rose*), horror (*The Man Who Changed His Mind*) and the adventure film (*King Solomon's Mines*). In truth there was never any serious suggestion that anyone other than Hitchcock would direct *The 39 Steps*; but the fact that the possibility was raised, if only briefly, once again suggests that the 'classic thriller sextet' of the 1930s should be seen not solely as Hitchcock films but also as Gaumont-British films.

Hitchcock later said that he had considered making a film of *Greenmantle* but opted for *The Thirty-Nine Steps* instead because it was 'a smaller subject'.[9] *Greenmantle* is a much more expansive narrative than *The Thirty-Nine Steps*: its action takes place across Europe and the Middle East and concerns an attempt by Germany to foment an Islamic uprising. *The Thirty-Nine Steps* was not only shorter and more compact – it is less than half the length of *Greenmantle* – but it also did not require overseas locations (or at least locations that could pass as overseas) as the action is confined to the British Isles. Another factor may have been that *Greenmantle* has certain parallels with the Arab Revolt during the First World War: in particular the character of Hannay's friend and fellow adventurer Sandy Arbuthnot is widely held to have been based on Colonel T. E. Lawrence – 'Lawrence of Arabia'. Alexander Korda harboured ambitions to make a film of Lawrence's *Revolt in the Desert* during the 1930s but was thwarted by a combination of the logistical difficulties involved and the political pressure brought to bear by the Foreign Office which did not wish to see a film that might upset the Turks who would be represented as villains.[10]

It has generally been maintained that the relationship between *The Thirty-Nine Steps* (novel) and *The 39 Steps* (film) is – to say the least – somewhat distant. Charles Barr, for instance, suggests that the film 'is virtually an original script'.[11] This seems to have been the consensus among contemporary reviewers who often described it as a 'loose' or 'free' adaptation and was endorsed at the time by Hitchcock himself:

> There can be no doubt that *The 39 Steps* [*sic*] is a rattling good book, but I couldn't see it as good film material. I found that by taking certain of the characters, part of the plot, and the excellent locales, I had the background for a very good screen story. Therefore I ignored the book as it stood, and developed the story with the screen in mind.[12]

Charles Bennett similarly averred that the film was more or less a screen original: 'Gradually, out of it all, we – I suppose, *I* – evolved the structure of the screenplay. All sorts of things in *The Thity-Nine Steps* [*sic*] – like the famous scene with the farmer's wife and things like that – none of this was in the novel. In fact very little of it was in the novel.'[13]

Hitchcock and Bennett made three significant changes in adapting the novel for the screen. One was to update the story from 1914 to the present: hence the film is set not on the eve of the First World War but in 1935.[14] Given that Hitchcock's next film, *Secret Agent*, would maintain the wartime setting of its source text, the decision to modernise *The 39 Steps* looks like a conscious strategy to locate it in the political context of the 1930s. In the course of doing so the film changed the meaning of the title: in the film 'the Thirty Nine Steps' is the code name of the enemy spy ring. Another major change was to introduce a romantic interest who is not in the book (though Buchan's Hannay acquired a love interest – and eventually a wife – in *Mr Standfast*) but who can be understood in terms of the film industry's imperative of providing a romantic couple. And a third important change was to turn Buchan's South African-raised protagonist into a Canadian. This can be seen as a strategy to appeal to the American market: Hannay becomes a 'mid-Atlantic' character with whom American as well as British audiences could identify. It may also have been influenced by the fact that at the time of making *The 39 Steps*, Buchan – elevated to the peerage as Lord Tweedsmuir – had just been appointed Governor-General of Canada.

There is much evidence that, unlike *The Man Who Knew Too Much*, *The 39 Steps* was seen right from the outset as a major production. It headed the

Gaumont-British production schedule for 1935 and was afforded a higher budget (initially set at £48,000 and rising to £58,500) than Hitchcock's previous film.[15] The higher budget should be seen in the context of Balcon's decision to orient production more towards the American market. This meant having to match the production values of Hollywood movies: the cost of *The 39 Steps* was around the same as the average picture cost of a middle-ranking studio such as Warner Bros. in the mid-1930s.[16] The casting of Robert Donat is further evidence that *The 39 Steps* was conceived with an eye on the American market. Donat was one of the few British actors with marquee value in America: he had recently starred in *The Count of Monte Cristo* (1934) for producer Edward Small and was much in demand by Hollywood due to his handsome good looks and lyrical speaking voice. Donat's co-star Madeleine Carroll, whose breakthrough role had been in Gaumont's *I Was A Spy*, had appeared in John Ford's *The World Moves On* (1934) and would return to Hollywood when David O. Selznick cast her as Princess Flavia in *The Prisoner of Zenda* (1937). Hence *The 39 Steps* exemplified Gaumont's international strategy both in its production values and in its casting. It was one of 'sixteen star-spangled specials' – films deemed to have a particular appeal for the American market – announced by Gaumont-British in the US trade press in June 1935.[17]

Balcon's own script notes on *The 39 Steps* reveal that he saw the film as 'an obvious international proposition' and was keen that it should not be too narrowly parochial in its content. He was concerned that the scene on the train with the travelling salesmen 'must be very foreign to an American audience' and advised that the script should be written with due regard to its intelligibility for the US market: 'I like the dialogue but it will have to be gone through most carefully as we must avoid all phrases which are purely of importance to a British Audience.'[18] He was also concerned that the scene where Hannay and Pamela share a room overnight at an inn would cause problems with the censors. In the event, however, the film had an easy passage through the BBFC. When the script was submitted for pre-production scrutiny on 15 January 1935, it was deemed 'harmless melodrama, with various very improbable incidents'. There were minor concerns about the dialogue of the salesmen on the train discussing women's underwear ('Delete reference to sex appeal') and one of the readers suggested omitting the character of the priest in the same scene. Otherwise one of the readers' concern about the scene where Hannay and Pamela are handcuffed together while laying on a bed ('This must be modified') was negated by the second reader who considered it 'perfectly harmless'. The BBFC scenario reports suggest that the script included a scene of the crofter and his wife in bed together: one reader objected ('Crofter and wife must not be shown in bed') whereas the other did not ('I see no harm in the way it is shown'). In the finished film there is no scene of the man and wife in bed. When the film was submitted for censorship on 16 May 1935, it was passed as an 'A' certificate with no deletions.[19]

The production of *The 39 Steps* appears to have been quite straightforward. It had a longer shooting schedule than *The Man Who Knew Too Much* with eight weeks on the studio floor between mid-January and mid-March 1935.[20] The street scene in a Scottish town where Hannay escapes from the Sheriff's office and hides among a Salvation Army parade was shot at Welwyn Studios in Hertfordshire as Lime Grove had no backlot or standing street sets. Assistant director Penrose Tennyson took a second unit to Scotland to shoot exteriors for the sequence of the police chasing Hannay across the moors: these were shot with doubles. Most accounts of the filming focus on Hitchcock's treatment of Madeleine Carroll: he allegedly called her 'the Birmingham tart' on set and one famous anecdote is that he pretended to have lost the key when Carroll and Donat were handcuffed together. This has generally been taken as evidence of Hitchcock's alleged misogyny and has been related to the victimisation of women in his later films such as the murder of Janet Leigh in *Psycho* and the gruelling ordeal of Tippi Hedren in *The Birds*.[21] However, this was Hitchcock's technique for drawing a sparkier performance from an actress whose screen image was rather cold and aloof. 'I had heard a lot about her as a tall, cold, blonde beauty, dignified and all that,' he told readers of *Film Pictorial*. 'After meeting her, I made up my mind to present her to the public as her *natural* self... In *The 39 Steps* the public is seeing a Madeleine Carroll who has no time to be calm and serene. She's far too busy racing over moors, climbing up and under embankments, and scrambling over rocks.'[22] Carroll was the archetypal 'Hitchcock blonde' – the first in a lineage that would also include Grace Kelly, Eva Marie Saint, Kim Novak and Tippi Hedren – and her spirited performance in *The 39 Steps* is her finest hour on screen.

Evidence that *The 39 Steps* was regarded as something of an 'event' was that it was accorded a high-profile première (at the New Gallery Cinema on London's Regent Street) attended by a number of prominent public figures including Home Secretary Sir John Simon and both the current Secretary of State for Air (Sir Philip Cunliffe-Lister) and his predecessor (Lord Londonderry). Also present was John Buchan himself, now Lord Tweedsmuir, who is reported as having said that the film was an improvement on the book.[23] There was even some talk of Buchan writing a new Richard Hannay adventure set in Canada to be made as a sequel to the film. Buchan had visited the set during production of *The 39 Steps* and had become friendly with Hitchcock. 'I can say that after I made the film "39 Steps" I used to see a lot of John Buchan, and I had lunch with him many times at the Union Club,' Hitchcock told Buchan's biographer Janet Adam Smith. 'We both attended a dinner to celebrate the premiere of the film in 1935. It was at this dinner that I was very flattered to hear John Buchan make the comment in his speech that I had improved up his novel.'[24]

It has become something of an orthodoxy in critical analyses of *The 39 Steps* to stress the film's difference from the book. This also reflects the continuing prevalence of the *auteur* theory in preference to genre criticism in relation to Hitchcock's work: hence *The 39 Steps* is claimed as Hitchcock's film rather than being seen as an adaptation of Buchan's novel. One example may suffice to represent a larger body of criticism. In an article for *Literature/Film Quarterly* in 1975, one critic writes of the film: 'Adapted from a novel by John Buchan, it is the quintessential Hitchcock, a blend of mirth, sexuality and suspense. When one examines Buchan's novel, where none of these qualities can be found, one realizes how markedly Hitchcock has changed his source.'[25] Yet this perspective seems flawed beyond the assertion that the novel contains no suspense (granted there is no sexuality and very little mirth). Many of the 'Hitchcockian' elements of *The 39 Steps* are in fact characteristics of the spy genre. The 'chaos world' of international intrigue and foreign spies, the narrative of flight and pursuit, the conspiracy to undermine the security of the British Empire and the abstract 'MacGuffin' that sets the plot in motion are all present in Buchan's novel. Even those arch *auteur* critics Rohmer and Chabrol saw *The 39 Steps* as 'a perfect example of the thriller in its pure state – so much so that it has as an essential characteristic the essence of every thriller'.[26]

Indeed it may be argued that the relationship of *The 39 Steps* to its source text is closer than has generally been allowed. It seems to me that the differences between film and book are largely on the surface: at a deeper structural and ideological level there are many more similarities than it would first appear. In fact the narrative structure of the book and the film are the same – a journey north from London to Scotland and back again – as is the double-hunt motif. Moreover several of the specific incidents in the film have direct or at least close parallels in the book: the murder of the spy in Hannay's flat, Hannay's escape from the enemy agents watching his flat disguised as a milkman, catching the train to Scotland, and scenes where Hannay stumbles by accident into the villain's home while fleeing from the police and where he has to improvise a speech at a political meeting. Even the film's celebrated scene at the crofter's cottage might have been suggested by a brief reference in the novel to Hannay spending his first night in Scotland lodging at 'a herd's cottage' where he takes 'the bed in the loft' and his hosts – a salt-of-the-earth couple – 'refused any payment'.[27] The scene in the film is a complete inversion of this situation: the crofter is characterised as a dour and suspicious type and as a miser who charges Hannay to sleep in 'a box bed' and later sells him out to the police after Hannay hands over all his money.

Hitchcock scholars see *The 39 Steps* as an exemplar of the classical narrative film. Charles Barr, for example, notes its 'exceptionally tight, symmetrical construction'.[28] Robin Wood suggests that, on the surface, *The 39 Steps* 'belongs to the "picaresque": an apparently inconsequential assemblage of episodes (the train, the crofter's cottage, the professor's mansion, the political meeting, etc.) whose common link is simply that each constitutes a further "adventure" for the protagonist'. 'In fact,' he amplifies, 'the film's structure is neither loose nor merely linear: each episode proves on closer inspection to be a component in a coherent scheme, each acquiring a deeper resonance when seen in relation to the others.'[29] Hitchcock's own account of the scripting of *The 39 Steps* was that he approached it 'as a film of episodes... As soon as we were through with one episode, I remember saying, "Here we need a good short story". I made sure the content of every scene was very solid, so that each one would be a little film in itself.'[30] Yet this also reflects the structure of the novel where each chapter is a separate incident – titles include 'The Adventure of the Literary Innkeeper', 'The Adventure of the Radical Candidate', 'The Adventure of the Spectacled Roadman', 'The Adventure of the Bald Archaeologist' and 'The Dry-Fly Fisherman' – that nevertheless slot into a coherent overall pattern. To this extent the novel provided the structural template for the film even if some of specific incidents are different.

It is not only in its narrative structure that Hitchcock's film resembles Buchan's book: the parallels extend to their themes and even to specific motifs. Michael Denning argues that Buchan's 'intensely nationalist tale' can be read as an examination of nationhood and class: these identities are explored through the motifs of impersonation and disguise. For the villains – the German agent known as the Black Stone and his associates – the role of impersonation is to pass themselves off as Englishmen: hence they 'are able to move across national boundaries impersonating figures of their own class, whether workers or gentlemen'. Hannay in contrast has no need (indeed probably no wish) ever to impersonate a foreigner: for him the role of impersonation is 'to move up and down the class structure while staying within and unifying the nationalities of the British Empire. So he can be a roadman one moment, a politician the next, a tramp, a mining engineer, a clubman.'[31] These patterns and motifs are maintained in the film of *The 39 Steps*. The professional spies move across national borders: Annabella Smith is stateless ('I have no country'), while Professor Jordan, the leader of the spy ring, passes as an Englishman living an outwardly respectable life in the 'big house' at Alt-na-Shellach, though it is strongly implied that he is foreign ('I live here as a respectable citizen... My whole existence would be jeopardised if it were known that I'm not – what shall we say? – not what I seem'). As a Canadian, Hannay stands outside the British class system: his outsider status is emphasised in the music hall at the beginning of the film where he is welcomed as 'a gentleman from Canada' and the crowd applaud.

One way of reading *The 39 Steps* is as a journey up and down the British class system. Hannay's ability to stay one step ahead of his pursuers arises from his adoption of different identities appropriate to the social milieu. He disguises himself as a milkman to evade the enemy agents watching his flat: he enlists the real milkman's assistance by pretending to be making his exit from an adulterous liaison ('Are you married?' 'Yes, but don't rub it in'). (A recurring motif of the film is that whenever Hannay tells anyone the truth – the milkman, Pamela, the Sheriff – they do not believe him: this is in contrast to the novel where characters he takes into his confidence such as the innkeeper and the parliamentary candidate Sir Harry accept his story without question.) He tells the suspicious crofter he is an unemployed motor mechanic and gives his name as 'Hammond'. Later he assumes the identities of a politician on the campaign trail (at the Assembly Hall) and of an eloping lover (at the Argyll Arms). In the latter scene the name and address he offers for the benefit of the landlady ('Mr and Mrs Henry Hopkinson, The Hollyhocks, Hammersmith') are so transparently false that it becomes a double impersonation: Hannay masquerades as a man pretending to be married. Hannay's social mobility allows him to navigate the class system: he is able to move freely between different social groups and to mould his own identity to fit the particular social environment. His mobility also extends across the United Kingdom from metropolitan London to rural Scotland: *The 39 Steps* may not be unique for a British film of the 1930s in including Scottish sequences (even if these were mostly filmed in London) but it was quite rare.

The broad parallels between book and film extend to specific motifs. Buchan's villain has a peculiarly distinguishing physical characteristic: he 'could hood his eyes like a hawk'. It is this feature that Hannay recognises when he stumbles into the Black Stone's home in Scotland. Similarly in the film Hannay recognises Professor Jordan as the enemy spymaster described by Miss Smith due to a distinctive physical characteristic: the missing top joint of his little finger. Robin Wood refers to this as a 'privileged signifier':

its appearances in the film mark important moments of plot revelation.[32] This may indeed be so: but the idea of the 'privileged signifier' is also present in the novel. So too is the 'MacGuffin'. In Buchan's novel this is represented by the murdered agent's notebook in which he has recorded details of the conspiracy in a secret code. Hannay succeeds in deciphering Scudder's code and learns of a German plot to steal a copy of the Admiralty's fleet dispositions so that upon the outbreak of war 'our coast would be ringed with mines, and submarines would be waiting for every battleship'.[33] At the time of the novel's publication this was a far from implausible scenario: a few months after the outbreak of war the battleship HMS *Audacious* had been disabled by a mine in the Irish Sea. In the film the 'MacGuffin' is the blueprint for a revolutionary new design of aircraft engine that will render it completely silent: it has been memorised by the music hall artiste Mr Memory in order that the Air Ministry will not realise the plans have been stolen. Evidence of how unimportant the 'MacGuffin' is to Hitchcock is that in the last scene the recital of the formula by the dying Mr Memory ('The first feature of the new engine is its greatly increased ratio of compression...') is garbled and compressed: the details hardly matter. It anticipates a similar moment in *North by Northwest* where the explanation of the 'MacGuffin' is drowned out by the noise of (ironically) an aircraft engine.

Another 'Hitchcockian' characteristic that might have been inspired to some extent by the novel is its narration. Hitchcock's films are notable for their extreme subjectivity: his systematic use of point-of-view and shot/reverse shot is seen as one of the means through which he expresses his authorial identity. David Bordwell suggests that, in Hitchcock's films, 'the narration confines us to a single character's point-of-view to a greater degree than is normal; this is reinforced by Hitchcock's unusual insistence upon optical subjectivity'[34] *The 39 Steps* privileges Hannay's point of view: other than two brief cutaways (the cleaning lady discovering the body and the crofter discovering the loss of his coat and hymn book) and two short scenes near the end of the film (Professor Jordan leaving his house and Pamela's visit to New Scotland Yard), Hannay is a participant and witness to everything that happens. This is a technique that Hitchcock would employ in many later films, perhaps most extensively in *Rear Window*. Evidence that at the time it was something of an innovation can be found in a review of *The 39 Steps* in the journal of the American Institute of Cinematography: 'You are allowed to see a thing or person only when the character you are accompanying sees it. As a consequence your reactions are the same as his.'[35] Yet this subjectivity has its origins in the novel: *The Thirty-Nine Steps* is written in the first-person and is

4 'May I come home with you?' Richard Hannay (Robert Donat) is propositioned by the mysterious 'Miss Smith' in *The 39 Steps* (Gaumont-British Picture Corporation, 1935).

seen entirely from Hannay's point of view. *The 39 Steps* was Hitchcock's first film adapted from a first-person narrative – a fact that might have some bearing on his adoption of such a highly subjective mode.[36]

For all these reasons, therefore, *The 39 Steps* has more in common with its source text than has hitherto been acknowledged. This is not to say, however, that it is a close adaptation or that it does not bring in elements that are not in the novel. An aspect of *The 39 Steps* that differs significantly from the book is the prominence of gender. Buchan's Hannay is to all intents and purposes sexless: this is the case even in the later books where he acquires a wife and family. In contrast the film features no fewer than three women who in different ways are set up as potential partners for Hannay. The first is 'Annabella Smith' (it is never clear if this is her real name or not) who attaches herself to him during the *mêlée* in the music hall and openly propositions him ('May I come home with you?' 'What's the idea?' 'Well, I'd like to'). Annabella is foreign and mysterious: Hannay first mistakes her for a prostitute ('Actress?' 'Not in the way you mean') and then thinks she is mad ('You ever heard of something called persecution mania?') until her murder persuades him she had been telling the truth. The second potential partner is the crofter's wife Margaret who is evidently attracted by Hannay's charm and cosmopolitan outlook: she is the only character in the film to believe in his innocence when she realises he is the suspected 'Portland Place murderer'. The third partner is Pamela whom Hannay first encounters on the train and who is initially resistant to him: unlike the crofter's wife she does not instinctively believe in his innocence and reveals his identity to the police. Pamela will eventually become a romantic partner for Hannay though only after she has suffered the indignities of being handcuffed to him and dragged under bridges and across streams as they escape from the two 'detectives' (actually enemy agents). The motif of the handcuffs has generally been read as a metaphor for marriage: Pamela is forced against her will to assume the role of Hannay's 'wife' at the inn until she learns from an overheard conversation that he has been telling the truth all along. It is at this point that Pamela becomes an ally and begins to look upon Hannay as a romantic partner. The memorable closing image of *The 39 Steps* is a close-up of Hannay and Pamela joining hands – the handcuffs still dangling from his wrist – to indicate their union.[37]

Another way of understanding *The 39 Steps* is in relation to the film culture of the time: it can be seen to have been influenced by a number of film styles and genres both from Britain and beyond. One of these – overlooked in narrowly focused *auteur* readings but picked up by film historians such as Mark Glancy – was the emergence of the so-called 'screwball' comedy in American cinema in the mid-1930s exemplified by films such as Frank Capra's *It Happened One Night* (1934) and Howard Hawks's *Twentieth Century* (1934).[38] The screwball comedy was characterised by its fast-paced narrative, witty dialogue and romantic banter: the films generally featured antagonistic couples thrown together in adverse circumstances who are nevertheless attracted to one another. In particular *The 39 Steps* bears certain parallels with *It Happened One Night* which has a similarly picaresque narrative and includes scenes in which the sparring couple – a runaway heiress (Claudette Colbert) and a down-on-his-luck newspaper reporter (Clark Gable) – have to share a motel cabin. Other influences that may be detected in *The 39 Steps* are the British regional comedy – the sequence where uniformed policemen pursue Hannay across the moors recalls the slapstick chase around Blackpool Pleasure Beach in the Gracie Fields film *Sing As We Go* (1934) with its use of accelerated motion (achieved by undercranking the camera) – and the musical: the closing sequence at the London Palladium even uses a dance number from Gaumont's Jessie Matthews musical *Evergreen* (1934). In a different tone the sequence at the crofter's cottage

5   Hannay encounters the suspicious crofter (John Laurie) and his trusting wife (Peggy Ashcroft) in *The 39 Steps* (Gaumont-British Picture Corporation, 1935).

with its acutely observed representation of an oppressive marriage and a pervading mood of gloom and despair – a sequence whose tone sets it apart from the rest of the film – is reminiscent of the style of French Poetic Realism of the 1930s. In the course of just eight minutes Hitchcock paints a picture of an oppressive marriage between the dour Presbyterian crofter and his vibrant younger wife longing for the lights of Sauchiehall Street that stands as one of the most effective critiques of patriarchy ever put on the screen. It is a tragic drama in miniature: for the woman, Margaret, there is no escape from a life of economic hardship and – as a short later scene reveals – domestic violence.

What about the politics of *The 39 Steps*? On the face of it, perhaps, *The 39 Steps* is as vague about the identity of the conspirators as *The Man Who Knew Too Much*. Annabella tells Hannay only that 'the very brilliant agent of a certain foreign power is on the point of obtaining a secret vital to your air defence', while Mr Memory is shot just as he is about to reveal the identity of the foreign power concerned: 'The Thirty-Nine Steps is an organisation of spies, collecting information on behalf of the foreign office of –.' So far so vague: *The 39 Steps* was of course constrained by the operation of censorship that prevented it from naming any foreign country as the villain. But there are certain visual and narrative clues that locate the film more directly in the ideological and geopolitical context of the mid-1930s than *The Man Who Knew Too Much*. Of the two enemy agents who pursue Hannay – minor characters who become more visible as the film progresses – one wears the sort of leather overcoat that is widely understood as visual shorthand for the Gestapo (the Nazi secret police) while the other sports what can only be described as a 'Hitler moustache'. Moreover the casting of German émigré Lucie Mannheim as Annabella hints strongly at the identity of the enemy. Annabella's comment 'I have no country' has usually been interpreted as meaning that she is a 'freelance' spy working for money, but it might equally be taken as a suggestion that she is an exile from her own country – which in the context of the time could only mean Germany. Might Annabella's remark that she will work for 'any country that pays me' be read as a comment on the fate of German exiles who found employment in Britain in the 1930s?

The 39 Steps represents a social landscape of Britain which suggests the tensions that exist beneath the 'thin protection of civilisation'. The rowdiness of the music hall at the start of the film spills over into violence – admittedly precipitated by a gunshot – and the film is characterised throughout by a sense of unease and uncertainty. At every stage of his journey Hannay encounters hostility and suspicion: this is in stark contrast to Buchan's novel where most of the people he meets are sympathetic and helpful. Indeed to watch *The 39 Steps* today is to be reminded that it was made against a background of economic uncertainty and social distress: the 1930s was the decade of the Jarrow Crusade and Walter Greenwood's *Love on the Dole* (1936). In hindsight historians have shown that the fears of social upheaval or even revolution were wide of the mark and instead have presented 1930s Britain as a nation of consensus: this was evident in the broad-based support for the National Government formed in 1931 as a response to the economic crisis and in the very narrow support for extremist political parties such as the Communist Party of Great Britain and the British Union of Fascists. Yet this was not necessarily evident to contemporaries for whom the anxieties of the time were very real. This is particularly evident in the scene at the Assembly Hall where the topics suggested for discussion are 'the herring fishery', 'unemployment' and 'the idle rich'. This might remind us that unemployment in Britain had reached record highs during the early 1930s: the worst month was in January 1933 when some 2,979,000 workers – representing 22 per cent of the insured workforce – were registered as unemployed.[39]

The closest that *The 39 Steps* comes to making a direct political statement is in the scene at the Assembly Hall where Hannay, having been mistaken for a politician who has come to support the local candidate, delivers an off-the-cuff speech. This sequence develops an episode from the novel where Hannay is asked by a prospective parliamentary candidate to address a meeting on the subject of Free Trade ('I had very few notions about Free Trade one way or the other,' Hannay muses, 'but I saw no other chance to get what I wanted').[40] In the film this becomes much more of a set piece in which Hannay, after a hesitant beginning, responds to a question about 'the idle rich' with an impassioned speech extolling the virtues of hard work and peaceful international relations:

Hannay: The idle rich? That's a bit of an old fashioned topic these days, especially for me because I'm not rich and I've never been idle. I've been pretty busy all my life and I expect to be much busier quite soon.

Voice: Have you ever worked with your hands?

Hannay: Indeed I have. And I know what it is to be lonely and helpless and to have the whole world against me – and those are things that no man or woman ought ever to feel. And I ask your candidate and all of those who love your fellow man to set for themselves a resolution to make this world a happier and better place to live in. Where no nation plots against nation, where no neighbour plots against another neighbour, where there is no persecution or hunting down, where everybody gets a square deal and a sporting chance, and where everyone tries to help and not to hinder – a world from which suspicion and cruelty and fear are forever banished. That's the sort of world I want. Is that the sort of world you want?

This is all vague enough not to associate it with any particular political party and therefore contains nothing to trouble the censor. Its expression of an idealistic sort of internationalism might at something of a stretch be seen as support for the League of Nations. On the one hand it identifies Hannay as socially and politically progressive, while on the other hand it stands as an eloquent demonstration of the power of the demagogue able to rouse his audience through empty rhetoric – a motif that was nothing if not ideologically charged in the political context of the 1930s.

For all these political references, however, there is no evidence to suggest that *The 39 Steps* was understood at the time as anything other than escapist entertainment. Following the success of *The Man Who Knew Too Much*, expectations were high for *The 39 Steps*: for the most part reviewers felt that it did not disappoint. The film press on both sides of the Atlantic was highly enthusiastic. *Kinematograph Weekly* was evidently not sure which genre

6 'I've got it!' Hannay and Pamela (Madeleine Carroll) at the London Palladium in *The 39 Steps* (Gaumont-British Picture Corporation, 1935).

category best described *The 39 Steps* (it settled for 'spectacular espionage comedy melodrama') but it admired Hitchcock's 'tongue-in-cheek' approach and 'brilliantly unorthodox treatment'. As with *The Man Who Knew Too Much*, *The 39 Steps* exhibited the sort of cinematic qualities too often lacking in British films: 'It scores because the nucleus of an excellent plot has been shrewdly and wisely adapted to conform to the technique of the screen.'[41] The *Monthly Film Bulletin* thought it an 'exciting film of espionage... very freely adapted, with complete success, from John Buchan's novel'.[42] The London critics of the US trade papers also attended the trade show and predicted that *The 39 Steps* would be a hit. *Motion Picture Daily* felt that it 'has the speed, suspense and imagination in detail characteristic of a director with an American sense of box-office values'.[43] And *The Hollywood Reporter* concurred that 'the picture has a definite market in America'.[44]

In Britain most of the national critics were also enthusiastic about the film. *The Times* called it 'a first rate film of adventure edged with comedy' and felt that the free adaptation of the book was a success: 'Readers may not find it easy to relate the Richard Hannay they knew in the novel to the happy-go-lucky adventurer who goes by the same name in this film, but they are bound to condone the freedom of an adaptation which has produced such excellent results'.[45] Much the same view was expressed by the *Manchester Guardian*, which thought it provided 'entertainment in the best sense of the word' and again approved of the freedom of the adaptation: 'Mr Hitchcock has approached the story a little less seriously than the author. He has explained less and has added some comedy... Few will quarrel with this, for the chase formula is no longer as serviceable as it was.'[46] Campbell Dixon of the *Daily Telegraph* thought it 'a very ingenious, exciting story... as good in its way as John Buchan's, and immensely cinematic'.[47] Perhaps the most prescient review in light of later tendencies in film theory came from Sydney Carroll in the *Sunday Times*. Most contemporary reviewers admired Hitchcock's direction for its technical skill, but Carroll went further:

> Every film of real quality bears the unforgettable stamp of its creator. Individuality is a rare and precious thing. In moving pictures it is exceptionally hard to discover. When it is there, however, it usually assumes a force and a distinction unmistakably attributable to its director alone. In *The Thirty-Nine Steps*, the identity and mind of Alfred Hitchcock are continuously discernible, in fact supreme.[48]

Carroll's review anticipates the discursive language of the later generation of *auteur* critics: it would seem that an early version of the *auteur* theory was alive and well in Britain two decades before *Cahiers du Cinéma* and three decades before Andrew Sarris.

However, there were a few dissenting voices who were less than wholly enthusiastic about the film. In particular there were criticisms of some of Hitchcock's technical tricks that were evidently seen as distracting. The film critic of the *New Statesman* felt that *The 39 Steps* 'is more satisfactory if accepted as entertainment than when considered strictly in terms of technique' and drew attention to 'so many little filmic tricks that are either unpardonably clumsy or, if deliberate, downright tiresome'. In particular the reviewer felt that the opening was marred by 'several awkward "cuts" [which] taint the film with a peculiar dilettantism quality which has hitherto marred 90 per cent of our talkies'.[49] Graham Greene, then the film critic of the *Spectator*, was also not a fan. In an article on the state of British cinema early in 1936, Greene described Hitchcock as being 'tricky, not imaginative': 'Hitchcock's films – especially *The Man Who Knew Too Much* – are simply made up of tricks, in their plots as well as their direction.' 'Some of his tricks are quite good tricks,' Greene conceded – he cited as an example the moment in *The 39 Steps* where 'the scream of the charwoman finding the murdered woman was cut to the shriek of the Flying Scotsman rushing north' – but he still disapproved of the implausibility of Hitchcock's films: 'Think of the ease in *The Thirty-Nine Steps* [*sic*] with which his hunted hero managed to get down from Scotland to the London Palladium, although all the way up to Scotland, and while he was in Scotland, his pursuers were always close on his heels.'[50]

The implausibilities of *The 39 Steps* did not harm its performance at the box office. *Variety* reported that it took $30,000 (around £6,700) per week during a five-week run at the New Gallery 'which is more than capacity'.[51] It also ran for eight weeks at the Marble Arch Pavilion and was held to be the second most successful film of the year in the West End after the Hollywood epic *Lives of a Bengal Lancer*.[52] This success seems to have been repeated in its national release during the autumn of 1935: it was comfortably among the year's top ten hits.[53] It was also successful in other parts of the British Empire. It was reported to have been a 'surprise hit' in Sydney where it ran for four weeks despite a summer heatwave.[54] And it was reportedly the most successful British film ever shown in Canada, where its release was timed to coincide with Buchan's arrival as Governor-General.[55]

However, it was America that was eyed as the big prize. Here the film first had to pass through the Production Code. As had also been the case with *The Man Who Knew Too Much*, the script of *The 39 Steps* had not been submitted for pre-production scrutiny. The PCA was particularly concerned with the scene at the inn where Hannay and Pamela share a bed while pretending to be a runaway couple. The PCA advised Gaumont's New York office that 'it was our first thought to delete the whole sequence when the girl and the man are on the bed. If we had had an opportunity to examine the script prior to the shooting of this scene we would have suggested changes or modifications to avoid this difficulty.'[56] In the event it insisted on deleting the shot where Pamela removes her stocking, Hannay's line 'Now for the operating table' and two shots of the sleeping Hannay rolling over and placing his hand on Pamela's leg.[57] Gaumont complained that removing the shots on the bed 'makes a very bad break in the action. It will be quite impossible to send a picture out with such a jump in the action. It would impair the value of the production to a great extent.'[58] However, the PCA remained implacable and insisted on the cuts being made. Gaumont learned its lesson: in future it would submit scripts in advance to the American censor as well as the British.

The critical reception of *The 39 Steps* in America – where it followed hot on the heels of *The Man Who Knew Too Much* – was overwhelmingly positive. It was generally thought to be superior to the previous film and some reviewers suggested that it did not merely match but even surpassed the entertainment and production values of American movies. *Time* said that it 'is the most effective demonstration yet of Director Alfred Hitchcock's method of artful understatement and its success, which has already been sensational abroad, should be a lesson to his Hollywood imitators'.[59] For Philip K. Scheuer of the *Los Angeles Times* it was 'the most perfectly told cinema within memory' and a sure sign that British cinema was on the map in America: 'All of our flattering notions about Hollywood films are upset when a picture like *The 39 Steps* come along... *The 39 Steps* makes the best of the home movies resemble so many twice told tales'.[60] And André Sennwald of the *New York Times* felt that it was 'one of the fascinating pictures of the year' and more sophisticated than the domestic product: 'By comparison with the sinister delicacy and urbane understatement of *The Thirty-Nine Steps* [*sic*], the best of our melodramas seem crude and brawling.'[61]

Like *The Man Who Knew Too Much*, *The 39 Steps* was most successful in the larger metropolitan centres. It seems to have done well from 'word of mouth' as well as from the favourable notices. Its greatest success came in New York where it was shown at the 6,000-seat Roxy Theatre where it was held over for a second week and grossed $77,000.[62] Arthur Lee of Gaumont-British's New York office wrote to Mark Ostrer: 'We're pretty bucked up by the success of *The 39 Steps* at the Roxy... This is the first time we have made money for the exhibitors.'[63] Hitchcock was named as runner-up in the New York Critics' choice of the best director of 1935 on the strength of both *The Man Who Knew Too Much* and *The 39 Steps* – the winner was John Ford for *The Informer*.[64] Elsewhere the reception of *The 39 Steps* was uneven: it enjoyed some success in Chicago, Newark, St Louis and Washington, DC, but less so in Denver, Detroit, Los Angeles and Philadelphia.[65] As ever when considering the popular reception of British films in America, the performance of *The 39 Steps* needs to be placed in context. On the one hand the success of this (and other Gaumont-British films) was less than the studio had hoped for and was limited to certain pockets: it did not receive a wide national release and even in locations where it was held over it did not necessarily do as well as some Hollywood films showing in other theatres. On the other hand, however, its success was not at all negligible. It was recognised by the US trade press as representing a new British cinema that could match the professionalism and production values of American films. It performed well in America's most cinephile city (New York) where it seems to have become something a cult hit: a '39 Steps Club' opened there whose members included James Thurber, author of *The Secret Life of Walter Mitty*. And – significantly – it was chiefly on the strength of *The 39 Steps* that Hitchcock began to receive overtures to work in Hollywood.

It is an indication of the extent to which *The 39 Steps* has come to be regarded as such a definitively 'Hitchcockian' film that later film and television adaptations of Buchan's novel have all taken the 1935 film as their point of reference more so than the source text. In fact Hitchcock himself had briefly considered remaking *The 39 Steps* in the late 1950s following his successful Hollywood remake of *The Man Who Knew Too Much* for Paramount Pictures. Angus MacPhail, who had co-written the American *The Man Who Knew Too Much*, sketched out a treatment for a new version of *The 39 Steps* featuring an opening sequence in the Whispering Gallery at St Paul's Cathedral where Hannay overhears a secret conversation between spies ('The submarine will be lying off Gleneagles. The rendezvous is at the foot of the Thirty Nine Steps') and suggested that 'Liberato the World's Greatest Escapologist' would take the place of Mr Memory.[66] MacPhail seems to have been keener on the idea than Hitchcock: 'I still don't understand what you mean by saying that *The Thirty-Nine Steps* can't be remade. In the first place, it hasn't been made. Any resemblances in your beautful film were purely coincidental.'[67] In the event the idea was abandoned when the Rank Organisation announced its intention to remake *The 39 Steps*.[68] As directed by Ralph Thomas, starring Kenneth More as Hannay and Swedish starlet Taina Elg as schoolmistress Miss Fisher, *The 39 Steps* (1959) was a modernised version of the story that has sometimes been described, erroneously, as a scene-for-scene remake of Hitchcock's film.[69] Truffaut felt that the remake 'was poorly directed' and singled out the scene where the foreign spies watch Hannay's flat: Thomas includes close shots of the spies in the street rather than staying with Hannay's point of view. Hitchcock concurred: 'It's really too bad; they miss the whole point. It's obvious that you can't change your viewpoint in the midst of a situation like that.'[70]

The Rank Organisation produced another version of *The 39 Steps* in 1978, written by Michael Robson and directed by Don Sharp. This film was closer in spirit to Buchan's novel: it is set in 1914 on the eve of the First World War and restores both the character of the murdered agent Scudder and the German conspiracy to steal the Admiralty's naval plans. Robert Powell is probably closest of all the actors to play Richard Hannay to the character of Buchan's romantic gentleman hero – he would reprise the role in a short-lived television series *Hannay* (1988) for Thames Television – and Sharp directs with a keen eye for period detail: this version of *The 39 Steps* is replete with vintage motor vehicles, trains and other heritage trappings. The decision to set the film in period rather than make it a contemporary adventure story might be seen as evidence that the amateur spy hero was now considered an outmoded archetype. It also situates *The 39 Steps* within a cycle of what might be called 'heritage spy' dramas that also included Rank's production of *The Riddle of the Sands* (1978) and the television series *Reilly: Ace of Spies* (1981). Even so the film's climax is more Hitchcock than Buchan – with a nod to Harold Lloyd and Will Hay – as Hannay hangs from the hands of Big Ben to prevent the detonation of a bomb attached to the mechanism.[71]

The BBC's 2008 television film of *The 39 Steps* – adapted by Lizzie Mickery, directed by James Hawes and starring Rupert Penry-Jones as Hannay – followed the 1978 film in maintaining the period setting and including a romantic interest, though in a nod to more progressive gender politics the character of Victoria Sinclair (Lydia Leonard) was both a Suffragette and a Secret Service Bureau agent. The decision to shoot on 35-millimetre film rather than high-definition video ensured a 'filmic' style and again this version was notable for its period trappings in the style of heritage drama. Nevertheless Hitchcock's influence was still evident in the set pieces. Penry-Jones, who also starred in the BBC's popular spy series *Spooks*, told one journalist: 'I said – jokingly, of course – that I wouldn't be in *The 39 Steps* unless the action included the famous chase scene in which Hannay is pursued by a biplane. I've always wanted to be chased by a plane like Cary Grant in *North by Northwest* and I was just delighted when it happened on our version of *Steps*.'[72]

The enduring legacy of Hitchcock's film of *The 39 Steps* may also be seen in the success of the stage version which ran for nine years at the Criterion Theatre in London from 2006 to 2015 and in the process became the fifth longest-running play in West End theatre history.[73] Adapted by Patrick Barlow from an original concept by Simon Corble and Nobby Dimon, *The 39 Steps* is a comedy in the style of Monty Python in which four actors perform all the roles, involving numerous fast changes and transitions. It includes dialogue references to other Hitchcock films, including *Strangers on a Train*, *Vertigo* and *North by Northwest*. Evidence that Hitchcock's film has so fully eclipsed its source text in the popular imaginary might be intuited from the fact that the play, known by its full title of *John Buchan's The 39 Steps* throughout its London run, became *Alfred Hitchcock's The 39 Steps* when it transferred to Broadway.

4

HITCHCOCK AND MAUGHAM:
SECRET AGENT (1936)

Neither *Secret Agent* nor *Sabotage*, the middle films of Hitchcock's 'classic thriller sextet', are as celebrated as *The 39 Steps*. To some extent this may arise from a degree of confusion over which film is which: *Secret Agent* was based on W. Somerset Maugham's *Ashenden* stories, while *Sabotage*, which followed *Secret Agent*, was, somewhat confusingly, an adaptation of Joseph Conrad's novel *The Secret Agent*. (To add further to the confusion, Hitchcock would make the similarly titled *Saboteur* in the United States in 1942.) The lesser critical status of these two films may also be attributable to their difference from those which came before and afterwards. While both containing their full share of 'Hitchcockian' elements, *Secret Agent* and *Sabotage* are more serious in tone and darker in mood than the other films. If *The Man Who Knew Too Much*, *The 39 Steps* and *The Lady Vanishes* belong to the sensational or magical lineage of the thriller, then *Secret Agent* and *Sabotage* exemplify the realist or existential thriller. This difference was due in large measure to the nature of their source texts: further evidence that Hitchcock's films need to be placed in their contexts of production and understood not solely as Hitchcock films.

Secret Agent marked a departure from Hitchcock's previous thrillers which had been derived from a tradition of popular fiction represented by authors like 'Sapper' and Buchan. W. Somerset Maugham (1874–1965) was a more 'respectable' or 'middle-brow' writer and playwright, best known for his novels *Of Human Bondage* (1915), *The Moon and Sixpence* (1919) and *The Painted Veil* (1925). His work is notable for its cosmopolitan outlook – for much of his life Maugham lived abroad – and for its acute observation of social manners and mores. Maugham's knowledge of Europe and his multi-lingualism resulted in his recruitment by the Foreign Office Intelligence Department during the First

World War: he was based in Switzerland and travelled regularly to France and Italy collecting intelligence under the guise of a writer undertaking research. *Ashenden* (some editions include the subtitle 'The British Agent') was published in 1928 and was semi-autobiographical in that it was inspired by his wartime experiences without being a memoir as such. As Maugham explained in his preface: 'This book is founded on my experiences in the Intelligence Department during the war, but rearranged for the purposes of fiction. Fact is a poor story-teller ... fiction should use life merely as raw material which it arranges in ingenious patterns.'[1] This echoes Hitchcock's oft-quoted remarks on facts ('To insist that a storyteller stick to the facts is just as ridiculous as to demand of a representative painter that he show objects accurately') and drama ('What is drama, after all, but life with the dull bits cut out') and helps to explain why the director would have been drawn to Maugham's work and to *Ashenden* in particular.[2]

Ashenden is neither a novel in the accepted sense nor a collection of stand-alone short stories with a recurring protagonist but rather a hybrid of the two: it is perhaps best described as an episodic or composite novel in that it includes a number of separate incidents which are linked only through the characters of Ashenden himself – a writer recruited into the secret service – and his controller, a colonel known only by the letter 'R'. Ashenden's experiences are far removed from the sensational heroics of Richard Hannay or Bulldog Drummond, and Maugham's account of the secret service is much more mundane than the high-society world of William Le Queux or E. Phillips Oppenheim. Maugham describes the work as 'extremely monotonous. A lot of it is uncommonly useless. The material it offers for stories is scrappy and pointless; the author has himself to make it coherent, dramatic and probable.'[3] Much of Ashenden's routine work involves gathering intelligence and paying spies for information: he seems more of a glorified courier than the heroic secret agent of popular imagination. The absence of a unifying narrative running throughout the book is a realistic device but also a structural weakness. Ashenden himself even reflects that, as a minor cog in a vast machine, 'he never had the advantage of seeing a completed action ... It was as unsatisfactory as one of those modern novels that give you a number of unrelated episodes and expect you by piecing them together to construct in your mind a connected narrative.'[4]

Ashenden may be little-known today but it was an important milestone in the history of spy literature. 'The stories in *Ashenden* ... were something new in spy fiction,' writes Julian Symons. 'After the easy absurd assumptions made by Buchan, "Sapper" and Oppenheim, the *Ashenden* stories have the reality of a cold bath.'[5] 'The foundation of a whole fictional literature about intelligence –

the putting on and penetration of masks in the zone of danger – lies in these Ashenden stories, reaching out in our own time to Ian Fleming, Len Deighton, John le Carré,' writes Anthony Curtis in his 'critical portrait' of Maugham. 'Maugham established for all time the peculiar relation between the agent (Ashenden), the chief R (here only a partially characterized figure) who manipulates him, and the victims whom he in turn tries to manipulate.'[6] The Ashenden stories not only represent the seedy reality of spying but often as not end in failure. Hence Ashenden's mission to intercept a German courier not only leads to the murder of the wrong person but also fails to find the secret documents ('The Hairless Mexican'/'The Greek'). And, perhaps to a greater degree than any other writer in the genre, Maugham considers the victims caught up in the world of international skulduggery: a governess who dies to keep her secret ('Miss King'), a loyal wife ignorant of her husband's treason ('The Traitor') and a businessman killed needlessly in a street battle during the Russian Revolution ('Mr Harrington's Washing').

Ashenden was not an easy book to adapt for the screen: its episodic structure and the absence of a romantic interest meant that there would again be significant changes in turning it into a film. The solution was to combine aspects from two of Maugham's stories and a play based on *Ashenden* by Campbell Dixon, the film critic of the *Daily Telegraph*. The stories were 'The Hairless Mexican' (in which Ashenden and a Mexican assassin are sent to Naples to intercept a Greek courier and the assassin kills the wrong man) and 'The Traitor' (in which Ashenden goes to Lucerne to persuade Caypor, an Englishman spying for Germany, to return to England in the knowledge that he will be arrested and shot). Hitchcock explained how these sources were worked into the film in a contemporary interview article for *Film Weekly*: 'We switched the two stories round completely; made Caypor the innocent victim; turned the Greek into an American; introduced a train smash for dramatic purposes; and obtained the love interest from the play.'[7] It is not clear whether the play was ever performed but the film acknowledges 'the play by Campbell Dixon' as a source ahead of 'the novel *Ashenden* by W. Somerset Maugham'. The writing credits of *Secret Agent* are just as opaque as the previous two films: Charles Bennett is credited for 'screen play', Ian Hay for 'dialogue', Alma Reville for 'continuity' and Jesse Lasky Jr for 'additional dialogue'. Lasky, whose father was one of the founders of Hollywood giant Paramount Pictures, was hired specifically to write dialogue for American characters: Bennett averred that he 'wrote a few lines and that is all'.[8]

To an even greater extent than *The 39 Steps*, Gaumont-British saw *Secret Agent* as a vehicle for the international market. Hitchcock initially wanted to reunite the star pairing of *The 39 Steps*. With Robert Donat unavailable – Donat was notoriously reluctant to commit to films – there was an attempt to secure Leslie Howard, then under contract to Warner Bros. Michael Balcon cabled Jack Warner: 'Had magnificent part for Leslie Howard in Secret Agent to be directed Hitchcock whose present picture sensational success London completing third month continuous run.'[9] Warner declined on the grounds that 'we have sold Howard pictures for two years and haven't made one'.[10] Unable to secure a bankable star name for the American market, Gaumont ensured that two of the supporting roles were beefed up. Peter Lorre, who had settled in Hollywood after *The Man Who Knew Too Much*, was recalled to play the 'Hairless Mexican', and Robert Young, a likeable American actor under contract to MGM, was cast in the part of Marvin, a love rival for Ashenden who turns out to be the German spy. Young also starred opposite Jessie Matthews in the musical comedy *It's Love Again* (1936): his presence in these films was an aspect of Gaumont's international strategy. With Madeleine Carroll as Ashenden's romantic interest Elsa Carrington, there was less need to find a star name for Ashenden himself: John Gielgud, who had appeared in Gaumont's *The Good Companions* (1933), was cast in his first starring role. Gielgud was always primarily a stage actor – while shooting *Secret Agent* he was alternating the parts of Romeo and Mercutio with Laurence Olivier in a celebrated production of *Romeo and Juliet* at the Old Vic – and by all accounts was uneasy in front of the camera.[11] Yet his uncertainty and introspection are ideal for the part of a reluctant protagonist who does not conform to the heroic archetype of the conventional thriller hero.

Secret Agent had a problematic passage through the film censors on both sides of the Atlantic. Gaumont-British initially submitted the book *Ashenden* to the British Board of Film Censors in July 1935: the internal reader's report indicated that a scene 'where the Mexican recalls his experiences with a lady spy, and how he slew her must not be shown in detail' but otherwise suggested there was no objection to the content.[12] However, it was a very different matter when the full screenplay was submitted some four months later. Colonel Hanna, the retired Indian army officer who was the BBFC's senior script reader, reported:

> The main difference between the book and this scenario, is that in the book Colonel R is never shown as suggesting or countenancing murder, as the means of obtaining his ends. In this scenario it is distinctly shown all along that Ashenden was aware that the Mexican's instructions meant murder. This makes a very fundamental difference to the story, and I am strongly of the opinion that this aspect should be removed. Caypor could meet his death as the result of a hand to hand fight or quarrel with the Mexican without any preconceived idea of murder, and the murder of Marvin can be avoided by showing him killed instead of stunned in the railway accident.[13]

For Hanna, therefore, the main issue at stake was the suggestion that the killing of the enemy spy was mandated by the secret service: this was some decades before any British secret agent in popular fiction held a 'licence to kill'. He also insisted on several deletions, including one piece of dialogue ('bloody murderer'), the 'comic business with coffin' in the opening scene ('This is in very bad taste') and 'silhouettes of three men hanging from gibbet'.

Hanna's colleague Miss Shortt – the daughter of former Home Secretary (and BBFC President) Sir Edward Shortt – also disliked the script though for different reasons:

> This is a bloodthirsty, stupid story, but I do not think it is possible to take exception to the main plot. I think it is a pity to make Ashenden so weak and nerveless [sic] and rather casts a slur on British agents. The scenes of the bombing of the train, and the three corpses hanging from the gibbet, must be carefully handled, and as the story differs somewhat from the book already, I think Marvin should be killed outright in the train accident and not shot defenceless by the Mexican. I do not like the impression given throughout, that Britain had to employ strong-nerved Mexicans to do the obviously unpleasant work of the British Agents.[14]

Miss Shortt therefore seems to have disliked *Secret Agent* for presenting its hero as weak and indecisive. Like Hanna she objected to the killing of the injured Marvin following the train crash: this was evidently a sticking point for the BBFC.

Further evidence that Gaumont-British was giving more thought to the US market is that Balcon was concerned that *Secret Agent* should not run foul of the American censor. His script notes reveal concerns over some of its racier moments: 'Think ought to take script for Hays office in view of investment ... I think scene 325 and scenes with Lili will definitely get us into trouble with the Hays organisation – the Elsa/Ashenden affair is quite dangerous enough.'[15] The decision to submit *Secret Agent* to the Production Code Administration prior to shooting was no doubt influenced by the problems encountered over *The Man Who Knew Too Much* and (to a lesser extent) *The 39 Steps*. Balcon's concern was justified: the American censor raised even more objections to *Secret Agent* than the British. An internal Production Code memorandum noted that the script 'presents a very serious problem'.[16] Vincent Hart detailed a long list of objections in a letter to Gaumont's Arthur Lee:

1. Based upon our experience with several pictures in which we have portrayed Mexicans as bandits and killers, we are of the opinion that the 'Hairless Mexican' should not be definitely characterized as a Mexican. Our suggestion is that he be portrayed as of a nondescript nationality and that you refrain from alloting him, either in

characterization, portrayal or dialogue, to any particular recognized nation.

2. The portrayal of the rooms in the hotel in which Ashenden and Elsa reside should be done in such a way as to clearly establish that they live in separate rooms, with no action taking place in a bathroom. We suggest that you strengthen the inference already in the script that there is no sexual relationship between Ashenden and Elsa and that they are merely posing as man and wife for spy purposes. Elsa's picturization as appearing clothed only in a bath towel, conducting her conversation from the bathroom, Ashenden's going into the bathroom and sitting on the edge of the tub and talking to her is objectionable from the standpoint of the Production Code. Elsa should be fully covered at all times.

3. The running 'gag' of the Mexican throwing coins and chocolates to girls in such a way that they drop down inside the dresses of the girls and then offering to retrieve them should be modified in such a way as to cut all business of the coins slipping inside the dresses. We suggest that some other less offensive gag be used.

4. We are somewhat concerned with the portrayal of the two murders committed by the 'Hairless Mexican' – a hired killer, a bandit and a fugitive from justice in his own country. In order that justice may finally prevail we are of the opinion that this murderer should not walk off free but should either be apprehended by the authorities of the country in which the final scene is laid or perhaps killed by a stray bullet or bomb in the fighting.

5. Careful consideration will have to be given to the scenes using the Swiss chocolate factory as the seat of spy operations, in order not to give offense to the Swiss nation.[17]

There followed a list of specific points, including the deletion of 'God' and 'damn' from the script, the removal or alteration of lines deemed offensive ('Ashenden's line "Does that go for either sex?" referring to the dogs should be modified to something less offensive') or too suggestive ('Marvin's remark, whispered in Elsa's ear, "Let's grab our key and go upstairs, honey" should be deleted') and the modification of the scenes between the young girl Lili and the Mexican in the latter's hotel room in order to 'definitely establish that there is no sexual interest or relationship between the two'. Like the British censor, Hart also expressed concerns over the scene showing dead bodies on a gibbet ('The portraying of the three human figures in silhouette and the accompanying dialogue as well as the impressionistic shot of a gibbet with Ashenden's lifeless body hanging from it should, in our opinion, be changed to something less gruesome') and the violence of the final scene on the train ('We recommend that this scene be modified to avoid undue gruesomeness and brutality, particularly in the closing scenes of the Mexican shooting Marvin as he drinks from the glass').

In the absence of any pre-production screenplays of *Secret Agent* in the archives, the British and American censors' reports are also revealing about the development of the script. It would seem that *Secret Agent* was intended as an even darker and psychologically more complex film than it became: the reference to an 'impressionistic shot' of Ashenden's body hanging from a gibbet (presumably reflecting Elsa's nightmare) suggests one of Hitchcock's trademark visual effects such as the glass ceiling in *The Lodger* or the gallows in *Murder!* There seems to have been more suggestion of an affair between Elsa and Marvin: the PCA insisted on removing the word 'lover' and a scene with Marvin in Elsa's bathroom. At the same time certain scenes identified as problematic by the censors survived into the film: the death of Caypor remained an act of premeditated murder and the shot of the bodies on the gibbet was included (though not the hallucinatory image of Ashenden's body). This would suggest there was some flexibility in the operation of film censorship: censors on both sides of the Atlantic were prepared to allow some leeway if the film-makers complied with other requests. As for the nationality of the 'Mexican': Gaumont acceded to the PCA's request by adding a line to the effect that he is not a Mexican national ('Why do they call him the Hairless Mexican?' 'He has a lot of unruly hair and isn't a Mexican') – in Maugham's story the moniker is literal in so far as the character is bald and Mexican – and by referring to him throughout the rest of the film as 'the General' rather than as 'the Mexican'. In any event it is unlikely that Peter Lorre's performance as the girl-chasing dandy could have been mistaken for the sort of Mexican bandit stereotype perpetuated in countless Hollywood movies.

The changes to the ending of *Secret Agent* reveal the hand of censorial intervention. Both the BBFC and the PCA had objected to the death of Marvin who was supposed to be killed in cold blood by the 'Mexican': the BBFC suggested that it would be better if Marvin died from his wounds while the PCA thought that justice would be served if the Mexican also died. According to C. A. Lejeune, two endings were shot:

The film, as Hitchcock originally shot it, ends in this way. The four, Ashenden and his wife [sic], the Mexican and the spy, come face to face on a train rushing eastward to Constantinople. The train is bombed by British aircraft. There is a crash, the carriages are telescoped; the others are shaken, but the spy is pinned under the wreckage. Ashenden's hands grope out to kill him, but he can't do it.

The Mexican, revolver in hand, takes out a brandy flask and drinks. 'Wasser' begs the spy, and gets the flask, but as he tips it to drink, the Mexican puts the gun against his heart and pulls the trigger.

Then there comes a terrible and moving shot – the sort of shot that a director only catches very rarely in a whole lifetime of pictures. The spy stops short, with the flask at his mouth – he turns on the Mexican one look of complete surprise and bewilderment – the brandy gushes out of his mouth, and he falls slowly. The Mexican picks up the flask, carefully, so as not to waste any, and drinks, with a satisfied little smile that he has earned his money and the business has been neatly done.

Now that is the end of the hunt as Hitchcock intended it, a logical rounding off of character and a reasonable disposition of the whole business. But the British Board of Film Censors wouldn't have this scene at any price, and Gaumont British had to rush to their shelves and get down a safety ending which had been shot as an emergency alternative.

Climax B, as approved by the Censor, sticks to the original version up to the moment of the train smash. Then you see a curious *volte face* of behaviour. The spy, terribly injured and in pain, is obviously dying under the wreckage. The Mexican, an Etonian for the first and last time in his career, slips him a gun under a package of cigarettes, and is shot in the stomach for his pains. At least, that's how it seemed to me. Other observers decided, on consideration, that the spy got the gun accidentally. At any rate, by putting the dirty dog on to the wrong man, the Board of Censors cleared their academic conscience.[18]

This describes the ending as it appears in the finished film: there is indeed some abiguity as to whether the assassin hands over his pistol in the expectation that Marvin will shoot him or whether he expects Marvin to commit suicide. The remark about the Mexican acting as 'an Etonian for the first and last time' might have been a reference to a line in the book: 'He hasn't had the advantages of a public-school education. His ideas of playing the game are not quite the same as yours or mine.'[19]

There is evidence to indicate that the alternate ending was shot at the studio's behest and that neither Hitchcock nor associate producer Ivor Montagu approved it. Montagu wrote to Balcon: 'The motive underlying this decision was, I am aware, the view that public taste would demand the death of the General ... As you know, both Hitch and I disagreed with this view, holding that the subsequent cheap conventionality and thematic muddle of the climax (and in retrospect of the whole story) would more than outweigh the possible popularity of the General's death.' In particular Montagu felt that the General's action in handing Marvin his pistol was out of character for someone hitherto represented as a ruthless professional assassin: 'Lorre, instead of being the vile thing with tempting outer charm that makes us forget his vileness until it suddenly unveils itself, becomes a charming thing never doing anything vile ...

7   John Gielgud as Brodie/Ashenden, the reluctant hero of *Secret Agent* (Gaumont-British Picture Corporation, 1936).

If Lorre instead is killed, then the vile thing the hero and heroine feared never happens, they are wrong, and become instead merely a couple of irresolute cissies whose shilly-shallying results in the death of their unwaveringly dutiful colleague.'[20] (The uncertainty over the ending of *Secret Agent* anticipates Hitchcock's Cold War spy thriller *Topaz* which similarly had different endings – three of them in fact. During production of the later film, Hitchcock looked back to *Secret Agent*: 'Well, to sum up, gentlemen, we have no ending to our picture . . . At least we don't have in the picture a character called R.'[21])

The flawed ending of *Secret Agent* is symptomatic of the film as a whole: it is the sort of film that is best described as 'uneven'. Hitchcock scholars generally regard *Secret Agent* as flawed in its narrative construction and overall tone. (As so often Raymond Durgnat is an idiosyncratic exception: he expresses a preference for the 'black hard mood' of *Secret Agent* over the 'dapper heroics' and 'easy levity' of *The 39 Steps*.[22]) Hitchcock attributed the failure of *Secret Agent* – relative to the previous two films – to the absence of a dynamic protagonist: 'There were lots of ideas in the picture, but it didn't really succeed and I think I know why. In an adventure drama your central figure must have a purpose . . . John Gielgud, the hero of *The Secret Agent* [*sic*], has an assignment, but the job is distasteful and he is reluctant to do it.'[23] Yet this explanation is not entirely convincing in so far as writers such as Eric Ambler and Graham Greene were able to fashion exciting thrillers with protagonists who are the most reluctant of spies: Ambler's Josef Vadassy (*Epitaph for a Spy*) and Charles Latimer (*The Mask of Dimitrios*) and Greene's Myatt (*Stamboul Train*) and Arthur Rowe (*The Ministry of Fear*) are all close relations of the Ashenden character who, like them, is an amateur caught up in the world of espionage rather than a professional spy. Moreover, there is evidence that for some critics, at least, the Ashenden character was a welcome change from more traditional screen heroes. As *Time* magazine observed: 'In contrast with old time fiction operatives like Sherlock Holmes, whose deductive gifts were superhuman, Ashenden belongs to the modern school of sleuths whose fallibility makes them plausible.'[24]

Charles Barr suggests that '[what] is unsettling about *Secret Agent* is the way in which it seeks to adapt Maugham's material within a *39 Steps* framework'.[25] Ashenden, like Hannay, is forced by circumstances into close proximity with a woman, including having to pass as husband and wife, which gives rise to a romantic relationship: to make the parallel even closer the woman is played in both films by the same actress (Madeleine Carroll). And, also like *The 39 Steps*, *Secret Agent* is structured narratively around a series of set pieces, including one on board a train. This reading may be extended further to argue that *Secret Agent* works as a counterpoint to *The 39 Steps* which mirrors but at the same time subverts the conventions of the previous film. In place of the extrovert and heroic Hannay we have the introverted and decidedly unheroic Ashenden; in place of the intelligent and sensible Pamela we have Elsa Carrington, who is initially characterised as a shallow thrill-seeker; and the role of the professional spy taken in *The 39 Steps* by Annabella Smith is transferred here to the grotesque character of the General. This counterpoint can also be seen in the film's sexual politics: whereas *The 39 Steps* had offered three potential romantic partners for Hannay (Annabella, Margaret, Pamela), *Secret Agent* instead offers a triangulation of suitors around Elsa (Ashenden, Marvin, the General). In this sense *Secret Agent* might be seen as a distorted mirror of *The 39 Steps*: it replays certain aspects of the previous film but from a much more equivocal and ambiguous perspective.

Most accounts of *Secret Agent* focus on the film's set pieces: this tends to support an auteurist reading of it as Hitchcock's film rather than as a genre film. Hitchcock explained the main set pieces – the scene in the church where Ashenden and the General discover the murdered agent, the killing of Caypor on the mountain, and the scene in the chocolate factory that turns out to be a spy 'post office' – in terms of using the locations: 'What do they have in

8   Ashenden meets his 'wife' Elsa in *Secret Agent* (Gaumont-British Picture Corporation, 1936).

Switzerland? They have milk chocolate, they have the Alps, they have village dances, and they have lakes. All of these national ingredients were woven into the picture.'[26] Leaving aside that Hitchcock's idea of Switzerland is just as much an imaginary cultural construct as the London of double-decker buses and shots of Tower Bridge and the Houses of Parliament, the set pieces can also be understood as conventions of the genre. Consider, for example, the chocolate factory. This is an extended suspense sequence (approximately seven minutes) that demonstrates Hitchcock's notion of 'pure cinema' in so far as the action is mostly 'silent' (as the background noise in the factory prevents dialogue from being audible) and where tension arises from whether Ashenden and the General's deception will be discovered before they have intercepted the coded message. Yet as well as being a characteristically 'Hitchcockian' sequence, the motif of an apparently normal location being a cover for spy activity is also a convention of the genre. In the spy thriller outward appearances are rarely what they seem: a suburban boarding house might be a spy hide-out (the 1938 British film *Strange Boarders*) or a gentleman's outfitters might be the front for the headquarters of a secret counter-espionage organisation (*The Man From U.N.C.L.E.*, an American television series of the 1960s). The British television series *The Avengers* – in which employment bureaus, marriage agencies, dancing schools, department stores and nursing homes are all fronts for various subversives – is merely the most parodic extreme of a motif that runs throughout the genre.

Secret Agent also exemplifies the themes of disguise and identity that inform the spy genre. Indeed *Secret Agent* is even more preoccupied with the idea of role-play than *The 39 Steps*: all of the principal characters are playing out roles. Elsa plays the role of Ashenden's wife: she has been instructed 'to be as conubial as possible' and Ashenden himself remarks that 'this girl's been issued to me as part of my disguise'. Marvin, the American playboy tourist and Ashenden's putative love rival, is a cover identity assumed by the German spy. The General is known as 'the Hairless Mexican' but this is also an assumed identity as he is neither hairless nor a Mexican. As for Ashenden himself: he is an entirely fictitious identity. The man known as 'Ashenden' is really a writer-soldier called Brodie: the opening sequence of *Secret Agent* features Brodie attending his own funeral ('It isn't often a soldier dies in his sleep these days') and being informed of his new persona and mission by secret service chief 'R' ('As in 'Aarrgh?' 'No, R for rhododendron'). (This is the 'comic business with the coffin' that Colonel Hanna of the BBFC deemed to be in poor taste: after the mourners leave, a one-armed attendant nonchalantly lights his cigarette from the candelabra standing on the coffin before suddenly knocking it over to reveal that the coffin is empty.) In this regard *Secret Agent* employs motifs that would feature in later spy films: the James Bond movie *You Only Live Twice* (1967) opens with Bond's apparent assassination – like Brodie's death it turns out to be a deception – while the idea of 'Ashenden' as an entirely fictitious identity anticipates Hitchcock's use of the same device in *North by Northwest*.

Where *Secret Agent* differs most markedly from Hitchcock's preceding spy thrillers, however, is in its pervading tone of moral ambiguity. *The Man Who Knew Too Much* and *The 39 Steps* had both dealt in moral absolutes: they exemplify Michael Denning's description of 'magical thrillers where there is a clear contest between Good and Evil with a virtuous hero defeating an alien and evil villain'.[27] In contrast *Secret Agent* inhabits a more ideologically ambiguous terrain: it explores issues of individual conscience and exhibits throughout a more pessimistic tone than either of its two predecessors. It adopts a distinctly ironic perspective towards patriotism ('Do you love your country?' 'Well, I've just died for it') and its protagonist is characterised as being thoroughly disillusioned with his job ('I'm fed up with this whole business. It isn't as if we've done any good since we've been out here.'). The fact that Ashenden's real identity is a soldier (a change in the film: Maugham's character has no military experience) associates him with the soldier poets of the Great War such as Siegfried Sassoon and Wilfred Owen: Ashenden shares their sense of disillusionment and *ennui*. He finds the idea of killing the German spy distasteful ('Oh, I know it's war, it's our job to do it. That doesn't prevent it being murder, does it? Simple murder!') and in the event cannot bring himself to participate in the killing of either Caypor or Marvin. The scene of Caypor's death is presented in a characteristically Hitchcock mode by turning Ashenden into a spectator: he watches from a distance through a telescope as the General (who has no such moral qualms) pushes Caypor to his death from a mountain ledge. Ashenden's impulsive cry of 'Look out!' might be understood as a means of trying to absolve him of guilt; but equally his inability to prevent the killing merely underlines his impotence as a hero.

Secret Agent seeks to distance itself from the sensational adventure narrative that had defined Hitchcock's previous two thrillers: it does this principally through the character of Elsa Carrington. R. Barton Palmer even suggests that 'Bennett and Hitchcock arguably make Elsa the moral (and then narrative) center of the film, effectively displacing Ashenden'.[28] (This might, of course, reflect the fact that Madeleine Carroll was a bigger star than John Gielgud.) Elsa is initially presented in a less than entirely sympathetic light. At their first meeting, she tells Ashenden that her interest in spying is to satisfy her craving for adventure ('I've come to Switzerland for a thrill – excitement, big risks, danger, perhaps even a little ...' – at which point she mimes firing a pistol with her fingers) and is evidently excited when Ashenden reports discovering the murdered agent in the church ('How thrilling!'). She even expresses her disappointment when she is left behind to accompany Mrs Caypor while Ashenden and the General 'have all the fun'. However, Elsa's mood changes from the moment she realises, from the howling of Caypor's dog, that the deed has been done: her sense of guilt increases when it is revealed that Caypor was not, after all, the German agent. Thereafter Elsa becomes increasingly disillusioned – even more so than Ashenden – and by the end of the film has undergone a complete ideological transformation to the extent that she attempts to prevent Ashenden and the General from going through with killing Marvin:

Elsa: I'm not going to let you do this. It's cold-blooded murder!

Ashenden: There's no use trying to stop us now. It's got to be done. I'm going to do it – it's my job.

Elsa: I'd sooner see you dead than let you do this.

9 A moment of reflection for Ashenden and 'The General' (Peter Lorre, *left*) in *Secret Agent* (Gaumont-British Picture Corporation, 1936).

Tom Ryall suggests that Elsa – a character who is not in Maugham's book – 'functions as an index of transition from light adventure tale to the gloomy world of espionage'.[29]

The ambivalence of *Secret Agent* is reinforced in its final images. The mission to kill the enemy agent has been accomplished – albeit through the intervention of the Royal Air Force in bombing the train rather than by Ashenden himself – and a short montage of troops and newspaper headlines accompanied by stirring martial music indicates the Allied victory. The very last shot is a double exposure of the smiling faces of Ashenden and Elsa over a postcard which says: 'Home safely but Never Again. Mr and Mrs Ashenden.' On one level this might be seen to anticipate the ending of *North by Northwest* in establishing the marriage of the romantic couple with characteristic Hitchcock economy. However, as Lesley Brill attests, 'the ending of *Secret Agent* is profoundly inadequate as a closure for the complex and sometimes sordid narrative that precedes it'.[30] The happy ending seems forced: it does not feel like a natural and inevitable outcome of the narrative as the marriage between Hannay and Pamela that in the event was cut from *The 39 Steps* was. Indeed it seems to have been an add-on: the scene was not in the shooting script.[31]

It would probably be fair to say that overall *Secret Agent* is the most uncertain film of the 'classic thriller sextet'. It features more elaborate suspense set pieces than any Hitchcock film to date but this was at the expense of the tightly constructed narratives of the other films. Its moral seriousness and psychological realism sit rather uneasily with its moments of broad comedy: the running joke about the General dropping coins or chocolates down ladies' *décolletage* is the sort of joke that would not have been out of place in a Marx Brothers film. The film's failure to integrate drama and comedy was noted in contemporary reviews. *The Times*, for example, noted Hitchcock's 'refreshing ability to mingle genuine humour with the macabre atmosphere of suspicion and detection', but added that on this occasion 'the balance is never adjusted … There is always the feeling that he is about to weld the two into a whole, in which humour and suspense will play proper and not contradictory parts.'[32] Overall *Secret Agent* had the sort of reception generally described as 'mixed'. *Kinematograph Weekly* thought it 'a worthy companion picture to *Thirty-Nine Steps*' and approved of its different approach to the subject matter: 'Although conventional in its fundamentals, this espionage drama differs vastly from the orthodox in its treatment. Instead of unfolding the tale with the directness usually associated with entertainment of this type, the producer reflects the story in the psychological reactions of the leading characters.'[33] Arthur Vesselo in the *Monthly Film Bulletin* praised the 'very skilful photography' and admired the film's settings ('In conveying atmosphere, Hitchcock shows himself a master, and his backgrounds – *e.g.* a chocolate factory which is also an espionage bureau, or a troop train going through enemy territory – are solid and realistic'), but felt that the narrative construction was flawed ('where Hitchcock fails is in the details of plot-construction, in leading up to and getting away from a climax, in making his general purpose clear') while the ending 'is brief and not very satisfactory'. 'There is much to be said for the technical quality and finish of this film,' he concluded; 'but the puzzling indeterminacy of outlook which pervades it makes it less than a completed whole.'[34] The US trade papers were more critical. *The Hollywood Reporter*, contrary to Arthur Vesselo, found it deficient in its technical qualities: 'The picture as a whole is marred by inexpert camera technique, film editing whose incorrectness hits one between the eyes, and strangely uneven sound recording.'[35] And the *Independent Exhibitors' Film Bulletin* felt that Hitchcock had become so obsessed with showing off his directorial flair that he had lost sight of the first principle of good direction – to tell the story: 'Alfred Hitchcock, "England's greatest director", hasn't done quite so well by this spy story. In effort to individualize the film he employed some dubious technical tricks to gain effect and turned out a jerky, halting job that will annoy many spectators, because it will befuddle them.'[36]

The most hostile review of *Secret Agent* came from Graham Greene in the *Spectator*, who felt that Hitchcock's control over the production was much to its detriment:

> How unfortunate it is that Mr Hitchcock, a clever director, is allowed to produce and even to write his own films, though as a producer he has no sense of continuity and as a writer he has no sense of life … [As] for Mr Maugham's *Ashenden*, on which this film is said to be based, nothing is left of that witty and realistic fiction.[37]

Greene, who had also disliked *The 39 Steps* for its narrative implausibility and lack of reality, elaborated on the reasons why he disliked Hitchcock's work:

> His films consist of a series of small 'amusing' melodramatic situations: the murderer's button dropped on the baccarat board; the strangled organist's hands playing the notes in the empty church; the fugitives hiding in the bell-tower when the bell begins to swing. Very perfunctorily he builds up to these tricky situations (paying no attention on the way to inconsistencies, loose ends, psychological absurdities) and then drops them: they mean nothing: they lead to nothing.[38]

Greene's hostility towards Hitchcock's films has been well documented though it remains a curious phenomenon given that their work shares so many common features. Hitchcock and Greene were both Catholics; they both specialised in the thriller genre; they both liked stories that plunged an ordinary person into extraordinary circumstances; and they both alternated throughout their careers between lighter works – what Greene called his 'entertainments' – and more psychologically complex subjects. *Secret Agent* was Hitchcock's nearest excursion into Greeneland: its moral ambiguity and unheroic protagonist locate it at the same end of the spy genre as Greene's novels of the 1930s such as *Stamboul Train*, *A Gun for Sale* and *The Confidential Agent*. Greene enjoyed a productive collaboration with another British director, Carol Reed, writing the screenplays for *The Fallen Idol* (1948) and *The Third Man* (1949), though he never worked with Hitchcock, even when Hitchcock was interested in Greene's novel *Our Man in Havana* in the late 1950s, which in the event was also filmed by Reed. Greene rejected Hitchcock's offer of £50,000 for the screen rights, later telling an audience at the National Film Theatre: 'I haven't got all that admiration for Hitchcock … and he was offering a rather derisory sum, and announced that he had bought it – so I said no.'[39]

5

HITCHCOCK AND CONRAD: *SABOTAGE* (1936)

Hitchcock followed *Secret Agent* with a film of Joseph Conrad's novel *The Secret Agent*, which necessitated a change of title to *Sabotage*. The confusion around the titles and sources of the two films is not merely academic: the fact that Hitchcock had used *Secret Agent* for his film of *Ashenden* would suggest that at that point he had not thought of the Conrad book as his next project. In a contemporary interview for the popular film press he claimed that the run of spy pictures had not been planned as such:

> It was purely a coincidence that three of my films in succession – *The Man Who Knew Too Much*, *The 39 Steps* and *Secret Agent* – should all have a background of spying. I am not setting out to be an expert on screen spies ... My next picture, which I am making with Sylvia Sidney (at present called *Sabotage*, though the title is to be changed), is a straightforward criminal thriller, without a spy in it, in spite of the coincidence that it is adapted from Conrad's novel, *The Secret Agent*.[1]

In another context, after finishing *Sabotage*, Hitchcock wrote: 'I know there are critics who ask why lately I have made only thrillers. Am I satisfied, they say, with putting on the screen the equivalent merely of popular novelettes? Part of the answer is that I am out to get the best stories I can which will suit the film medium, and I have usually found it necessary to take a hand in writing them myself.'[2]

Quite apart from Hitchcock's somewhat disingenous suggestion that the film would be 'a straightforward criminal thriller, without a spy in it', *The Secret Agent* could hardly be classed as a 'popular novelette': indeed it was perhaps the most high-brow source text that Hitchcock would ever adapt. Paula Marantz Cohen contends that *Sabotage* was 'the one movie of his career that is based on an irrefutably great work'.[3] Joseph Conrad (1857–1924) was one of the first English modernists: his novels – including *Heart of Darkness* (1899), *Lord Jim*

(1900), *Nostromo* (1904), *The Secret Agent* (1907) and *Under Western Eyes* (1911) – were characterised by their moral pessimism and their introspective, rootless protagonists. In certain respects Conrad might seem an unusual choice of author for Hitchcock to adapt. Hitchcock had usually looked to the work of more popular, even low-brow, writers such as Marie Belloc Lowndes (*The Lodger*) and John Buchan (*The 39 Steps*). The fact that he would follow *Sabotage* with films of novels by Josephine Tey (whose *A Shilling for Candles* was the source text of *Young and Innocent*), Ethel Lina White (whose *The Wheel Spins* was turned into *The Lady Vanishes*) and Daphne du Maurier (*Jamaica Inn*) highlights how much the Conrad adaptation stands out in the sequence of Hitchcock's films. Hitchcock professed that he was not interested in filming more 'literary' novels. He told Truffaut that he would never be able to film a work such as *Crime and Punishment* because 'in Dostoyevsky's novel there are many, many words and all of them have a function ... [To] really convey that in cinematic terms, substituting the language of the camera for the written word, one would have to make a six- to ten-hour film.'[4]

However, and as Matthew Paul Carlson has argued, there is a sense in which Conrad and Hitchcock were closer in spirit than sometimes assumed. [5] While Conrad had never been a best-seller – his novels were admired by literary critics but did not find a wide public until the success of *Chance* (1913) – he conceived *The Secret Agent* (subtitled 'A Simple Tale') as a more 'popular' text. As he told his agent: 'There is an element of popularity in it. By this I don't mean to say that the thing is likely to be popular. I merely think that it shows traces of capacity for that sort of treatment which may make a novel popular.'[6] While Conrad was ambivalent about writing for a mass market, Hitchcock unashamedly courted popular appeal; but at the same time his films were characterised by their 'artistic' flourishes that also made him the darling of the critics. His British films looked to straddle a middle ground between the populist appeal of Hollywood on one hand, exemplified in his preference for fast-paced narratives and star appeal, and the stylistic influence of European, especially German, films on the other. Hitchcock was a regular at the Film Society in London, the premier venue for screening European 'art' films, as was his friend and associate producer Ivor Montagu, one of the founders of the Film Society and an active participant in the alternative film culture of the interwar years.[7] H. G. Wells, another founding member of the Film Society, provides a link between Conrad and Montagu in so far as Wells was the dedicatee of *The Secret Agent* and had also lent his name to a trio of experimental comedy shorts produced by Montagu and Adrian Brunel in 1928: *Bluebottles*, *Daydreams* and *The Tonic*.[8] Carlson suggests that *The Secret Agent* and *Sabotage* are linked by more than just the latter being an adaptation of the former: he argues that 'both Conrad's novel and Hitchcock's film are distinguished by their preoccupation with the tensions between high and low as well as between the desires for critical success and popular appeal'.[9]

Conrad's dedication of *The Secret Agent* to 'the historian of the ages' describes it as a 'simple tale of the XIX century'. [10] The novel is set in 1886 but the real incident that inspired it – the failed attempt by a French anarchist called Martial Bourdin to blow up the Greenwich Observatory – happened in 1894. *The Secret Agent* centres on Verloc, an *agent provocateur* who becomes involved in a plot to bomb the observatory at the behest of his paymasters at the Russian Embassy. Russia seeks to pin the blame on anarchist émigrés based in London: the aim is to provoke a public outrage in order to force the British government's hand in signing an international treaty to proscribe the activities of such émigrés by preventing them from living in London. It is impossible not to read *The Secret Agent* in the light of Conrad's own background: he was an émigré whose parents had been political dissidents persecuted by the Tsarist regime over their support for Polish nationalism. To this extent *The Secret Agent* tapped into two ideological currents in British politics: the distrust of autocratic regimes in Europe – it was written shortly after the Revolution of 1905 in Russia which caused Tsar Nicholas II to implement some limited political reforms – and the liberal idea of Britain as a safe haven for dissidents and refugees from such regimes. This was also the theme of Edgar Wallace's near-contemporaneous *The Four Just Men* (1905) – in which a secret society plots to assassinate a politician planning to introduce an 'Aliens and Political Offences Bill' – and can therefore be seen as a motif of the genre rather than being unique to Conrad.

That said, Conrad's story was rather more sophisticated than Wallace's sensational 'shocker': indeed the influential literary critic F. R. Leavis went as far as calling *The Secret Agent* 'one of Conrad's two supreme masterpieces' – the other was *Nostromo* – and 'one of the two unquestionable classics of the first order that he added to the English novel'.[11] What distinguishes *The Secret Agent* from run-of-the-mill genre fiction is its psychological and moral complexity. Conrad is less interested in the mechanics of anarchist plotting than he is in the behaviour and motivation of his characters. *The Secret Agent* paints a bleak picture of a world of corruption, both political and moral, populated by repulsive characters and seedy locations. It is not just the anarchists who are ideologically ambiguous – Verloc himself is not even a true anarchist but a paid *agent provocateur* – but also the policemen and officials who seek to track them down. Hence the Chief Inspector (most characters are known by their titles rather than by name) suppresses evidence of his informant Verloc's involvement in the conspiracy and tries to implicate another man in his place: this in turn is discovered by the Assistant Commissioner who uses the case to advance his own career.[12] If *The Thirty-Nine Steps* marks the origin of the sensational spy thriller, then *The Secret Agent* can claim to represent the origin of the realist or existential thriller. Conrad's 'Author's Note' added to the 1920 edition of *The Secret Agent* acknowledged the 'sordid surroundings and moral squalor of the tale'. 'But still,' he added, 'I will submit that in telling Winnie Verloc's story to its anarchistic end of utter desolation, misery and despair, and telling it as I have told it here, I have not intended to commit a gratuitous outrage on the feelings of mankind.'[13]

Given that the source text was so different from Hitchcock's other films, the decision to film *The Secret Agent* requires some explanation. His biographer Donald Spoto speculates that 'Hitchcock must have chosen Conrad's novel because he shared several of its concerns: the banality of evil, the transference or assumption of guilt, the disaffection and unsteadiness in human relationships, the duplicity inherent in the enterprise of espionage and the enterprise of tracking down spies.'[14] Rohmer and Chabrol posit another explanation that has as much to do with Hitchcock's own professional and artistic ambitions as the nature of the source text. They aver that *Sabotage* was 'a film whose sole purpose was personal prestige' and that he undertook it in order to demonstrate 'that he was a director of "international" status'.[15] In this reading he chose Conrad because the source offered an opportunity to make the more serious type of film that critics such as John Grierson had long wanted him to do: he adapted the story 'with sufficient fidelity to prevent charges of betrayal' but at the same time he set out to direct it 'with such dazzling virtuosity that it would evoke the best of Hollywood without sacrificing a certain British chic'.[16] *Sabotage* was therefore intended both to prove to his critics that Hitchcock was more than just 'the world's best director of unimportant pictures' and to provide his ticket to Hollywood. It is no coincidence that Hitchcock's first visit to the United States in the spring of 1937 was to promote the release of *Sabotage*.[17]

At the same time, however, the production of *Sabotage* also needs to be seen in the context of Gaumont-British's international strategy in the mid-1930s. It was one of 24 feature films made by the studio for its 1936–7 programme which – according to its own publicity – 'will all be Class "A"... produced on an increased budget arrangement. Several Hollywood stars, directors, writers and technicians will participate in their production, in London.'[18] Among the other Gaumont-British films offered for US distribution at the same time as *Sabotage* were the historical picture *Tudor Rose* (under its working title *Nine Days a Queen*) starring Nova Pilbeam, *The Great Barrier* about the building of the Canadian Pacific Railway with American star Richard Arlen, the First World War drama *Everything Is Thunder* starring Constance Cummings and Douglass Montgomery, and a film of Rudyard Kipling's *Soldiers Three* starring Victor McLaglen and directed by Raoul Walsh (which in the event was not completed). The employment of US talent was representative of a trend across the British film industry as a whole in the mid-1930s which also saw William Cameron Menzies directing *Things To Come* (1936) and Marlene Dietrich starring in *Knight Without Armour* (1937) – both for Alexander Korda – while other Hollywood stars whose names were linked with British films included Maureen O'Sullivan and Cary Grant.[19] Michael Balcon had secured Sylvia Sidney – a stage actress whose film breakthrough came with the title role in *Madame Butterfly* (1933) – for the role of Mrs Verloc on a visit to Hollywood in 1935.[20]

Like *Ashenden*, *The Secret Agent* had been adapted for the stage: Conrad dramatised his own novel but the play ran for only a few performances in London in 1922.[21] It is not clear whether Hitchcock actually saw the play: Marantz Cohen states that he did though it has not been possible to verify this.[22] Charles Barr suggests it is unlikely that he did as 'it does not seem that Hitchcock and his collaborators referred to it'.[23] *Sabotage* – which for a while during pre-production was known as *The Hidden Power* – has similarly opaque credits as Hitchcock's other Gaumont-British films: Charles Bennett is credited for 'screen play', Ian Hay and Helen Simpson for 'dialogue', Alma Reville for 'continuity' and E. V. H. Emmett for 'additional dialogue'. Of the two newcomers to the writing team, Helen Simpson was a crime writer – she was the co-author, with Clemence Dane, of *Enter Sir John*, the novel on which *Murder!* was based, as well as author of *Under Capricorn*, which Hitchcock would film in 1949 – while E. V. H. Emmett was best-known as the 'voice' of the newsreel Gaumont-British News though he also undertook occasional script-writing jobs and would later join Ealing Studios when Michael Balcon was head of production there. As with the other films, individual contributions are difficult to untangle, though the survival of some pre-production script materials for *Sabotage* means that the process of adaptation can be documented more thoroughly. What becomes evident is that the adaptation of *The Secret Agent* into *Sabotage* was influenced by a range of political and formal considerations.[24]

Although *Sabotage* is closer to its source text than most of Hitchcock's films, there are nevertheless a number of significant changes between the novel and the film. The first – as had also been the case with *The 39 Steps* – was to update the story to the present. This had the effect of detaching the narrative from its historical roots in the 1880s and repositioning it in the context of the ideological tensions of the 1930s. Conrad's references to anarchists and socialists were removed and there was no suggestion that Russia (or any other power for that matter) was behind the bomb outrage. This was no doubt in order to comply with the policy of the British Board of Film Censors which had consistently vetoed any films that identified specific nations as committing unfriendly acts. A previous – entirely unrelated – scenario titled *Sabotage* submitted by Gaumont-British in 1933 about the Metropolitan-Vickers trial had been rejected on the grounds that it was 'political propaganda'.[25] The state-sponsored political terrorists of Conrad's novel therefore became – like the villains of *The Man Who Knew Too Much* – a group of conspirators of indeterminate national origin whose motivation may have been as much mercenary as ideological. The shooting script includes the following exchange between undercover policeman Ted Spencer and Superintendent Talbot:

> *Ted:* What's the idea, Sir? What's the point of all this wrecking?
>
> *Talbot:* Making trouble at home to take our minds off what's going on abroad. Same as in a crowd. One man treads on your toe and while you're arguing with him his pals pick your pocket.
>
> *Ted:* Who's behind it?
>
> *Talbot:* Ah, they're the ones you and I'll never catch. It's the men they employ that we're after.[26]

Barr finds this 'unconvincingly nebulous, and a demonstration of the importance to the political thriller of getting the MacGuffin right; however lacking in detail, it needs to assure us that something significant is at stake behind the personal experiences that we follow, and I don't find that this happens with *Sabotage*'.[27] Yet it is entirely consistent with Hitchcock's oft-repeated assertion that the 'MacGuffin' was really of no importance: that its function was merely as a catalyst for the action or drama. In contrast I would contend that the conspiracy plot of *Sabotage* (a group of unspecified conspirators plan to set off a bomb at the Lord Mayor's Show) is no more and no less politically significant or dramatically urgent than the conspiracy plot of *The Man Who Knew Too Much* (a group of unspecified conspirators plan to assassinate an unnamed statesmen at the Royal Albert Hall).

Other changes were of a formal nature. Conrad's sprawling, non-linear narrative was condensed into a linear four-day period: Hitchcock favoured this structure which he had used in *The 39 Steps* and would employ in later films including *Rear Window*, *North by Northwest* and *The Birds*. The fact that Charles Bennett was involved in writing both *The 39 Steps* and *Sabotage* might suggest that the tighter narrative structure reflected his input: Bennett's original play

Blackmail also demonstrates the sort of tight construction that characterises his collaborations with Hitchcock in the 1930s. And a key scene that occurs off-stage in the novel – the death of Mrs Verloc's younger brother Stevie when he is blown up by a bomb in the parcel he is carrying across London – became a major set piece in the film. This was one of the moments of 'dazzling virtuosity' that would showcase Hitchcock's direction, though he later said that he came to regret including the sequence in the film:

> I made a serious mistake in having the little boy carry the bomb. A character who unknowingly carries a bomb around as if it were an ordinary package is bound to work up a great deal of suspense in the audience. The boy was involved in a situation that got him too much sympathy from the audience, so that when the bomb exploded and he was killed, the public was resentful.[28]

Yet to call the sequence 'a grave error', as Hitchcock did, is not only to ignore the salient fact that Stevie also dies in Conrad's book even though it happens off-stage – to this extent if it was a mistake then it was as much Conrad's mistake as Hitchcock's – but also that his death is dramatically necessary for the ending of the film where Mrs Verloc kills her husband after learning he had sent Stevie to carry the time bomb. Hitchcock's suggested after-the-event alternative ('The way to handle it would have been for Homolka to kill the boy deliberately, but without showing that on the screen, and then for the wife to avenge her young brother by killing Homolka') is closer to what actually happens in the book.[29]

Another significant change was to the ending of the film. In the novel Mrs Verloc kills her husband with a carving knife when she learns of his culpability for Stevie's death: she then flees to the Continent with one of Verloc's fellow conspirators but commits suicide by jumping into the English Channel when the other man deserts her. This, evidently, was far too bleak for the film. Hitchcock and his writers introduced a romantic relationship between Mrs Verloc and policeman Ted Spencer – a sanitised character who has no resemblance to the policemen in the book – but were still faced with a knotty problem: while killing Verloc was necessary in both dramatic and psychological terms, the BBFC would surely not allow a murderer to 'get away' with the crime nor would it countenance a policeman covering up the killing because he is in love with the woman. This was a sticking point when the script of *Sabotage* was submitted to the BBFC. 'I find no objection to the main plot of this story,' reported Miss Shortt, 'but I think there should be some alteration in the end. Verloc could die in some other manner and so avoid Ted putting his love before his duty.'[30] A revised ending was submitted while the film was being shot, which now satisfied the censor: 'Ted Spencer, the detective, being quite convinced that Sylvia [*sic*] is not guilty of the murder of her husband, is shown for a very brief period hesitating between love and duty, but Sylvia's action in reporting to the Police Inspector prevents him from any breach of duty.'[31] In the event Hitchcock (and no doubt Bennett) borrowed from the ending of *Blackmail* in which the detective similarly attempts to cover up his fiancée's responsibility for killing Crewe and the police assume the blackmailer Tracy (now also dead) was the guilty party: in *Sabotage* Mrs Verloc confesses to killing her husband at the point where a bomb explodes destroying all evidence of what happened in the cinema and Superintendent Talbot is left confused ('Is that woman psychic? She said he's dead before the bomb went off ... Or was it after?').

The production of *Sabotage* would prove to be more problematic than Hitchcock's previous Gaumont-British films. Hitchcock had originally hoped to cast Robert Donat as the romantic lead Ted Spencer: Donat's casting was indeed announced in May 1936.[32] However, Donat withdrew on the grounds of ill health shortly before shooting commenced: John Loder – a stolid British actor who had made several films in Hollywood in the early 1930s – was a late replacement. Hitchcock felt that Loder 'simply wasn't the right man for the part' and told Truffaut that consequently 'I was forced to rewrite the dialogue during shooting'.[33] He was also dissatisfied with Sylvia Sidney's performance as he felt she lacked the necessary emotional range: 'I must admit that I found it rather difficult to get any shading into Sylvia Sidney's face, yet on the other hand she had nice understatement.'[34] The casting of Austrian émigré Oscar Homolka, who had just played Kruger in Gaumont's *Rhodes of Africa* (1936), was more propitious. Homolka's physical appearance closely matched Conrad's description of Verloc: 'His eyes were naturally heavy; he had an air of having wallowed, fully dressed, all day on an unmade bed.'[35] For Homolka, *Sabotage* would be the start of a long career playing character parts in spy films that culminated with his mischievous but sympathetic Soviet spymaster Colonel Stok in *Funeral in Berlin* and *Billion Dollar Brain*.

The shooting of *Sabotage* also took place against a background of institutional uncertainty at Gaumont-British. There is no record of its cost (the best estimate is around £60,000) but its shooting during the summer of 1936 coincided with a financial crisis at the studio. In 1935 Gaumont-British had made a small overall profit of £12,000 – the success of films such as *The 39 Steps* and *The Iron Duke* had been offset by others which did not meet expectations – but in 1936 it recorded a loss of £97,000.[36] In hindsight, Balcon felt that the studio's strategy of 'internationalism' had been misconceived:

Throughout 1934 and 1935 we had maintained our very substantial output, including a number of highly successful films like *The Thirty-Nine Steps* [sic] and

> *Tudor Rose*, but on the whole our films in those years were not as good as they
> should have been, and they were costing more than they should have. The
> financial results might have been different if we had had a sufficiently powerful
> and effective global selling organisation, but we did not; also the policy of using
> American artists had not paid off and the attack on the American market again
> fizzled out ... I am quite sure that these were mistaken decisions artistically, and
> financially they were unrewarding.[37]

The downturn in Gaumont-British's fortunes affected the production of
Sabotage. Hitchcock had wanted to build a full-scale replica of a tram for the
sequence where Stevie is delayed on slow-moving public transport: Balcon and
Montagu both felt this unnecessarily extravagant and insisted that a less
expensive bus would suffice. On this occasion the economic mandates of the
producers prevailed over the artistic whims of their star director.[38]

Sabotage is very much the odd-one-out of Hitchcock's 'classic thriller sextet':
its more sombre tone and its refusal to allow a happy ending set it apart from
the other films with which it is usually grouped. To an even greater extent than
Secret Agent it exemplifies the existential lineage of the thriller: this is usually
seen as the reason for its commercial failure in comparison to Hitchcock's
other Gaumont-British films. It marks a shift away from the narratives of
movement that had characterised *The Man Who Knew Too Much*, *The 39 Steps*
and *Secret Agent* and focuses instead on mood and atmosphere. It is also the
only film of the sextet to explore espionage from within (in the sense that it
focuses on the perpetrator Verloc) rather than from outside (such as a Bob
Lawrence or Richard Hannay who stumbles upon the conspiracy by accident,
or even an Ashenden figure whose assignment is to discover the identity of an
enemy spy). *Sabotage* combines the narrative of international espionage with
elements drawn from other genres. Foremost among these is the domestic
melodrama: there are echoes of previous Hitchcock films such as *The Lodger*
and *The Manxman* in the romantic triangle (Verloc, Mrs Verloc, Ted) that lies at
the centre of the film. To this extent *Sabotage* anticipates Hitchcock's later
Notorious (1946) which similarly combines aspects of the spy film and the
melodrama: the difference is that in *Notorious* these elements are more
seamlessly interwoven whereas *Sabotage* seems less assured in its construction.

It seems to me that the strengths and weaknesses of *Sabotage* as a film
largely derive from its relationship to its source text. Hitchcock seems to
have been constrained by the need to maintain a degree of fidelity to the
source: there would be little point in adapting Conrad – with all the cultural
capital that would attach to the film – if the treatment then turned out to
be as free as *The 39 Steps*. That said, there are some significant changes.

10 A meeting of spies at the London Zoo Aquarium: Verloc (Oscar Homolka, *right*) and his contact in *Sabotage* (Gaumont-British Picture Corporation, 1936).

In the novel Verloc is the proprietor of a pornographic bookshop: in the film he has become the manager of a suburban cinema. This might well have been another change deemed necessary to satisfy the censors (though Howard Hawks's film of *The Big Sleep* (1946) would manage to maintain the pornographic bookshop of Raymond Chandler's novel without censorial intervention); at the same time it also associates *Sabotage* more closely with the cultural mileu of its audiences (assuming of course that more people frequented the cinema than pornographic bookshops). The film's most memorable moments – the meeting between Verloc and a fellow conspirator in the atmospheric location of the London Zoo aquarium and the brilliantly drawn-out suspense sequence of Stevie on the bus that marks Hitchcock's most schematic application to date of the montage techniques of Soviet cinema – are cinematic rather than literary in their effects. At the same time, however, some incidents in the film may have arisen indirectly from the book. For example, could the opening act of sabotage which plunges London into darkness following a power cut (there is no equivalent scene in the novel) have been inspired by Conrad's description of the city as a 'cruel devourer of the world's light'?[39]

Mark Osteen argues that 'although *Sabotage* strays quite far from Conrad's brilliantly ironic novel in many respects, Hitchcock ingeniously invokes one of its main themes: the indeterminate nature of all action and the consequent difficulty in assigning blame'.[40] Unlike the sensational thriller variant, where the ideological and moral issues are always clear cut, in *Sabotage* the issues are clouded: it is a film that deals in shades of grey rather then black and white. The introduction into the film of a romantic triangle that is not present in the novel presents Mrs Verloc as being torn between her husband and her would-be suitor Ted: one an agent of chaos, the other a symbol of law and order. Yet in certain respects Verloc emerges as the more sympathetic character: he has provided for his wife and her brother (as in the novel it is suggested that she has married Verloc for security rather than love) and he initially attempts to distance himself from the bomb plot ('I'm not going to be connected with anything that might mean loss of life ... I won't touch it') until he is more or less blackmailed into it. Verloc's humdrum domestic life – exemplified in his repeated complaint about the vegetables not being cooked properly – marks him out as a rather pathetic figure: the very essence of what Spoto terms 'the banality of evil'. In contrast Ted, the notional hero-figure, is both manipulative – in this sense he prefigures Cary Grant's Devlin in *Notorious* (though John Loder's too-chirpy performance is far removed from Grant's cynical understatement) – and seems ready to allow his attraction to Mrs Verloc to override his duty as a policeman.

Conrad is interested in the nature and causes of political terrorism: the novel's focus is on the motivation and psychology of Verloc rather than on the consequences of his actions. In contrast the film is much more concerned with its practical implementation: its focus is as much on the 'how' as the 'why' of political violence. *Sabotage* opens with a dictionary-style definition of its own title ('Wilful destruction of buildings or machinery with the object of alarming a group of persons or inspiring public uneasiness') and significantly it changes the principal act of violence from an attack on the Royal Observatory at Greenwich (a location on the outskirts of London) which in the event fails to an attack on Piccadilly Circus (the heart of London's West End) which succeeds in so far as the explosion causes numerous fatalities. In this sense it would seem that *Sabotage* was quite consciously tapping into contemporary anxieties around subversion and political terrorism. The British government was sensitive to acts of political violence following the success of the Irish Republican Army (IRA) during the civil war in Ireland (1919–22), while the assassination of King Alexander I of Yugoslavia in 1934 seemed to

11   Superintendent Talbot (Matthew Boulton, *left*) and Ted Spencer (John Loder) in *Sabotage* (Gaumont-British Picture Corporation, 1936).

some like a throwback to Sarajevo 1914. Evidence that 'bomb outrages' of the sort depicted in *Sabotage* were considered a real threat at the time can be seen in the introduction of heightened security measures at public buildings and landmarks. In 1939, for example, the staff at Hampton Court Palace outside London were issued with a directive concerning 'precautionary measures [to be] taken against bomb outrages in State Apartments, Wine Cellars, Tudor Kitchen, & Mentagna Gallery'.[41] This was in all likelihood a response to a 'declaration of war' at the start of the year by the IRA. The threat was a very real one: on 25 August 1939 – a week before the outbreak of the Second World War – the IRA carried out a bomb attack on Coventry city centre which killed five people and injured seventy.[42]

All this would point towards *Sabotage* being a more political film than has generally been allowed. Indeed there is evidence that the film's representation of political violence was a cause of some anxiety in certain quarters. The British authorities in Palestine, for example, banned its release there, stating that 'the story of a scheme organised by foreign saboteurs to destroy London [is] entirely undesirable for exhibition'.[43] The fear was that it might inflame Arab unrest and encourage attacks on British targets. It was banned in Quebec on the grounds that 'sympathy [is] created for premeditated murders' and that it represented 'terrorists with bombs'.[44] And in Brazil it was withdrawn shortly after its release because it was deemed 'an incitement to terrorism and a threat to public disorder': at the time there was a communist-inspired revolutionary movement that sought to overthrow the authoritarian government.[45] In Britain the main threat to internal security as perceieved by the Security Service (MI5) for most of the interwar period was Communist Party infiltration of the trade unions and docks, though in the mid-1930s its focus shifted to the British Union of Fascists and its links with Nazi Germany and Fascist Italy.[46] While *Sabotage* is deliberately vague about the identity of the conspirators, the casting of the German-speaking Oscar Homolka as Verloc and Verloc's forenames (Karl Anton – changed from Adolphe in the book) hint strongly at Germany.[47] There had been similarly veiled hints in *The 39 Steps* (the First World War setting of *Secret Agent* meant there had been no need to disguise the identity of the enemy in that film): to this extent the politics of *Sabotage* were consistent not only with Hitchcock's other British thrillers but also with the ideological outlook of Gaumont-British in the 1930s.

Sabotage is perhaps the most realistic of Hitchcock's Gaumont-British films. It is realistic both in a psychological sense – the principals are more believable than the heroic protagonists of films like *The Man Who Knew Too Much* and *The 39 Steps*, for example – and in a formal sense. Even John Grierson conceded that 'Hitchcock is the only English director who can put the English poor on the screen with any verisimilitude'.[48] The representation of the suburban cinema in *Sabotage* and its environs demonstrates the same sort of attention to surface detail as the boarding house in *The Lodger* and the tobacconist's shop in *Blackmail*: Hitchcock had always demonstrated a particular knack for representing lower middle-class locales. *Sabotage* also makes more extensive use of real locations than most of Hitchcock's other British films: these include London Zoo, Trafalgar Square and Simpson's restaurant in The Strand. Hitchcock also shot actuality footage of the Lord Mayor's Parade which is cut in with a studio reconstruction in the film. The authenticity of the locations – even when using back-projection plates – has the effect of making the conspiracy plot of *Sabotage* seem closer to home than in Hitchcock's other British spy films.

At the same time, however, another interpretation of *Sabotage* – particularly among Hitchcock scholars – has been to see it as an early example of meta-cinema: a film that both comments on and draws attention to its own status as a film. Of course this might be seen as equivalent to modernist fiction's interest in its own fictionality: but it also exemplifies the transformation of a 'literary' novel into the modern medium of film. In this context changing Verloc from a shopkeeper to a cinema proprietor becomes an integral part of the film rather than a just cosmetic change. *Sabotage* was produced at a time when – in the oft-quoted words of historian A. J. P. Taylor – cinema-going was 'the essential social habit of the age'.[49] In 1936 there were over 4,500 cinemas in Britain and an estimated 917 annual cinema admissions.[50] The Bijou Cinema that Verloc runs with his wife is representative of the hundreds of small independent cinemas to be found throughout Britain in the 1930s. It is evidently not one of the sumptuous picture palaces of the West End but rather the sort of establishment known in popular parlance as a 'flea-pit'. This is evident both from its working-class patrons and from its programme: the Bijou evidently specialises in low-brow fare including Westerns (a poster advertises a Western starring 'Tom McGurth') and horror films (the film cans which Stevie carries for Verloc – and from which Ted is able to identify him following the bus explosion – contain a supporting feature titled *Bartholomew the Strangler*). The cinema setting locates *Sabotage* within a familiar social environment that contemporary audiences would instantly have recognised as being part of their own experiences: this is another reason why *Sabotage* seems one of the more realistic of Hitchcock's British films.

It has been suggested that *Sabotage* might be understood in a semi-autobiographical context. The Bijou is somewhere in the 'SE5' postcode area: in the 1930s this covered the London boroughs of Southwark, Lewisham and Greenwich.[51] This was not far from where Hitchcock grew up: his family moved from Leytonstone to Stepney in 1906 when Alfred was six. Hitchcock was an avid film-goer during his formative years. In subsequent interviews he expressed his preference for the cinema over theatre and testified that American films were his favourites. He told Truffaut: 'Though I went to the theatre very often, I preferred the movies and was more attracted to American films than to the British.'[52] *Sabotage* therefore recalls the London that Hitchcock knew from his childhood: the fact that its cinema is next door to a greengrocer's shop strengthens this autobiographical association as Hitchcock's uncle owned a number of groceries and fish-and-chip shops in the East End.[53]

Yet the cinema is more than just a physical space in *Sabotage*: the film is replete with references to film and film culture. The cinema is presented both as a site of entertainment but also as a socially disreputable space. There are frequent allusions to popular film tastes. For example, when Verloc remarks that he is 'off to a trade show' – a cover story for meeting his paymaster at the aquarium – Ted (in his own cover identity as a shopkeeper's assistant) asks him

12   Mrs Verloc (Sylvia Sidney) realises the truth in *Sabotage* (Gaumont-British Picture Corporation, 1936).

to 'pick up a good one. You know, plenty of murders. This love stuff makes me sick.' Verloc's reply ('Women like it, though') indicates his understanding of the market as well as reinforcing perceived gender differences. There are also references to the idea of the cinema as a pernicious influence. When Ted tries to prise information out of Mrs Verloc about her husband's activities ('What goes on after hours in that cinema of yours?'), her reply ('Deeds of darkness') refers to the view of some moralist critics of cinema that the darkness of the cinema auditorium turned it into a place for socially inappropriate behaviour: from its earliest days there had been social anxieties around single women attending the cinema. And the shopkeeper's apologetic response when Verloc learns that his neighbour had allowed an undercover policeman to work in his shop ('You must have been showing some funny sort of films, I dare say. You know – a bit too hot') might be seen as another oblique reference to the novel where Verloc's business had been running a pornographic bookshop. Elsewhere, film performs a significant plot function. The fact that nitrate film was not allowed to be carried on public transport due to its inflammability initially prevents Stevie from catching a bus and therefore contributes to the delay to his journey: later he is indulged by a friendly conductor who allows him on board – with tragic consequences for all the passengers. And towards the end of the film the trigger for Mrs Verloc to kill her husband is the moment in the cinema when she sees an excerpt from a Walt Disney cartoon *Who Killed Cock Robin?*: the death of the cartoon character – accompanied by boisterous laughter from the audience – 'directs her to recognize her brother's murderer and to suggest that she avenge herself'.[54]

Sabotage continually elides the real world and the fictional world of the screen: there are several points in the film where the 'real' and 'reel' worlds merge into each other. One of these is towards the end of the aquarium sequence where Verloc imagines the buildings of Piccadilly Circus collapsing following a bomb explosion: his mental image is projected onto the glass front of one of the fish tanks as if it were a cinema screen. (As an aside, the shape of the 'screen' is wider than the standard Academy ratio of the time: it is almost as if Hitchcock was anticipating the emergence of widescreen processes in the 1950s.) Another is the scene in the Verlocs' parlour – which can be reached only by passing through the cinema itself – where Ted reacts to the sudden noise of a woman's scream:

Ted: I thought someone was committing a murder.
Verloc: Someone probably was – on the screen there.

Here Verloc makes the distinction between fiction and reality: but ultimately this distinction will turn out to be illusory for him when at the end of the film murder does indeed cross over from the screen into the domestic space. Mrs Verloc will stab her huband in the very same parlour: hence Ted's 'I thought someone was committing a murder' becomes in retrospect an ironic anticipation of an event to come.

Sabotage divided critics even more than *Secret Agent*: about the only point on which there was any consensus was that it demonstrated Hitchcock's technical brilliance. The extent to which it polarised critical opinion is highlighted in the very contrasting views of two prominent critics for the weekly press: Graham Greene and C. A. Lejeune. Greene, as we have seen, was not among Hitchcock's admirers: he had been severe on *The 39 Steps* for its narrative implausibilities and condemned *Secret Agent* as a 'deplorable adaptation of Mr Maugham's *Ashenden*'. But his review of *Sabotage* was surprisingly positive:

I have sometimes doubted Mr Hitchcock's talent. As a director he has always known exactly the right place to put his camera (and there is only one right place in any scene), he has been pleasantly inventive with his sound, but as a producer and as a writer of his own scripts he has been appallingly careless: he has cared more for an ingenious melodramatic situation than for the construction and continuity of his story. In *Sabotage* for the first time he has really 'come off'.[55]

While Greene evidently did not appreciate that Hitchcock had been just as fully involved in scripting *Sabotage* as his other films ('This melodrama is convincingly realistic, perhaps because Mr Hitchcock has left the screenplay to other hands'), he felt that the film 'retains some of the ruthlessness of the original' and that for once Hitchcock's directorial flourishes did not detract from the story: 'This ingenious and pathetic twist' – in reference to the *Who Killed Cock Robin?* sequence – 'is stamped as Mr Hitchcock's own, but unlike so many of his ideas in the past it is an integral part of the story.' Otherwise Greene felt that 'Hitchcock has been helped by admirable dialogue, written by Mr Ian Hay and Miss Helen Simpson, and a fine cast ... with only two weak members' (those were John Loder and child actor Desmond Tester as Stevie for whose 'prep school accent I feel an invincible distaste').

In contrast Lejeune, usually one of Hitchcock's champions, disliked *Sabotage* with a vengeance. While she felt it 'is the cleverest picture Alfred Hitchcock has made since the arrival of the talkies', she also found it 'the least likeable of them all'. Her review explained that while she appreciated its technical excellence, calling it a 'quite masterly piece of film technics', the tone of the film was simply too bleak:

> The keynote of *Sabotage* is complete destruction. Not only is the main plot concerned with a conspiracy to blow up Piccadilly Circus and terrorise London, but everything that is human and innocent and ordinary in the picture seems consecrated to the needs of ruthlessness. The young schoolboy brother of the heroine, the only really sympathetic character in the piece, is smashed to pieces with a time bomb in a London omnibus. With him go a puppy, an amiable old lady, a friendly conductor, and all the most cheerful group of sentimental commonplaces that Hitchcock can gather together into one locale. Following this event, the heroine sticks her husband in the stomach with a carving knife, and a kindly old anarchist blows the corpse and himself to glory with another hand grenade, leaving the murderess free to marry the Scotland Yard detective. And all this destruction is neatly contrived from two pots of explosives kept in the back bedroom of a bird-shop, and labelled, with cherubic Hitchcock malice, 'Tomato Ketchup' and 'Strawberry Jam'.[56]

Lejeune conceded that the bus sequence 'is superbly timed' and 'calculated to wring every whither in the audience. But I believe – and I stick to it – that there is a code in this sort of free-handed slaughter, and Hitchcock has gone outside the code in *Sabotage*.' Hitchcock – who paid more attention to critics (or at least some critics) than his public statements would allow – seems to have taken Lejeune's criticism to heart: his later comment to Truffaut that the bus sequence 'was a grave error on my part' was a reply to Truffaut's suggestion that the killing of a child in a film 'comes close to an abuse of cinematic power'.[57]

Greene and Lejeune represented the extremes of critical opinion: otherwise the reception of *Sabotage* was the very definition of 'mixed'. Most reviewers noted that the film preferred the mechanics of suspense over the psychological aspects of Conrad's novel, but there was no consensus whether this was a good thing or not. On the one hand *The Times* felt that 'Mr Hitchcock concentrates so much on the building up of an atmosphere of suspense, with typical and rather too frequent expressions of Cockney humour, that he does not realize how much he is thinning that atmosphere by becoming absorbed in the timing and theatrical mechanics of the bomb.'[58] In contrast the *Monthly Film Bulletin* praised the film for the very same reason: 'Whereas in the book interest centres on the psychology of Verloc, the film is mainly a drama of suspenses. The individual genius of Hitchcock is very clearly shown in the distinctive and original direction.' It added that '[the] scene on the bus is unforgettable'.[59] The *Manchester Guardian* made a similar point ('instead of Conrad's air of mystery we have Hitchcock's atmosphere, and instead of Conrad's prose Hitchcock's screen technique'), but felt that Hitchcock was beginning to repeat himself: 'It is excellent that there should be in the British film industry a director who can impress his personality on his pictures; but when those pictures are all of the same type there is a sameness about his work.'[60]

Sabotage was the one Hitchcock film of the 1930s that did not find an appreciative audience. There is no hard evidence of its box-office performance but according to John Sedgwick's statistical analysis of popular film preferences it was outside the top fifty films of 1936 in Britain: *Secret Agent* – released earlier the same year – is ranked seventeenth.[61] Some indication of how Hitchcock was seen by ordinary cinema-goers rather than by professional critics is suggested by Leslie Halliwell's memoir *Seats in All Parts*:

> Until *The Lady Vanishes* we did not follow Alfred Hitchcock's name or even then understand a director's function, but I remember thinking *Secret Agent* a rambling mess and *Sabotage* rather unpleasant after some striking early scenes. *The Thirty-nine Steps* [*sic*] was quite another matter. A revival of its tongue-in-cheek adventure, laced with humour and chilling suspense, warmed us up on a December night when the [Bolton] Hippodrome's heating system broke down.[62]

In this regard the eight-year-old Halliwell and his mother seem to have been representative of audiences more generally in preferring the fast-paced action of *The 39 Steps* to the bleaker tone of *Sabotage*. This, certainly, was the lesson that Hitchcock drew from the reception of *Sabotage*: for his next film, *Young and Innocent* (1937), the only one of the 'classic thriller sextet' not featuring an espionage theme, he would return to a more light-hearted mode.

The reception of *Sabotage* in the United States – where it was released in 1937 under the title *The Woman Alone* – was generally more positive than in Britain. Frank S. Nugent of the *New York Times* called it 'a masterly exercise in suspense... imperfect narrative, but perfect dramaturgy'. 'Always the master of his picture's destiny,' he went on, 'Mr Hitchcock has reduced *The Woman Alone* to the bare essentials of its narrative, selecting only those incidents which he could bend to his melodramatic will.'[63] For the *Los Angeles Times* it was 'one of the best pictures that has come out of Britain' and demonstrated 'Mr Hitchcock's skill as a director at its best though his subject is scarcely heart-warming or cheering. But it is tense, exciting, terrifying, the characteristic understatement of the British being admirably suited to the grimly sensational episodes because it is inspired by acutely intelligent dramatic instinct and timing.'[64] Ezra Goodman in *Cinema Progress* felt that the sequence building up to the explosion of the bus was 'one of the truly memorable sequences in the entire history of the cinema and worthy of ranking with the scene where the baby-carriage careens down the steps in Eisenstein's *Potemkin*'.[65] The *Motion Picture Herald* felt that it should appeal both to cinephiles and general audiences: 'Definitely an out-of-the rut picture, it can be handled to attract the film connoisseur without losing the masses.'[66] *Harrison's Reports*, however, thought it '[a] thrilling melodrama; it should appeal to intelligent audiences. The one drawback, as far as the masses are concerned, is the slow-paced action. Otherwise, the story is extremely interesting and holds one in tense suspense throughout.'[67]

Sabotage has continued to divide opinion in subsequent critical assessments. For many Hitchcock scholars it tends to be regarded as an interesting failure that does not fit into the overall pattern of his Gaumont-British films. William Rothman, for example, contends that '*Sabotage* is not a major achievement. It does not successfully integrate its moments of horror with the theatricality demanded by the Hitchcock thriller format, which for the first time seems to constrict rather than liberate Hitchcock.'[68] Charles Barr finds the disparate elements of the film problematic: '*Sabotage* is at once a political thriller, a Conrad adaptation, and a psychodrama, and the three layers don't fully mesh; in a sense, it is delivering three stories in one, in a rich and uneven narrative that lasts barely 75 minutes.'[69] In contrast Raymond Durgnat – rarely one to side with the consensus – considers *Sabotage* 'the profoundest film of Hitchcock's thriller period, and perhaps of his career'.[70] And Neil Sinyard concurs that 'the solidity of the settings and supporting characterizations, the ruthless outrageousness of its plotting, and the tragic and ironic love story that is its core, give the film a profundity and compassion beyond anything Hitchcock made in this country'.[71]

6

AGE OF APPEASEMENT: *THE LADY VANISHES* (1938)

The Lady Vanishes – the last of the 'classic thriller sextet' – stands apart from the preceding Gaumont-British films in its production context. For one thing it was not strictly a Gaumont-British production at all but rather a Gainsborough picture 'presented' by Gaumont-British.[1] The structural reorganisation of the Gaumont-British combine in 1936–7 was occasioned by several factors – including Michael Balcon's decision to leave the company to take charge of MGM's British production arm, a takeover attempt by John Maxwell of ABPC, the closure of the Shepherd's Bush studio, and the slump that affected British film production following the boom period of the mid-1930s – and led to a consolidation of film-making activities under the banner of Gainsborough Pictures. Edward Black, Balcon's successor as head of production, oriented the studio towards genre films for the home market: this strategy was exemplified in the prominence of comedy films for music-hall stars Will Hay and the Crazy Gang in the late 1930s.[2] And for another thing most of Hitchcock's key collaborators on the preceding films were not involved in making *The Lady Vanishes*. In particular it was the first film since *The Man Who Knew Too Much* without any script credit for Charles Bennett: Bennett decamped to Hollywood in 1938 – where he would be joined a year later by Hitchcock.

Rohmer and Chabrol describe *The Lady Vanishes* as 'an excellent English film, an excellent Hitchcock film'.[3] It is often seen as Hitchcock's most quintessentially English film and the most perfectly realised film of the sextet – perhaps even more so than *The 39 Steps*. However, *The Lady Vanishes* was not originally to have been a Hitchcock film at all. Gaumont-British had bought the rights to Ethel Lina White's novel *The Wheel Spins* in 1936 and a screenplay titled *The Lost Lady* had been written by Frank Launder and Sidney Gilliat.

It was to have been directed by Roy William Neill, an Irish-born Hollywood director who made several films in Britain in the late 1930s including George Arliss's last, *Dr Syn* (1937).[4] Hitchcock came on board at a relatively late stage and by his own account his role in the development of the film was limited to fine-tuning the screenplay. In 1967, for example, he told one enquirer that 'a script had been prepared by Sidney Gilliat and Frank Launder. I then spent a month with Frank Launder revising and adding extra material to the script and so the final version of the film was based on this rewritten script.'[5]

The Lady Vanishes was unusual for Hitchcock, therefore, in so far as he had not been involved in the origins of the film but picked up a project initially earmarked for another director. This was different enough from his usual *modus operandi* that it requires some contextualisation. After completing *Young and Innocent* towards the end of 1936, Hitchcock had set his sights on Hollywood: he felt less at home at Gaumont-British following Balcon's departure and at the same time was attracted by the higher budgets and production values of the US film industry. Hitchcock's own account in the Truffaut interview – 'As soon as I had finished work on *The Lady Vanishes*, I went to America for the first time and stayed there for ten days' – is misleading in so far as his first visit to the United States in the summer of 1937 predated the production of *The Lady Vanishes*.[6] Hitchcock's visit Stateside was ostensibly to promote the US release of *Sabotage* and to capitalise on a reissue of *The Man Who Knew Too Much* and *The 39 Steps*, though he also took the opportunity to meet leading producers such as Walter Wanger and David O. Selznick. He had one picture left on his Gaumont-British contract: to this extent picking up a film that already had a script in place upon his return to London might be seen as a means of facilitating his move to a new career in Hollywood. In the event the negotiations with Selznick dragged on for a year: it was not until the summer of 1938 – and after a second visit to the United States – that Hitchcock finally agreed terms with Selznick.[7] Following *The Lady Vanishes*, he would direct one more film in Britain – the costume drama *Jamaica Inn* (1939) for Mayflower Pictures, an independent producer set up by Erich Pommer and Charles Laughton – before moving permanently to America.

The fact that *The Lady Vanishes* was not a Hitchcock-initiated project problematises the question – so often taken for granted – of Hitchcock's authorship. Indeed there is a strong case to make that it was as much a Launder and Gilliat film as a Hitchcock film. Launder and Gilliat were screenwriters whose careers paralleled each other throughout the late 1920s and early 1930s until their first collaboration with *Seven Sinners* (1936) – a remake of the silent train-based thriller *The Wrecker* – for Gaumont-British. Gilliat was credited on two Hitchcock films – for the titles of *Champagne* and for 'research' on *The Manxman* – though perhaps his most significant credit in view of their later collaboration on *The Lady Vanishes* was for 'scenario and additional dialogue' for *Rome Express*. The prominence of trains in Launder and Gilliat's early work – which, as well as *Rome Express* and *Seven Sinners*, also included *Night Train to Munich* (1940), directed by Carol Reed and often seen as a sequel of sorts to *The Lady Vanishes* – is no more than a superficial reason for locating *The Lady Vanishes* in their *œuvre* as much as in Hitchcock's. And in any event Hitchcock had featured trains in *Number Seventeen*, *The 39 Steps* and *Secret Agent*. A more convincing reason for attributing the primary authorship of *The Lady Vanishes* to Launder and Gilliat is that the qualities that have been most admired in the film – notably its adroit blending of the thriller and comedy modes and its thematic interest in the idea of Englishness – also characterise their later work. Their jointly authored scripts following *The Lady Vanishes* included several comedy-thrillers – *Inspector Hornleigh on Holiday* (1939), *Night Train to Munich*, *Crooks' Tour* (1940) and *The Girl in the News* (1940) – in addition to a stage play, *The Body Was Well Nourished*, performed at the Lyric Theatre in the summer of 1940, while Launder also wrote *Inspector Hornleigh Goes To It* (1940), one of the early wartime cycle of fifth-column thrillers with a climax on another night train, this time from Carlisle to London. When they graduated from writing to producing and directing their own films, Launder and Gilliat occasionally returned to the comedy-thriller with *I See A Dark Stranger* (1946) and *Green for Danger* (1946), while *State Secret* (1950) also has some echoes of *The Lady Vanishes* in its tale of a surgeon caught up in political intrigue in a fictitious Central European country.

The extent to which *The Lady Vanishes* may be described as either a Hitchcock film or a Launder and Gilliat film is further complicated by the film's relationship to its source text. Ethel Lina White (1876–1944) is now less remembered than other British crime writers of the interwar period such as Agatha Christie and Dorothy L. Sayers though at the time she was popular enough for Hollywood to produce films of several of her books, including *Some Must Watch* (filmed as *The Spiral Staircase* in 1945) and *Midnight Hour* (as *The Unseen* in 1945). Her 1936 novel *The Wheel Spins* may be placed within a cycle of train-related crime fiction in the 1930s: other examples included Graham Greene's *Stamboul Train* (1932) – filmed in Hollywood as *Orient Express* (1934) – and Agatha Christie's *Murder on the Orient Express* (1934), as well as films such as *Rome Express* and *Seven Sinners*. The vogue for train-related fiction in the 1930s may be related to the increasing popularity of Continental travel for the middle classes and the democratisation of foreign holidays. A throwaway line in *The Lady Vanishes* ('Don't tell me Cook's are running cheap tours here!') is a reference to the travel agency Thomas Cook & Son, which had been offering organised tours of Continental Europe since the late nineteenth century. And the travel motif in which a diverse group of characters are brought together in adverse circumstances is an ideal narrative for exploring national identity: social attitudes and national characteristics are exaggerated when displaced from the domestic scene and contrasted with 'foreign' values.

The Wheel Spins has been so overshadowed by the film of *The Lady Vanishes* that later editions of the novel have adopted the film's title. However, many aspects of the film are present in White's original. The basic situation concerning the disappearance of a middle-aged English governess on an express train in an unspecified Central European country is taken from the novel, as is the heroine Iris Carr (Henderson in the film) who attempts to find Miss Froy and to persuade the sceptical fellow passengers of her disappearance. Thematically the novel is replete with observations about the English character:

> 'It was my fault,' declared Mrs Barnes. 'I know people think I'm curious. But, really, I have to force myself to show an interest in my neighbour's affairs. It's my protest against our terrible national shyness.'

> 'But we're proud of that,' broke in Miss Rose. 'England does not need to advertise.'[8]

Miss Froy herself is characterised as something of a conservative who regrets the inevitability of social change and admires the upper classes for their paternalism:

> 'Those people are English,' she whispered to Iris, not knowing that they had met before. 'They're part of an England that is passing away. Well-bred, privileged people, who live in big houses, and don't spend their income. I'm rather sorry they're dying out.'

> 'Why?' asked Iris.

> 'Because, although I'm a worker myself, I feel that nice leisured people stand for much that is good. Tradition, charity, national prestige. They may not think you're their equal, but their sense of justice sees that you get equal rights.'[9]

In contrast Iris is characterised as a modern 'society girl' whose outward demeanour offends the other English characters but conceals an underlying decency that is demonstrated when she is the only person who tries to help the missing Miss Froy.

The style of *The Wheel Spins* anticipates the film in a number of respects. It is a very 'cinematic' text: written in short chapters and featuring cinematic allusions such as White's description of the scenery passing outside the train window ('Iris had the impression that the whole scene was flickering like an early motion-picture') and the aura of movie stardom that envelops the 'honeymoon' couple travelling under the name of Todhunter ('The bride wore the kind of elaborate travelling-costume which is worn only on journeys inside a film studio').[10] It includes a self-reflexive dimension as Iris's reluctant helper Max Hare discusses the mystery of Miss Froy's disappearance in terms of a detective story: 'Could you write a detective thriller? ... I've got it to fit. Bit of jiggery-pokery in parts, but it hangs together. Now would you like to hear an original story called "The Strange Disappearance of Miss Froy"?'[11] The novel also anticipates the oneiric dimension that critics have identified in the film: Iris lapses in and out of consciousness and her experiences are several times described through dream-like imagery. Early in the journey Iris, who is suffering from sunstroke, is described as 'beginning to feel heady and unreal, as though she were in a dream, where every emotion is intensified'.[12] And later an apparently friendly doctor suggests that Miss Froy is a hallucination caused by Iris's sunstroke: 'You saw someone who is not there ... She is nothing but a delirium – a dream.'[13] This explanation is also put forward by Dr Hartz in *The Lady Vanishes*. As in *The 39 Steps*, Hitchcock's use of subjective narration and his directorial flourishes to depict Iris's delirious state – such as the scene where she sees Miss Froy's face superimposed on the faces of the other passengers around her – can be traced back to the source text rather than being seen solely as an expression of his own authorship.

The changes made by Launder and Gilliat in writing the screenplay may be seen not as radical alterations but rather as building upon the inherent cinematic qualities of the novel. As in *The 39 Steps* a romantic interest is added for Iris in the form of musician Gilbert who is evidently attracted to her despite their initial antipathy ('Confidentially I think you're a bit of a stinker too') and who takes the place of two characters in the book – a rugby international called Max Hare and a prissy professor of languages who acts as a reluctant translator. The reason for the kidnapping of Miss Froy is changed from a local matter in the novel, where she is a governess who has unwittingly come into a politically sensitive secret, to a matter of far greater international import: in the film she is a spy masquerading as a governess who is conveying to the Foreign Office a code that contains 'the vital clause of a secret pact between two European countries'. (This is an explanation that Max Hare posits in the book – 'Miss Froy is a spy who's got some information which she's sneaking out of the country. So she's got to be bumped off. And what better way than on a railway journey?' – only to reject it as too implausible: 'I only told you how things *might* be worked out. But I'm just like the old lady who saw a giraffe for the first time. Honestly, "*I don't believe it.*"'[14]) Some of the minor characters of the book are maintained – the Baroness and the Todhunters, for example – while a pair of spinster sisters become middle-aged bachelors. Evidence that these interventions were Launder and Gilliat's rather than Hitchcock's is that the two cricket-obsessives Charters and Caldicott – memorably played by Basil Radford and Naunton Wayne – would feature in other Launder and Gilliat-scripted films including *Night Train to Munich, Crooks' Tour* and their wartime directorial debut *Millions Like Us* (1943).[15] The final-act shoot-out sequence – an addition suggested by Hitchcock – also provides a more cinematic climax.[16]

The Lady Vanishes was the first film under a new distribution agreement between Gaumont-British and MGM whereby the latter would act as distributor for the studio's films at home and abroad.[17] On the one hand, the MGM deal was seen at the time as evidence of the growing interest in British films in America; on the other hand, it was also a symptom of Gaumont-British's failure to establish its own distribution network in the United States. Unlike previous Hitchcock films such as *The 39 Steps* and *Secret Agent*, there was nothing in the production of *The Lady Vanishes* to indicate that it made any concessions to American tastes. The stars Margaret Lockwood and Michael Redgrave were both relative newcomers with only a handful of appearances in British films to their names, while of the supporting cast only Paul Lukas (as the chief villain Dr Hartz) and Dame May Whitty (Miss Froy) had any Hollywood experience. Moreover the script of *The Lady Vanishes* is replete with the sort of 'parochial' references to English culture and habits that Balcon had sought to minimise in *The 39 Steps*. This point was noted by C. A. Lejeune, writing as London film correspondent for the *New York Times*, who wondered whether American audiences would understand the recurring joke about Charters and Caldicott wanting to get back in time to see the end of a Test Match: 'I don't know how this very national joke will go down in, say, Kansas City, but over here it looks like being the season's best running gag.'[18]

Further evidence that *The Lady Vanishes* was produced without taking American sensibilities into account is that it was not submitted for pre-production scrutiny to the Hays Office. This may have been a consequence of Gaumont-British closing its New York office: nevertheless the company's change of policy – since *The 39 Steps* it had regularly submitted scripts to the American censor as well as the British prior to production – suggests that it was less concerned about the American reaction. And there was much in *The Lady*

Vanishes to which the Production Code Administration took exception when the film was submitted for approval on 4 October 1938. The PCA advised that it 'is basically in conformity with the requirements of the Production Code' but appended a long list of scenes and dialogue that required modification. It objected in particular to the characters of 'Mr and Mrs Todhunter' and required the deletion of several bits of dialogue 'in order to remove the portrayal of this adulterous relationship which apparently is unnecessary to the plot'. It also objected to Gilbert's lines 'always supposing you were born in wedlock, which I doubt' and 'My father always taught me never desert a lady in trouble – he even carried it as far as marrying my mother'.[19] It is interesting that neither these lines nor the Todhunters' adultery had been such a concern for the British censor who had allowed them: this was an instance where the American censor seemed more puritanical in enforcing its moral code. The PCA files do not make it clear but there may also have been – as there had with *The Man Who Knew Too Much* – a view that Hollywood producers would feel aggrieved if British films were treated by different standards than American movies.

Nor did *The Lady Vanishes* obviously orient itself towards the American market in terms of its production values. There is no information regarding its cost but it looks to have been produced on a lower budget than *The 39 Steps*, *Secret Agent* or *Sabotage*. *Young and Innocent* had been shot at the newly opened and well-equipped Pinewood Studios: *The Lady Vanishes* in contrast had to make do with Gainsborough's tiny Islington Studios. It was shot – according to Hitchcock – on 'one of the smaller Islington stages, on a set ninety feet long. We used one coach; all the rest were transparencies or miniatures'.[20] The confined sets were a speciality of art director Alexander Vetchinsky whose work exhibits a practical minimalism in contrast to the style of Alfred Junge and Oscar Werndorff who had designed the previous films of the thriller sextet. Hitchcock's extensive use of models and back projection prompt different responses. For Truffaut they simply did not matter: 'I tell myself each time [I see it] that I'm going to ignore the plot, to examine the train and see if it's really moving, or to study the camera movements inside the compartments. But each time I become so absorbed by the characters and the story that I've yet to figure out the mechanics of that film.'[21] For Charles Barr in contrast its evident artificiality is one of the salient features of *The Lady Vanishes*: the opening shot – as the camera moves through 'a toytown set' replete with model trains and vehicles – is 'as blatantly artificial as anything in *Number Seventeen* or *Young and Innocent*', while the models 'announce that this is not realism but a construction, a fantasy'.[22]

The reading of *The Lady Vanishes* as a fantasy – as exemplified in its oneiric narration and its unspecified 'Mittel Europa' setting – is a familiar one in Hitchcock scholarship. Like David Lean's *Brief Encounter* (1945) – another film that has been read as a highly subjective fantasy rather than as the straightforward realist drama suggested by contemporary reviews – *The Lady Vanishes* is exceptionally and, one might say, deliberately vague in relation to the specifics of time and place. On the one hand, the early scenes suggest that the film is set during the spring: the opening shot shows a covering of fresh snow and there are references in the dialogue to 'spring avalanches' as the reason for the delay to the train. On the other hand the Test Match that Charters and Caldicott are so keen to attend would place the film at some point during the English summer: Barr points out that there was indeed a Test Match in Manchester in July 1938 between England and Australia that – as in the film – was abandoned due to heavy rain.[23] As for place, the unnamed country of the novel has become 'Bandrika' in the film ('Bandrika is one of Europe's few undiscovered corners'): culturally it occupies the same imaginary geography as the 'Ruritania' of Anthony Hope's *The Prisoner of Zenda* – already filmed several times, most recently by David O. Selznick in 1937 – or the 'Vosnia' of Launder and Gilliat's post-war spy thriller *Secret State*. (As an aside, there is an irresistible temptation to link these imaginary places in a historical taxonomy of British popular fiction: are they the same country by different names? Perhaps Ruritania – a predominantly feudal kingdom in which the pomp and pageantry of monarchy is a means of projecting an image of state authority – became Bandrika following the break-up of the Austro-Hungarian Empire at the end of the First World War. The deference shown to the Baroness in *The Lady Vanishes* suggests the persistence of an aristocracy. At some point between 1938 and 1950 there was a *coup d'état* and Bandrika became the military dictatorship known as Vosnia.)

The comparison between *The Lady Vanishes* and *Brief Encounter* may be taken even further in so far as both are fundamentally concerned with the representation, or construction, of Englishness. *The Lady Vanishes* is replete with references to the English character: to this extent it may be seen within a lineage of films and other fictions dealing with English people in overseas and often exotic locations that also includes *Innocents in Paris* (1953), *A Passage to India* (1984), *A Room With A View* (1986) and *The Best Exotic Marigold Hotel* (2011). These films all focus on encounters between English characters displaced from their usual comfortable environments and other cultures: this may be treated either for drama or comedy or (as in *The Best Exotic Marigold Hotel*) a combination of both. In *The Lady Vanishes* the treatment is comedic:

13 'I'm enquiring about the Test Match in Manchester!' The archetypal Englishmen abroad, Charters (Basil Radford, *left*) and Caldicott (Naunton Wayne, *right*) in *The Lady Vanishes* (Gainsborough Pictures, 1938).

the first act of the film, especially, as characters gather in a crowded hotel to await the delayed train, plays out as a comedy rather than a thriller. Much of the humour arises from Charters and Caldicott, two clubman stereotypes brilliantly realised through a combination of script and the droll performances of Radford and Wayne. Charters and Caldicott are (on the surface at least) so insular in their attitudes that one wonders why they are travelling abroad at all: they are put out by the inept service at the hotel ('Third-rate country, what do you expect?') and are comically embarrassed when the maid, who has vacated her room for them, returns to change her clothes. Indeed *The Lady Vanishes* is uncharacteristic of Hitchcock's British films in that its exposition is so leisurely: for the first 25 minutes the focus is as much on Charters and Caldicott as on the ostensible protagonist Iris, and it is only when a pair of hands reach out to strangle a folk singer (it is later revealed that the song contains a secret code) that a sense of menace intrudes upon the comedy.

Yet there is much more to the representation of Englishness in *The Lady Vanishes* than Charters and Caldicott dressing formally for dinner in a Central

14   Gilbert (Michael Redgrave) and Iris (Margaret Lockwood, *centre*) find Miss Froy (Dame May Whitty) in *The Lady Vanishes* (Gainsborough Pictures, 1938).

European backwater or using sugar cubes to describe the field placements in a cricket match. The English characters of *The Lady Vanishes* all represent different social and gender types. The heroine Iris – an engagingly sparky performance by a young Margaret Lockwood – exemplifies a type that Sue Harper has described as 'Wholesome Sensible Girls who projected an air of competence and energy, and had the forthright manner of a socially emergent group'.[24] Indeed Iris and her all-female friends are so socially confident as they take over the hotel at the beginning of the film that Caldicott thinks they are Americans – a comment that says as much about attitudes towards gender as nationality (in the sense that Caldicott cannot accept that young women can be so assertive). Gilbert (Michael Redgrave) exemplifies the bohemian intellectual who is the only one of the English characters thoroughly conversant with the local language and customs ('I am putting on record for the benefit of mankind one of the lost folk dances of Central Europe'). It is significant that on the train he is initially separated from the others as he prefers to travel in a third-class carriage where he can converse

15 'Pacifist, eh? Won't do, old boy. Early Christians tried it and got thrown to the lions.' Caldicott proves his mettle in a crisis while 'Mrs Todhunter' (Linden Travers) looks on in *The Lady Vanishes* (Gainsborough Pictures, 1938).

with the locals. Miss Froy, who like Gilbert exhibits a more cosmopolitan outlook, belongs squarely to the archetype of indestructible Little Old Ladies exemplified by the likes of Agatha Christie's Miss Marple and who would find their screen apotheosis in Katy Johnson's Mrs Wilberforce of Ealing's *The Ladykillers* (1955). Her parting comment before leaving the besieged train carriage at the film's climax ('I'd better be getting along now') is a classic piece of English understatement. The Todhunters – in fact an adulterous couple rather than honeymooners as others suppose – are by some distance the least sympathetic of the English characters: they are also the most insular and self-interested. Charters and Caldicott's obsession with cricket ('You can't be in England and not know the Test score!' the former thunders down a telephone to an unknown recipient) marks them out as the most stereotypically English of all the passengers. Unlike Todhunter, however, they are gentlemen who will prove their mettle at the moment of crisis. Charters's stoical reaction when he is shot in the hand is a beautifully judged demonstration of the English stiff upper lip. To this extent *The Lady Vanishes* can be read as much as a fond endorsement of traditional notions of Englishness as a critique of those values.

The Lady Vanishes asserts its Englishness at every opportunity: even the social ritual of afternoon tea serves a plot function towards the end of the film when Gilbert points out that all the English passengers will be in the dining car taking tea. The film includes numerous references to English popular culture. At one point Gilbert impersonates Sherlock Holmes and comedian Will Hay (who of course starred in a popular cycle of films for Gainsborough Pictures in the late 1930s and early 1940s including the railway-themed *Oh Mr Porter!*, which included a story credit for Frank Launder) and later remarks that he 'once drove a miniature engine on the Dymchurch line' (a reference to the Romney, Hythe and Dymchurch Light Railway which opened in 1927). These culturally specific references root the film in a distinctively English idiom: to this extent the Englishness of *The Lady Vanishes* might be seen to anticipate the celebrated Ealing comedies after the Second World War. (The Ealing comedies of course were produced by Michael Balcon who by then had moved away from the policy of 'internationalism' that had defined his tenure at Gaumont-British: again it is significant that *The Lady Vanishes* – the most parochially English of Hitchcock's thriller sextet – was produced after Balcon had left the company.) *The Lady Vanishes* even includes a reference to that specifically English institution: the Oxford–Cambridge university rivalry. An officer who boards the train to demand the handing over of Miss Froy explains his excellent English by mentioning that he was at Oxford: Gilbert hits him over the head with a chair and remarks '*I* was at Cambridge'. That this reflected the input of Launder and Gilliat rather than Hitchcock may be inferred from the fact that a similar joke occurs in *A Yank at Oxford* (1937) – Gilliat was one of many contributors to the script of MGM's first British production – and that a plot point in *Night Train to Munich* revolves around Caldicott recognising Dickie Randall from Oxford ('We were at Balliol together … He used to bowl slow leg breaks. Played for the Gentlemen once. Caught and bowled for a duck, I remember.')

On the face of it the imaginary 'Mittel Europa' of *The Lady Vanishes* seems as much a fantasy construct as its English stereotypes. Bandrika – a country seemingly populated by gesticulating comedy foreigners speaking broken English ('The train is a little bit up-hold') – is no more realistic than the Art Deco Venice of the Astaire-Rogers musical *Top Hat* (1935) or the highly stylised European locations of horror films such as *Frankenstein* (1931) which owe as much to the cinema of German Expressionism as to any real place. Yet on closer inspection there are some clues as to which country Bandrika might represent as a surrogate. The shooting script of *The Lady Vanishes* locates it 'somewhere in southern Europe'.[25] This is consistent with the book, where the train is en route to Trieste: Yugoslavia would therefore suggest itself as the most likely location. However, the evidence of the film itself is more suggestive of Central Europe. Charters and Caldicott are en route from Budapest and want to make a connection at Basle: this would seem to suggest it is set in Austria as lying more or less between Hungary and Switzerland. However, a complicating factor is the presence on the train of 'Dr Hartz of Prague' who is ostensibly en route to perform an operation at 'the national capital': hence the imaginary Bandrika might also be Czechoslovakia. On one level of course none of this matters: in any event the imaginary geography of *The Lady Vanishes* should be seen in the context of the British Board of Film Censors' mandate against representing any foreign nation in a negative light. On another level, however, it matters a great deal: if *The Lady Vanishes* is set either in Austria or in Czechoslovakia then it locates the film squarely in the context of contemporary geopolitics. The parallels here are quite irresistible: the shooting of *The Lady Vanishes* during the early months of 1938 coincided with the *Anschluss* between Germany and Austria proclaimed on 13 March – a political union between the two nations that had been specifically forbidden by the Treaty of Versailles – while its British release in September 1938 coincided with the Sudetenland Crisis as Germany demanded annexation of the German-speaking areas of Czechoslovakia. 'A thing like this might cause a war,' remarks Caldicott in *The Lady Vanishes*: the film was released in London shortly after Prime Minister Neville Chamberlain flew to Munich to negotiate directly with Hitler and returned to Britain declaring 'peace for our time'.[26]

The coincidence of the release of *The Lady Vanishes* and the Sudetenland Crisis was precisely that: the film was 'in the can' months before the Munich Agreement (29 September 1938) and therefore cannot have been intended as a parable or allegory of the deal that saw Britain and France accede to Germany's annexation of the Sudetenland while guaranteeing the integrity of the rest of Czechoslovakia. Yet the historical context of its release overlays a political dimension onto *The Lady Vanishes* that regardless of its intent resonates today as it would undoubtedly have done at the time. The climax of the film contains what seems like nothing so much as a conscious allusion to the policy of appeasement pursued by the British government towards Hitler's Germany. The train has been isolated on a branch line where it is surrounded by militia who exchange gunfire with the remaining – all British – passengers. It is at this point that Charters and Caldicott reveal their true colours and rally to the cause. At the same time the character of Eric Todhunter – played by Cecil Parker, a character actor who specialised in stuffy upper middle-class types – advocates surrender:

> *Todhunter:* I won't be a party to this sort of thing. I don't believe in fighting.

> *Caldicott:* Pacifist, eh? Won't do, old boy. Early Christians tried it and got thrown to the lions.

Shortly later Todhunter steps off the train waving a white handkerchief and is promptly shot dead: affirmation of Caldicott's assertion that pacifism (for which read appeasement) 'won't do'. Todhunter's waving of his handkerchief is almost too perfect a parallel of Chamberlain waving his piece of paper while declaring 'peace for our time' that it is necessary to remind ourselves again that *The Lady Vanishes* had been completed before Munich. Nevertheless the parallel was noted in some of the contemporary reviews. The *New Statesman*, for example, remarked that 'the film contains a number of lines rendered almost embarrassingly topical by the events of the past few weeks'.[27] It is a reading that has gained currency over the years. Andrew Sinclair, for example, writing in the preface to a published version of the screenplay, remarks that '*The Lady Vanishes* is Hitchcock at his most worldly and assured. Yet beneath the entertainment, there is the menace of a Europe about to plunge into the horror of war.'[28] And Matthew Sweet avers that '*The Lady Vanishes* is the most political film that Hitchcock ever made. It is a parable about Britain during the appeasement years.'[29]

The extent to which *The Lady Vanishes* was indeed a parable of Britain during the age of appeasement needs to be nuanced. On the one hand it needs to be considered that the policy of appeasement commanded wide public and political support. Appeasement was not the dirty word that it later became. The Munich Agreement came as a relief to the majority of the British public and Chamberlain was lauded for having averted a general European war: critics of Munich were a vocal but small minority at the time. Indeed the historian A. J. P. Taylor later argued that Munich 'was a triumph for all that was best and most enlightened in British life'.[30] If *The Lady Vanishes* is to be understood as an anti-appeasement tract, therefore, then it was ideologically against the grain of British public opinion in 1938.[31] On the other hand *The Lady Vanishes* was by no means the only British film to offer a critique of government policy. Herbert Wilcox's *Sixty Glorious Years* (1938) – the second of a brace of films produced and directed by Wilcox starring his wife Anna Neagle – was released a month after *The Lady Vanishes* and included an even more explicit reference to foreign policy as Queen Victoria admonishes her Prime Minister, William Gladstone, for his tardiness in sending a mission to relieve General Gordon at Khartoum: 'I am haunted by the dread that we may be too late. That is the danger to which this country so often exposes itself. One day it may be our undoing.' For Khartoum read Munich: and in this case the anti-appeasement message was evidently intentional as *Sixty Glorious Years* included a 'scenario and dialogue' credit for Sir Robert Vansittart, the former Permanent Under-Secretary of State at the Foreign Office and a known critic of the government's policy towards Germany.[32]

Yet even if the interpretation of *The Lady Vanishes* as a warning against appeasement should be nuanced, the film may nevertheless be read at least in part as a commentary on contemporary politics. An early exchange between Miss Froy and Charters makes this clear:

Miss Froy: I always think that Bandrika is one of Europe's few undiscovered corners ... The people are just like happy children, with laughter on their lips and music in their hearts.

Charters: It's not reflected in their politics.

Miss Froy: I never think you should judge any country by its politics. After all, we English are quite honest by nature, aren't we?

While this mild reference to political duplicity was not sufficient to trouble the censors, a more direct political reference did not make it into the film. The shooting script contains this exchange between Gilbert and Caldicott as they cross the border:

Caldicott: Glad it's all over, aren't you? The Government will play the devil about this when we get back. No knowing what they'll do.

Gilbert: (abruptly) Nothing.

Caldicott: (staring at him) I say, you're not a Socialist are you? We're all on the same boat nowadays – even the Liberals.[33]

This might just have been too much for the censor, who disapproved of explicit mention of political parties. The line 'all on [sic] the same boat' seems like a reference to the National Government – a coalition which, following the general election of 1935, was dominated by the Conservative Party. It was the National Government which pursued the foreign policy of appeasement – opposed by the socialist Labour Party – though which also embarked upon a programme of military and naval rearmament in the second half of the 1930s in response to the worsening international situation. In the film Caldicott simply acknowledges the truth of Gilbert's frank assessment of diplomatic *realpolitik* with a thoughtful nod.

The topicality of *The Lady Vanishes* informed its critical reception even if only in an indirect way: several reviews suggested that it came as a welcome light relief following the war scare of September 1938. *The Lady Vanishes* had the best notices since *The 39 Steps* and was held by some as Hitchcock's best film to date. The reviews contain very few references to Ethel Lina White or Launder and Gilliat: the contemporary reception discourse positioned *The Lady Vanishes* very much as a Hitchcock film. For the *Monthly Film Bulletin*, 'Alfred Hitchcock has directed *The Lady Vanishes* with all his individual expertness of touch and this is an out of the ordinary and exciting thriller'.[34] *The Times* agreed that Hitchcock 'waves his directorial wand' and that 'his touch has never been surer nor his power to hold our attention more complete. He, alone among English directors, has an unmistakable style. He loves all that is sinister and bizarre – murder, espionage, and crime – and as a teller of all such stories he has no equal in the cinema.'[35] For C. A. Lejeune it demonstrated that Hitchcock 'has reached the point when every new film of his can be regarded as a blind date for connoisseurs of mystery fiction – something we can go to as safely as we would ask for a new Ellery Queen, a new Margery Allingham, or a new H. C. Bailey from the library'.[36] Campbell Dixon – reviewing it for *World Film News* – averred that '*The Lady Vanishes* is his best picture. I would go further and say that it is easily the best thriller ever made in this country.'[37] In the same journal Marion Fraser suggested that 'Hitchcock retains his reputation as the most consistently entertaining of British directors perhaps because he sticks to a type of film with which he has become thoroughly familiar. In his hands the technique of the spy drama has reached a high standard not so much because he is a master of melodrama but because he has a genius for combining horror, suspense and comedy.'[38]

When *The Lady Vanishes* opened in New York at Christmas 1938 it was such an immediate hit with the critics that Hitchcock was voted the year's best director – the best film was MGM's *The Citadel* – and described as 'England's greatest director' by Frank S. Nugent of the *New York Times*, for whom it was the comedy elements of *The Lady Vanishes* that were the most memorable: 'If it were not so brilliant a melodrama, we should class it as a brilliant comedy. Seeing it imposes a double, a blessedly double, strain: when your sides are not aching from laughter your brain is throbbing in its attempts to outguess the director.'[39] Alistair Cooke, reporting from New York, testified that it was a popular success: 'I have never known an audience in a movie theatre anywhere applaud so whole-heartedly together as the Broadway audiences are applauding *The Lady Vanishes*.'[40] However, the trade critics were somewhat more equivocal and evidently felt that the film would be a hard sell beyond

New York. *The Hollywood Reporter* thought it 'a very British affair of the spy mystery school, with a definite question mark as to the extent of its appeal to American audiences as a whole'.[41] And for *Variety* it was '[another] British triumph from the directorial and photographic standpoint, but just how it will fare with American audiences is problematical ... But for Hitchcock's directorial genius, picture would have been relegated to Class B.'[42]

Like *The 39 Steps*, the reputation of *The Lady Vanishes* has grown over the years to the extent that it is now regarded as one of Hitchcock's – and British cinema's – finest hours. For Philip French, the long-serving film critic of the *Observer*, it is 'the most perfectly judged comedy-thriller ever made'.[43] It seamlessly combines its thriller-genre motifs – the apparently insoluble mystery, Iris's increasing paranoia as no one will believe her story, the conspiracy of silence she faces, the moment of revelation and the final dramatic denouement – with the conventions of a light romantic comedy and a whiff of topicality. It represents the final maturity of the style that Hitchcock had developed throughout the 'classic thriller sextet' and would become the model for all future comedy thrillers with a train setting including its own semi-sequel *Night Train to Munich* and Hollywood films ranging from *Lady on a Train* (1945) to *Silver Streak* (1976). It might also have marked the first occasion on which Hitchcock consciously parodied his own work. 'I'm half inclined to believe that there's some rational explanation for all this,' Caldicott remarks as the bullets fly: this might be taken as a comment on the most frequent criticism of Hitchcock's thrillers – their implausibility. One of the chief delights of *The Lady Vanishes* is both that there is a rational explanation and that at the same time it does not matter in the slightest what it is.

The seamless construction of *The Lady Vanishes* – and the extent to which this may be attributed to Hitchcock's direction – is highlighted through a comparison with *Night Train to Munich* (1940). This was produced by Twentieth Century-Fox as one of its British quota films: it was shot at Gaumont-British's newly reopened Lime Grove Studios with the same producer (Edward Black) and the same art director (Alexander Vetchinsky) as *The Lady Vanishes*. Launder and Gilliat scripted the film, which was adapted from an original magazine story by Gordon Wellesley.[44] Margaret Lockwood starred alongside Rex Harrison and Austrian émigré Paul Henreid. It is the presence of Basil Radford and Naunton Wayne as Charters and Caldicott that provides the direct narrative link between *Night Train to Munich* and *The Lady Vanishes*. Critical opinion is divided between those who regard *Night Train to Munich* as a lesser film than *The Lady Vanishes*, largely on the grounds that it did not exhibit the Hitchcock 'touch', and those who rate it as a film in its own right. For Graham

Fuller, *Night Train to Munich* is 'a leaden thriller ... in which director Carol Reed squanders both the train sequence and Margaret Lockwood'.[45] In contrast Peter William Evans describes *Night Train to Munich* as 'one of the most brilliant thrillers of the British cinema'.[46]

On one level there are important differences between *Night Train to Munich* and its illustrious predecessor. Most obviously the ideological context had changed entirely: with the outbreak of the Second World War there was no longer any need to disguise the identity of the enemy. ('I presume the Film Censorship previous ban on this type of story is now lifted,' says a note in the BBFC scenario report when the initial treatment for *Night Train to Munich* – under the original title of *Report on a Fugitive* – was submitted in November 1939.[47]) *Night Train to Munich* is more specific about time and place than *The Lady Vanishes*. An opening caption states that the events in the film take place 'during the year preceding the war and on the night of September 3rd 1939': in fact the film begins with the German annexation of Czechoslovakia in March 1939, though most of the narrative is compressed into the days immediately prior to the outbreak of war. It concerns the efforts of the British secret service to rescue a Czech scientist and his daughter from the Gestapo in order to prevent his revolutionary new formula for armour plating from falling into the hands of the Germans. The *Manchester Guardian* approved of the fact that the enemy was now real: 'War has done one service to films: they can make their villains real men, not Ruritanians; their spies can be full-blooded Teutons and not vague Levantines with a vague grudge against Britain.'[48]

It would be fair to say that *Night Train to Munich* is stylistically less cohesive a film than *The Lady Vanishes*. In contrast to the Hitchcock film, where the thriller and comedy elements are seamlessly combined, Reed's film demonstrates a tension between the thriller and comedy modes. On the one hand, the newsreel montage of German tanks and troops that opens the film and the scene where a prisoner in a concentration camp is quite brutally beaten by the guards link the film to the reality of Nazi aggression. On the other hand, the sequences where British secret service agent Dickie Randall infiltrates the German High Command in Berlin by masquerading as monocled Prussian officer Major Herzoff plays out as a *Boy's Own* adventure that bears as little resemblance to the real world as a Bulldog Drummond story. It is the comedy elements of *Night Train to Munich* that emerge more forcefully as the film goes on, to the extent that by the mid-way point it seemingly ceases to take itself at all seriously. This is demonstrated by a scene in Germany in which a minor functionary who grumbles about the excessive bureaucracy ('*This* is a fine country to live in!') is reprimanded by a superior who accepts his explanation that he had been misheard ('I said this is a *fine* country to live in!') and who then remarks to no one in particular 'This is a bloody awful country to live in!' The casting of a gentle English character like Raymond Huntley as a Nazi bureaucrat should perhaps be taken as a sign that *Night Train to Munich* does not take itself too seriously.

Yet in other respects *Night Train to Munich* successfully rehearses some of the motifs of *The Lady Vanishes*. Charters and Caldicott are still the stereotypical Englishmen abroad: thwarted in his attempt to buy *Punch* at a German railway kiosk ('English magazine – very humorous'), Charters opts instead for a copy of *Mein Kampf* ('I understand they give a copy to all the bridal couples over here,' he tells his companion. 'Oh, I don't think it's that sort of book, old man,' is the reply). And again the film is replete with references to English popular culture, including Gilbert and Sullivan ('I was a member of the Foreign Office Operatic Society,' reveals Dickie Randall. 'Did you know I was once Pooh-Bah to the Foreign Secretary's Koko?') and cricket (Caldicott, recognising his old university acquaintance, sends him a note to warn him his disguise has been rumbled, telling him 'you are batting on a sticky wicket'). And, like *The Lady Vanishes*, *Night Train to Munich* includes several topical references, including to the Nazi-Soviet Pact of August 1939 ('I see that fellow Ribbentrop's gone to Moscow'. 'Hmm. So did Napoleon') which locate it in a specific historical context. The most direct reference is the film's title which must have been intentionally ironic: 'Munich' – for audiences in 1940 – would surely have brought to mind the now-discredited Munich Agreement. *The Lady Vanishes* may or may not have been intended as a critique of appeasement; in *Night Train to Munich*, in contrast, the allegory seems quite clear.

Like *The 39 Steps*, *The Lady Vanishes* has been remade for both film and television. The Rank Organisation, which had released Don Sharp's film of *The 39 Steps* in 1978, was also involved the same year with a remake of *The Lady Vanishes*, directed by Anthony Page, written by George Axelrod and produced by Tom Sachs for Hammer Film Productions – the British studio best known for its horror films of the 1950s and 1960s now making its last foray into production. Axelrod seemingly held the original film in little regard:

> What we're competing with here is not the real picture but people's memory of it. Hitchcock's film had some brilliant things in it, but as a whole picture you'd have to admit it's pretty creaky. The four or five things people remember from the original version receive a homage in our version – which raises the question of when a homage becomes a rip off.[49]

In fact the 1978 *The Lady Vanishes* follows the structure of the original film fairly closely and maintains that film's alterations from the source text including the characters of Charters and Caldicott – here played by Arthur Lowe and Ian Carmichael. Four decades on it was no longer necessary to place the film in the imaginary country of Bandrika: the remake locates events in southern Germany (Bavaria) on the eve of the Second World War (August 1939). Otherwise the most significant change from the original was to turn the leads into Americans – a *Life* magazine reporter called Robert Condon (Elliott Gould) and madcap heiress Amanda Kelly (Cybill Shepherd) – presumably with an eye on the US market. Gould and Shepherd are both woefully miscast: neither is able to play their role as anything other than a contemporary American tourist rather than as sophisticated international travellers of the 1930s.

The most recent version of *The Lady Vanishes* was a 90-minute television film by the BBC in association with Masterpiece Films of America in 2013. This was shot on location in Budapest and sets the action in pre-war Yugoslavia. According to producer Annie Tricklebank:

> Originally we thought it was just the Hitchcock film. But when we started digging into it, we realised it was actually adapted from a book called *The Wheel Spins*, written, I think, in 1936 ... It's a complete delight and beautifully written. So, rather than go back to the film, we decided to go to the book. To be purists, really.[50]

This rather begs the question why the television version maintained the title of the Hitchcock film rather than reverting to the book's original title. Otherwise it is an authentic adaptation: Miss Froy (Selina Cadell) is a governess who has witnessed a murder rather than a spy and it is Max Hare (Tom Hughes) who comes to the assistance of Iris Carr (Tuppence Middleton) as she searches for the missing women. There are no Charters and Caldicott, though White's spinster sisters the Misses Floodporter (Geraldine James and Stephanie Cole) are restored in their place. The critical reception was lukewarm. When it was screened in America, the *New York Times* called it 'a perfectly adequate television mystery of the week'. 'But,' the review went on, 'it foregoes the crackling pace, light touch and surprisingly sophisticated sexual banter of the original, opting for melancholy, ominousness and sentimentality. It's about five minutes shorter than the Hitchcock, but its deliberate pace makes it seem longer.'[51] Even after 75 years, it seems, *The Lady Vanishes* could not escape from Hitchcock's shadow.

PART II

HOLLYWOOD

7

HITCHCOCK AND AMERICAN CINEMA

Hitchcock's relocation to Hollywood in 1939 marked a decisive turning point in his career. Although Hitchcock would return to film in Britain occasionally – *Under Capricorn* (1949), *Stage Fright* (1950) and *Frenzy* (1972) as well as some of the locations for his remake of *The Man Who Knew Too Much* (1956) – these were really American films made in Britain rather than British films *per se*. In fact the only two fully British films he directed after 1939 were a brace of short propaganda subjects for the Ministry of Information in 1944 – *Bon Voyage* and *Aventure Malgache* – which received limited distribution. For the rest of his career Hitchcock was based permanently in Los Angeles and was essentially an American film-maker – or if one prefers, a British film-maker working in Hollywood, though he took American citizenship in 1955 – and his work therefore needs to be positioned within the institutional and economic contexts of the US film industry.

In Britain there were mixed views about Hitchcock's move to America. C. A. Lejeune felt that his first two American films – *Rebecca* (1940) and *Foreign Correspondent* (1940) – fully justified his decision:

> In the unlikely event that anyone – except, of course, Hitchcock himself – should have been anxious about the influence of Hollywood on England's chubby No. 1 director, *Foreign Correspondent*, coming on top of *Rebecca*, should reassure him.
>
> Hitchcock is all right. Hitchcock, one might fairly say, has fulfilled himself. Like Ernst Lubitsch, and like Lubitsch alone of Europe's great directors, Hitchcock has found in the New World the full flowering of his talents. The films he made in this country were, at best, brilliant tentatives, graced by individual touches. The two films he has made in Hollywood are mature works, in which the touch is barely distinguishable from the whole.[1]

In contrast Lindsay Anderson, writing in 1949, believed that the quality of Hitchcock's films suffered when he went to Hollywood. For Anderson,

'Hitchcock's best films are in many ways very English, in their humour, lack of sentimentality, their avoidance of the grandiose and the elaborately fake' and these qualities were lost when he signed a contract with the extravagant Hollywood producer David O. Selznick: 'Almost in advance Hitchcock was committed to all that is worst in Hollywood – to size for its own sake (his first picture for Selznick was 2,000 feet longer than any he had directed previously), to the star system for its own sake, to glossy photography, high-toned settings, [and] lushly hypnotic musical scores.'[2]

There were also some voices in the British film industry who believed that Hitchcock had deserted his native country in its hour of need during the Second World War: that he was one of those who – as it was put at the time – had 'Gone With the Wind Up'.[3] It was not that Hitchcock or other members of the British colony in Hollywood – including actors Charles Laughton and Laurence Olivier – were being accused of cowardice, but rather that they should have been working in Britain making films to support the British war effort. In the event several of the 'Hollywood British' did return: David Niven rejoined his army regiment and starred in *The Way Ahead* (1944), Laurence Olivier joined the Fleet Air Arm and made the patriotic epic *Henry V* (1944), and Leslie Howard directed and starred in *Pimpernel Smith* (1941) and *The First of the Few* (1942). Hitchcock's decision to remain in California drew the ire of his old friend and mentor Michael Balcon, who as Head of Production at Ealing Studios would be responsible for producing some of the best British films of the Second World War. In August 1940 Balcon fired a broadside in the form of a feature article in the *Sunday Dispatch*, provocatively entitled 'Deserters!', which referred to 'a plump young junior technician in my studios whom I promoted from department to department. Today, one of our most famous directors, he is in Hollywood, while we who are left behind are trying to harness films to the great national effort.'[4]

Balcon's attack on Hitchcock as a 'deserter' was unfair in several respects. For one thing Hitchcock's decision to relocate to the United States predated the outbreak of war: his contract with Selznick was signed in July 1938 and came into effect in April 1939.[5] And for another the British government had stated publicly that British actors and film-makers based in Hollywood could best serve their country by making films promoting the British cause in America – especially given that the United States remained neutral until December 1941. The British ambassador to Washington, Lord Lothian, more or less told the British community to stay put in Hollywood 'because they are consciously championing the British cause in a very volatile community which would otherwise be left to the mercies of German propagandists, and because the continuing production of films with a strong British tone is one of the best and subtlest forms of British propaganda'.[6] This was a time when 'Hollywood British' films – American films with a strong British flavour – were popular with American audiences: these ranged from literary adaptations such as *Wuthering Heights* (1939) and *Pride and Prejudice* (1940) to adventure films such as *The Adventures of Robin Hood* (1938) and *The Sea Hawk* (1940).[7] Hitchcock himself contributed to the 'Hollywood British' cycle with *Rebecca* and *Suspicion* (1941) – both featured English settings and starred British actors – while *Foreign Correspondent* was set largely in London. Hitchcock was also involved in the preparation of *Forever and a Day* (1943) – an episodic pro-British feature film conceived and produced by members of the 'Hollywood British' community (in the event Hitchcock was busy with other projects and his segment was directed by French exile René Clair) – and undertook several wartime projects for the British Ministry of Information: he re-edited the documentary films *Men of the Lightship* (1940) and *Target for Tonight* (1941) for their US release and directed the two Francophone shorts, *Bon Voyage* and *Aventure Malgache*, in 1944.[8]

Hitchcock, then, 'did his bit' for the British war effort, but the primary reason for his move to Hollywood was not to make pro-British propaganda but the opportunity of working with the bigger budgets and technical resources of the US film industry. The price – at least in the short term – was to sacrifice some of the autonomy he had enjoyed at the Gaumont-British Picture Corporation. Following lengthy negotiations, Hitchcock had signed a non-exclusive contract with Selznick International that committed him to making one film a year with the option of making films for other producers between his Selznick projects.[9] A former MGM executive, Selznick had set up as an independent producer in the mid-1930s and specialised in 'prestige' productions with the highest production values: these included *The Prisoner of Zenda* (1937), *The Adventures of Tom Sawyer* (1938), *Intermezzo* (1939) and most famously of all *Gone With the Wind* (1939). For a while it was mooted that Hitchcock's first film for Selznick would be a melodrama of the sinking of the *Titanic* though in the event they settled on an adaptation of Daphne du Maurier's *Rebecca*: Hitchcock's last British film had also been based on a du Maurier novel (*Jamaica Inn*) thus providing a neat symmetry between the end of his British period and the start of his Hollywood career. The relationship between Hitchcock and Selznick would prove to be fertile and frustrating in equal measure. In the event Hitchcock would direct only three pictures for Selznick – *Rebecca*, *Spellbound* (1945) and *The Paradine Case* (1947) – but during the period of his Selznick contract he made seven other films either while on loan to other producers or as a freelance.[10]

Hitchcock's move to Hollywood coincided with the zenith of the studio system as a mode of production: 1939 is now widely regarded as Hollywood's *annus mirabilis* with more recognised classics than any other year. The list includes – but is not limited to – *Beau Geste, Gunga Din, The Hunchback of Notre Dame, Mr Smith Goes to Washington, Ninotchka, Only Angels Have Wings, Stagecoach, The Wizard of Oz, Young Mr Lincoln* and *Gone With the Wind*.[11] However, Hollywood's 'golden age' would be short lived and by the late 1930s there were already indications that significant changes were looming for the film industry. In 1938 the US Justice Department had signalled its intent to challenge the major studios' ownership of movie theatres which was deemed an unfair monopoly: the lawsuit was postponed until after the war but the issue remained pending like a Sword of Damocles over the heads of the studios. The Second World War was a boom period for cinema-going and the studios reaped the benefits. At the same time it was a period of rising production costs: the average feature film budget increased from $336,600 in 1942 to $554,386 by 1945.[12] Hollywood's major studios reoriented their production strategies to concentrate on fewer but bigger films in order to exploit their monopoly of the first-run theatres. The 'Big Five' (Paramount, MGM, Twentieth Century-Fox, Warner Bros. and RKO Radio Pictures) reduced their annual programmes of around fifty films each to an average of thirty between 1942 and 1946.[13]

It was this combination of circumstances – increasing attendances combined with the reduction in output from the majors – that created the space for independent producers such as Selznick. There were differing levels and degrees of independent production, ranging from in-house units based at particular studios, such as Cecil B. De Mille at Paramount and Walter Wanger at United Artists, to genuine 'outsider' producers such as Selznick and Samuel Goldwyn who turned to the majors for distribution and exhibition of their films. A feature of the war years was that a number of major pre-war Hollywood directors – including Frank Capra, John Ford, Howard Hawks and William Wyler – became independent producer-directors not tied to long-term studio contracts. These film-makers enjoyed greater creative and administrative freedom, which in turn brought about innovation in style and technique. Hitchcock was unique among Hollywood's leading talent in that he worked both as a 'house' director for a major producer (Selznick) and as a freelance director at other studios including RKO (*Mr and Mrs Smith, Suspicion, Notorious*), Universal (*Saboteur, Shadow of a Doubt*) and Fox (*Lifeboat*). It was not until 1947 that Hitchcock finally broke away from Selznick but in the meantime his Selznick contract remained his security blanket as he gained experience of the business and administrative side of the film industry as well as the creative side.

Although his most successful films of the war years were Selznick pictures – *Rebecca* (with a domestic box-office gross of $3 million) and *Spellbound* ($4.9 million), with *Rebecca* also winning the Academy Award for Best Picture of 1940 – Hitchcock seems on the whole to have preferred his other assignments where he evidently enjoyed greater creative freedom. Selznick was a notoriously interventionist producer who liked to supervise all aspects of the film-making process, including matters usually left to the director such as camera angles and alternative takes. Hitchcock's habit of 'cutting in the camera' and his leisurely approach to studio filming differed from the Hollywood norm and became a bugbear for his producer. As Selznick set out in a memo during the shooting of *Rebecca* in September 1939:

> Cutting your film with the camera and reducing the number of angles required is highly desirable, and no one appreciates its value more than I do; but certainly it is of no value if you are simply going to give us less cut film a day than a man who shoots twice as many angles ... As somebody said the other day, 'Hitchcock shoots like [W. S.] Van Dyke – except that he gets one third as much film', which means that you cut your film with your camera the way Van Dyke does but that he gets three times as much cut film per day ...
>
> There are various things about your methods of shooting which I think you simply must correct, because even if we permitted you to follow them on *Rebecca*, you would have to cure them on your next picture and succeeding pictures because nobody in Hollywood would stand for them, so we might as well clamp down on you for this picture.[14]

Although in the event the memorandum was not sent, it stands as an effective summary of the differences in working practices between the British director and the Hollywood studio system (W. S. Van Dyke – who went by the nickname of 'One-Take Woody' – was a prolific director of the 'journeyman' variety renowned for his ability to complete films on schedule: it was hardly a flattering comparison by Selznick and this may be one reason why the memo was not sent). Hitchcock later sought to distance himself from *Rebecca*: he told Truffaut that 'it's not a Hitchcock picture; it's a novelette really'.[15]

Rebecca was an unusual film for Hitchcock in that it was not a suspense thriller but rather a romantic novel that he turned into a psychological drama. It also relied more on camera movement than Hitchcock's customary montage technique in its narration. In fact Hitchcock's films of the 1940s demonstrate a greater variety of subject matter and directorial style than at any point of his career since the late 1920s and early 1930s. They included a screwball comedy (*Mr and Mrs Smith*), a war film (*Lifeboat*), a courtroom drama

(*The Paradine Case*) and a costume picture (*Under Capricorn*) alongside three spy pictures – *Foreign Correspondent, Saboteur* and *Notorious* – and four films perhaps best described as psychological thrillers: *Suspicion, Shadow of a Doubt, Spellbound* and *Rope*. Hitchcock enjoyed setting himself technical challenges: *Lifeboat* confined the entire action of the film to a restricted location and *Rope* experimented with continuous ten-minute takes in order to shoot the film in 'real time'. For much of the decade Hitchcock alternated between fairly mainstream commercial films – *Foreign Correspondent, Saboteur, Spellbound* and *Notorious* would all fit into this category – and more personal projects such as *Shadow of a Doubt, Lifeboat* and *Rope*. It is the latter group that by and large has proved more interesting to *auteur* critics: in contrast – and with the sole exception of *Notorious* – Hitchcock's genre films have generally been accorded less attention.

The fact that Hitchcock made fewer spy pictures following his move to Hollywood – three between 1940 and 1946 compared to five in Britain between 1934 and 1938 – reflects to some extent the lesser profile of the genre in American cinema. Hitchcock claimed that early during his Hollywood career he had difficulty in attracting major stars to his thrillers because the genre was held in low critical esteem:

> In Europe, you see, the thriller, the adventure story is not looked down upon. As a matter of fact, that form of writing is highly respected in England, whereas in America it is definitely regarded as second-rate literature; the approach to the mystery genre is quite different. When I had completed the script of *Foreign Correspondent*, I went to Gary Cooper with it, but as it was a thriller, he turned it down. This attitude was so commonplace when I started to work in Hollywood that I always ended up with the next best – in this case Joel McCrae. Many years later Gary Cooper said to me, 'That was a mistake. I should have done it.'[16]

The spy film in particular was at best a marginal presence in American cinema before 1940 and tended to be confined to the realms of B-movie production: short supporting features intended for the bottom half of a double bill such as the 'Mr Moto' series starring Peter Lorre and based on the Japanese secret agent created by American author John P. Marquand which combined aspects of the sensational thriller – fast-moving action, secret societies and unlikely assassination plots – with the conventions of the detective story.[17] The few A-class spy films produced in the 1930s such as MGM's *Mata Hari* (1931) and Warner's *British Agent* (1934) were more in the style of romantic melodramas than contemporaneous British films with a flavour of political intrigue such as *Rome Express* and *The Man Who Knew Too Much*. More characteristic of American cinema was the gangster film. This had emerged in the early 1930s – exemplified by *Little Caesar* (1931), *The Public Enemy* (1931) and *Scarface* (1932) – and was largely an outcome of the Great Depression: gangster protagonists were characterised as tragic heroes and their criminality was presented as a consequence of social and economic conditions. Following pressure from the Hays Office, which was concerned about the possibly harmful effects of these films on juvenile audiences, the ideological strategy of the gangster film shifted in the mid-1930s with the emergence of the G-Man film – examples included *G-Men* (1935) and *Bullets or Ballots* (1936) – which focused on the efforts of federal agents in combating organised crime and which shared some common ground with the spy film in that its protagonists were usually government agents.[18]

The emergence of the spy film as a significant production trend in Hollywood can be dated quite precisely to 1939 when the major studios released twelve spy or espionage themed films. How can we account for the sudden proliferation of spies and saboteurs on America's movie screens? This would seem to be an example of how motion pictures responded to the ideological climate in so far as the end of the 1930s witnessed a 'spy scare' in America with a heightened level of anxiety over the existence of a German 'fifth column' or 'Trojan Horse' in the United States.[19] This anxiety extended from Washington, DC, into society at large and manifested itself in various ways. The panic sparked by Orson Welles's infamous radio broadcast of *The War of the Worlds* in October 1938, for example, was a product of this climate: the evidence suggests that those who were taken in by the broadcasts may not have literally believed that Martians had landed in New Jersey but rather that a foreign power (probably Germany) had launched an attack on the United States.[20] It was also seen in the proliferation of films in which secret agents and detectives foiled attempts to sabotage the US defence industries. Ronald Reagan starred in a series of secret service films for Warner Bros. in 1939–40 (*Secret Service of the Air, Code of the Secret Service, Smashing the Money Ring, Murder in the Air*), while other screen detectives engaged in the war against saboteurs included Nick Carter (Walter Pidgeon in *Nick Carter, Master Detective*) and reformed jewel thief Michael Lanyard (Warren William in *The Lone Wolf Spy Hunt*). The identity of the enemy agents and subversives tended to remain vague in order to appease the censors: to this extent the content of American cinema was as tightly regulated as it was in Britain. However, this situation changed when Warner Bros. produced *Confessions of a Nazi Spy* in 1939.

Confessions of a Nazi Spy was an account of how the Federal Bureau of Investigation (FBI) uncovered a German spy ring operating in the

United States. On one level *Confessions of a Nazi Spy* can be seen as a variation on the G-Man formula – its star Edward G. Robinson was associated with the genre through films such as *Bullets or Ballots* – while its journalistic style anticipated the emergence of the semi-documentary spy film after the Second World War such as *The House on 92nd Street* (1945) and *I Was a Communist for the FBI* (1951). What differentiated *Confessions of a Nazi Spy* from other spy films was that it was based on a true case – the infiltration of the German-American Bund by FBI agent Leon G. Turrou as recalled in his book *The Nazi Spy Conspiracy in America* – and explicitly identified Germany as the instigator of subversive activities in the United States. It is more a collection of scenes than a conventional narrative: newsreel footage of the German invasion of Czechoslovakia is juxtaposed with fictional scenes of the operation of the spy ring and speeches by an orator in Nazi uniform who declares that 'Germany must save America from the chaos that breeds with democracy and racial equality' and 'All our efforts must now be directed against the strongest remaining democracy – the United States'. The film sits squarely within Warner's tradition of making films informed by topical current affairs and its politics reflected the influence of German émigrés including director Anatole Litvak and co-star Paul Lukas, as well as Edward G. Robinson and writer John Wesley who were both involved in anti-fascist causes.[21]

As might be expected, *Confessions of a Nazi Spy* was a highly controversial film. Jack Warner pressed ahead with it in the face of opposition both from the industry and from the German government. The Production Code office was concerned that the film would violate its 'national feelings' clause that mandated against the negative representation of any foreign nations. 'Are we ready to depart from the pleasant and profitable course of entertainment, to engage in propaganda, to produce screen portrayals arousing controversy, conflict, racial, religious and nationalistic antagonism, and outright, horrible human hatred?' an internal PCA memorandum asked rhetorically when Warners submitted the script. It added: 'I fear it will be one of the most memorable, one of the most lamentable mistakes ever made by the industry.'[22] However, as the film was based on recorded events there was little the PCA could do to block its production: instead Joseph Breen appealed to the studio's commercial interests in suggesting that it 'risked political censorship at home and abroad'.[23] *Confessions of a Nazi Spy* was indeed banned in Germany, Italy, Spain, Ireland and throughout much of South America, while in Britain it was allowed in a cut version in the summer of 1939 and reissued uncut in 1940.[24] Yet this did not harm the film's performance at the box office: it returned $797,000 from the domestic (North American) market and a further

$734,000 from overseas markets, which ensured a profit against its modest production cost ($681,000).[25]

Hollywood's first major spy cycle lasted from 1939 until 1946 with the production of spy films peaking in 1942–3 following America's entry into the Second World War. As ever genre boundaries are fluid: spy and espionage themes crossed over into other genres such as the Western (*Cowboy Commandos, Valley of Hunted Men*), adventure (*Tarzan's Desert Mystery*), comedy (*My Favorite Spy*) and even horror (*Invisible Agent*). The following table lists all the titles I have identified produced by the eight major Hollywood studios (MGM, Paramount, Twentieth Century-Fox, Warner Bros., RKO, Columbia, Universal and United Artists) and by leading independents (Walter Wanger, for example, produced *Foreign Correspondent*) in which spying or espionage is the main focus of the narrative. It includes Anglo-American productions – films

Year	Films
1939	*Confessions of a Nazi Spy, Secret Service of the Air, Espionage Agent, Code of the Secret Service, Television Spy, The Lone Wolf Spy Hunt, Nick Carter – Master Detective, Conspiracy, They Made Her a Spy, Mr Moto's Last Warning, Mr Moto in Danger Island*
1940	*Foreign Correspondent, British Intelligence, Murder in the Air, Phantom Raiders, Enemy Agent, Charlie Chan in Panama*
1941	*Man Hunt, Confirm or Deny, Dangerously They Live, One Night in Lisbon, Mystery Sea Raider*
1942	*Spy Ship, Across the Pacific, Saboteur, This Gun for Hire, Secret Enemies, Madame Spy, Escape from Hong Kong, Nazi Agent, Secret Agent of Japan, Little Tokyo USA, Berlin Correspondent, Sabotage Squad, Underground Agent, Counter-Espionage, Sherlock Holmes and the Voice of Terror, The Great Impersonation*
1943	*Background to Danger, Journey into Fear, Appointment in Berlin, Above Suspicion, They Met in the Dark, Appointment in Brittany, Passport to Suez, Sherlock Holmes and the Secret Weapon, Sherlock Holmes in Washington, They Came to Blow Up America, Five Graves to Cairo, The Fallen Sparrow, Escape to Danger (*), The Adventures of Tartu (*), Yellow Canary (*), Squadron Leader X (*)*
1944	*Ministry of Fear, The Mask of Dimitrios, Hotel Reserve (*), The Conspirators, Action in Arabia*
1945	*The House on 92nd Street, Hotel Berlin, Confidential Agent, Escape in the Fog, Cornered*
1946	*Notorious, Cloak and Dagger, O.S.S., 13 Rue Madeleine*

shot by the Hollywood studios in Britain in order to utilise their 'frozen' dollar revenues (these films are marked with an asterisk) – but not British films distributed by the majors in North America.[26] Nor does it include serials featuring espionage activities such as Republic's *Spy Smasher* (1942) or Columbia's *Batman* (1943).

Even excluding espionage-themed films in other genres, these films represent a range of different styles and narrative templates. As in Britain during the 1930s, Hitchcock's films marked the top end of a genre that was dominated largely by B-grade material. The Mr Moto, Charlie Chan and Sherlock Holmes films, for example, were series films in which the great detectives investigated espionage and foiled spy rings. (In the case of Universal's modernised Sherlock Holmes films this was consistent with the original stories. Several of Conan Doyle's stories, including 'The Naval Treaty', 'The Second Stain' and 'The Bruce-Partington Plans', were built around the recovery of stolen documents. In 'His Last Bow' Holmes came out of retirement to foil the German master spy Von Bork in 1914: aspects of this story – updated to the Second World War – featured in *Sherlock Holmes and the Voice of Terror*. In *Sherlock Holmes and the Secret Weapon*, Holmes prevented his arch-enemy Professor Moriarty, now working for the Nazis, from acquiring the Norden bombsight: this was a real bombsight developed by the Dutch-American inventor Carl L. Norden.) When the Charlie Chan series moved from Twentieth Century-Fox to Monogram Pictures in 1944 the first film was *Charlie Chan in the Secret Service*. There would be more films in the list if the minor studios were also included: the genre was particularly suited to low-budget production.

Otherwise several trends can be identified. One notable feature is the prominence of films based on British authors of spy fiction. *Man Hunt* (1941), for example, was a film of Geoffrey Household's novel *Rogue Male*: Twentieth Century-Fox had offered the property to Hitchcock before it was handed to Fritz Lang.[27] Other Hollywood adaptations of British spy writers included two films of novels by Helen McInnes – MGM's *Above Suspicion* (1943) and *Assignment in Brittany* (1943) – and *The Great Impersonation* (1942) by the old master of the genre E. Phillips Oppenheim updated by Universal from the First to the Second World War. In particular it was during the war that the work of Graham Greene and Eric Ambler came to the attention of Hollywood. (There had been a film of Greene's *Stamboul Train* – retitled *Orient Express* – in 1934 but it retained none of the flavour of the novel: it became a melodrama more in the style of *Grand Hotel*.) Paramount had bought the rights to Greene's *A Gun for Sale* in 1936 but did not film it until 1942 – under the title *This Gun for Hire*.[28] A triptych of wartime excursions into 'Greeneland' was completed by

Ministry of Fear (1944), directed by Fritz Lang for Paramount, and *Confidential Agent* (1945), directed by Herman Shumlin for Warner Bros. The same studio was responsible for adaptations of Eric Ambler's *Uncommon Danger*, directed by Raoul Walsh as *Background to Danger* (1943), and *The Mask of Dimitrios* (1944), directed by Jean Negulesco, while RKO made *Journey into Fear* (1943), directed by Norman Foster (possibly with uncredited assistance from Orson Welles), and *Hotel Reserve* (1944), an adaptation of *Epitaph for a Spy* shot in Britain with no fewer than three credited directors, Victor Hanbury, Lance Comfort and Max Greene.[29] It is a matter of conjecture why Hitchcock never filmed any of Ambler's books: they were good friends – Hitchcock was best man at Ambler's wedding to Hitchcock's script assistant Joan Harrison in 1958 – and Ambler's stories of accidental spies caught up in political intrigue fitted the formula of the Hitchcock thriller. Greene's antipathy towards Hitchcock is well known and no doubt helps to explain this omission. Greene later testified that in the late 1950s he had declined an offer from Hitchcock for the film rights to *Our Man in Havana* as 'I haven't got all that admiration for Hitchcock, that we'll say M. Truffaut has ... And he was offering a rather derisory sum, and announced that he had bought it – so I said no.'[30]

Another context for Hollywood's wartime spy cycle was that it coincided with the emergence of *film noir* in American cinema: a style or mode of film-making characterised by its extreme stylisation – low-key cinematography, chiaroscuro lighting and fragmentary *mise- en-scène* – and by its pervading mood of cynicism and despair. The term *film noir* originated in France after the Second World War: the critic Nino Frank seems to have coined it in reference to certain American movies – including *The Maltese Falcon, Double Indemnity, Laura* and *Murder, My Sweet* – released in France after the Occupation.[31] As a critical term rather than an industry category, *film noir* has always been a fluid idea and the canon of what constitutes *film noir* has been much debated by film critics and historians. Most agree that the core films of the *noir* cycle are private-eye thrillers (*The Maltese Falcon, Murder, My Sweet, The Big Sleep*), films about maladjusted ex-servicemen (*Somewhere in the Night, Deadline at Dawn, The Blue Dahlia*) and what can perhaps best be described as *femme fatale* thrillers (*Double Indemnity, The Postman Always Rings Twice, The Lady from Shanghai*), though *noir* characteristics have also been detected in other genres including the social problem film (*The Lost Weekend*), costume drama (*Gaslight*) and the Western (*Pursued*). It is not unusual to find films from the spy cycle included in *noir* filmographies. In 1955, for example, Raymond Borde and Étienne Chaumeton's *Panorama du Film Noir Américain* identified a corpus of 22 '*films noirs*' including *Journey into Fear* and *The Mask of Dimitrios*.[32]

And *This Gun for Hire* is often cited as a foundational text of *film noir*: it was the success of Warner's remake of Dashiell Hammett's private-eye novel *The Maltese Falcon* (1941) that caused Paramount to go ahead with a property that had sat on their shelves for six years.[33]

There were various industrial and ideological contexts for the emergence of *film noir* – including wartime material restrictions on the film industry which mandated an economical mode of production (most *noirs* were low- or at best middle-budget films) and the existential social anxieties of the war and post-war years – while the *noir* style drew upon a diverse range of cultural influences including the cinema of German Expressionism (it is significant that many of the directors and cinematographers specialising in *noir* were German émigrés) and the 'hard-boiled' school of American crime fiction (Dashiell Hammett, Raymond Chandler, James M. Cain and Cornell Woolrich among others). Hitchcock has not usually been seen as an important figure in the history of *film noir*, though Borde and Chaumeton identify *Rebecca* and *Suspicion* as formative films in the emergence of *noir* and recognise *Shadow of a Doubt* as a 'major work', while suggesting that *Notorious*, *The Paradine Case* and *Rope* also represent *noir* 'in different degrees'.[34] Yet there is a case to make that Hitchcock's films of the 1940s can be placed within the mainstream of *film noir* rather than being positioned 'on the margins of *noir*'.[35] Hitchcock employs the characteristic *noir* motifs of expressionist cinematography and chiaroscuro lighting – indeed these motifs had been a feature of his film-making practice from his early career in Britain – while *film noir*'s themes of suspicion and paranoia were grist to Hitchcock's mill. Hitchcock's interest in popular psychoanalysis, particularly evident in *Spellbound* and *Rope*, was also consistent with the themes of *film noir*. Indeed it might be said that Hitchcock was perfectly at home as a practitioner of *film noir*: another reminder that even an *auteur* director should be seen in relation to the prevailing styles and conventions of the film industry and film culture in which they work.

In this context it is instructive to compare Hitchcock's wartime films to those of his closest rival in the thriller genre: Fritz Lang. Lang's films in Weimar Germany, including *The Spiders* (*Die Spinnen*, 1919–20), *Dr Mabuse, the Gambler* (*Dr Mabuse, der Spieler*, 1922) and *Spies* (*Spione*, 1928), were characterised by their combination of sensational melodrama (master criminals, improbable plots, fast-paced action) and extreme visual stylisation that work 'to develop a paranoid vision of a world where everything seems to fit together as part of an ever-widening web of conspiracy'.[36] Lang's work of the 1930s, including his last films in Germany, particularly *M* (1931), and his early films in Hollywood, *Fury* (1936) and *You Only Live Once* (1937), suggested a shift towards psychological realism and social problem films, though for most of his Hollywood career Lang would specialise in genre films, thrillers especially. Lang never achieved the same degree of control over his own films as Hitchcock enjoyed and his Hollywood career has often been characterised as a period of professional frustration. His own account of *Ministry of Fear*, which he undertook as a director for hire, is a good case in point: 'I was handed a script which had practically none of the quality of the Graham Greene book. When I wanted to have some changes made in it, the writer resented it deeply. Then, when I wanted to step out of the picture, my agent told me that I was contractually obliged to complete it.'[37]

Like Hitchcock, Lang directed three spy films between 1940 and 1946 – *Man Hunt, Ministry of Fear* and *Cloak and Dagger* (1946) – between other assignments including two Westerns (*The Return of Frank James, Union Pacific*), a war film (*Hangmen Also Die*) and several psychological thrillers (*The Woman in the Window, Scarlet Street, Secret Beyond the Door*). Lang was the third choice (after Hitchcock and John Ford) to direct the film version of Geoffrey Household's *Rogue Male*: *Man Hunt* is the story of a British big-game hunter, Thorndike (Walter Pidgeon), who is captured in Germany shortly before the outbreak of war while undertaking what he terms 'a sporting stalk' of Hitler. Thorndike is savagely beaten by Gestapo thugs in an attempt to make him sign a confession that he was acting on behalf of the British government, but escapes back to England where he is pursued by sinister German agents. Produced before the United States had entered the war, *Man Hunt* troubled the Production Code who insisted that the violence must be toned down – hence Thorndike's beating takes place off screen – and should not be made into a 'hate picture'.[38] The film was compared favourably to Hitchcock's work by the reviewer of *The Nation*, who felt that 'Fritz Lang seems able to give a few lessons in the technique of suspense even to Alfred Hitchcock, and he has created out of a maze of improbabilities, inaccuracies, and poor performances a really exciting picture.'[39] *Man Hunt* features some 'Hitchcockian' set pieces, notably the sequence in the London Underground where Thorndike evades and dispatches one of his pursuers, though Lang's film is bleaker than Hitchcock's and his Nazis are more thuggish than Hitchcock's suave villains in *Foreign Correspondent* and *Saboteur*.

Lang himself may have been dissatisfied with *Ministry of Fear* and the film itself is only partially successful as an adaptation: the internal psychological dimension of Greene's novel is lost in the film which becomes a double-hunt thriller where one improbable incident follows on swiftly from another with scant regard for narrative plausibility. Yet if seen on its own terms rather than as an adaptation, *Ministry of Fear* is a marvellous paranoid thriller replete with *noir* elements. It is perhaps the most 'Hitchcockian' of Lang's films: it features a protagonist plunged by chance into the 'chaos world' of conspiracy and espionage (a man newly released from a mental hospital stumbles across a German spy ring in wartime Britain when he accidentally uses one of their code phrases while passing time at a village fête) and includes such motifs as a microfilm hidden in a cake, a charity organisation ('Mothers of Free Nations') that acts as a front for a spy ring, fake spiritualists and a blind man who turns out to be an assassin. Indeed, Thomas Elsaesser contends that *Ministry of Fear* 'could almost be seen as a spoof of British Hitchcock'.[40] In contrast *Cloak and Dagger* for producer Milton Sperling's United States Pictures was a rather more routine affair about an American physics professor parachuted into wartime Germany to retrieve scientific secrets from the Nazis. It was one of a cycle of films immediately after the war – also including *O.S.S.* and *13 Rue Madeleine* – dramatising the 'now it can be told' activities of the Office of Strategic Services.[41] The presence in these films of stars such as Gary Cooper (*Cloak and Dagger*) and James Cagney (*13 Rue Madeleine*) suggested that the espionage thriller was no longer looked down upon as it had been only a few years before. However, the material was less amenable to Lang's usual style: the imperative of a semi-documentary approach mandated against his characteristic expressionist treatment. Interestingly when Hitchcock attempted a similar subject two decades later in *Torn Curtain* – featuring a nuclear physicist on a mission to East Germany during the Cold War – the result was also somewhat lacklustre.

Andrew Sarris – for whom Lang, like Hitchcock, was one of the 'pantheon' directors – wrote that 'Lang's cinema is the cinema of the nightmare, the fable, and the philosophical dissertation'.[42] As a director Lang has much in common with Hitchcock: both are masters of *mise-en-scène* whose films construct a self-contained fictional universe characterised by their pervading mood of threat, conspiracy and existential paranoia. It is not difficult to imagine a *Man Hunt* or a *Ministry of Fear* directed by Hitchcock and a *Notorious* (though perhaps not a *Foreign Correspondent*) directed by Lang. But at the same time there are also important differences between the two directors. Lang is less concerned with the mechanics of suspense than Hitchcock and makes less extensive use of subjective narration and point-of-view. And Lang's films are not only more violent but also tend to be morally bleaker than Hitchcock's. While *auteur* criticism stresses the differences between Hitchcock and Lang, a genre-based approach focuses more on what they have in common and the extent to which the similarities in their work was due to the narrative and visual conventions of the genre in which they both specialised and the working practices of the US film industry as a whole.

As with his British spy films of the 1930s, therefore, Hitchcock's wartime American spy films need to be seen not just as Hitchcock films but in the context of the film industry more widely. They demonstrate not only the development of Hitchcock's film-making style during his early years in Hollywood but also how the ideological context in which he was working changed during the Second World War. *Foreign Correspondent* was a 'Hollywood British' film produced before America had entered the war but including a clear propaganda message in its appeal to Americans to prepare for war. *Saboteur* was produced immediately following Pearl Harbor and its propaganda is of a different sort: it exploits political anxieties over spies and fifth columnists to warn against the danger of an enemy within. And *Notorious* – released a year after the end of the war but in development since late 1944 – used the framework of romantic melodrama to explore anxiety over the possibility of Nazi revivalism. And the films also reveal how Hitchcock's style adapted to working in Hollywood: while *Foreign Correspondent* and *Saboteur* recall the style of his British adventure thrillers such as *The Man Who Knew Too Much* and *The 39 Steps*, *Notorious* demonstrates the extent of Hitchcock's assimilation into the style of American *film noir*.

8

'A MASTERPIECE OF PROPAGANDA':
FOREIGN CORRESPONDENT (1940)

Foreign Correspondent was Hitchcock's second Hollywood film, following *Rebecca* (1940), and his first spy picture in America. It is generally seen as a transitional film between Hitchcock's British and American careers. On the one hand, *Foreign Correspondent* looks back to Hitchcock's Gaumont-British spy thrillers: in particular it reunited Hitchcock with screenwriter Charles Bennett and returned to the subject matter of international intrigue in contemporary Europe that had featured in *The Man Who Knew Too Much, The 39 Steps* and *The Lady Vanishes*. On the other hand, *Foreign Correspondent* anticipates certain features of Hitchcock's American films in its higher production values (its negative cost of $1.4 million was four times more than *The 39 Steps*) and its relationship to American politics. There is a neat symmetry in that Hitchcock's last British film (*Jamaica Inn*) and first American film (*Rebecca*) were both adaptations of Daphne du Maurier without any political content, while his second Hollywood picture mirrors his penultimate British film (*The Lady Vanishes*) in being a contemporary spy thriller with a strong political flavour. The parallel extends even further in that both films went against the grain of the prevailing political ideology at the time: *The Lady Vanishes* was an anti-appeasement narrative released at the time of the Munich Agreement, which represented the high-water mark of appeasement, while *Foreign Correspondent* was a strident call for American intervention in the Second World War made at a time when US public opinion remained strongly in favour of neutrality.

The production history of *Foreign Correspondent* also mirrors *The Lady Vanishes* in so far as it was not a project that Hitchcock initiated himself. Walter Wanger had bought the rights to Vincent Sheean's *Personal History* in 1936. Sheean was a foreign correspondent for an American news syndicate:

Personal History is a memoir of his experiences in Europe and around the world in the 1920s. These included a Rif uprising in Morocco and the civil war in China. *Personal History* is essentially a narrative of adventure (Sheean admits he was 'sorry when the war ended' and seized the opportunity to travel after missing military service) but is also characterised by an acute understanding of international politics. In particular Sheean has an anti-colonialist outlook and reveals a liberal sympathy for people living under foreign control, such as the Jewish population of Palestine. Sheean casts himself as a naïve idealist negotiating the world of international *realpolitik*. His account of the Lausanne Conference of 1923 – held to resolve a dispute between Italy and Greece – is a good example:

> I perceived for the first time the most persistent of diplomatic truths: that morality, in international relations, was measured only on the scale of interest – that one nation's heroism was another nation's crime. No doubt the Italians who bombarded Corfu felt that they were striking a blow for King and Country, defending the sacred heritage of the Latin race, etc., etc. To the parliamentarians of Paris and London they were offenders against a chimæra called 'civilization'. In such a disingenuous system of state relationships was it possible that nobody ever believed in a principle? That nobody was ever on the side of the right simply for the right's sake?[1]

Although little of *Personal Journey* would survive into *Foreign Correspondent*, the narrative of an American innocent with no political awareness thrust into the arena of world politics would be carried through into the film.

It is easy to see why *Personal History* appealed to Walter Wanger. He was one of Hollywood's more liberal and internationalist producers: he had served on Woodrow Wilson's staff at the Paris Peace Conference of 1919 following wartime service in US Army Intelligence. After working at Columbia, MGM and Paramount he became an independent producer in the mid-1930s: his films – distributed by United Artists – included *You Only Live Once* (1937), a crime melodrama that included a significant element of social criticism, and *Blockade* (1938), a romantic melodrama set against the background of the Spanish Civil War. *Blockade* ran foul of the Production Code Administration, which insisted that all political references should be dropped from the script. Hence it is never stated explicitly that its peasant hero (Henry Fonda) is fighting for the Republican side and there is no mention of General Franco anywhere in the film. It has been claimed that the film's poor performance at the box office was due to the intervention of Will H. Hays, President of the Motion Picture Producers and Distributors of America, who prevailed upon the major cinema chains not to show it.[2] Wanger – like other independents such as Samuel

Goldwyn and David O. Selznick – depended upon the majors for distribution and exhibition of his films.

Personal History seems to have been something of a pet project for Wanger: he had spent $200,000 on scripts and treatments before Hitchcock became attached to the film.[3] It went through various iterations. *Personal History* was originally slated for Lewis Milestone, the acclaimed director of *All Quiet on the Western Front* (1930), who worked on a first draft. Milestone soon dropped out, whereupon Wanger assigned *Personal History* to the *Blockade* team of writer John Howard Lawson and director William Dieterle. They fashioned Sheean's rambling narrative into the story of an American college student called Joe Sheridan (Sheean himself was a graduate of the University of Chicago), who is prompted to travel to Europe after seeing a newsreel of world events. It is evident from this script that the anti-isolationist theme of *Foreign Correspondent* predated Hitchcock's involvement. Early in the script Joe makes an impassioned speech:

> Webster College has a beautiful campus and a swell view of the mountains – but those mountains are walling us in from the entire living world. The only whiff of life we get is in the newsreels – and we turn our backs on them.

> (passionately)

> How many students know what's going on in the world? How many of us know what we believe? What is the truth about Communism? We don't know! How about Fascism! We don't know! What do we mean when we talk about Democracy? We don't know![4]

It is difficult to read this as anything other than a critique of American isolationism: the repetition of 'we don't know' in reference to both Communism and Fascism might be an allusion to the censorship policy which prevented overt political content in Hollywood films. The rest of the script follows Joe's journey to Europe where he witnesses events in Spain and Germany, helping the Jewish Dr Bergemann escape from the Nazis to Switzerland and then returning to rescue Bergemann's daughter Miriam who travels with Joe to the United States. It is no surprise that the script, including direct references to the persecution of German Jews, ran foul of the censor. Joseph Breen informed Wanger that it contained 'pro-Loyalist, pro-Jewish, anti-Nazi propaganda', and, while conceding that it did not technically violate the Production Code, advised that the content 'would inevitably cause enormous difficulty, when you come to release the picture'.[5] Privately Breen told Will Hays that the script addressed 'controversial racial and political questions' and predicted that it would 'arouse audience feeling against the present German regime, in the matter of its treatment of the Jews'.[6]

Wanger's decision not to proceed with *Personal History* at this point was probably as much to do with the box-office failure of *Blockade* as the intervention of the censor, who in the event did not reject the script outright but advised that if the film were made it should avoid any 'derogatory' portrayals of the German police. John Howard Lawson later claimed that it was Wanger's creditors at the Bank of America who scuppered the film: 'Just before it was to go into production, the sets were built and the actors were all engaged, Walter called us in ... He said, "The whole thing is off. I have to get my money from banks and I'm told I'll never get another penny if this anti-Nazi film goes into production."'[7] Nevertheless the project refused to die: *Personal History* was announced several times in the trade press during 1938 and 1939. The outbreak of war in Europe in September 1939 gave the film a new lease of life. Warner's *Confessions of a Nazi Spy* – released shortly before the outbreak of war – had indicated that anti-Nazi films were no longer box-office poison. MGM moved ahead with two films of novels with an anti-Nazi theme: Ethel Vance's *Escape* and Phyllis Bottome's *The Mortal Storm*. Immediately upon the outbreak of war, Wanger announced that *Personal History* – now based on a script by John Lee Mahin, co-writer of *Scarface* – would be released before the year's end. The imperative of shooting quickly was driven by the fear that if the war ended soon the film's topicality would be lost.[8]

Hitchcock became involved in the project during the autumn of 1939 when Selznick agreed to Wanger's request to loan his services as soon as Hitchcock had finished *Rebecca*. The arrangement had advantages for all parties. For Selznick the loan-out provided a much-needed cash injection at a time when he had two major films in post-production (*Gone With the Wind* and *Rebecca*) whose revenues would not accrue until 1940: Wanger paid Selznick $5,000 a week for Hitchcock's services meaning that Selznick profited from the deal as the director's regular weekly salary was $2,500.[9] For Hitchcock it was a welcome opportunity to work with a producer much more *laissez-faire* than the notoriously interventionist Selznick and to return again to the thriller genre that had established his reputation following the two du Maurier adaptations. And for Wanger it brought a director who, as a specialist in the suspense thriller, was a perfect match for the material. With Hitchcock on board any idea that *Personal History* would be a 'quickie' was soon forgotten: Wanger seems to have allowed Hichcock *carte blanche* over the production and did not balk as the cost rose from an original estimate of $1 million to a final negative cost of $1,484,167.[10]

Hitchcock rejected all the existing scripts and worked on his own treatment in association with his secretary Joan Harrison. Nevertheless their 'original story' of November 1939 carries some echoes of John Howard Lawson's script. The treatment begins:

> This is the story of a young American newspaperman who goes to Europe with certain fixed ideas of what is right and what is wrong. In his opinion Europe in the year 1939 has only itself to blame for its political troubles and the rapidly approaching war crisis. He learns, however, through bitter experience that European life is more complex than he had imagined and that methods and ideas which may be perfectly right for a new nation and continent cannot always be applied in a more sophisticated civilization. He learns, too, that an enemy may not always adopt the expected guise – that a seeming fool may be a very wise man – and that love may come where you least desire to find it.[11]

Hitchcock therefore fashioned the material even more strongly into a narrative of ideological conversion that would initially contrast American and European values ('The young man leaves for Europe, very confident in himself, his ability to do his job, and that America and American methods are always right') before the protagonist learns to curb his chauvinism and comes to accept that he does not necessarily know it all.

Hitchcock's initial treatment for *Personal History* is different from the finished film of *Foreign Correspondent* in specific detail and incident but the underlying structure of the film can be recognised. The unnamed protagonist is sent to Geneva to cover a World Peace Conference: on the boat to Europe he meets Buxton, leader of the World Peace Brotherhood, and, without initially realising who she is, Buxton's daughter Kay. Following the (apparent) assassination of the Dutch delegate, the action moves swiftly to Holland, where 'Our Hero' is sent to 'get a human angle on the dead man from his widow', and then to London, where it is revealed that Buxton has in fact kidnapped the Dutch delegate in order to extract information that he intends to sell to Germany. There is an echo of Ealing's film of *The Four Just Men* (1939) in the fact that Buxton is a Member of Parliament. The treatment describes incidents that are included in the finished film such as the villains' hide-out inside a windmill and the final act on board the Clipper back to America which is fired on by a German battleship on the day war is declared. Otherwise two points about the treatment are especially noteworthy. One is that it hints at an Oedipal dimension to the relationship between Kay and her father ('she's reported to be a tough nut – no use for men, either – appears to be a bit of an Oedipus complex in that set-up'): in this context the marriage between 'Our Hero' and Kay represents a form of ideological repositioning as it detaches her from the influence of her father.

The other feature of the treatment that warrants mentioning is the character of another journalist – an apparently foppish and lackadaisical Englishman –

who becomes a secondary hero: 'The American meets several of the other foreign correspondents, among them one on the English "Times", Ian Fleming, whom he rather despises, for his apparent effeminacy, suede shoes and affected drawl.'[12] This is clearly intended as a caricature of the future creator of James Bond: Ian Fleming had indeed been a foreign correspondent during the early 1930s – he covered the Metropolitan-Vickers show trial in 1933 for the Reuters News Agency – and was known for his somewhat affected manner. It is not clear whether Hitchcock and Fleming had met at this point – they were casual acquaintances after the Second World War when Fleming travelled regularly to the United States – though evidently Hitchcock knew of Fleming before he achieved fame as an author. In the treatment Fleming seemingly represents the worst kind of amateur ('when the American, who cannot understand his apparent lack of keenness and organization, asks why he is doing nothing, he merely remarks that it seems such an old story'), but it is Fleming who exposes Buxton as a spy. He also outrages the American by suggesting that he should use his relationship with Kay to get at Buxton ('All right, old boy, but if you think that just because of your American ideas of chivalry I'm going to let you sacrifice thousands of lives, you're mistaken'). In this sense the Fleming character serves an ideological function: to demonstrate that the apparent complacency of the English is merely an act that disguises a ruthlessly pragmatic nature beneath.

The script of *Personal History* was developed during the spring of 1940: there were half a dozen drafts between the start of the year and the end of May. Among the writers who contributed to the screenplay were Charles Bennett, the British author James Hilton (whose novels *Lost Horizon* and *Goodbye, Mr Chips* had both recently been made into films) and the American humourist Robert Benchley (who would have a cameo role in the film as an amiably drunken journalist).[13] On the film itself Bennett and Joan Harrison are credited with 'screenplay' and Hilton and Benchley for 'dialogues'. Bennett later claimed that Hitchcock 'asked me as a favor if I'd mind letting her name [Joan Harrison] be on the picture. She had only been his secretary. She had never come up with a solitary idea, or a solitary thought.'[14] According to Hitchcock, 'Joan was a secretary, and as such she would take notes while I worked on a script, with Charles Bennett, for instance. Gradually she learned, became more articulate, and she became a writer.'[15] Bennett may have been peeved about the co-credit for Harrison when *Foreign Correspondent* was nominated for the Academy Award for Best Screenplay. (*Rebecca* – on which Harrison shares the writing credit with Robert E. Sherwood – was also nominated: the Oscar for Best Screenplay went to

Donald Ogden Stewart for *The Philadelphia Story*.) There were evidently also
many uncredited contributions. According to Richard Maibaum: 'I was writer
about number thirty on *Foreign Correspondent*, and primarily I rewrote the
Albert Basserman part of the old statesman who was kidnapped.'[16] As with
some of Hitchcock's British films, it is difficult to untangle the various
contributions as the draft scripts do not include the name of the writer or
writers. Nevertheless it is possible to document the changes. The unnamed
protagonist of Hitchcock's treatment became Johnny Jones, Buxton became
Stephen Fisher, head of the Universal Peace Party but no longer an MP, Kay
Buxton became Carol Fisher, and Ian Fleming became Scott ffolliott. The
character of Stebbins, a cynical American correspondent in London ('All this
fuss about sandbags and gas masks is just English indifference'), was a late
addition written for Robert Benchley.[17]

The most significant change during the scripting process, however, was the
gradual rewriting of the protagonist. The character of Johnny Jones – surely a
conscious reference to the blundering protagonist of George M. Cohen's
musical *Little Johnny Jones* who travels to Europe on the eve of the First World
War – was transformed over the course of various drafts from a knowledgeable
if opinionated political commentator to a naïve American abroad. Thus, in the
first 'White Script' (undated but probably written in January or February 1940)
he is described as 'a very smart political observer, with a couple of books to his
credit, and the ability to set down his ideas in honest, straightforward
language'. The 'Yellow Script' (26 March 1940) includes the following
exchange between Jones and his editor:

> *Powers:* You give quite a lot of thought to European politics, don't you?
>
> *Johnny:* If you can call that shilly-shallying they're doing over there 'politics'.[18]

At this point, however, it was evidently decided that Jones should not be so
politically aware, as in the 'Pink Script' (23 April 1940) the scene has changed
entirely:

> *Powers:* What do you think of the present European crisis, Mr Jones?
>
> *Johnny:* What crisis?
>
> *Powers:* I'm referring to the impending war, Mr Jones.
>
> *Johnny:* Oh that. (*He smiles*). To be very frank, sir, I haven't given it much
> thought.[19]

This is the scene as it appears in the finished film. The production records do
not indicate the reason for this change but it seems reasonable to speculate

that the decision to turn Johnny Jones into a character unaware of European events was taken with a view to making him a more representative American everyman type. All the evidence suggests that a majority of Americans outside the metropolitan centres of the East and West coasts were not well informed about the European situation. This view persisted even after America's entry into the war. In 1943 the British consul-general in Chicago reported: 'The majority of people in the Middle West are ill-informed and ignorant; as they have little interest in anything outside America their opinions are valueless and unascertainable.'[20] Yet the 'Middle West' was also an important market for American films: to this extent the changes to *Foreign Correspondent* – as *Personal History* had become by the end of April 1940 – were a conscious strategy to challenge the perceived ignorance of American audiences about world affairs.

Yet at the same time Hitchcock and Wanger had to proceed cautiously. In 1940 the mood of political and public opinion in the United States was strongly isolationist. There was support for Britain and the Allied cause at the top of government – President Franklin D. Roosevelt was a noted Anglophile – though this support fell a long way short of intervention in the war. American isolationism had historical and ideological roots: the experience of the First World War had left many Americans embittered – there was a widely held view that America had been tricked into a war through Allied (specifically British) propaganda – while the economic and social problems of the Great Depression had turned America into a more inward-looking nation. Hence the publicity materials for *Foreign Correspondent* set out to downplay its political elements. As one journalist reported in the *New York Times*: 'Foreign Correspondent will have as little political significance as it has to the Vincent Sheean book, which is none at all. The title was changed from *Personal History* because of Wanger's refusal to compromise the Sheean yarn or profit from the mislabeling.'[21] This was also the view of the PCA when the script of *Foreign Correspondent* was submitted for pre-production scrutiny. Joseph Breen felt that *Foreign Correspondent* 'has not the remotest resemblance to the story that we were so concerned about two years back'.[22]

Foreign Correspondent went before the cameras on 18 March 1940. Hitchcock had wanted Gary Cooper as his star but had to settle for the likeable but more lightweight Joel McCrea, with Laraine Day as Carol. The principal cast was completed by Herbert Marshall, a decade after starring for Hitchcock in *Murder!*, as Stephen Fisher and George Sanders, who had just appeared in *Rebecca*, as Scott ffolliott. Marshall and Sanders – along with Edmund Gwenn as the mild-mannered assassin Rowley – were members of Hollywood's 'British colony' whose presence in the film enhances the 'British' feeling of *Foreign Correspondent*. Other key roles went to German émigré Albert Basserman – nominated for an Academy Award for Best Supporting Actor – as the kidnapped/assassinated statesman Van Meer and the craggy-faced Italian-born Eduardo Cianelli as the 'heavy' villain Krug ('a member of the Borovian Embassy staff'). *Foreign Correspondent* was shot entirely in the studio with just a few back projection plates of Amsterdam by second-unit cameraman Osmond Borrodaile: these had to be retaken when the originals were lost when the Dutch freighter SS *Rijnstroom* was sunk on its journey across the Atlantic.[23] The film's most spectacular set piece – a plane crash into the sea – was staged in a water tank by Hitchcock and William Cameron Menzies, the leading Hollywood production designer here credited for 'special production effects'.

Foreign Correspondent needs to be seen within a cycle of what, following Mark Glancy, may be termed 'Hollywood British' films. The late 1930s and early 1940s saw a rise of British-themed Hollywood films ranging from quality literary adaptations such as MGM's *Goodbye, Mr Chips* (1939) and *Pride and Prejudice* (1940) and costume swashbucklers such as Warner's *The Sea Hawk* (1940) to contemporary war movies such as Twentieth Century-Fox's *A Yank in the RAF* (1941), Warner's *International Squadron* (1941) and Wanger's own *Eagle Squadron* (1942), all variations on the narrative formula of American volunteers in the Royal Air Force. Alexander Korda's *That Hamilton Woman* (1941) – released in Britain itself as *Lady Hamilton* – was the most overtly pro-British of Hollywood films produced before the United States entered the Second World War. The reasons for the emergence of 'Hollywood British' films at this time were both political and economic. On one level it has been argued that the production of films presenting a favourable picture of Britain as a democratic and peace-loving nation represented an ideological campaign to persuade Americans that Britain was in fact much like America with a shared culture and political values in order to prepare the ground for America's entry into the war – an event which in turn mandated the production of even more stridently pro-British films such as MGM's *Mrs Miniver* (1942) and *The White Cliffs of Dover* (1944) and RKO's *Forever and a Day* (1943).[24]

On another level, as Glancy has ably demonstrated, Hollywood's Anglophilia was underpinned by hard-headed economic considerations. By the 1930s the US film industry drew half of its total revenues from overseas markets: for a major A-class feature film it was the foreign earnings that often made the difference between breaking even and returning a profit. Britain was by some measure the most lucrative overseas market: between 50 and 60 per cent of all Hollywood's overseas revenues came from Britain.[25] The British market was especially lucrative because Britain was a highly cinephile country – there were over 4,000 cinemas and some 900 million annual cinema attendances by the end of the decade – where there was no need to incur costs in dubbing or subtitling films and without the punitive taxes of some other European territories. The British market became even more important between 1939 and 1941 when other European markets were closed off. Germany banned all American films in 1940 and the German occupation of France and the Low Countries in the same year effectively closed off those markets for the duration of the war. By 1941 the 'Hitler circuit', as the trade press called the markets that had fallen under German control, included Austria, Belgium, Bulgaria, Czechoslovakia, Denmark, France, Greece, Hungary, Luxembourg, the Netherlands, Norway, Poland, Romania and Yugoslavia. With the Latin American and Far Eastern markets providing tiny returns in comparison, Britain became the most important of all overseas markets. Some sources even indicate that during the Second World War, Britain accounted for up to 90 per cent of all Hollywood's foreign revenues: it was little wonder that the US film industry would look to produce films geared towards Britain.[26]

In this context the historical 'moment' of *Foreign Correspondent* was important. It was released in the late summer of 1940 at precisely the moment that Germany achieved military hegemony of Western and Central Europe so those markets were closed to American films. According to United Artists' records, *Foreign Correspondent* returned total rentals of $2,202,238. When the domestic and foreign revenues are broken down, however, it is revealed that the film did not quite break even in the domestic (North American) market where it returned $1,428,538 (against a negative cost of $1,484,167) and so was reliant on foreign earnings for its profit. Furthermore, of the film's total foreign earnings of $772,700, Britain accounted for $480,000 with a further $292,700 from markets outside Europe and nothing from Continental Europe.[27] In short: the British market accounted for nearly 22 per cent of the total revenues of *Foreign Correspondent* and 62 per cent of its foreign revenues. In this context the ideological imperative that had prevailed during the production of the film – to maintain a distance from real European politics (Germany and Hitler are never mentioned as instigators of the conspiracy) in order to appease both the American censor and European markets – had been overtaken by external events by the time of its release.

The main narrative of *Foreign Correspondent* is set immediately prior to the outbreak of the Second World War: an insert shot of a telegram dated 19 August 1939 establishes the opening date and the main action ends on the day that war was declared (3 September 1939). This ensured that the film's content would not date even if the war situation changed before its release: the eve-of-war narratives of near-contemporaneous films such as *Night Train to Munich* and Leslie Howard's British production *Pimpernel Smith* (1941) adopted the same strategy. *Foreign Correspondent* therefore differs from Hitchcock's British spy films in that it is set at a specific historical moment in the recent past rather than in the present. It is surely no accident that the film begins only four days before the signing of the Nazi-Soviet Pact. This pact – an agreement of convenience between Hitler and Stalin – caught the Western powers by surprise: it had the effect of isolating Poland – whose independence had been guaranteed by Britain and France – and made clear Germany's territorial ambitions. *Foreign Correspondent* is set against a background of mounting international tension and a war scare: the 'MacGuffin' – as in *The Lady Vanishes* – is a secret treaty known only to the kidnapped statesman Van Meer ('keynote to the European situation today... Holland's strong man'). Against this background the wording of the telegram from foreign correspondent Stebbins ('According to high official it is believed absolutely no chance of war this year account of late crops') is clearly intended as ironic: it irresistibly recalls that the *Daily Express* – a leading mass-circulation British newspaper – had confidently predicted 'No War This Year' in a now infamous front-page banner headline as late as 7 August 1939.[28]

Foreign Correspondent belongs squarely within the sensational lineage of the thriller: it is a narrative of action and rapid movement with little respect for either plausibility or psychological complexity. Johnny Jones, a crime reporter, is sent to Europe by his editor to discover what is going on ('There's a crime brewing in that bedevilled continent...'): he soon finds himself caught up in a conspiracy involving kidnapping, assassination and a fake peace organisation that is cover for a spy ring. It might be stretching the interpretation a little far to suggest that the Universal Peace Party (whom Jones dismisses as 'well-meaning amateurs') is a metaphor for the failure of appeasement in the face of German aggression: nevertheless the same motif had featured in late 1930s British films such as *Bulldog Drummond at Bay* and *The Four Just Men*. It is never made clear whether the villain Fisher is himself German or a Nazi sympathiser, though his description of the enemy for Jones's benefit is quite evidently also a description of himself: 'They're fanatics! They combine a mad love of country with an equally mad indifference to life – their own as well as others. They're cunning, unscrupulous – and inspired!' *Foreign Correspondent* is nothing if not direct in its symbolism: as Jones escapes from heavies over the roof of his Amsterdam hotel, he accidentally knocks out two letters in the neon sign so that 'HOTEL EUROPE' becomes 'HOT EUROPE'.

16 *Foreign Correspondent* (United Artists/Walter Wanger Productions, 1940): the assassin ...

Foreign Correspondent further exemplifies the sensational thriller in its employment of set pieces. These not only demonstrate Hitchcock's mastery of film technique but can also be seen as a means through which Hitchcock incorporated aspects of European film-making practices into his American films. The film's first major set piece – the assassination of Van Meer – is clearly influenced by the montage techniques of Soviet cinema: the set-up on the steps and the sudden 'impact' close-up of Van Meer's face spattered with blood after he is shot by the assassin are nothing if not a direct homage to the Odessa Steps sequence of Sergei Eisenstein's *Battleship Potemkin* (1925). The assassin's escape in the rain, through a maze of umbrellas, also brings to mind the Dutch documentarist Joris Ivens's *Rain* (1929) – albeit that the Amsterdam of *Foreign Correspondent* is a studio set rather than the real place – while at the same time anticipating Jacques Remy's *The Umbrellas of Cherbourg* (1964). (As an aside it might be noted that there is quite a high level of casual violence in *Foreign Correspondent*: the assassin shoots a policeman and a passing bicyclist during his escape. It is surprising this did not bother the censors as the assassin is not brought to justice in the course of the film.) In contrast the scene inside the

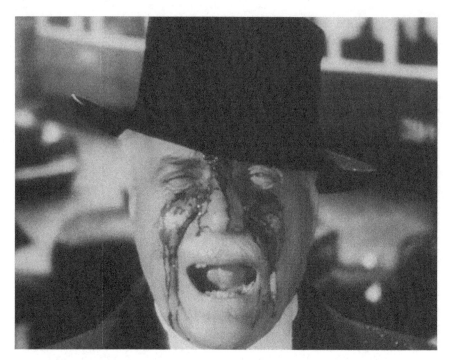

17   *Foreign Correspondent* (United Artists/Walter Wanger Productions, 1940) ...and his victim – demonstrating Hitchcock's use of Soviet-style montage.

windmill where Jones discovers Van Meer is not dead after all (a double was shot to make the world think he is dead) eschews montage in favour of a highly expressionist *mise-en-scène* of shadows and angles in the style of the German silent cinema: these are visual echoes of Hitchcock's time working at the UFA Studios in Munich. The inclusion of these very 'European' aspects of visual style into *Foreign Correspondent* can be seen as an example of how classical Hollywood assimilated aspects of the European avant-garde into its own formal system: Hitchcock was not the only director to do this of course – German émigrés such as Fritz Lang and Douglas Sirk were also naturally inclined to expressionist motifs – though his films are particularly notable examples.[29]

Yet in most other key respects *Foreign Correspondent* exemplifies the narrative and ideological strategies of the Hollywood cinema in which Hitchcock was now working. Most obviously it features two parallel lines of narrative: on one level the narrative of Johnny's transformation from ill-informed American abroad to a position of political knowledge and on another level the narrative of his relationship with Carol. 'Your childish mind is as out of place in Europe as you are in my bedroom,' Carol remarks pointedly when

Johnny seeks refuge in her hotel room while escaping from two heavies masquerading as policemen: the film therefore links the two narratives in so far as it is Johnny's relationship with Carol that brings about his conversion from cynical isolationist to committed internationalist. Another ideological strategy that is as much a part of classical Hollywood as it belongs to Hitchcock is the Oedipal trajectory of the narrative. Johnny's relationship with Carol cannot be fulfilled until she has rejected her own father for him: for her part Carol cannot accept Johnny until she learns the truth about her father. Fisher emerges as a more sympathetic conspirator than others in Hitchcock's films: he is partly redeemed by his love for his daughter. He apologises for his deception ('I'm sorry for using the tactics of the country I grew up with' – again it is not entirely clear whether he means Germany or the fictitious third-party agitator Borovia) and ultimately sacrifices his own life following the plane crash into the Atlantic.

The shooting script of *Foreign Correspondent* ended with Johnny, Carol and Scott rescued by a US Navy destroyer: with a little subterfuge Johnny manages to radio his editor to tell the story despite the captain's insistence that this would violate American neutrality. (It is not evident why revealing the story is against the Neutrality Acts or why the US Navy could not rescue the survivors of an aeroplane shot down by a German ship: the film makes it very clear that the US Navy is not involved in the fighting.) The principal photography of *Foreign Correspondent* was finished by the middle of June 1940: the later stages of shooting coincided with the German Blitzkrieg against Holland, Belgium, Luxembourg and France. At a late stage of production it was decided to add a coda to the film. An additional scene was written by Ben Hecht in which Johnny – now a fully fledged war correspondent – broadcasts to America from London during an air raid. Hitchcock had made a brief return visit to London in June 1940 to wind up his affairs there: the Blitz on London and other British cities would not start for another two months but the nation was already braced for the expected air attacks following the fall of France and the evacuation of the British Expeditionary Force from Dunkirk. In the new coda of *Foreign Correspondent*, Johnny is in the middle of a regular radio broadcast when the air raid warning sounds. He stays by the microphone:

> I can't read the rest of the speech I had because the lights have gone out, so I'll just have to talk off the cuff. All that noise you hear isn't static. It's death coming to London. Yes, they're coming here now. You can hear the bombs falling on the streets and the homes. Don't tune me out. Hang on a while, this is a big story and you're part of it. It's too late to do anything here now except stand in the dark and let them come. It's as if the lights were all out everywhere. Except in America.

18   'Hello America, hang on to your lights – they're the only lights left in the world!' Johnny Jones (Joel McCrae) turns propagandist in *Foreign Correspondent* (United Artists/Walter Wanger Productions, 1940); Carol Fisher (Laraine Day) looks apprehensive.

> Keep those lights burning there. Cover them with steel. Ring them with guns.
> Build a canopy of battleships and bombing planes around them. Hello America,
> hang on to your lights – they're the only lights left in the world!

During this speech the noise of bombs gradually fades and 'The Star-Spangled Banner' rises on the soundtrack until it plays loudly over 'The End'.

The coda of *Foreign Correspondent* is an important sequence in both formal and ideological terms. Formally it marks a point of rupture within the film which hitherto has conformed to the principles of the classic realist text in maintaining a sense of verisimilitude: the broadcast breaks this verisimilitude by having the protagonist speak directly to the public – the public listening on the radio but by extension also the audiences watching the film in cinemas. In an article on propaganda in cinema, Steve Neale distinguishes between clear-cut propaganda films and other films that are not in themselves propaganda but nevertheless serve a 'propagandist function' depending upon their contexts of production and reception. He uses as examples two German films released in the same year as *Foreign Correspondent*: the notorious anti-Semitic 'documentary' *Der Erwige Jude* (*The Eternal Jew*) and the feature film *Jud Süss* (*Jew Süss*). While the two films are 'closely related in producing an anti-Semitic position', Neale argues that *Der Erwige Jude* is propaganda in so far as it breaks from the conventions of the classic realist text and employs a different mode of address to the spectator, whereas *Jud Süss* exemplifies the classical film that serves a propagandist function in the ideological context of the cinema of the Third Reich.[30] In these terms most of *Foreign Correspondent* – comprising the film as originally shot – would exemplify Neale's definition of a film serving a propagandist function: a classic realist text whose ideological import arises from the context of its release in the summer of 1940. However, the coda invokes a different mode of address as Johnny Jones/Joel McCrea speaks directly to the American public: hence its propaganda content is made more explicit and direct.

The coda is also significant on an ideological level. It was originally to have been set in Paris: this was changed to London following the fall of France.[31] It anticipates, uncannily, the reporting of the Blitz by American journalists such as Edward R. Murrow of CBS, whose broadcasts from London during the Blitz made an enormous impact in the United States, and Quentin Reynolds of *Collier's Weekly*, who narrated a short film titled *London Can Take It!* produced by the GPO Film Unit in October 1940, intended initially for distribution in the United States but also shown in Britain under the title *Britain Can Take It!*[32] Reynolds's insistence in his commentary on the authenticity of the bombing ('These are not Hollywood sound effects') recalls the same point made by Johnny ('All that noise you hear isn't static') in *Foreign Correspondent*. The ideological strategy of Johnny's speech is to create a sense of familiarity between Britain and America ('I'm speaking to you from a part of the world as nice as Vermont and Ohio, Virginia, California and Illinois') and to impress upon Americans that the war in Europe was their war too. It stops short of calling for American intervention in the war: to this extent Johnny's 'off the cuff' speech is finely calculated as there is nothing to which isolationists could take offence. It ends with a rousing call to America to take up arms in defence of the last bastion of liberty: an assertion of American patriotism that would resonate with isolationists and interventionists alike.

Foreign Correspondent was released in America in late August 1940 and in Britain two months later: its reception differed on each side of the Atlantic. Most American critics regarded it as a superior entertainment: for Richard L. Core of the *Washington Post* it was 'the year's most engrossing mystery yarn'.[33] Philip K. Scheuer of the *Los Angeles Times* predicted that it 'will be a classic in cinema annals. It is Alfred Hitchcock's triumph – and thus Hollywood's, and thus America's, and thus, in a way, England's too.'[34] The political aspect of the film seems not to have bothered reviewers who felt that it worked primarily as a melodrama. *Harrison's Reports*, for example, called it 'a thriller of the first order ... The story has a significant political angle; but it is of secondary importance to the melodramatic action, which is absorbing.'[35] Others were slightly less fulsome in their praise: the film was generally well received though for some critics it strayed too far into implausibility. *Variety* suggested that it 'might well qualify as one of the best of the year to date were the plot not so heavy on the artificial side'. It amplified: 'It's not the kind of phoniness apparent to much of a film audience – there's far too much suspense and action for that – but there are a few too many points that won't hold liquid for a cooler-headed jury of critics unless they, too, are captivated by the Hitchcock brand of nerve-jingling.'[36] And Bosley Crowther, senior film critic of the *New York Times*, complained that '*Foreign Correspondent* is simply not logical. For a story which is so artificial and unblushingly hokey as this one, the fulsome dedication which it bears to the "clear-eyed" foreign correspondents, plus the flag-waving sequence which has been tagged on at the end, strike us as being oddly unbecoming.'[37]

British critics were also divided over *Foreign Correspondent*. The fact that it was released in Britain at the height of the Blitz on London meant that its prescient coda acquired an even greater significance. The contrasting positions on the film were neatly exemplified by the views of the two 'Sunday ladies'. C. A. Lejeune of the *Observer*, usually one of Hitchcock's champions, thought it 'grim melodrama' and 'a less likeable film than *Rebecca*'. She felt that '*Foreign Correspondent* is all tied up with these grisly days, a topicality that may give it a quick response and a short appeal' and averred that the coda struck a false note: 'Hitchcock has been too long out of England to understand the mind of the bombed. The assault on London didn't happen this way. That may not matter. The assault on London couldn't happen this way. That does matter.'[38] In contrast Dilys Powell called it 'genuine Hitchcock' and thought it was 'worth fifty Rebeccas'. She rejected the criticisms made by Bosley Crowther, averring that 'there is no need to be put off by the dedicatory caption about the far-sightedness of the foreign correspondents, nor, indeed, by the solemn appeal of the final speech ... This is not a hortatory picture; the message is only a postscript.'[39]

The coda of *Foreign Correspondent* was also the subject of an argument in the pages of *Documentary News Letter*. This was a minority journal, published by an independent body called Film Centre, established in the late 1930s by John

Grierson, the leading advocate of documentary film in Britain. *Documentary News Letter* was the successor to *Cinema Quarterly* and *World Film News* as the voice of progressive film culture in Britain. It was not habitually given over to praising Hollywood films but nevertheless found much to admire in *Foreign Correspondent*, which it selected as its 'film of the month' for November 1940. In a review that ran against the consensus which held that Hitchcock was the primary influence on his own films, *Documentary News Letter* attributed the politics of *Foreign Correspondent* to its producer. It described Wanger as 'Hollywood's most alert and liberal minded producer' and detected his hand in the concluding propaganda set piece:

> The importance of the sequence is that it is a message to the States – and not to us – sent out by an American journalist and, in fact, conceived at script conferences at which Walter Wanger had the last word. It is neither warlike nor a political piece of propaganda; it stimulates thought, and its message should strike home on the other side of the Atlantic; to us over here it does at least bring evidence of a goodwill backed by clear thinking.[40]

This review in turn prompted a rebuttal in the next issue of the journal, written by the documentarist and film critic Paul Rotha and signed by several luminaries of British cinema including Michael Balcon and Alberto Cavalcanti as well as critics Ritchie Calder and Dilys Powell (despite her own favourable review of the film) and the Labour MP Michael Foot. Rotha wrote 'to place on record my deep resentment' at the review of *Foreign Correspondent* and especially its comments about the closing speech which, he felt, revealed 'a grave lack of knowledge of public opinion here in Britain' and 'implies that the British people no longer have faith in democracy in their own country'. He took particular exception to the suggestion that America's lights were 'the only lights left in the world':

> I can assure these leaders of the British documentary film that the people who are really suffering as well as fighting this war do not share this view that the lights are even dimmed in Britain. If they did, the Fascist propagandists might well claim to have already won the war ... In their editorial the Editors of *DNL* divide the British nation into two camps of US and THEM; I invite these leaders of the documentary group to remember that democracy in practice needs only one camp – WE.[41]

Rotha's letter seems to have been prompted by an erroneous suggestion that John Grierson – who at the outbreak of war had taken up a new post as head of the National Film Board of Canada – had written, or at least influenced, the speech at the end of *Foreign Correspondent*. His objection to *Foreign Correspondent* should be understood in the context of the journal's left-leaning politics and its advocacy of the idea of the 'people's war': Rotha evidently felt that the ending of *Foreign Correspondent* went against the spirit of documentary films such as *Britain Can Take It!* – released in Britain at the same time as *Foreign Correspondent* – with its emphasis on the stoical resistance of British civilians to German bombardment.

In the event this was little more than a storm in a teacup: *Documentary News Letter* was a small-circulation specialist magazine that was probably not widely read outside the film industry and was certainly not reflective of popular film taste. And British audiences do not seem to have been put off by the falseness that Rotha detected in *Foreign Correspondent*: according to the trade press it was the second most popular general release in Britain in 1940 – the first was *Rebecca*.[42] Its British revenues, as we have seen, were essential for the ultimate box-office success of *Foreign Correspondent*. Wanger and Hitchcock both had good reason to be satisfied with the film which was nominated for the Academy Award for Best Picture – in the event losing out to *Rebecca*, for which Selznick, as the producer, accepted the Oscar – and also picked up nominations for cinematography (Rudolph Maté) and art direction (Alexander Golitzen) as well as those for Best Original Screenplay and Supporting Actor. It also received an endorsement from an unexpected quarter. None other than Joseph Goebbels, the Reich Minister of Popular Enlightenment and Propaganda in Nazi Germany and an avid cinephile himself, saw *Foreign Correspondent* (probably, Hitchcock speculated, acquiring a print through neutral Switzerland) and evidently liked it, describing it as '[a] masterpiece of propaganda, a first-class production which no doubt will make a certain impression upon the broad masses of the people in enemy countries'.[43]

9

THE ENEMY WITHIN: *SABOTEUR* (1942)

If *Saboteur* – an original screenplay not to be confused with the similarly titled *Sabotage* – is generally regarded as a second-division Hitchcock film, this is due at least in some measure to the director's own retrospective critique of what he evidently regarded as a flawed project. In hindsight Hitchcock felt that 'the script lacks discipline. I don't think I exercised a clear, sharp approach to the original construction of the screenplay. There was a mass of ideas, but they weren't sorted out in proper order; they weren't selected with sufficient care.'[1] He was also dissatisfied with the casting: the male lead Robert Cummings lacked sufficient *gravitas* ('a competent performer, but he belongs in the light-comedy class of actors'), while female lead Priscilla Lane 'simply wasn't the right type for a Hitchcock picture'.[2] Yet these flaws did not prevent *Saboteur* from being a popular success, while Hitchcock's disparaging view has had the effect of marginalising a film that in fact has significant ideological import: *Saboteur* – along with the more acclaimed *Lifeboat* (1944) – represents Hitchcock's contribution to the anti-Fascist cinema of the Second World War.

Like *Foreign Correspondent*, Hitchcock made *Saboteur* while on loan from Selznick: it was a Frank Lloyd Production for Universal Pictures. Universal – rather like RKO Radio Pictures for whom Hitchcock had made *Mr and Mrs Smith* (1941) and *Suspicion* (1941) – was at the time a second-rank Hollywood studio whose staple products in the early 1940s were star-genre combinations such as the romantic musicals of Deanna Durbin and the comedies of Bud Abbott and Lou Costello. Universal was one of the so-called 'Little Three' (alongside Columbia and United Artists) which unlike the 'Big Five' (MGM, Paramount, Warner Bros., Twentieth Century-Fox and RKO) did not own its own cinemas. In the early 1940s it adopted a policy of buying in pre-packaged A-class film projects that could be produced and released through Universal. Frank Lloyd, who produced *Saboteur* with Jack H. Skirball, was best known as director of the film version of Noël Coward's *Cavalcade* (1933) – produced for the Fox Film Corporation – and MGM's *Mutiny on the Bounty* (1935).

The production context of *Saboteur* demonstrates the changes in production ecologies that occurred in the US film industry during the 1940s that would in time lead to the eclipse of the studio system and the rise of independent producers and 'package' deals. Selznick developed *Saboteur* as a package with script and director in place which he sold to Universal for $200,000 plus 10 per cent of the gross receipts.[3] There were advantages for both parties in this arrangement. For Selznick it was a means of generating income at a time when he was taking a temporary rest from active production following the rigours of *Gone With the Wind* and *Rebecca*. He made money on the deal as the fee for Hitchcock's services was more than the director's contracted salary and Selznick pocketed the difference. For Universal it was a means of saving time and expense on preparation of the film as it came with a script already in place. It was also a means of getting films into the lucrative first-run theatres: the vehicles of Deanna Durbin and Abbott and Costello played more in the so-called 'mom and pop' theatres than in the larger cinemas in major metropolitan centres. In addition to his fee Hitchcock received 10 per cent of the gross once it passed 170 per cent of the negative cost. It was a lucrative deal: *Saboteur* cost $753,109 and by the end of 1946 had grossed $1,747,924. Hitchcock's share of the profits amounted to $32,734.[4]

The production history of *Saboteur* spanned America's entry into the Second World War: the development of the script reflected the changing ideological context. Hitchcock began working on the script in the summer of 1941 in collaboration with Joan Harrison. Like *Foreign Correspondent*, their 'Untitled Original Treatment' of 20 August is recognisable as the blueprint of the finished film. It sketches out a childhood friendship between two orphans, Barry and Ken, who as adults go to work in an aircraft factory in Los Angeles. Barry, characterised as clumsy and accident-prone, is suspected of arson and murder when the factory is destroyed in a fire that kills Ken: in reality the fire-extinguisher he used had been filled with gasolene by a saboteur. The treatment follows the same narrative trajectory as the finished film as Barry flees from the authorities and seeks to identify the real culprit. Much of the detail of the finished film is present: the name of the arsonist-saboteur (Fry), Barry escaping the police by jumping into a river, the circus caravan with its complement of 'freaks', the chase through Radio City Music Hall in New York and the climax atop the Statue of Liberty.[5] Hitchcock evidently drew freely

19   Hitchcock was not happy with the casting of either Robert Cummings or Priscilla Lane in *Saboteur* (Universal/Frank Lloyd Productions, 1942).

upon aspects of his previous work. In particular the treatment reworks various elements from *The 39 Steps*, including the innocent protagonist plunged into the chaos world of spies and saboteurs, the picaresque cross-country narrative, the outwardly respectable chief villain, the initially sceptical heroine and even the motif of the handcuffs. To this extent *Saboteur* might be seen as the first occasion on which Hitchcock set out to remake a previous success – a strategy that would also bear fruit with the second *The Man Who Knew Too Much* and *North by Northwest*.

The treatment was fleshed out into a full screenplay by Peter Viertel, a young writer on Selznick's payroll who was the son of Austrian émigré director Berthold Viertel – the elder Viertel had made several films for Gaumont-British in the 1930s – with an uncredited contribution from John Houseman, co-producer of Orson Welles's *Mercury Theater on the Air* who also had a period under contract to Selznick in the early 1940s. It is entirely a matter of speculation that the protagonist's surname of Kane was Houseman's reference to Welles: Houseman had been involved in the early development of *Citizen Kane* (1941) but had split from Welles following creative differences.[6] By the end of October the childhood opening had been dropped and the script opened with the scene at the aircraft factory that is the site of the initial act of sabotage.[7] The humourist and short-story writer Dorothy Parker was then drafted in to add scenes and polish the dialogue. The untitled 'White Script' of 12 December 1941 is credited to Parker, Harrison and Viertel. At this point there was no indication of the nationality of the saboteurs though there was a suggestion that their motivation might have been mercenary rather than ideological: Barry Kane remarks that Fry 'is a saboteur – a man that doesn't mind killing Americans for money'.[8]

The script was barely completed, however, before it was overtaken by events. On the morning of 7 December 1941, the Japanese launched a surprise aerial attack on the US Navy base at Pearl Harbor in Hawaii. The attack – without a formal declaration of war – precipitated the United States' entry into the Second World War: America's subsequent declaration of war on Japan (8 December) was followed by Japan's allies Germany and Italy declaring war on America (11 December). The production of *Saboteur* must therefore be understood within a very specific set of historical and ideological circumstances. It was on 12 December 1941 – only five days after Pearl Harbor and one day after Germany's declaration of war – that the 'White Script' was submitted to the Production Code Administration. At this point official policy regarding the role of the film industry in supporting the war effort had yet to be determined: it was not until June 1942 that an Office of War Information (OWI) was set up.[9] In the absence of official guidelines regarding film propaganda, the PCA took it upon itself to ensure that movies supported a patriotic outlook and did not contain anything that might be deemed defeatist or subversive. And in this context *Saboteur* presented certain problems. The PCA told Universal that 'the basic story seems acceptable under the provisions of the Production Code'. 'However,' it added, 'there is one disturbing element which appears, from time to time, throughout this script and that is the great number of seemingly anti-social speeches and references. It is essential that such statements be rewritten to avoid giving this flavour.' Among the lines it singled out were one that cast aspersions on the wealthy ('Just because he's got a big ranch and a fancy house and a million-dollar swimming pool – that doesn't say he's a good guy') and another that suggested defiance of the law ('I have my own ideas about my duties as an American citizen. They sometimes involve disregarding the law').[10] With America now a nation at war, it seems that the PCA was not prepared to accept any suggestion that all Americans were anything but law-abiding patriots.

Hitchcock and Universal realised that America's entry into the war made *Saboteur* a timely and topical picture: the imperative now was to press ahead as

20 The travelling circus 'freaks' represent social outsiders in a scene added to *Saboteur* (Universal/Frank Lloyd Productions, 1942) following Pearl Harbor.

quickly as possible. The script was hurriedly revised in the early weeks of 1942. The 'anti-social speeches' noted by the PCA remained, but they were now counterbalanced by the addition of several set-piece speeches asserting the virtues of America and its democracy. In the 'Blue Script' of 8 January 1942 the scene where Barry encounters a circus troupe who hold a vote on whether to hand the fugitive over to the police was revised to include a reference to the wartime context:

> *Bones:* In this situation I find a parallel for the present world predicament – we stand defeated at the outset – you, Esmerelda, have sympathy, yet you are willing to remain passive and let the inevitable happen. I have a belief, yet, I am tempted to let myself be over-ridden by force. The rest of you, with the exception of this malignant jerk here, are ignorant of the facts, and therefore confused.[11]

Given the historical context it is difficult to read this as anything other than a commentary on America's entry into the war: many Americans were indeed confused and knew little of the international situation. The 'malignant jerk' is an antagonistic midget – known in the film as 'The Major' – who rejects the democratic process ('No vote: I'm against voting!') and is subsequently denounced as a 'fascist'. Another addition was a speech by Barry in which he responds to the villain-in-chief Tobin's declaration of support for totalitarianism ('When you think about it, Mr Kane, the competence of totalitarian nations is much higher than ours') with a rousing defence of democratic values:

> *Barry:* Let me tell you something. The last four or five days I've learned an awful lot... I've met ruthless guys like you... and I've met a whole lot of others... people that are warm and helpful and eager to do the right thing – people that are alive – people that get a kick out of helping each other. They feel proud to be fighting the bad guys. Love and hate – the world is choosing up sides. I know who I'm with, and I know there are a lot of people on my side – millions of us in every country, and we're plenty strong. We'll fight standing up on our feet, and we'll win. Remember that Mr Tobin. We'll win no matter what you guys do. We'll win if it takes us from now until the cows come home.[12]

This speech would be slightly shortened and modified in the finished film, but it is entirely characteristic of the propaganda strategies of American cinema of the Second World War: it would become common practice to insert into films of all genres a set-piece speech affirming faith in America and its democratic values.

The amendments seem to have satisfied the PCA. Its comments on the revised script pages no longer picked up on the 'anti-social' speeches: now its concern was that some of the dialogue was 'overly sex suggestive and must be rewritten to avoid this flavour'. One line to which it took exception was when Barry and his reluctant companion Patricia are trying to keep warm in the desert at night and he implies sharing bodily warmth: 'Well, I didn't want to insult you by not trying.'[13] It also objected to Barry's line: 'She picked me up and... *(he smiles)*... she was a pretty girl – Maybe it was a little risky – but there you are.'[14] However, the fact that both these lines remained in the finished film demonstrates that the PCA's directives were not absolute. The PCA was also concerned about a sequence towards the end of the film where the police pursue the saboteur Fry through a cinema 'in the course of which a man is shot and the audience is thrown into a panic'. The PCA regarded this scene as 'very dangerous' on the grounds that it 'might excite a panic among the audience viewing the picture'. It did not prohibit the sequence but advised that 'great care must be taken in shooting these scenes to get away from the possibility of causing a panic'.[15] *Saboteur* was reviewed by the PCA on 25 March 1942 and awarded a seal of approval without cuts.

The tendency among Hitchcock critics has typically been to see *Saboteur* in relation to Hitchcock's British thrillers: it is usually found wanting in comparison. Lindsay Anderson noted 'its barefaced pilfering from almost every film Hitchcock had ever made': he felt that 'individual episodes are directed with enjoyable virtuosity – the aircraft factory fire at the beginning, a gunfight in a cinema, the final megalomaniac climax on the Statue of Liberty – but the film as a whole has the over-emphasis of parody'.[16] Rohmer and Chabrol similarly regard it 'a potpourri of his English work, returning to certain features and elaborating them to the point of exaggeration'.[17] In particular *Saboteur* tends to be seen as a reworking of *The 39 Steps* transposed to an American setting: the innocent protagonist, the double-hunt motif and the heroine who becomes a reluctant travelling companion are all echoes of the earlier film. Furthermore, most of the set pieces of *Saboteur* have parallels in Hitchcock's Gaumont-British films of the 1930s: the explosion at the aircraft factory that sets the plot in motion (*Sabotage*), Barry arriving at Tobin's ranch only to find that he has walked straight into the villain's lair (Hannay at Professor Jordan's house in *The 39 Steps*), Barry escaping from the police by jumping off a bridge into a river (Hannay jumping off the train in *The 39 Steps*), Barry sheltered by the kindly blind hermit Philip Martin (who might be seen as a counterpart of the crofter's wife in *The 39 Steps*), the sequence where Barry and Patricia find themselves trapped in public at the charity ball in New York (the political meeting in *The 39 Steps*) and the chase through the cinema (*Sabotage*). Other 'Hitchcockian' motifs that would feature in later films include the villain's housemaid holding Barry at gunpoint (*North by Northwest*) and the climax on the Statue of Liberty (prefiguring Hitchcock's use of Mount Rushmore at the end of *North by Northwest*). Freeman, the insecure and overly fastidious henchman, is a close relation of the homosexual Leonard in *North by Northwest*.

Yet to see *Saboteur* just as 'a loose remake of *The 39 Steps*' (to quote Robin Wood) is limiting in several respects.[18] For one thing it ignores the quite salient fact that *Saboteur* is an American film. Although *Saboteur* was Hitchcock's fifth American film it was only his second to be set in America – the first was the uncharacteristic screwball comedy *Mr and Mrs Smith* – and his first really to suggest an American atmosphere in its locales and *mise-en-scène*. The highways lined with advertising billboards and the Western 'ghost town' of Soda City locate *Saboteur* within a culturally specific iconography of 1940s Americana, while Hitchcock's adroit combination of studio and location anticipates the style of post-war *film noir* such as *They Live by Night* (1948). A characteristic Hitchcock motif is the advertisement that feeds Barry's sense of paranoia ('You're being followed – by the cars that don't use Comet Oil'). The clearest visual reference to America is the film's climactic sequence on the Statue of Liberty: the symbolism of the villain Fry falling to his death from a world-famous symbol of American democracy is nothing if not obvious. Hitchcock's British films had not on the whole made such use of iconic British landmarks – the one major exception is the British Museum in *Blackmail* – but it was a motif he would develop in his American work including the Jefferson Memorial in Washington DC (*Strangers on a Train*), the Golden Gate Bridge in San Francisco (*Vertigo*) and of course Mount Rushmore (*North by Northwest*).

Another important difference between *Saboteur* and *The 39 Steps* is to be found in their social politics. Like Richard Hannay, Barry Kane finds himself assigned to the role of a fugitive from justice who is therefore outside the social order; but there the comparison ends. In *The 39 Steps* Hannay moves with ease up and down the class system and is able to assume different identities to fit the social milieux in which he finds himself. In *Saboteur*, however, Barry lacks Hannay's social mobility: he is never anything other than a blue-collar worker and feels ill at ease when he is propelled into unfamiliar environments. This is particularly evident in the scenes at Deep Springs Ranch and later at the charity ball: 'You're not even dressed!' declares a distinguished-looking elderly gentleman when Barry tries to warn him of the danger. Barry's inability to navigate the class system like Hannay is a fundamental point of difference between *Saboteur* and *The 39 Steps*. It is an indication of the different cultural influences on Hitchcock's British and American films. The Hannay of *The 39 Steps* belongs in spirit to the tradition of 'clubland heroes' who populated early twentieth-century British popular fiction; the protagonist of *Saboteur* in contrast is drawn from the same background as the working-class heroes of American cinema represented by actors such as Clark Gable and James Cagney. In certain respects, indeed, the film to which *Saboteur* bears the closest resemblance is not *The 39 Steps* but Frank Capra's *It Happened One Night* (1934) in which the proletarian newspaperman hero (Gable) finds himself on a picaresque journey with a runaway heiress (Claudette Colbert): the heroine of *Saboteur* is a billboard model rather than an heiress but the social differences between her and Barry are just as evident.

Saboteur was also the product of a different set of historical and ideological contexts than *The 39 Steps*. Released in the United States in April 1942, *Saboteur* was one of the first war-related films produced in Hollywood. In the opening scene there are references to the wartime context: Barry mentions the President by name ('Mr Roosevelt should clear that' – a reference to a 'bottleneck' at the factory) and makes a joke about the importance of wartime industry ('Just goes to show you what a little blonde can do hold up national defence' – when he and Ken accidentally collide with Fry because they had been eyeing up a pretty female co-worker). For once there is no 'MacGuffin' as such: no secret documents or stolen plans. The aim of the conspirators is to disrupt America's war effort: in the film's climax Barry thwarts their plot to detonate a bomb at the Brooklyn Navy Yard. It is also suggested that the saboteurs are planning to blow up the Boulder Dam – completed as recently as 1937 – and that they had sunk the French liner *Normandie* in New York: this is implied by the smirk on Fry's face as he passes the wreck (in fact the liner had been gutted by an accidental fire). The latter was a late addition that arose during shooting. Hitchcock later said that 'the Navy raised hell with Universal about those three shots because I implied that the *Normandie* had been sabotaged, which was a reflection of their lack of vigilance in guarding it.'[19]

Thomas Schatz has documented the emergence of cycles of war-related films following Pearl Harbor and notes in particular 'the prominence of spy, espionage, and war-related crime thrillers in the early years of the war, especially 1942, and the subsequent surge in home-front dramas and combat films in the later war years'.[20] As far as espionage subjects were concerned, *Saboteur* represents the upper end of a genre that was dominated largely by B-grade material: *Sabotage Squad, Underground Agent, Secret Enemy, Unseen Enemy, Counter-Espionage, Madame Spy* and *Escape from Hong Kong* were among the glut of films released in 1942 featuring spies (usually German), saboteurs and secret agents, while espionage subjects also featured in other genres including the Western (*Cowboy Commandos, Valley of Hunted Men*), the serial adventure (*Spy Smasher*), comedy (*My Favourite Spy*) and even horror (*Invisible Agent*). The proliferation of films about spies and saboteurs operating in the United States was such that in September 1942 the OWI's Bureau of Motion Pictures expressed its concern that these films 'tended to give the public an exaggerated idea of the menace'.[21] The OWI exerted pressure on the film industry to reduce production of espionage films: such films did indeed tail off between 1943 and 1945. Instead the OWI encouraged the production of combat movies which first became a distinctive cycle in 1943 (*Air Force, Bataan, Sahara, Corvette K225, Wake Island, Guadalcanal Diary*) and which supplanted spy and espionage subjects in the public's favour. *Saboteur* was therefore a perfectly timed film: it came at the right moment to tap into early wartime paranoia around espionage but before the official mandate to shift away from home-front espionage to combat-front subjects.

Although there is no hard evidence, it is possible that *Saboteur* may have been made in response to an official mandate. In the late 1930s and early 1940s J. Edgar Hoover, the powerful Director of the Federal Bureau of Investigation (FBI), campaigned energetically to persuade the American public in general and policy-makers in particular of the danger of a 'fifth column' in America. Francis MacDonell attests that Hoover 'repeatedly characterized America's "Trojan Horse" as a serious threat to national security'.[22] Anticipating the sort of rhetoric later adopted by Senator Joseph McCarthy during the anti-communist 'witch hunts' of the 1950s, Hoover warned about an 'enemy within – composed of people who believed that the Government of the United States [could] be overthrown'.[23] In hindsight it is apparent that Hoover significantly exaggerated the threat of an Axis fifth column in the United States: the real aim of his campaign had been to whip up hysteria in order to build up the FBI – which expanded from 898 agents in 1938 to 4,886 by 1945 – and to consolidate his own power base.[24] In fact the only significant German spy ring in America, the Duquesne ring, was rounded up within a month of Pearl Harbor.[25] Nevertheless *Saboteur* is so insistent on the threat of the enemy within – and the complacency of the American public – that it seems reasonable to speculate that it might have been influenced by Hoover's rhetoric.

The ideological strategy of *Saboteur* is to present the contest between Fascism and democracy in relation to domestic politics. It is significant that the conspiracy is not directed from an external source – as *Confessions of a Nazi Spy* or the post-war anti-Nazi spy thriller *The House on 92nd Street* (1945) which was also made with the support of the FBI – but is internal to the United States. *Saboteur* posits the existence of a group of fifth columnists within the upper echelons of American society: Tobin is a wealthy rancher and Mrs Sutton, who is evidently aware of the full extent of the conspiracy, is an esteemed society hostess. Tobin is therefore another member of that group of outwardly respectable Hitchcock villains that also includes Professor Jordan (*The 39 Steps*), Stephen Fisher (*Foreign Correspondent*), Alexander Sebastian (*Notorious*) and Philip Vandamm (*North by Northwest*). A recurring theme of *Saboteur* is the refusal to accept that people like Tobin or Mrs Sutton can possibly be traitors: Patricia is sceptical ('It's hard to believe that about any American') and Barry's attempts to warn Mrs Sutton's guests that they are in the middle of 'a hot bed of spies and saboteurs' are met with disbelief as he is assumed to be drunk or playing a practical joke. For his part Tobin rejects his American identity ('I've suddenly had enough of this country – the war has made it grim') and plans to leave for Cuba after his latest act of sabotage ('I am a refugee. I have at last joined that revolting group of world travellers. One ultimately turns into the thing one despises most.'). Hitchcock averred that Tobin and his supporters were based on the so-called 'America First' groups: 'We were in 1941 and there were pro-German elements who called themselves

America Firsters and who were, in fact, American Fascists. This was the group I had in mind while writing the scenario...'[26] In fact the main American Fascist groups were the German-American Bund and the Legion of Silver Shirts which had become proscribed organisations after the outbreak of war: Tobin mentions the suppression of these groups ('The new law threatens all of – *us* – with the death penalty').[27]

Saboteur explicitly links Fascism to wealth: Robin Wood observes how it 'gradually reveals that power in America is *literally* Fascist'.[28] It is the rich and powerful who support Fascism: they are supported by the police (the Sheriff whom Patricia meets after escaping from Soda City turns out to be 'a particularly good friend of the Nazis') and are funded by the unwitting participants in Mrs Sutton's charity ball. The idea that wealthy Americans would benefit from Fascism is made explicit in a key ideological exchange:

> *Barry:* Why is it that you sneer every time you refer to your country? You're doing pretty well. I don't understand.
>
> *Tobin:* No, you wouldn't. You're one of the ardent believers, a good American. Oh, there are millions like you, people that plod along without asking questions. I hate to use the word stupid, but it seems to be the only one that applies. The great masses, the moron millions. Well, there are a few of us who are unwilling to just troop along, a few of us who are clever enough to see that there's more to be done than just to live small, complacent lives, a few of us in America who desire a more profitable type of government. When you think about it, Mr Kane, the competence of totalitarian nations is much higher than ours. They get things done.

This speech – and other similar references in the film – anticipate Hitchcock's more subtle examination of the totalitarian mindset in *Lifeboat*.

Saboteur's suggestion of internal treachery might have proved politically problematic – such 'unAmerican' sentiments came under intense scrutiny during the McCarthy-inspired witch hunts of the post-war period – were it not for the fact that elsewhere the film is insistent upon the goodness of American values and the American people. 'That has always seemed to me to be the real way to learn about the country – as well as the surest test of the American heart, in all its degrees of size and temperature', remarks the blind hermit Philip Martin when Barry mentions that he is hitch-hiking across the country. Barry's riposte to Tobin ('The last four or five days I've learned an awful lot... I've met ruthless guys like you... and I've met a whole lot of others... people that are warm and helpful and eager to do the right thing – people that are alive – people that get a kick out of helping each other') and Esmeralda the Bearded Lady's faith in Barry's innocence which she intuits from Patricia's responses ('It's the good people that stick when anybody's in trouble.

21   The Statue of Liberty (reconstructed in the studio) provided a suitably iconic setting for the climax of *Saboteur* (Universal/Frank Lloyd Productions, 1942).

There aren't many good people in the world. And I think that we – all of us – know that better than most') are reminiscent of the sentiments of Frank Capra's films of the 1930s such as *Mr Deeds Goes to Town* and *Mr Smith Goes to Washington*. It is significant in this regard that those who help Barry are either Capra-esque 'little people' or those on the margins of society: the friendly truck driver who misdirects the police, the blind man who offers him food and shelter, and the circus 'freaks' who accept him as an outcast like themselves. The America of *Saboteur* is not quite the socially and politically united nation of most wartime films: the real patriots turn out to be those on the margins rather than the wealthy and privileged.

Hitchcock later suggested that he made a 'serious error' with the climax of *Saboteur*. A chase sequence inside the Statue of Liberty ends with Barry confronting Fry on top of the statue's torch: Fry falls over the railing and is left clinging to the torch as Barry attempts to haul him back up; but Fry's jacket sleeve tears and he falls to his death. Hitchcock felt that this was a mistake as the villain rather than the hero was the one in jeopardy: 'If we'd have had the hero instead of the villain hanging in midair, the audience's anguish would have been much greater.'[29] He would 'correct' this mistake in *North by Northwest* where the position is reversed. Yet the climax of *Saboteur* seems no less suspenseful from the fact that it is Fry who takes the fall: his abject terror is superbly conveyed by actor Norman Lloyd and there is still suspense to be generated from the fact that Barry wants Fry alive in order to establish his own innocence ('I'll clear you – I swear I will!' Fry gasps as Barry reaches for his arm). In any event if Hitchcock made an 'error' in *Saboteur* it was one he repeated at the end of *To Catch A Thief* (1955) where it is the real thief rather than the hero who is hanging on for their life.

The critical reception of *Saboteur* was very similar to *Foreign Correspondent*: most reviewers regarded it as polished entertainment with topical interest though there were some reservations about its implausibilities. This was best summed up by Bosley Crowther:

> To put it mildly, Mr Hitchcock and his writers have really let themselves go. Melodramatic action is their forte, but they scoff at speed limits this trip. All the old master's experience at milking thrills has been called upon. As a consequence – and according to Hitchcock custom – *Saboteur* is a swift, high-tension film which throws itself forward so rapidly that it permits slight opportunity for looking back... So fast, indeed, is the action and so abundant the breathless events that one might forget, in the hubub, that there is no logic in this wild-goose chase.[30]

Much the same point was made by the exhibitor's journal *Harrison's Reports*:

> A thrilling timely melodrama about the subversive activities of fifth columnists. The picture catches one's interest at the beginning and never loses its hold. Although the melodramatic sequences become far-fetched towards the end to a point where intelligent audiences might find them laughable, they do not lessen its entertainment value for the masses.[31]

For some critics, the implausibilities of *Saboteur* were simply too much. Nelson B. Bell of the *Washington Post* found it 'a pretty tawdry carnival of extravagance... In its mounting eagerness for thrills, *Saboteur* loses force as a valuable public document in direct proportion to its lack of plausibility and conviction.'[32]

British critics seem to have been less concerned with the film's implausibilities than their American counterparts. Dilys Powell felt that it 'displays both Hitchcock's talent for the chase and his taste for contrasting the normal, the banal, with the eccentric and the macabre'.[33] William Whitebait saw it as a throwback to Hitchcock's British thrillers in so far as 'the adventures belong to the pre-war Hitchcock world of chase and suspense ... Not all the turns in *Saboteur* are new, but the pace is kept up. The phoney thrill leads up to a real thrill.' He particularly liked the Statue of Liberty climax: 'Every second in this final thrill is prolonged, but the real Hitchcock touch lies in the paradox. It's absurd, but it grips; it's melodramatic, but the whole incredible event has been witnessed by a huddle of tourists who gape as we do.' Overall Whitebait felt that '*Saboteur* just falls below the master's best'.[34]

Saboteur may indeed have lacked plausibility; it may have lacked discipline in story construction; and it may have suffered in the casting of the main parts (though Norman Lloyd drew good notices for his small role as the saboteur Fry); but it was a solid box-office success that reaffirmed Hitchcock's status as the pre-eminent director of thrillers and suspense films. It would also turn out to be the last pure chase-and-pursuit film that he would make. His later spy films would demonstrate a shift away from the breathless pacing and swift transitions of films like *Foreign Correspondent* and *Saboteur* in favour of more character-focused films such as *Notorious* and the remake of *The Man Who Knew Too Much* which privileged psychological realism over action and movement. And even when Hitchcock returned to the narrative of chase and pursuit in *North by Northwest* it would be cast in a more ideologically and morally ambiguous mode than the didacticism of *Saboteur*.

10

THE WOMAN WHO KNEW TOO MUCH: *NOTORIOUS* (1946)

Notorious – one of Hitchcock's most successful films – did not start out as a spy picture. In 1945 Hitchcock and screenwriter Ben Hecht were looking for a follow-up to their successful collaboration on the psychological thriller *Spellbound* for David O. Selznick. This had been Hitchcock's first American film with top-rank stars (Ingrid Bergman and Gregory Peck) and his most successful at the box office since *Rebecca*. Hitchcock was particularly keen to work again with Ingrid Bergman and told Selznick's story editor Margaret McDonell that he had in mind 'a story about confidence tricks on a grand scale in which Ingrid could play the woman who is carefully trained and coached in a gigantic confidence trick which might involve her marrying some man'.[1] McDonell drew Hitchcock's attention to a short story by John Taintor Foote called 'The Song of the Dragon', which Selznick had bought as a possible vehicle for Vivien Leigh following *Gone With the Wind*.[2] Foote's story, originally published in the *Saturday Evening Post* in 1921, was about a young actress recruited as a spy during the First World War and tasked with sleeping with the head of a German spy ring in New York in order to gather intelligence: the first part of the story told how she accomplished her mission, while the second part focused on her anxiety that her fiancé would reject her because of her compromised past. From this premise Hitchcock and Hecht developed *Notorious*, which, however, became so far removed from its original source that Foote did not even warrant a screen credit.

Notorious was initially developed as a Selznick production. After a three-year break following *Rebecca*, Selznick had returned to active production with the wartime melodramas *Since You Went Away* (1943) and *I'll Be Seeing You* (1944). *Spellbound* was conceived as a vehicle for Selznick's most valuable contract star,

Ingrid Bergman, who had recently won an Academy Award for *Gaslight*. Hitchcock liked working with Bergman: following *Notorious* he would direct her for a third time in *Under Capricorn*. He also evidently enjoyed working with Ben Hecht. Best known as co-author (with Charles MacArthur) of the play *The Front Page*, a satire of the newspaper industry that had been filmed twice, under its own title in 1932 and again in 1940 as *His Girl Friday*, Hecht was one of Hollywood's top screenwriters, whose credits included *Nothing Sacred*, *Gunga Din* and *Wuthering Heights*. Hecht, known for his ability to write quickly, had provided the coda for *Foreign Correspondent*. In some respects Hecht was not a typical Hitchcock collaborator: the speedy working methods of the Hollywood professional were in sharp contrast to the director's slow and measured approach to story construction. Hecht did not come cheap – his salary for *Notorious* was on a par with Hitchcock's at $5,000 per week – and Selznick seems to have agreed to employing him in the belief that the screenplay would be finished quickly.[3] In the event, however, Hitchcock and Hecht would spend ten months writing *Notorious*, whose screenplay cost $126,485.[4]

As ever the production of *Notorious* needs to be understood in its various ideological and economic contexts. The story was updated from the First World War to the end of the Second World War: Hitchcock was always more comfortable with contemporary rather than period subjects. *Secret Agent*, which had been set during the First World War, had not been one of his more successful films. At the time that Hitchcock and Hecht began working on the scenario in the winter of 1944–5 the end of the war was in sight but Germany had yet to be defeated. The plot would concern a Nazi underground movement in Rio de Janeiro after the war. The threat (albeit as it happened unfounded) of Nazi revivalism informed a number of post-war films including *Cornered* (1946) and *Berlin Express* (1948). Its use in *Notorious* may have been influenced by official policy: in December 1944 Hitchcock and Hecht were involved in scripting an informational film for the US State Department looking ahead to post-war foreign policy and explaining the rationale for the formation of the United Nations. The film was released as *Watchtower Over Tomorrow* (1945): Hitchcock was not credited on the film and it is not certain whether he had any input beyond the initial idea but the fact that it coincided with the preparation of *Notorious* is worth noting.[5]

The decision to set the film in Rio de Janeiro (though like *Foreign Correspondent* it would be shot entirely in the studio with the location suggested only by background plates) was informed by both economic and political contexts. With Continental Europe still closed to American movies until the end of the war, the Latin American market, especially Brazil and

Argentina, had grown in importance. During the war the MPPDA had embarked upon a strategy to grow the Latin American market, which accounted for around 12 per cent of Hollywood's foreign revenues – though the film industry's attempts to court Latin audiences with a cycle of exotic musicals starring the 'Brazilian bombshell' Carmen Miranda were met with derision south of the Rio Grande.[6] Another factor was that, while most South American nations remained neutral during the war, there were some, notably Argentina, that were more sympathetic to the Axis powers than the Allies. At the end of the war some Nazis, the most infamous being Adolf Eichmann, found refuge in South America: the idea of a Nazi spy ring operating in the region was therefore a plausible plot device.

The story and shape of *Notorious* evolved over the course of several draft treatments and full screenplays by Hecht and Hitchcock (who did not take a credit) between January and November 1945. The narrative centred on a young American woman of 'loose' morals – variously known as Alicia Wyman, Alicia Homer and Alicia Huberman – who learns that her father was a member of a Nazi underground movement plotting World War Three. Alicia's 'notorious' reputation arises from her guilt: 'I have lived like a fool, blindly and selfishly – unaware that my home was a nest of Nazi snakes, that my father was a traitor – that I was helping betray my country by my stupidity and selfishness.'[7] Alicia is recruited by American intelligence agents to infiltrate the Nazi spy ring – a role she undertakes in order to redeem herself and atone for her father's treachery. She is tasked with seducing Alexander Sebastian, a friend and colleague of her father who is 'the head Nazi brain in Brazil and head of the Gestapo underground in the U.S.'[8] However, Alicia falls in love with the American agent who has recruited her, and he in turn is torn between his love for Alicia and his duty to his country. There had been precedents for this situation – known in the intelligence community as a 'honeytrap' – during the Second World War. In particular *Notorious* recalls the case of Mildred Fish Harnack, an American woman living in Germany who at the behest of her own husband carried on an affair with an officer of the Abwehr (German military intelligence) in order to gather information for the Soviet Union.[9]

This basic narrative was present in all drafts of *Notorious* but the end of the film kept changing. The first draft was closest to the finished film as the American agent (here known as Walt Boone) rescues Alicia from Sebastian's house while Sebastian is left to his fate at the hands of his Nazi colleagues. Alicia is rewarded with a presidential citation and all ends happily.[10] The second draft divided the role of the agent (Captain Prescott) and Alicia's lover (Captain Wallace Fancher of the US Army Air Force) and concluded with

Fancher fighting Sebastian on a cliff top and both falling to their deaths. This version was told in flashback, framed by scenes in a Colón nightclub where Alicia's notoriety as something of a *femme fatale* has made her the star attraction: there are some similarities between these scenes and the Rita Hayworth vehicle *Gilda* (1946), to which Hecht made an uncredited contribution.[11] A third draft again combined the role of the intelligence agent and Alicia's lover, now called Devlin, but concluded with Devlin's death at the hands of the Nazis.[12] Yet another draft had Devlin rescuing Alicia from Sebastian's mansion only for her to die after being poisoned with arsenic by Sebastian and his mother: a coda has Devlin sitting in a Rio café reading a letter from the President commending Alicia's bravery.[13]

It is clear from these treatments that Hitchcock saw *Notorious* as being quite different from his previous spy films. There is none of the rapid movement that characterised *The Man Who Knew Too Much*, *The 39 Steps*, *Foreign Correspondent* or *Saboteur*. Instead the tone is serious and the focus is on Alicia's emotional make-up and psychological motivation. As Captain Prescott reflects at the end of the second draft: 'He has often thought of her – of the burden she was bearing – widow of the notorious Sebastian – and her lover dead believing her a traitor like her parents. And the world scorning her for the same reasons.'[14] *Notorious* lacks the ideological certainty of films like *Foreign Correspondent* and *Saboteur*: its overriding sense of moral ambiguity locates it squarely within the realist-existential lineage of the spy thriller. It features a heroine who is more or less forced to prostitute herself in the service of her country and a hero (the character finally known as Devlin) who is willing to let her do it. Indeed, Devlin is the least conventionally heroic Hitchcock protagonist since Ashenden in *Secret Agent*: this was a matter of concern for Selznick who was concerned that no major star would want to take the role. Selznick disliked the characterisation ('Devlin just doesn't make sense to anybody but Ben Hecht') and felt that the neo-Nazi conspiracy would date by the time the film was completed ('I urge avoiding references to Nazis who are going to be pretty dead ducks nine months from now'). He was particularly critical of the structure ('It's just a lot of dialogue, it has no construction – no beginning, no middle, no end') and felt that Hecht – renowned for his witty dialogue – had become 'bored and stale on the subject'.[15]

Hitchcock, for his part, was struggling with the 'MacGuffin': he found it difficult to work out the purpose of Alicia spying on Sebastian and his associates. The early treatments made vague references to German U-boats operating in the South Atlantic but Germany's surrender in May 1945 made this device no longer topical. Another idea was the building of an underground army to carry on the war. It was at some point during the spring of 1945 (the precise timing is not clear) that Hitchcock and Hecht hit upon the idea of using uranium ore as their plot device. This was the basis of what became the major suspense set piece in the film as Alicia steals the key to Sebastian's wine cellar so that she and Devlin can discover what is hidden there: the uranium in the wine bottles would become one of Hitchcock's best 'MacGuffins'. Uranium was the essential component in the development of the first atomic bomb. Hitchcock was quite vague – perhaps deliberately so – how he learned about the bomb:

> A writer friend of mine had told me that scientists were working on a secret project some place in New Mexico. It was so secret that once they went into the plant, they never emerged again. I was also aware that the Germans were conducting experiments with heavy water in Norway. So these clues brought me to the uranium MacGuffin. The producer was skeptical, and he felt it was absurd to use the idea of an atom bomb as the basis for our story. I told him that it wasn't the basis for the story, but only the MacGuffin, and I explained that there was no need to attach too much importance to it.[16]

The 'secret project' Hitchcock referred to was the Manhattan Project, based at Los Alamos, New Mexico, and involved a team of scientists led by J. Robert Oppenheimer. As the project was top secret and as the first atomic bomb test was not until 19 July 1945 it is unclear how Hitchcock could have known about it: the most likely explanation is that he was embellishing the story in hindsight to claim knowledge of something he did not know about until later.

The decision to link the conspiracy in *Notorious* to the development of the atomic bomb meant that the film would tap into current political anxieties. The Manhattan Project was so secret that President Harry S. Truman did not even divulge the existence of the atomic bomb to America's British and Soviet allies until it was ready for testing. During the war the FBI foiled an attempt by a German spy ring to penetrate the Manhattan Project: this became the subject of the post-war feature *The House on 92nd Street* (1945), produced by Louis de Rochemont for Twentieth Century-Fox. *The House on 92nd Street* was shot in a semi-documentary style that would influence other thrillers in the late 1940s such as *Call Northside 777* (1947), *The Street With No Name* (1948) and *The Naked City* (1948). Yet as it turned out it was not the Axis powers that were a threat to America's atomic secrets but the Soviet Union. It was subsequently revealed that the Soviets had a mole inside the Manhattan Project in the person of Klaus Fuchs, the German-born nuclear physicist who fled to Britain after Hitler came to power and was cleared to join the programme despite his Communist sympathies. Fuchs was responsible for leaking secrets about nuclear fission to the Soviets, including details of 'Little Boy' bomb: he was arrested in Britain in 1949 and imprisoned under the Official Secrets Act (a quirk of British law meant that he could not be charged with treason as the Soviet Union had been an ally at the time).[17] In the course of their research Hitchcock and Hecht spoke to scientists at the California Institute of Technology: Hitchcock averred 'that afterward the FBI had me under surveillance for three months'.[18]

However, it was not the uranium plot device but rather the moral tone of the film that bothered the Hays Office. When a temporary screenplay of *Notorious* was submitted to the PCA in May 1945, it was rejected out of hand by Joseph Breen who told Selznick that it was 'definitely unacceptable under the provisions of the Production Code'. Breen elaborated:

> This unacceptability is suggested principally by the characterisation of your lead, Alicia, as a grossly immoral woman, whose immorality is accepted 'in stride' in the development of the story and who, eventually, is portrayed as dying a glorious heroine. There is, too, in contrast, an almost complete absence of what might be called 'compensating moral values'.
>
> In addition, the frequent references throughout the story to Alicia's gross immorality, even when those references are intended, possibly, to point up and emphasize her attempts at regeneration, add, we think, very considerably to the overall unacceptability of this story.[19]

Breen offered an olive branch of sorts by suggesting 'that it might be possible to tell this story if you were to establish it early that Alicia is, possibly, a lady who lives by her wits – a gold-digger, perhaps, but not specifically a prostitute'. A note in the PCA files reveals that at a subsequent meeting with the film-makers 'it was agreed that the characterization of the female lead would be changed in such a way as to avoid any direct inference that she is a woman of loose sex morals'. In addition, 'Mr Hecht indicated that they now expect to have the girl not die in the end but live and marry the hero. It was made clear that, in that case, it would be absolutely necessary to avoid any suggestion of sex promiscuity or looseness on her part.'[20] Hence, through the intervention of the censor, *Notorious* would return to something closer to the first treatment – and, indeed, to the original source story in which the heroine is able to marry her fiancé – than the bleaker one envisioned by Hitchcock and Hecht.

Breen also raised another point: the film's representation of the American intelligence services. He told Selznick:

> In addition, you will have in mind, I think, the need for your taking some counsel about this story with representatives of the FBI, the Navy Department, and the Brazilian Government. I think you know that the industry has had a

22 The censors were concerned that Alicia (Ingrid Bergman) should not be portrayed as a woman of 'loose sex morals' in *Notorious* (RKO Radio Pictures, 1946).

kind of 'gentleman's agreement' with Mr J. Edgar Hoover, wherein we have practically obligated ourselves to submit to him, for his consideration and approval, stories which importantly involve the activities of the Federal Bureau of Investigation.[21]

Hoover took a keen interest in the movies. He had extended the Bureau's cooperation to Fox for *The House on 92nd Street*, which was an account of a successful FBI operation. However, *Notorious* was a very different case. Hoover asked Selznick 'that all references to the Federal Bureau of Investigation be omitted'.[22] In the finished film Devlin and his colleagues are working for the American government but are not identified with any specific agency.

It was at this point that Selznick decided not to produce *Notorious* under his own *imprimatur* but rather to sell it as a package to another studio. A number of factors may have influenced this decision, including the problems with the censors, the mounting costs of the script, and the fact that Selznick wanted to focus his efforts on the production of *Duel in the Sun* (1946), the lavish Western that he saw as his follow-up to *Gone With the Wind*. He went first to Hal Wallis at Paramount, and, when that deal fell through, sold it to RKO Radio Pictures. RKO was the smallest and least prestigious of the 'Big Five': by the mid-1940s the studio that had produced *King Kong* and *Citizen Kane* was dependent on outside producers for its prestige product. It was a good deal for Selznick: RKO paid $250,000 for the package of script and Hitchcock as producer-director, picked up the bill for producing *Notorious*, and agreed to share the profits fifty-fifty with Selznick.[23] The RKO deal also brought Cary Grant into the frame as Grant was under contract to the studio. Hitchcock had worked with Grant on *Suspicion*, which had been the first film to suggest a darker side to Grant's screen image that made him ideal for the role of Devlin. Within a few weeks of the RKO deal (finalised on 23 July 1945), the United States employed atomic bombs against the Japanese cities of Hiroshima (6 August) and Nagasaki (9 August) in order to bring the Second World War to a conclusion. *Notorious* now had an element of topicality that no one had ever envisaged.

That said there were still problems to be overcome. RKO brought in Clifford Odets, a playwright whose screen credits included the Cary Grant vehicle *None But the Lonely Heart* (1944), to revise the screenplay, but this was once again rejected by the Production Code office. The sticking point was the same as before. Breen informed RKO's William Gordon:

> We again wish to stress the fact, that before this picture can be approved, it will be necessary to remove the present indications that your sympathetic lead is a woman of loose sexual habits. This flavour arises, not only from the fact that it is indicated that she is living with a man in the early part of the picture, but also from numerous undenied accusations and imputations on the part of a great number of people throughout the script.[24]

There followed a list of specific objections, including the lines 'How far can you trust a woman of that sort?' and the description of Alicia as 'a tramp, ready to die for her country'. Other lines were deemed suggestive of 'undue intimacy', including Alicia's 'Who ... undressed me?' and Devlin's 'I rubbed you down too' after they are caught in a rain shower. A month later, Breen advised Gordon that a further revised script 'is still in violation of the Production Code': now an additional problem was the inclusion of a party scene where the PCA cautioned that 'none of the people in the party should be shown offensively drunken'.[25] In a further letter covering later script pages, Breen took exception to a particular line ('Then maybe you can assist the Sebastians in a nice clean divorce') 'as being very questionable, particularly when spoken by an officer of the United States government'.[26]

The censors' interventions over *Notorious* are significant in two particular respects. For one thing the political anxiety that might have arisen over the film's references to the atomic bomb was being displaced onto anxiety around its representation of sexuality: in this regard the intervention of the censors anticipated later critical readings of the film's narrative. And for another thing *Notorious* was one of several films at the time to challenge the Production Code's dictates regarding sexual morality: MGM's *The Postman Always Rings Twice*, Columbia's *Gilda* and Selznick's *Duel in the Sun* were all released in 1946. In the event the case of *Notorious* would demonstrate how the relationship between the studios and the censors involved a degree of give-and-take on both sides. Hitchcock circumvented one of the Code's dictates against 'excessive and lustful kissing' by directing a love scene between Alicia and Devlin in which they kiss continuously while moving across the hotel room in a close embrace: the censor could not object as they are not sitting or lying down. Hitchcock explained the unusual staging thus: 'I conceived that scene in terms of the participants' desire not to interrupt the romantic moment. It was essential not to break up the mood.'[27]

After a year in development, *Notorious* went before the cameras in October 1945. At a final cost of $2,375,000 it was Hitchcock's most expensive film to date: almost half the budget went on 'above-the-line' costs (script, direction and stars).[28] The star pairing of Cary Grant and Ingrid Bergman was supported by Claude Rains as Alexander Sebastian and the Czech émigré 'Madame Konstantin' as his domineering mother. Gregg Toland, the cinematographer of *Citizen Kane*, was sent to Rio to shoot back-projection plates – Ted Tatzlaff was the principal director of photography on *Notorious* – and the film also marked Hitchcock's first collaboration with costume designer Edith Head. Hitchcock seems to have been at his most assured during the shooting of *Notorious*, which includes some of his most memorable scenes: the elaborate crane shot which begins as a high angle looking down the stairs of Sebastian's mansion and gradually dollies in to a close-up of Bergman's hand hiding the key to the wine cellar – an effect that Hitchcock had previously employed in *Young and Innocent* – is justly famous. The fact that Ingrid Bergman towered over her screen 'husband' Claude Rains was disguised by building a ramp on the studio floor for Rains to walk on in long shots: for close shots the old trick of Rains standing on a box was sufficient.[29]

Notorious was submitted to the PCA for approval in June 1946. The censor insisted on cuts to the first reel: it required the removal of an early scene 'to get away from the suggestion that Ernest and Alicia have been having an illicit sex affair' and to 'reduce the drinking and drunkenness as much as possible throughout'.[30] Ernest was a minor character whom Alicia takes up with after her father's imprisonment. William Gordon confirmed that the entire Alicia-

23   A passionate interlude for Devlin (Cary Grant) and Alicia (Ingrid Bergman) in *Notorious* (RKO Radio Pictures, 1946).

Ernest scene would be deleted and the drunken party 'will be reduced in footage'.[31] With those cuts, *Notorious* had finally completed its arduous passage through the Production Code.

Notorious is highly regarded within the Hitchcock canon. For William Rothman, '*Notorious* is, with *Shadow of a Doubt*, the greatest achievement of Hitchcock's first decade of work in America'. He sees it as a transitional film for Hitchcock: '*Notorious* transforms the Hitchcock thriller of the thirties into a fully American film, as *Foreign Correspondent* and *Saboteur* do not: it creates a Hitchcock paradigm, with Hitchcock's subsequent Cary Grant vehicles – *To Catch a Thief* and *North by Northwest* – among those cast in its mold.'[32] His biographer Donald Spoto writes that '*Notorious* is in fact Alfred Hitchcock's first attempt – at the age of forty-six – to bring his talents to the creation of a serious love story, and its story of the two men in love with Ingrid Bergman could only have been made at this stage of his life.'[33] (It has often been suggested that Hitchcock harboured sexual feelings for Bergman: the intense and passionate love scenes in *Notorious* might be understood as a way of playing out his infatuation by proxy. *Rear Window* – starring Hitchcock's other favourite actress Grace Kelly – also includes an extended kissing scene shot in extreme close-up.) Only Lindsay Anderson dissents: he regarded *Notorious* as demonstrating the worst excesses of Hitchcock's American films with their 'tendency to overplay, to inflate, [a] tendency which in *Notorious* swelled to an obsession and produced a film which shares with its successors, *The Paradine Case* and *Rope*, the distinction of being the worst of his career'.[34]

Thomas Leitch sees *Notorious* as the 'pivotal film' of Hitchcock's career that 'marks a turning point in Hitchcock's development'. 'Before *Notorious*,' Leitch explains, 'Hitchcock made many different kinds of films; after *Notorious*, he would with rare exceptions make one kind of film, sticking not only to thrillers but to thrillers of a very particular sort.'[35] While Leitch perhaps overstates the case – Hitchcock's post-*Notorious* films included a courtroom drama (*The Paradine Case*), a costume picture (*Under Capricorn*) and a black comedy (*The Trouble With Harry*) – there is nevertheless much substance to his argument that *Notorious* represents a point of convergence between the two most distinctively 'Hitchcockian' genres: the spy film on the one hand and the domestic crime melodrama exemplified by films such as *The Lodger, Murder!, Young and Innocent, Suspicion* and *Shadow of a Doubt* on the other. These two strands in Hitchcock's work converge in *Notorious*, which removes the activity of spying from the public arena of films such as *The Man Who Knew Too Much, The 39 Steps, Foreign Correspondent* and *Saboteur* and relocates it in the domestic space. This anticipates Hitchcock's later spy films – including the remake of *The Man Who Knew Too Much, Torn Curtain* and *Topaz* – which focus as much on the family and personal relationships as on the external threat to national security. Leitch further suggests that *Notorious* exemplifies several characteristic 'Hitchcockian' motifs that would be reworked over and again in later films: these include the emphasis on psychological rather than physical violence, the use of dramatic irony rather than mystery, and the emergence of the character of the monstrous mother (Mrs Sebastian in *Notorious* can be seen as a forerunner of later Hitchcock mothers in *Strangers on a Train, Psycho, The Birds* and *Marnie*).[36]

Notorious may be an exemplary Hitchcock film but it is also representative of the narrative and formal strategies of American cinema in the mid-1940s. It exemplifies a trend for more female-centred films that emerged during the war – others included *Now, Voyager* (1942), *Since You Went Away* (1943), *Gaslight* (1944) and *Mildred Pierce* (1945) – that were partly a reflection of wartime changes in women's social status and partly an outcome of the temporary shortage of male stars due to military service. Such films have often been labelled 'women's pictures' on account of their female-centred narratives

24   The famous crane shot demonstrates Hitchcock's directorial virtuosity in *Notorious* (RKO Radio Pictures, 1946).

and their assumed interest for female audiences. *Notorious* can be positioned within this tendency as it places its female protagonist at the centre: Alicia is very much the focus of the narrative and Ingrid Bergman is privileged in terms of close-ups despite Cary Grant's top billing. *Notorious* was an important film for Bergman as it marked the first occasion on which she had played a 'loose' or 'fallen' woman following a series of saintly heroines in films such as *Casablanca* (1942), *For Whom the Bell Tolls* (1943) and *Going My Way* (1945). To this extent her role in *Notorious* was a case of art anticipating life: a few years later Bergman would become *persona non grata* in Hollywood following her affair with Roberto Rossellini while making *Stromboli* (1949).

Notorious may also be aligned with the *film noir* cycle of the 1940s. This can be seen on several levels. The *mise-en-scène* of *Notorious* exemplifies the extreme visual stylisation of *film noir*: high-angled shots, chiaroscuro lighting, a preponderance of close-ups and compositions which foreground oversized objects such as the poisoned coffee cup. Of course this stylisation may also be attributed to Hitchcock's authorship: he had employed similar devices many times before, such as the drugged glasses of brandy in *The Lady Vanishes* and the oversized revolver in *Spellbound*. What seems different about *Notorious*, however, is that Hitchcock's camera effects are more fully integrated into the formal system of the film as a whole than they had been before: this is probably what Leitch is referring to when he avers that 'no Hitchcock film is more fully achieved, with fewer false steps'.[37] Hence the tilted point-of-view shots (such as when Alicia sees Devlin standing in the doorway when she wakes with a hangover) and the celebrated dolly shot as the camera closes in on the key in Alicia's hand are combined with more characteristic Hollywood practices of the 1940s such as longer takes and deep-focus (such as the long shot from Sebastian's point of view as he spies on Alicia and Devlin from the other side of the room). Hitchcock's personal style of direction and the aesthetics of *film noir* came together perfectly in *Notorious*: both exemplify what David Bordwell calls 'the bounds of difference' – the degree of permissible deviation from stylistic norms – within classical Hollywood cinema.[38]

Notorious also shares the moral and ideological cynicism of *film noir*. It expresses profound scepticism over the values of patriotism and duty – values that had informed so many wartime films – and is highly equivocal about the ethics of counter-espionage. When Devlin appeals to Alicia's patriotism, for example, her response is cynical in the extreme: 'That word gives me a pain. Thank you, I don't go for patriotism or patriots ... Waving the flag with one hand and picking pockets with the other, that's your patriotism!' To this extent the Hitchcock film it most resembles is *Secret Agent* in which both the male and female leads had questioned their duty to their country. Alicia's cynicism is justified when it turns out that the 'work' her country has in mind ('My department authorised me to engage you to do some work for us, there's a job in Brazil') involves her to all intents and purposes prostituting herself in the service of the state. Furthermore, the nominal hero-figure Devlin is complicit in this process until he realises that he loves Alicia and belatedly discovers a moral compass of some sort. This cynicism about the behaviour of the US intelligence services – represented as politically pragmatic but morally bankrupt – anticipates Hitchcock's later Cold War spy films *North by Northwest* and *Topaz*.

Notorious also exemplifies *film noir* in its gender politics. As E. Ann Kaplan writes: 'The *film noir* world is one in which women are central to the intrigue of the films, and are furthermore usually not placed in safely familiar roles.'[39] This is certainly true of *Notorious*, where Alicia is central to the intrigue and is assigned to a role that is not only unfamiliar but actually transgressive. Alicia – compromised both by her father's treachery and by her own promiscuity that is explained as a consequence of her father's actions ('When he told me a few years ago what he was, everything went to pot: I didn't care what happened to me') – is recruited by US intelligence agent Devlin who suggests that working for the government will provide a form of atonement for her father's treason ('You could make up a little for some of your daddy's peculiarities') and is tasked with seducing Alexander Sebastian in order to gain access to his inner circle ('She's good at making friends with gentlemen, and we want someone inside his house, in his confidence'). The fact that she accomplishes this assignment with consummate ease ('You may add Sebastian's name to my list of playmates') reinforces her reputation for promiscuity in her employer's eyes ('A woman of that sort ... None of us has any illusions about her character'). While Alicia is not a fully fledged *femme fatale* in the mould of a Phyllis Dietrichson (*Double Indemnity*) or an Elsa Bannister (*The Lady from Shanghai*), *Notorious* nevertheless explores the anxiety around predatory female sexuality that was a characteristic of the *femme fatale* films of the mid-1940s.

The association between spying and female sexuality identifies *Notorious* with real spies such as Mata Hari: Alicia even refers to herself as such.[40] The common view of Mata Hari – an erotic dancer with a 'notorious' past executed by the French as a suspected German spy in 1917 – is of a seductress who used her sexuality to trade secrets. More recently it has been suggested that Mata Hari probably was not a spy at all but was duped by her German lover and made a scapegoat by the French authorities. Hollywood turned the Mata Hari story into one of its early 1930s exotic melodramas: Greta Garbo starred in MGM's *Mata Hari* (1931). *Notorious* might also be seen in the context of a wartime propaganda discourse that associated 'loose' women with Axis spies: posters such as 'Loose Lips Sink Ships' (America) and 'Keep Mum, She's Not So Dumb' (Britain) identified female sexuality as a threat to national security. The emergence of the *femme fatale* cycle during the war – exemplified by films such as *Double Indemnity*, *Murder, My Sweet* and *The Postman Always Rings Twice* – further reinforced this association between sexuality and transgression.

For feminist critics such as Tania Modleski, 'a film like *Notorious* begins to expose some of the problems of women's existence under patriarchy'.[41] *Notorious* makes a direct association between patriarchy and nationhood: this is made explicit when Alicia refers to America as 'Uncle Sam' ('When do I go to work for Uncle Sam?'). The fact that Alicia is more or less obliged to place her body in the service of the state implies a collapsing of the distinction between public and private: the narrative seeks to legitimate this by presenting Alicia's mission as a vital matter of national security. Yet, for all that *Notorious* places the woman at the centre of the narrative, it denies her any real narrative agency of her own. All Alicia's decisions are left to the men who control her:

she even has to ask intelligence chief Paul Prescott whether she should accept Sebastian's marriage proposal. Alicia's rival suitors represent different forms of male oppression: Devlin is aloof and manipulative (and on one occasion physically violent: he punches her and knocks her out when he thinks she is about to become hysterical), while Sebastian, despite professing his love, nevertheless attempts to murder her by slow poisoning when he discovers she has deceived him. Alicia is therefore one in a long line of Hitchcock heroines who becomes a victim of male violence or (at best) psychological cruelty: others include Alice White (*Blackmail*), the second Mrs de Wynter (*Rebecca*), Lina McLaidlaw (*Suspicion*), Margot Wendice (*Dial M for Murder*), Judy Barton (*Vertigo*), Marion Crane (*Psycho*) and Marnie Edgar (*Marnie*).

It is more an indication of the theoretical preoccupations of film scholarship than a criticism of their work to note that critics such as Modleski and Robin Wood place *Notorious* within the discursive terms of Hollywood melodrama – hence their emphasis on its gender politics and representation of patriarchal codes – rather than analysing it as a spy film: indeed they see the espionage plot as secondary to the film's real thematic concerns with gender and sexuality.[42] It would be fair to say that *Notorious* sits less squarely within the genre of the spy film than Hitchcock's previous excursions into the world of international espionage: or rather, perhaps, that it combines the conventions of the spy thriller with elements drawn from other genres. This would also be a feature of Hitchcock's remake of *The Man Who Knew Too Much*, which like *Notorious* merges the spy film with the domestic melodrama. At the same time, however, the public narrative of *Notorious* should not be dismissed as inconsequential. The uranium 'MacGuffin' – albeit regarded as insignificant by Hitchcock himself – assumes greater significance when understood in its historical context. The dropping of atomic bombs on Hiroshima and Nagasaki ended the Second World War but at the same time inaugurated a nuclear arms race between the United States and the Soviet Union that would define the Cold War. The Soviet Union detonated its first atom bomb in 1949: its nuclear programme had been accelerated due in large measure to secrets revealed by the so-called 'atomic spy ring' including Karl Fuchs and Julius and Ethel Rosenberg. In this context the espionage plot of *Notorious* reflected very real contemporary anxieties over nuclear secrets.

All that said *Notorious* is ostensibly less political than either *Foreign Correspondent* or *Saboteur*: other than one violent exclamation from Alicia's father at his trial ('You can put me away. But you can't put away what's going to happen to you and the whole country next time! Next time we are going to –') there are none of the set-piece speeches in support of totalitarianism or democracy that had featured in the previous two spy films. Nevertheless it is more direct than either *Foreign Correspondent* or even *Saboteur* in identifying Germany as the enemy: Devlin refers to 'some of the German gentry who were paying your father' and Sebastian's circle of fellow conspirators are visually coded as Nazis with Aryan features and Teutonic accents. Other than Sebastian, who is another of Hitchcock's suave and charming villains, the Nazis are characterised as entirely ruthless: they dispose of one of their own, Eric Huber, when his behaviour threatens to expose them ('Something must be done about Eric'). Yet for once the identity of the enemy spies is not particularly important: *Notorious* does not set out to be an anti-Fascist propaganda film like *Saboteur* or *Lifeboat*. Indeed, had it been made only a year or so later it is perfectly conceivable that the Nazi conspirators could have been changed to Communists without making any real difference to the film. Instead the narrative and ideological strategy of *Notorious* is to map geopolitics onto its sexual politics through the romantic and sexual triangle between Devlin, Alicia and Sebastian. Devlin recruits Alicia to spy on Sebastian before realising he is in love with her; Alicia loves Devlin but goes along with the plan to seduce Sebastian because she believes it is what Devlin wants; Sebastian loves Alicia and is jealous of Devlin, whom he suspects (rightly) of being his wife's lover. Of course the romantic triangle is a standard device of melodrama – Hitchcock had employed it as long ago as *The Manxman* – though in *Notorious* it takes on an added political dimension. Devlin (American) and Sebastian (German) are rivals for Alicia: in this sense the contest between them for Alicia can be read politically as a contest between American democracy on the one hand and German Fascism on the other. Alicia – who has a German father but is herself an American citizen – has divided loyalties though ultimately she makes the 'right' decision in choosing Devlin/America over Sebastian/Germany.

Even so the conclusion of *Notorious* is riddled with ambiguity. This is another reason for placing *Notorious* alongside the *film noir* cycle: one of the characteristics of *noir* deemed subversive by some was that it often featured an uneasy resolution that did not conform to the conventional Hollywood happy ending – and even if happy endings were sometimes tacked on by studios or at the insistence of the censors they were often not very convincing. The ending of *Notorious* encapsulates the emotional and moral complexities of the film. Devlin, having realised that Alicia is being slowly poisoned, goes to Sebastian's mansion to rescue her: she is sick but manages to walk to Devlin's car with his assistance. Devlin and Alicia are helped by Sebastian who realises that if Alicia is exposed as an American agent in front of his Nazi colleagues they will kill him. Once outside the house Sebastian begs to leave with Devlin and Alicia but

Devlin locks him out of the car. The last shot of the film has Sebastian walking slowly back to the house in the sure knowledge of his own imminent demise. It is not just that Devlin somewhat callously leaves Sebastian behind that makes the conclusion of *Notorious* unsettling (Sebastian has partly redeemed himself by assisting their escape) but that Alicia's fate is left uncertain: the film ends with Devlin driving her to the hospital but as it stands there is no indication whether she lives or dies. (An additional scene in the shooting script provides the answer. A secretary who has been typing the case notes closes a file with Alicia's name on it: her surname 'Sebastian' is crossed out and – after a brief pause – 'Devlin' is written in by hand. It is a neat and elegant way of indicating a happy outcome, but the decision to leave it out of the final cut is more consistent with the film's overall tone.[43])

Notorious met with an overwhelmingly positive reception when it was released in August 1946. Bosley Crowther, who had been critical of the narrative implausibilities of both *Foreign Correspondent* and *Saboteur*, found *Notorious* 'another taut, suspenseful film' and suggested that 'the distinction of *Notorious* as a film is the remarkable blend of love story with expert "thriller" that it represents'.[44] Philip K. Scheuer felt that '*Notorious* reveals a more polished Hitchcock. Like all his films, it is the work of a master story-teller.'[45] For Howard Barnes of the *Washington Post* it was 'a literate and star-studded thriller, directed as only Alfred Hitchcock can shoot a picture'.[46] The trade press was equally enthusiastic. *Variety* noted its 'outstanding production value' and labelled it 'a romantic drama of top-fire caliber that will pay off big'.[47] *Harrison's Reports* found it 'an intriguing mixture of romance and counter-espionage, presented in a manner that holds one's interest undiminished from start to finish'.[48] And *Film Bulletin* contended that 'Alfred Hitchcock's superb directorial skill, combined with luminous acting by Ingrid Bergman and Cary Grant, make *Notorious* a topnotch thriller'.[49] *Notorious* did indeed 'pay off big': its domestic rentals of $4.8 million made it the eighth biggest box-office attraction of 1946 behind *The Best Years of Our Lives*, *Duel in the Sun*, *The Jolson Story*, *The Yearling*, *Saratoga Trunk*, *The Razor's Edge* and *Night and Day*.[50] It was nominated for Academy Awards for Best Original Screenplay and Best Supporting Actor for Claude Rains.

In hindsight *Notorious* has come to be seen as a watershed film for Hitchcock. It was the first occasion on which Hitchcock acted as his own producer and the first time in his Hollywood films that he was able to assemble a first-choice cast. The reception discourse of *Notorious* suggests that it was the star appeal of the film that accounted in large measure for its success. To this extent it anticipated later successful Hitchcock star vehicles such as *Rear*

Window (James Stewart and Grace Kelly), *To Catch A Thief* (Cary Grant and Grace Kelly), *The Man Who Knew Too Much* (James Stewart and Doris Day) and *North by Northwest* (Cary Grant and Eva Marie Saint). Following on the heels of *Spellbound*, also a big box-office hit, Hitchcock's stock was high. He was keen to break free from Selznick – their last collaboration would be the stodgy courtroom drama *The Paradine Case* (1947) – and to embark upon a career as a fully fledged independent producer-director. For some time Hitchcock and Sidney Bernstein – managing-director of the Granada cinema chain in Britain and special adviser to the Films Division of the Ministry of Information during the war – had been looking to set up their own production company: this became a reality with Transatlantic Pictures in 1947. Hitchcock made two films under the Transatlantic banner: *Rope* (1948) and *Under Capricorn* (1949). These were notable for their radical formal experimentation in their use of long camera takes as well as being Hitchcock's first films in colour. However, neither was successful at the box office and while *Rope*, at least, has been the object of sympathetic re-evaluation by *auteur* critics, their commercial failure spelled the end of Transatlantic Pictures. As the 1940s came to a close Hitchcock was therefore at something of a crossroads: little can he have known that his most successful years were still ahead of him.

11

UPSCALING THE GENRE: *THE MAN WHO KNEW TOO MUCH* (1956)

The two versions of *The Man Who Knew Too Much* make an exemplary case study for comparing the respective qualities of British Hitchcock and American Hitchcock. On the one hand, champions of British Hitchcock prefer the original for its narrative pace and economy, while regarding the remake as too slickly Hollywoodised. John Pett, for example, disliked 'the glossy over-decorated style' of the American version: 'It had very little of the freshness of impact of the original and was too lengthy and slow to sustain any pitch of excitement.'[1] On the other hand, proponents of American Hitchcock tend to regard the first film as lightweight and shallow, whereas the remake exemplifies the greater complexity and psychological depth of Hitchcock's later work. For Rohmer and Chabrol it is self-evident that the second version is superior, which they attribute to Hitchcock's maturity as an artist: 'The point is that he was not content merely to improve the form, to probe the characters, or to update the story: what we are given is a veritable transfiguration. In its new form, this film is one of those in which the Hitchcockian mythology finds its purest, if not its most obvious expression.'[2] Hitchcock, for his part, famously remarked that 'the first version is the work of a talented amateur and the second was made by a professional' – an answer that satisfies either camp depending on their preference for the 'amateur' British or 'professional' Hollywood version.[3]

To compare the two films is natural enough yet from a historical perspective not very instructive as they are products of very different institutional contexts. We have seen how the British *The Man Who Knew Too Much* was representative of the production strategies and working practices of the British film industry in the 1930s. Similarly, the American *The Man Who Knew Too*

Much exemplifies trends within the US film industry in the 1950s: its longer running time and its employment of major stars (James Stewart and Doris Day), colour and widescreen were all hallmarks of Hollywood's strategy in the 1950s as it responded to the rise of television as a rival mass-entertainment medium by offering higher production values and spectacle. To this extent the remake of *The Man Who Knew Too Much* exemplifies the process that US film historians Kristin Thompson and David Bordwell have described as the 'upscaling' of genres: the production of what had once been supporting feature material with 'A'-feature budgets and values.[4] Hitchcock's return to the spy film a decade after *Notorious* needs to be understood in relation to the contexts of the US film industry in the mid-1950s. And to appreciate *The Man Who Knew Too Much* properly it is necessary to consider it in its own right rather than seeing it solely as a remake of the earlier film.

Hitchcock had harboured ambitions to remake *The Man Who Knew Too Much* for nearly twenty years. He had first mooted the idea as early as 1938: in a profile for the *New Yorker* – coinciding with the visit to America that set up his contract with David O. Selznick – he described the scene in the bazaar where the greasepaint disguise comes off the face of the murdered secret agent.[5] He had tried to interest Selznick in the project in the early 1940s, and Selznick had gone as far as buying the remake rights from Gaumont-British. In late 1941 Hitchcock and John Houseman sketched out a scenario transposing the narrative to America with the ski resort of Sun Valley replacing St Moritz for the opening scenes, the Metropolitan Opera House in New York in place of the Albert Hall and the target of the assassination plot being the Brazilian president.[6] This outline may have been deemed too similar to *Saboteur* which Hitchcock was about to shoot: in any event the project went no further. *The Man Who Knew Too Much* was also one of the possibilities mooted by Hitchcock and Sidney Bernstein for Transatlantic Pictures after the war. Although Selznick held the remake rights to *The Man Who Knew Too Much*, Hitchcock and Bernstein were able to buy the rights to the original story (credited to Charles Bennett and D. B. Wyndham Lewis) from the Rank Organisation.[7] However, the failure of *Rope* and *Under Capricorn* spelled the end of Transatlantic Pictures. It was not until the mid-1950s that Hitchcock was finally able to realise his ambition to remake *The Man Who Knew Too Much* for Paramount Pictures.

Following the end of the Transatlantic venture, Hitchcock joined Warner Bros. as an independent producer-director and made four films for the studio: *Stage Fright* (1950), *Strangers on a Train* (1951), *I Confess* (1952) and *Dial M for Murder* (1953). Hitchcock experienced a relative degree of autonomy at Warners though the corollary was that he was obliged to work with lower budgets and lesser stars than he had with Selznick: it is no slur on their names to suggest that Michael Wilding (*Stage Fright*), Farley Granger (*Strangers on a Train*) or Ray Milland (*Dial M for Murder*) were not in the first-rank of stars, and even Montgomery Clift (*I Confess*), who was, did not have the same marquee value as Cary Grant or James Stewart. This was the context for Hitchcock's move to Paramount Pictures in a highly lucrative deal negotiated by his agent Lew Wasserman of MCA. He was able to choose his own projects and exercised control over all aspects of production from script and casting to costumes and advertising. He would be paid $150,000 per picture plus 10 per cent of the profits once the films had recouped twice their negative cost, and, uniquely, his contract included a reversion clause that gave Hitchcock ownership of the films eight years after their initial release.[8]

Hitchcock's status as an independent producer-director at Paramount exemplified a trend across the US film industry as a whole in the 1950s as the studios wound down their in-house operations and looked instead to operate chiefly as financers and distributors rather than as producers. This transition was partly a response to the 'Paramount Decree' of 1948: the US Supreme Court's ruling that the major studios must divest themselves of their cinema chains as their ownership of the lucrative first-run theatres constituted an unfair monopoly.[9] As this meant that the major studios no longer had a guaranteed market for their own films, the Supreme Court ruling necessitated changes in the ways in which Hollywood operated. One of the consequences was that the studios focused more on distribution and began to act as facility houses for independent producers to supply their product rather than producing films themselves. Paramount led the way in this regard. Since the early 1940s Cecil B. De Mille had been based at the studio as an independent producer: in the 1950s he was joined by Hungarian fantasy specialist George Pal and by directors George Stevens and William Wyler. Thomas Schatz explains how Hitchcock was particularly well placed to benefit from the changing conditions in the film industry:

> Among Hollywood's top talent, no one made the transition into the New Hollywood more successfully than Alfred Hitchcock. Certainly none was better prepared. Hitchcock was the only major producer-director from the studio era who had never worked as a house director under long-term studio contract. Thus he had developed his administrative and business skills, and he was accustomed to dealing with studios as rental facilities and distribution companies. Equally importantly, Hitchcock had already developed his own trademark style. By the 1950s a 'Hitchcock picture' was a known commodity in the movie marketplace, a story type and narrative technique that had become familiar to millions of viewers.

That put Hitchcock at a tremendous advantage as the very notion of film style shifted from a studio-based to an individual context.[10]

Hitchcock's Paramount years are generally regarded as representing the zenith of his Hollywood career. He made six films for the studio – *Rear Window* (1954), *To Catch A Thief* (1955), *The Trouble With Harry* (1955), *The Man Who Knew Too Much* (1956), *Vertigo* (1958) and *Psycho* (1960) – as well as a last film for Warner Bros. (*The Wrong Man*) and one for MGM (*North by Northwest*). He also acted as executive producer of the television drama anthology series *Alfred Hitchcock Presents* (1955–62) on the CBS network. Ephraim Katz summarises the consensus view when he describes the Paramount years as 'a period in which Hitchcock's art reached its full maturity ... These films culminated one of the most illustrious careers in the history of cinema.'[11] Ironically the film that was least well received at the time (*Vertigo*) has since been critically rehabilitated to such a degree that in 2012 it toppled *Citizen Kane* in *Sight & Sound*'s once-a-decade poll of the best films of all time. Hitchcock was at the top of his professional form during these years: as he told Truffaut, 'I was feeling very creative at the time, the batteries were well charged'.[12]

Yet the extraordinary burst of creativity that Hitchcock enjoyed in the 1950s was surely due to more than just his batteries being 'well charged'. At Paramount Hitchcock enjoyed a more stable working environment than at any time since his arrival in Hollywood. He was able once again to work with stars of the calibre of Cary Grant (*To Catch A Thief*), James Stewart (*Rear Window, The Man Who Knew Too Much, Vertigo*) and Grace Kelly (whom he first directed in *Dial M for Murder*, followed in quick succession by *Rear Window* and *To Catch A Thief*, before his favourite female star married Prince Rainier of Monaco and retired from the screen). Another reason for Hitchcock's success during the 1950s was that – as at Gaumont-British in the 1930s – he was able to work with many of the same production personnel on most of his Paramount films. These included writer John Michael Hayes (*Rear Window, To Catch A Thief, The Trouble With Harry, The Man Who Knew Too Much*), composer Bernard Herrmann (who joined Hitchcock on *The Trouble With Harry* and worked on every subsequent film up to and including *Marnie*), cinematographer Robert Burks (who followed Hitchcock from Warner Bros. and again shot every one of the director's films until *Marnie* with the sole exception of *Psycho*) and editor George Tomasini (who edited every Hitchcock film from *Rear Window* to *Marnie* with the exception of *The Trouble With Harry*). While not denying that Hitchcock was now an *auteur* in the complete sense who supervised every aspect of the production of his

25   Ben McKenna (James Stewart) is *The Man Who Knew Too Much* (Paramount Pictures, 1956).

films, the presence of the same people in important creative and technical roles undoubtedly had some bearing on the emergence of the distinctive Hitchcock style: the 'look' and 'sound' of his films between the mid-1950s and early 1960s, especially, was due in no small measure to Robert Burks and Bernard Herrmann. Hitchcock's core creative team was completed by graphic designer Saul Bass, who provided the highly stylised title sequences of *Vertigo*, *North by Northwest* and *Psycho*.

The Man Who Knew Too Much was conceived from the outset as a vehicle for James Stewart. Stewart was consistently among the top box-office stars of the 1950s with films such as *Winchester 73* (1950), *The Greatest Show on Earth* (1952) and *The Glenn Miller Story* (1954) to his name. Doris Day might have seemed an unusual choice as a Hitchcock heroine – Hitchcock had briefly hoped to reunite Stewart with his *Rear Window* co-star Grace Kelly – though her casting was consistent with the director's preference for working with 'name' stars. *The Man Who Knew Too Much* would be a transitional film for Day between the saccharine musicals of the early 1950s and the more mature romantic comedies of the 1960s. *The Man Who Knew Too Much* was budgeted at $1,342,000 excluding the salaries of Hitchcock, Stewart and Day, which were deferred to be paid from the box-office receipts.[13] The budget was far from exceptional by the standards of the 1950s and did not mark the film out as being particularly expensive. It was planned to shoot the film over 48 days, with seven days on location in Morocco and twelve in London.[14] In the event the budget and schedule would prove optimistic: the final 'below-the-line' cost of *The Man Who Knew Too Much* was $1,834,858 with the excess due largely to running 34 days over schedule.[15]

The production of *The Man Who Knew Too Much* was overshadowed by a dispute over the screenplay credit that ultimately led to Hitchcock's estrangement from screenwriter John Michael Hayes. Hayes objected to sharing the writing credit with Angus MacPhail: the matter was referred for arbitration to the Screenwriters' Guild who ruled in Hayes's favour.[16] MacPhail had been the story editor at Gaumont-British in the 1930s – he had some input into scripting the original version of *The Man Who Knew Too Much* – and then followed Michael Balcon to Ealing Studios in the 1940s. He collaborated with Hitchcock on the two wartime shorts, *Bon Voyage* and *Aventure Malgache*, as well as on *Spellbound*. It has been suggested that MacPhail had little input into the remake of *The Man Who Knew Too Much* and that in supporting his claim to a credit Hitchcock was doing a favour for an old friend down on his luck.[17] However, the script materials held by the Margaret Herrick Library demonstrate that MacPhail played a full role in the development of the film. It had been determined from the outset that the English couple of the original film would be replaced by an American couple in the remake and that the opening scenes would be set in Morocco. MacPhail's notes show that he was concerned to remedy what he regarded as flaws in narrative logic in the original film: 'I think the set-up was weak in the original: it would be much weaker today; and with the husband-and-wife set-up I fear this conduct would seem more than rash.'[18] It was MacPhail who suggested that the casting of Doris Day allowed the possibility of making her character a singing star: '[In] terms of the potential Miss Day, it might be fun to play the pub scene referred to in the original but not shown.'[19] Sadly the idea of Doris Day 'whooping it up at the Prospect of Whitby' did not survive beyond the early drafts. MacPhail also devised the remake's opening scene on a public bus in Morocco that introduces the Lawrences (or the McKennas as they would become) and the secret agent Louis Bernard rather than writing him in as an established friend: Bernard intervenes to calm a tense situation when their young son Hank accidentally pulls the veil from a Muslim woman's face.[20] And the substitution of the Sidney Street-style gun battle between the conspirators and the police for a new ending in a foreign embassy (originally the Russian Embassy) was also MacPhail's idea.[21]

The updating of *The Man Who Knew Too Much* reflected changes in global politics since the original film. While the first version featured anarchists of indeterminate national origin, the remake initially cast the Soviet Union as the instigator of the assassination plot. *The Man Who Knew Too Much* was made at the height of the Cold War: even following Stalin's death in 1953 there was profound distrust of Soviet influence in Eastern Europe. An early outline by MacPhail makes this clear:

> The Russians, pursuing usual tactics, have decided to put the Western Allies in the wrong. It so happens that the Hungarian Prime Minister is paying an official visit to London. He will be the guest of honour at a special programme of Hungarian music, to be given at the Festival Hall. Subsequently, he will be the guest of honour at a reception given by the Russian Ambassador at the Russian Embassy in London. The Russians intend to arrange that this Prime Minister, their own stooge, shall be assassinated at the Festival Hall.[22]

This scenario was clearly influenced by the case of Imre Nagy, the Hungarian Prime Minister appointed in 1953 who followed a more independent policy than Moscow would accept and who was consequently forced out of office and expelled from the Communist Party in 1955. To this extent the second version of *The Man Who Knew Too Much* was originally rooted much more directly in contemporary politics than the first film had been.

John Michael Hayes was brought on to *The Man Who Knew Too Much* around March 1955. MacPhail had not provided a complete screenplay: Hayes's input was significant as he not only completed the script but also changed the emphasis in important ways. For one thing Hayes downplayed the politics – direct references to Russia or the Communists were removed to the extent that the nationality of the conspirators became almost as vague as in the original – and focused instead on the relationship between the married couple who stumble into the plot. Hayes's first draft fleshed out the characterisations of the McKennas to better fit the star personae of James Stewart and Doris Day. It was Hayes who suggested that Jo McKenna – a singing star known as Jo Conway who has retired to raise their young son – is impatient to resume her career. This is the cause of some tension with her husband, a doctor:

Jo: Don't you ever want me to go back to work?

Ben: Jo – how can we run two careers in two different places and still have one family?

Jo: But my career won't be very long. These are the good years – and I've already lost some of them.

(He looks at her)

Not 'lost'. Given up. Now it's your turn to give up something. One more show.

Ben: It's hard to say yes – and harder to say no.[23]

Hayes also added the scene in which, following their son's kidnapping, Ben makes Jo take a sedative before breaking the news. Ben rationalises his action as being necessary to prevent her from becoming hysterical: it has been read by Hitchcock scholars as an example of the motif of patriarchal oppression that characterises his American films.

However, Hitchcock was never entirely happy with Hayes's script. In particular he was concerned about the scenes in London and the characterisation of the Addisons – the kindly middle-aged English couple who turn out to be enemy agents known as the Draytons in the finished film – and the policeman Inspector Buchanan. Hitchcock therefore brought MacPhail back onto the film – much to Hayes's annoyance – in order to revise the English characters and scenes. MacPhail felt that 'the Addisons ... emerge as rather boring characters: for which we are all three to blame' and suggested making the man 'meek and nervous' and hen-pecked by his wife. He also felt that Inspector Buchanan – an expanded role for the policeman which partly filled a gap left by the removal of the comic-relief Uncle Clive – 'needs some careful work. I think, for example, that he should be extremely incisive ... This character, above all, I feel, should illustrate the impressive, sympathetic aspect of English understatement.'[24] Hitchcock agreed and tried to mollify Hayes. A memorandum from Hitchcock to Hayes hints at the tensions brewing over MacPhail's role in the scripting process:

> I know, John, that this is a very difficult job to do, and I think we should possibly try to find some examples to guide you. Buchanan is not at all a 'John Williams' type – that is to say, not what we would call a 'silly ass' type ...
>
> I get the joke of Chappell, Sr, calling 'Junior', but I am afraid this is very American for a precise, very elderly Englishman. Perhaps if he called out 'Son', it might be all right. Frankly, I am out of touch with the English and we might check with Angus on this. Chappel, Jr's remarks of 'quit' again raises the question of English flavour.[25]

Hitchcock's sense that after living for so long in America he was out of touch with the English idiom reflected his increasing detachment from his country of birth. Coincidentally it was during the preparation of *The Man Who Knew Too Much* – on 20 April 1955 to be precise – that Hitchcock became an American citizen.[26]

The first version of *The Man Who Knew Too Much* had been enormously problematic for the Production Code Administration: the remake was much less so, though there were still two points of concern. One was the subject of child kidnapping. Geoffrey Shurlock, Joseph Breen's successor as head of the PCA, reminded Paramount that this was prohibited by the Production Code but suggested that 'the danger of running afoul of this provision can be obviated by making it absolutely clear that the child is held merely as a hostage, with no actual threat to his life'. Shurlock recommended removing a scene where the villain Drayton holds a pistol to Hank's head and suggested that he should point it at Ben instead. Shurlock was also concerned about the character of Drayton who, as a consequence of Hitchcock's desire to make him less boring, had become a fake clergyman. The PCA was always mindful of the characterisation of religious groups and on this occasion suggested that 'it would be well if some means could be found earlier, when we pick him up in the chapel, to put more emphasis on the fact that he is not actually a minister'.[27] The latter point was also evidently a concern for the studio, which was anxious not to cause offence lest it damage the film's prospects at the box office. On this occasion it was not the powerful Roman Catholic lobby – as represented by the Legion of Decency – which was the concern but Protestants. As Luigi Luraschi, Paramount's Director of Censorship, told Hitchcock: 'I feel that in order to avoid offending any religious-minded group, but particularly the Protestants, it isn't enough to establish Drayton as a preacher for a non-denominational congregation. We have to establish very clearly and much earlier that he is a phony ...'[28] This concern followed the controversy stirred by Charles Laughton's *The Night of the Hunter* (1955), where Robert Mitchum played a murderous preacher who 'develops into such an offensive character that very strong protests are in the offing on the part of the Protestants as a group'.[29]

The shooting of *The Man Who Knew Too Much* was evidently not an easy process: to this extent it was unusual for Hitchcock who had not had time for the meticulous preparation he was accustomed to. In Morocco the unit found that local conditions were not conducive to speedy progress. The fact that they were shooting in high temperature and during the Muslim holy month of Ramadan did not help. Location manager 'Doc' Erickson reported that crowd scenes were especially problematic:

> The people are practically unmanageable even when we have more police than we have extras. It is, undoubtedly, due to the particular period we have chosen, that is the Ramadan celebration. We hire people for Frs 550 per day and find shortly after that they have sold their tickets for Frs 250 per day. We try to line up the extras when we hire them but, invariably, there are quite a number who turn

up with two or three tickets and so our original number is somewhat reduced each day. Between 12 and 3 pm we can scarcely hold on to approximately 20% of the extras hired.[30]

The script was also being rewritten while on location, which did not suit Hitchcock. 'Hitch keeps saying, "who wrote this sequence into the picture?"', Erickson reported. 'As usual, he was ready to go home as soon as he arrived. He's not even keen about going on to London, but he's committed himself to those damned interiors up there now.'[31]

One of Hitchcock's reasons for remaking *The Man Who Knew Too Much* was to be able to film the concert sequence again. In the original film this had been shot in the studio: Hitchcock had resolved that for the remake it would be shot on location. Initially it was to have been staged at the Festival Hall on London's South Bank but camera tests found that it would require extensive supplementary lighting to be able to film there in colour.[32] In the event it was possible to shoot the sequence in the Albert Hall itself, with Bernard Herrmann conducting the London Symphony Orchestra in a performance of 'Cantata, Storm Clouds by Arthur Benjamin'. Erickson explained that 'the Albert Hall operation has proved to be extremely slow ... Some of our crews have worked 24 hours and longer without a rest break. We worked until 11 o'clock last night at the Albert Hall in order to finish the Choir.'[33] Other scenes shot in London were the street exteriors, with the Park Lane Hotel doubling for the lobby and staircase of the now unnamed foreign embassy. Hitchcock and MacPhail were still rewriting the script and the unit 'has been shooting off the cuff as script is delivered to them daily'.[34] It seems to have come as a relief to Hitchcock when the unit returned to Hollywood: the studio sequences were completed over the summer of 1955.

Yet for all the travails of its production, *The Man Who Knew Too Much* emerged as a polished and characteristically 'Hitchcockian' film. Evidence that the studio was very happy with it is to be found in a cable from one of its executives: 'Ran *The Man Who Knew Too Much* today in rough form without dubbing and scoring and think it is one of Hitchcock's and Jimmy Stewart's best pictures ... It has a warm and very suspenseful personal story along with production size and scope.'[35] A preview screening in Pasadena was highly positive with three-quarters of the test audience rating the film as 'excellent' ('America is blessed to have Hitchcock', says one of the comment cards), though there were a few comments suggesting that it was 'too long'.[36] The film's length has since become an issue for British critics who prefer the original version of *The Man Who Knew Too Much*. Leslie Halliwell, for example, describes the 1956 film as a 'flaccid remake ... twice as long and half as entertaining'.[37] And Raymond Durgnat thought it had been 'painstakingly and boringly reworked for the family market... The sumptuousness is souped up to indulge the full appeal of local colour, or rather, vicarious tourism.'[38]

While comparisons between the two films are inevitable, it is necessary to consider the Hollywood version of *The Man Who Knew Too Much* on its own terms and in its own contexts rather than seeing it solely as a remake of the original film. And in these respects *The Man Who Knew Too Much* is entirely representative of the formal strategies of American cinema in the mid-1950s. The use of colour and widescreen was consistent with industry practice at a time when Hollywood saw spectacle and production values as a means of luring movie-goers back into theatres in face of the growing competition from television. Hitchcock was not a natural convert to widescreen photography, which was more suited to panoramic compositions *à la* David Lean than to Hitchcock's montage-based technique. However, he adapted successfully to Paramount's VistaVision process, which provided sharper resolution without stretching the image through an anamorphic lens as the alternative CinemaScope did. *The Man Who Knew Too Much* also exemplified the trend in the 1950s for overseas location shooting – what Durgnat dismissed as 'vicarious tourism' – exemplified by various genres including the costume epic (*Ivanhoe*, 1953, shot in Britain), the romantic drama (*Three Coins in the Fountain*, 1954, in Italy), war (*The Bridge on the River Kwai*, 1957, in Ceylon) and the musical (*South Pacific*, 1958, on the island of Kauai). The visual appeal of 'exotic' locations such as Morocco in *The Man Who Knew Too Much* should again be seen in the context of the film industry's response to television. (One of the comments on the preview cards – possibly not intended entirely seriously – was that the film 'needs more camels'.)

While the narrative structure of both versions of *The Man Who Knew Too Much* is essentially the same – the initial exposition with the family on holiday abroad (Switzerland/Morocco), the murder of the secret agent and the subsequent kidnapping of the child in order to guarantee the father's silence, the return to London and the father's investigation to follow up a lead (dentist in the first film, taxidermist in the remake), the confrontation in the chapel, the Albert Hall, and the final climax (the Wapping siege/the embassy) bringing about the rescue of the child and the restoration of the family – there are nevertheless some important differences between them. The McKennas are an American family whereas the Lawrences are British, and they are both professionals (he is a general practice doctor, she is a famous singing star) unlike the Lawrences who have no stated profession and appear to be a couple of leisure. The two most significant differences between the films are the characterisation of the mother and the sex of the child. Jo McKenna in the American film is cast as a 'career woman' who has given up her singing career in order to become a full-time mother: she has less narrative agency than Jill Lawrence whose expertise as a markswoman enables her to save Betty in the British version. (This is not to say that Jo is entirely sidelined: it is Jo who works out that Ambrose Chapel is a place not a person and Jo who prevents the assassination at the Albert Hall by screaming at the crucial moment as in the original. But it is her husband who rescues their son at the film's climax while Jo distracts the guests – and in the process sends a signal to the kidnapped boy – by singing 'Que Séra, Séra' at the piano.) The switch from the daughter Betty in the British film to the son Hank in the American film has provided Hitchcock scholars with plentiful ammunition for Freudian readings of *The Man Who Knew Too Much* in which Jo, denied both her career and a second child, sees the son as a substitute or compensation.[39] This reading is also lent substance by dialogue between Ben and Jo that is present in the final draft screenplay but not in the finished film:

> *Jo:* Ben, glamor is a costume I put on once. It never fit too well. I'd rather live my own life than one written for me.
>
> *Ben:* Including sleeping with a man who always smells of ether?
>
> *Jo:* I don't have to look seductive at breakfast and worry if the *Times* reviewer doesn't like my scrambled eggs.
>
> *Ben:* Then, if that's the way you feel about the stage – do me a favour, huh?
>
> *Jo:* Anything you say.
>
> *Ben:* (*kindly*) Stop trying to make a chorus boy out of Hank.
>
> *Jo looks hurt*
>
> Oh, I know it's just a song and a dance here and there ... but it's all he thinks about. Show business.
>
> *Jo:* Ben, you're setting a trap for me.
>
> *Ben:* He has a good mind. Give him a chance to develop it.
>
> *Jo:* You mean give him a chance to be a doctor?
>
> *Ben:* I didn't say that.[40]

This scene – written by John Michael Hayes – clearly suggests a subtext about the parents having different ambitions for their son: although not used in the film, it would nevertheless tend to support the view of Hitchcock scholars that the American version of *The Man Who Knew Too Much* is more about the family than it is about international politics.

Ina Rae Hark reads *The Man Who Knew Too Much* as a 'revalidation of patriarchy': its representation of the family, and especially its characterisation of Jo as a mother first and foremost, is informed by the conservative attitudes of Eisenhower-era America towards the role and place of women in society. Hark contends that 'the attitudes about women and family current in middle-class and mid-fifties America, combined with the availability of James Stewart as an icon of the American male and Doris Day as an icon of femininity, would provide the ideal opportunity for a new *Man Who Knew Too Much* that redresses the balance between husband and wife by restoring familial authority to the father and making it clear that motherhood is a woman's best hobby or profession'.[41] This can be seen in several ways in the film from the *contretemps* about the accidental removal of the Muslim woman's veil (though Hark is wrong in suggesting that this scene is presided over by Hitchcock in his customary cameo appearance: there is a passenger who slightly resembles Hitchcock but the director's cameo comes later, in the scene with the acrobats) to Ben's insistence upon being the breadwinner and his refusal to consider relocating his practice to New York to facilitate Jo's stage career. It is probably too simplistic to suggest that the film is drawing a parallel between the patriarchal codes of Arab society and the American family: rather the suggestion would seem to be that all women are subject to forms of male oppression regardless of their culture. One of the most commented-on scenes in *The Man Who Knew Too Much* is where Ben administers Jo a sedative before telling her about Hank's kidnapping: Hark refers to it as 'Ben's almost brutal drugging and forcible restraint of Jo'.[42] In contrast Bob Lawrence in the British version simply hands his wife the kidnapper's note. Ben's rationale is that Jo is likely to become hysterical: hence the scene reinforces a traditional though somewhat stereotyped distinction between men as rational and women as emotional. This distinction can also be seen in the fact that it is Jo's feminine intuition that first casts suspicion upon Louis Bernard ('Mr Bernard is a very mysterious man'); Ben dismisses this as her pique that Louis has not recognised her ('You're sore the feller didn't ask you any questions'). There is none of the flirtation between the wife and Louis Bernard as in the British film: clearly this would have been unacceptable for Doris Day's squeaky-clean screen persona.

My own reading of *The Man Who Knew Too Much* is that it represents a moment of transition from the sensational thrillers that had characterised Hitchcock's British career and the more psychologically complex direction signalled in American films such as *Notorious*. On the one hand, *The Man Who*

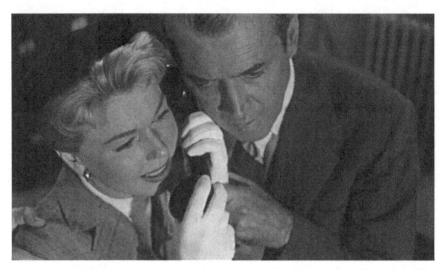

26   The anguish of the parents is more central to the remake of *The Man Who Knew Too Much* (Paramount Pictures, 1956).

Knew Too Much includes most of the elements of the magical or sensational thriller: it is a narrative of action and suspense featuring various improbable and dangerous situations in which there is a clear moral distinction between Good and Evil. As much as we may question Ben McKenna's action in drugging his own wife, there is no question that he is anything other than a decent man doing his best to protect his family. On the other hand, *The Man Who Knew Too Much* also rehearses some of the elements of the realist-existential thriller. The characterisations are psychologically more realistic – Jo's hysterics and Ben's response seem more plausible than the behaviour of the Lawrences in the British film: in particular Ben comes across as more genuinely anguished about his child's kidnapping than Bob Lawrence – and the film's greater emphasis on the family adds layers of meaning that are perhaps less evident in the British film. That the remake is as much about the family as it is about international politics is asserted in a caption immediately after the main titles: 'A single crash of Cymbals and how it rocked the lives of an American family.' For Robin Wood, this emphasis on the family in *The Man Who Knew Too Much* is evidence of its superiority over the original: 'The British version of *The Man Who Knew Too Much* is generically quite unproblematic. To raise the issue of genre is to suggest one of the ways in which the American version is so enriched: the simple action thriller is complicated by the intrusion of a genre that in the '50s reached one of its peaks of significance and expressiveness, the domestic

27 Jo McKenna (Doris Day) sings 'Que Séra, Séra' at the (unnamed) foreign embassy in *The Man Who Knew Too Much* (Paramount Pictures, 1956).

melodrama.'[43] To this end he places *The Man Who Knew Too Much* in the same cultural-historical context as the classic melodramas of the 1950s such as *Rebel Without a Cause* (1955), *Written on the Wind* (1956) and *Imitation of Life* (1959).

All that said, it would be wrong to ignore the espionage plot of *The Man Who Knew Too Much* entirely. Indeed the film may be seen as marking a transitional moment in the spy and espionage genre. The late 1940s and early 1950s had seen a cycle of anti-Communist films in Hollywood – including *The Iron Curtain* (1948), *The Red Menace* (1949), *I Married a Communist* (1949), *I Was a Communist for the FBI* (1951), *Big Jim McLain* (1952) and *Pickup on South Street* (1953) – which explicitly associated Communists with espionage and plotting to overthrow the American government. These films were very much products of the hysterical climate of the early Cold War and fed upon the paranoia around the 'red menace' fuelled by Senator Joseph McCarthy and the notorious 'witch hunts' conducted by the House UnAmerican Activities Committee (HUAC). It would be fair to say that none of these films were very good (with the exception of *Pickup on South Street*) and that by and large they were not successful: the Hollywood studios produced them more in order to assert their own anti-Communist credentials than in the expectation of making money. Hitchcock believed that 'the public doesn't care for films on politics. How else would you account for the fact that most of the pictures dealing with the politics of the Iron Curtain are failures?'[44]

The early draft treatments of *The Man Who Knew Too Much* associate it with the anti- Communist cycle in so far as its conspirators were originally to have been the Russians. Yet the cycle had already run its course: Hollywood's anti-Communist hysteria had peaked and the cycle faded quickly following the censuring of McCarthy who was exposed during the televised hearings in 1954 as a ranting demagogue and bully. This probably accounts for the decision to remove direct references to Russia or the Soviet Union from *The Man Who Knew Too Much* in favour of an unnamed (though implicitly East European) power. In the finished film there are a few oblique references to the Cold War ('Trying to liquidate one of their own big shots – I wish they'd stick to their usual custom and do it in their own country', remarks Inspector Buchanan) and a brief though amusing scene with a kitchen maid that suggests an Eastern bloc power ('Always something funny going on in this embassy ... Give me the Swiss Embassy any time – there's neutrality for you'). However, the assassination plot is detached from international politics – in the original film it was compared explicitly to Sarajevo as an event that could precipitate a world war – and becomes instead a matter of internal politics. It is the ambassador of the foreign power who is the conspirator-in-chief: he plots to dispose of his own prime minister during an official visit to London, presumably in order to engineer a *coup d'état* ('In a few moments I have to welcome our prime minister as my guest of honour when I hoped and expected that he would be completely unable to attend').

The Man Who Knew Too Much may also be related to British Cold War politics. In Angus MacPhail's draft the couple finally known as Mr and Mrs Drayton (who take the place of Peter Lorre's Abbot in the original version) are described as 'Russian agents in Britain'.[45] In the finished film they have become an English couple who by implication are Communist sympathisers: 'You English intellectuals will be the death of us all,' the ambassador remarks scornfully when he learns that they have brought the kidnapped boy to the embassy. The association between Communism and 'intellectuals' was a common theme of British Cold War culture. Although the Communist Party of Great Britain had only very narrow electoral base, its supporters and fellow travellers included public figures such as historians Eric Hobsbawm and E. P. Thompson, writers Philip Toynbee and Doris Lessing, and scientists John Maynard Smith and J. B. S. Haldane. Among those in the British film industry suspected of being Communist sympathisers were actors Ferdy Mayne, Sam Wanamaker and Mai Zetterling.[46] It has since emerged that Ivor Montagu, Hitchcock's friend and collaborator from his Gaumont-British days, supplied information to the Soviet Union when he worked for the Ministry of

Information during the Second World War. And in 1951 the British Intelligence community had been rocked by the defection of two Foreign Office diplomats (and MI6 – Secret Intelligence Service – officers) Guy Burgess and Donald Maclean who were about to be exposed as Soviet moles. Hitchcock was fascinated by the Burgess and Maclean affair and at various times considered making a film about them: in the event the closest he got was *Torn Curtain* which started from the premise of how the wife or girlfriend of a defector would react to their defection.

The Man Who Knew Too Much was generally well received by US critics, who saw it as a characteristic 'Hitchcockian' film. The idea that the spy thriller was seen as Hitchcock's genre is evident in the review from the *Los Angeles Mirror-News*: 'After experimenting with whimsy, romantic jewel thievery and pictures filmed entirely on one set, Director Alfred Hitchcock returns to a more familiar forte … His subject is international intrigue.'[47] (Those 'experiments' were Hitchcock's previous three films for Paramount: *The Trouble With Harry*, *To Catch A Thief* and *Rear Window*.) Most reviewers commented on the fact that *The Man Who Knew Too Much* was a remake of Hitchcock's 1934 film: opinions differed whether it improved upon the original. Bosley Crowther felt that Hitchcock had successfully adapted to new film-making practices: 'Alfred Hitchcock shamelessly reverted to an old story and to the cinematic style that made him famous in the Thirties … [It] shouldn't distress his ardent public to learn that he has cleverly combined his old style and modern screen processes of VistaVision and color in his new picture.'[48] In contrast Hollis Alpert of the *Saturday Review*, while finding it 'a plush suspense film in what might be termed his vintage manner', thought that bigger did not necessarily mean better: 'The cast is a fine one, the production is lavish, the settings (which include some well-photographed locations in Marrakech) are unusual, but those of us who were delighted with the earlier Hitchcock will never be satisfied completely until he forgets some of these big-budget trimmings. The ones we liked best were the little films, holes in plot and all.'[49] (This was a reference to Hitchcock's comment – quoted in the review – regarding his 1930s films: 'One would not accept that sort of film anymore. Too preposterous. Too many holes in the plot.') Philip K. Scheuer – who for some reason dated the original as 1925 and seems to have remembered it as a silent picture – felt that *The Man Who Knew Too Much* was not among Hitchcock's best but was still a highly effective thriller: '[If] his new film is out of the second drawer – and I am inclined to believe that it is – it is still as shrewd, sharp and suspenseful as many right off the top layer of other moviemakers.'[50]

In Britain the reception of *The Man Who Knew Too Much* was framed much more by comparison to the original film – with the new version generally found wanting. A recurring theme of the reviews was that the remake was slower and not necessarily improved by colour photography and widescreen. The consensus was summed up by the *Monthly Film Bulletin*:

> This remake of Hitchcock's 1934 success alters and expands the original (which ran only 75 minutes). Although a quite entertaining thriller with some caustic Hitchcock touches, it is likely to disappoint devotees of the first film. It lacks the earlier pace and excitement; the peculiarly English charm of the original has been exchanged for a vague VistaVision and Technicolor cosmopolitanism; the dentist episode and the siege climax are unhappily missing. Unfortunately significant is the comparative mishandling of the Albert Hall sequence, where the suspense is calculately drawn out and finally dissipated.[51]

The *Manchester Guardian* similarly felt that it 'suffers by comparison ... with the original *Man Who Knew Too Much*' and attributed this largely to its slower pace: 'In this new version the master has the help (or hindrance) of VistaVision: he is working in terms of the new gloss and grandeur and slow tempo of the wide screen ... But the slower the tempo, the longer the audience's opportunity to see the flaws in the film.'[52] And C. A. Lejeune in the *Observer* concurred that 'the first *Man Who Knew Too Much* was stronger in every way'.[53]

The reception of *The Man Who Knew Too Much* therefore highlighted two dominant themes: the idea that its content was 'vintage' Hitchcock – thereby reasserting the association between Hitchcock and the spy thriller – and the view, especially in Britain but shared by some of the American critics, that the film was generally inferior to the original version. That said, neither the British nor the American critics seem to have regarded it as a particularly important film: Hitchcock was a master story-teller and a supreme technician of cinema but he was still not seen as a serious artist or a profound film-maker. It was a very different case in France, however, where Hitchcock was starting to be taken very seriously indeed within the critical culture and where the release of *The Man Who Knew Too Much* coincided with the emergence of *la politique des auteurs*. It was not just Rohmer and Chabrol who saw *The Man Who Knew Too Much* as a film 'in which the Hitchcockian mythology finds its purest, if not its most obvious expression'. Jean-Luc Godard, reviewing *The Man Who Knew Too Much* for *Cahiers du Cinéma*, argued that what other critics regarded as its narrative *longueurs* and slow pace was in fact evidence of the maturity of Hitchcock's style as it allowed the director to focus on small details that enhanced the film's psychological realism: 'This is perhaps the most improbable of Hitchcock's films, but also the most realistic. What is "suspense"? Waiting, and therefore a void to be filled, and more and more Hitchcock has to fill it with asides which have little bearing on the event ... Let us love Hitchcock when, weary of passing simply for a master of taut style, he takes us the longest way around.'[54]

The Man Who Knew Too Much was one of five Hitchcock pictures – the others were *Rope*, *Rear Window*, *The Trouble With Harry* and *Vertigo* – for which Hitchcock retained the commercial rights: the reversion clause in his Paramount contract meant that full ownership of the films passed to him eight years after their initial release. Hitchcock's decision to keep these films out of circulation and off television during the 1970s has been understood both as a commercial decision to provide a legacy for his daughter and as a means of maintaining some control over his posthumous reputation.[55] The reissue of the five films in 1983–4 saw a revival of critical and popular interest in Hitchcock (who had died in 1980) and brought about a reassessment of these particular films. In particular the critical reputation of *Vertigo* was rehabilitated – a film regarded at the time as a misfire was now claimed as a masterpiece – and *Rear Window* came to be understood as much more than a romantic suspense thriller. The reissue of *The Man Who Knew Too Much* prompted a sympathetic reassessment from America's leading *auteur* critic Andrew Sarris, who felt 'that the 1956 *The Man Who Knew Too Much* has been underrated largely because it has been misunderstood'. He explained why he thought it a better and more mature work than the original:

> The 1956 remake is a much more high-powered and elaborately orchestrated exercise in suspense. The amiable set pieces in the 1934 thriller took place in locations – St Moritz, London – that the director knew first hand, and could therefore sketch in with knowingly realistic touches. The atmosphere is cozily low-key, and it is possible to discern a behavorial identification between the director and his players ... By 1956 Hitchcock had placed himself at a greater distance from his characters and milieu than he was capable of doing in 1934. What he lost in the warmth and sweetness of bumbling imperfections, he gained in the brilliance and savagery of his moral paradoxes. The 1956 *The Man Who Knew Too Much* is a thrilling piece of cinema for anyone who can appreciate the working out of formal problems as a means of stirring the murky depths of the unconscious. If you come out of the movie relieved that Stewart and Day are back together and happy again with their surprisingly sissyish little boy, then you have missed the whole point of Stewart's implacability and Day's delirium. This is no ordinary nuclear family. Trust Hitchcock to set it off with a bang, and then let the moral fall-out poison the ostensibly 'happy' ending.[56]

For Sarris, therefore, *The Man Who Knew Too Much* was a deeper and more profound film than its original reception would suggest, and deserved to be ranked alongside *Rear Window* and *Vertigo* among Hitchcock's 'rediscovered' masterpieces of the 1950s. This reassessment was based entirely on an auteurist reading of the films as expressing characteristic 'Hitchcockian' themes: critics such as Sarris and Robin Wood preferred the American *The Man Who Knew Too Much* because they saw it as more than just a genre film. At the same time, however, the American *The Man Who Knew Too Much* should also be regarded as an important milestone in the history of the spy thriller. It is high time that the American *The Man Who Knew Too Much* was understood not just as a remake (whether superior or inferior) of the British original, but rather in its own right as representing the transformation of the spy film in the 1950s as it embraced A-feature production values – a process that would culminate in Hitchcock's next spy thriller: *North by Northwest.*

12

'THE HITCHCOCK PICTURE TO END ALL HITCHCOCK PICTURES': *NORTH BY NORTHWEST* (1959)

North by Northwest was not initially regarded as one of Hitchcock's more important films: it was a fast-moving spy caper that offered a *divertimento* between the high artistic ambition of *Vertigo* (1958) and the macabre horror of *Psycho* (1960) – both films that challenged critics and audiences and became key texts in the *auteur* debates that emerged in Anglo-American film criticism in the 1960s. Hitchcock himself lent credence to the view that it was a minor work when he told interviewers that '*North by Northwest* is an adventure film, treated with a certain levity of spirit. *Vertigo* is much more important to me than *North by Northwest*.'[1] Yet the critical standing of *North by Northwest* has since been elevated to such a degree that now it is not only universally regarded as one of its director's best films but as the one that most fully represents his approach to film-making. Screenwriter Ernest Lehman averred that his aim had been 'to write the Hitchcock picture to end all Hitchcock pictures ... Something with wit, glamour, sophistication, many different colourful locales, a real *movie* movie.'[2] This idea has informed later critical assessments to the extent that *North by Northwest* is now regarded as a quintessentially 'Hitchcockian' film. François Truffaut put it to Hitchcock that '*North by Northwest* is the picture that epitomizes the whole of your work in America'.[3] And Lesley Brill suggests that 'the whole of Hitchcock's career ... can be understood in terms of the themes, underlying assumptions, and techniques that shape the central meanings of *North by Northwest*'.[4]

The production history of *North by Northwest* was unique in that Hitchcock produced and directed it on a one-picture deal for MGM. It was the only film he ever made for MGM, and was the outcome of a particular set of institutional contexts and circumstances. During the 'golden age' of Hollywood in the 1930s and 1940s, MGM had been the most prestigious of the major studios: it famously boasted 'more stars than in heaven' and was associated with high-end production values. Many of the top box-office stars had been under contract to MGM – including Clark Gable, Joan Crawford, Spencer Tracy and Myrna Loy – and the studio had produced such classics as *Grand Hotel, Mutiny on the Bounty, San Francisco, Goodbye, Mr Chips, Pride and Prejudice, Mrs Miniver, Meet Me in St Louis* and *National Velvet* as well as the popular Tarzan, Thin Man and Andy Hardy series. By the 1950s, however, MGM was an ailing giant that had failed to keep pace with changing conditions in the film industry. It was the last of the major studios to hold on to its cinema holdings following the Paramount Decree: indeed it was not until 1959 that MGM belatedly complied with the Supreme Court ruling and separated its exhibition side from its production and distribution activities. And at a time when other studios were cutting back overheads by releasing stars and other personnel from long-term contracts and opening their doors to independent producers, MGM clung stubbornly to its star contracts and centralised production system. The studio was further hampered during the 1950s by a series of boardroom struggles within its parent company Loew's Incoporated that led to the exit of long-serving head of production Louis B. Mayer, his successor Dore Schary, and senior executives Nicholas Schenck and Arthur Loew. The incoming president Joseph Vogel and new head of production Sol Siegel were more open to bringing in independent producers than the previous regimes: in 1956 Siegel announced a 'succession of deals with Hollywood's independent producers to put MGM on a competitive par with its more alert rivals'.[5] The first of these deals was with Hitchcock.

To some extent the MGM-Hitchcock collaboration was a marriage of convenience. For Hitchcock the timing was propitious as it came at a time when *Vertigo* had been delayed and he had no other projects lined up. His deal with Paramount was non-exclusive: in 1957, for example, he had also made *The Wrong Man* for Warner Bros. From MGM's perspective, Hitchcock was a 'name' director who had an excellent recent track record at the box office. Like all the studios, MGM had been hit by declining profits in the 1950s: in 1957 it recorded a loss for the first time in its history.[6] It had been overtaken in Hollywood's premier league by other studios, notably Paramount and Universal-International, which had adjusted more flexibly and successfully to changing industrial and economic conditions. Above all it was badly in need of a hit: there had been no outstanding successes since the glory days of the

Technicolor musicals produced by Arthur Freed in the late 1940s and early 1950s. To this extent MGM needed Hitchcock more than Hitchcock needed MGM: this was reflected in the highly favourable terms that he was able to negotiate for a one-picture deal.

Thomas Schatz observes that the deal to produce *North by Northwest* was 'a striking indication of the changing power structure and production values in Hollywood, particularly where top stars and filmmakers were concerned'.[7] MGM agreed to finance and distribute the film – initially budgeted at $3.1 million – with Hitchcock receiving a flat fee of $250,000 and star Cary Grant (preferred over James Stewart) receiving $300,000. In addition Hitchcock and Grant would be entitled to a percentage of the profits: Hitchcock's share was 10 per cent once the film had grossed twice its negative cost. Hitchcock also held out for a clause allowing him 'approval of all elements of production' – including the right of 'final cut'.[8] The fact that a studio for whom he had never worked was prepared to agree to this demand is further indication of the prestige that Hitchcock's name held. In the event of course *North by Northwest* was a major box-office success: North American grosses of $13.2 million ensured that the studio recovered its investment from the domestic theatrical release alone.[9]

A further indication of the power relationship between the director and the studio was that MGM had originally contracted Hitchcock to make a different film entirely but that he unilaterally decided to embark upon a new project of his own. MGM wanted him to film a property that the studio owned: *The Wreck of the Mary Deare* by British author Hammond Innes. The screenwriter assigned to the project was Ernest Lehman, who had adapted *Sabrina* (1954) for Billy Wilder and *The Sweet Smell of Success* (1957), based on his own story, for Alexander Mackendrick. Hitchcock and Lehman evidently enjoyed working together but neither could summon up much enthusiasm for *The Wreck of the Mary Deare*, which after a brilliant opening 'hook' – a cargo ship found abandoned in the English Channel with no crew on board – became a rather heavy-going courtroom drama. Hitchcock said that he had told the studio that 'the story wouldn't work out and suggested we do something else'.[10] He no doubt remembered that his previous venture into courtroom drama (*The Paradine Case*) had not been one of his more successful films. The change of project is confirmed by an internal studio memorandum of September 1957:

> On September 19, Mr Hitchcock met with Mr Thau, Miss Thorson and myself and explained that he was temporarily putting aside work on *The Wreck of the Mary Deare* and was going to assign Ernest Lehman to develop an original story which we will call, merely for purposes of identification and temporarily,

> *In A Northwest Direction.* It deals with the [*sic*] espionage and counter-espionage in
> the United States with locales in New York, Detroit, Mount Rushmore and Alaska,
> among others.[11]

Hitchcock never returned to *The Wreck of the Mary Deare*, which in the event
was made by British director Michael Anderson from a script by Eric Ambler,
starring Gary Cooper and Charlton Heston.

It was at this point that Hitchcock instructed MGM to pay $1,000 to *New
York Herald Tribune* journalist Otis L. Guernsey for the rights to a story idea that
Guernsey had pitched to Hitchcock over a lunch at the 21 Club in New York
some years before. Guernsey had suggested a situation in which an American
salesman on a business trip in the Near East is mistaken for a spy by the 'Bad
Guys' – the twist being that the spy turns out to be a decoy invented by the
'Good Guys' in order to confuse the enemy. The salesman seeks to solve the
mystery of mistaken identity and 'in the course of his searches he meets a girl
who is part of the "Good Guys" plan to establish the fictional masterspy, and,
finally, that he contributes to the downfall of the bad guys in a flurry of
denouement and romance'. 'The idea of an innocent man suddenly saddled
with a highly romantic and dangerous identity still sounds to me like a good
one for a picture,' Guernsey told Hitchcock, though he added that his own
attempt to flesh out the story 'does not seem to work, instead developing faults
of (a) logic (b) corn or (c) overcomplicated devices in order to establish
situations'.[12] Hitchcock – who had never been unduly concerned about flaws
in narrative logic – accepted Guernsey's offer to '[do] whatever you wish with
the idea – abandon it, or cause it to be worked on'. In a separate letter Guernsey
suggested that the idea was 'vaguely based on something which actually
happened in the Middle East during World War II'.[13] It was a long way from
Guernsey's thinly sketched outline to *North by Northwest* but the germ of the
idea was there: a man mistaken for a spy who does not exist but turns out to be
a decoy invented to confuse the enemy. The fact that Hitchcock made a token
payment to Guernsey suggests that he saw it as the origin of *North by Northwest*.

The scripting process of *North by Northwest* provides an excellent case study
of Hitchcock's working methods and his approach to story construction.
At this stage in his career Hitchcock preferred working with one writer rather
than the team-based approach of his British films. He and Lehmann began
holding story conferences in the late summer of 1957 with Lehmann then
working on the screenplay – which went under various working titles
including *In A Northwesterly Direction, Breathless!, The CIA Story* and *The Man on
Lincoln's Nose* – while Hitchcock shot *Vertigo* during the fall. Hitchcock
thought primarily in terms of scenes. One of these was a chase over the

presidential monument at Mount Rushmore: this was earmarked for the climax of *North by Northwest* from an early stage.[14] Another was a scene in a Detroit car factory that he described in some detail to Truffaut:

> I always wanted to have a long dialogue scene between Cary Grant and one of the factory workers as they walk along the assembly line. They might, for instance, be talking about one of the foremen. Behind them a car is being assembled, piece by piece. Finally, the car they've seen being put together from a simple nut and bolt is complete, with gas and oil, and all ready to drive off the line. The two men look at it and say. 'Isn't it wonderful!' Then they open the door to the car and out drops a corpse![15]

However, this scene is not to be found in any of the draft scripts or treatments: Hitchcock and Lehman dropped it because 'we couldn't integrate the idea into the story'.[16]

Lehman said that after scouting locations in New York, Chicago and North Dakota, 'I returned to California and started the endless task of writing a screenplay in my lonely office #206, the Thalberg Building, MGM, while Hitch finished *Vertigo* and took a desperately needed vacation in the British West Indies'.[17] By May 1958 Lehman had three-quarters of the screenplay complete: what was still missing was the final act at Mount Rushmore. Some of the motifs, such as the heroine who turns out to be part of the decoy plot, can be traced back to Guernsey's original idea. But there are also significant differences: the narrative was set wholly in America rather than overseas – the suggested Near Eastern setting might have seemed too close to *The Man Who Knew Too Much* – and substituted a spy ring (implicitly though never directly identified as foreign Communists) for Guernsey's arms smugglers. The hero became a Madison Avenue advertising executive called Roger Thornhill, described in the script as 'tall, lean, faultlessly dressed (and far too original to be wearing the gray-flannel uniform of his kind)' – a reference, no doubt, to the Gregory Peck film *The Man in the Grey Flannel Suit* (1956) recently adapted from Sloan Wilson's satire of the New York advertising industry – and gives every impression of having been written all along for Cary Grant despite the suggestion until some way into the pre-production process that *North by Northwest* might have been a vehicle for James Stewart. In the early drafts the villain is called David Mendoza and the non-existent spy for whom Thornhill is mistaken is known as George Rosen. Some of the names were changed on the advice of MGM's Legal Department: Mendoza became Phillip Vandamm and Rosen became George Kaplan. One significant difference from the finished film was the inclusion of a voice-over narration before the opening credits which it was suggested might be spoken by Hitchcock himself:

> Would it not be strange, in a city of seven million people, if one man were *never* mistaken for another … if, with seven million pair [*sic*] of feet wandering through the canyons and corridors of the city, one pair of feet *never* by chance strayed into the wrong foot steps?
>
> (a pause)
>
> Strange, indeed.[18]

The mistaken identity theme links the film to *The Wrong Man*, which had focused on a man arrested and tried for robbery on account of his resemblance to the real culprit: Hitchcock had introduced the film in a piece to camera instead of his customary cameo appearance. The voice-over remained in every draft up to and including the shooting script.[19]

Lehman injected a good deal of humour into *North by Northwest*. This suggests that the film was conceived from the outset as a parody of the spy thriller rather than as a straight example of the genre. Indeed the early script drafts are more self-referential than the finished film: they include a reference to another Hitchcock film ('We're just strangers on a train,' Eve remarks suggestively to Thornhill) and an aside against the 'Method' school of acting that Hitchcock disliked (the villain tells Thornhill – believing him to be an undercover agent acting out a role – that 'you chaps could stand a little less coaching from J. Edgar Hoover and a little more from Lee Strasberg'). The latter line was changed to 'the Actors' Studio' in the film. It was Lehman who came up with incidental details such as Thornhill's match folder bearing his initials 'ROT' (the 'O' stands for nothing) that becomes a plot device towards the end of the film. Perhaps mindful of the difficulties experienced over *Notorious*, the script indicates that the unnamed government agency responsible for creating the fictitious agent 'should suggest CIA without being so specific as to betray cosmic secrets to charwomen'. One idea that did not make it into the finished film was Thornhill blacking up his face when he disguises himself as a railway porter. This was no doubt deemed too racially sensitive: in the finished film Grant appears without a blacked-up face. This would prompt a cynical observation from one correspondent following the film's release: 'If you can find a caucasian redcap in a station in this country, something has happened to their Union! Or perhaps you did this in order to escape the protests of Southern Censors?'[20]

That said, there were some aspects of the script that caused concern within the studio. The main issue was the characterisation of the villain's henchman Leonard as a homosexual: this is evident from the description of his appearance ('He wears horn-rimmed glasses that are too large for his face and his attitudes are unmistakably effeminate') and in his dialogue ('Call it my women's intuition if you like, but I've never trusted neatness').[21] (Horn-rimmed glasses were a film industry visual shorthand for a homosexual male: Humphrey Bogart's Philip Marlowe wears a pair in *The Big Sleep* (1946) when he adopts the persona of a prissy intellectual to case out a pornographic book shop.) Robert Vogel, who acted in the same role as Luigi Luraschi at Paramount as the script watchdog and liaison with the Production Code office, cautioned that 'Leonard is going to be skating on very thin ice. He doesn't have to be the very essence of manliness, but if his "unmistakably effeminate attitudes" give audiences, the Code people, or the Legion of Decency a feeling that he is a pervert, we're in trouble.'[22] Vogel was also concerned about a reference in the script to Thornhill's 'two ex-wives' which he felt would alienate the Catholic Legion of Decency and advised Hitchcock to change it as the film 'will stand on its own dramatic and melodramatic feet and won't be helped by an inference that it contains material which is "morally objectionable" to Catholics'.[23]

Hitchcock was used to fighting battles with the censors – indeed on occasion he seems to have gone out of his way to challenge the Production Code, as he did with *Notorious* and would do again with *Psycho* – and despite his Jesuit schooling he cared little for the opinions of America's Catholics about his films. In the event the passage of *North by Northwest* through the Production Code was relatively smooth in comparison to some others: the fact that Hitchcock was able to keep certain points to which the censor objected demonstrates the extent to which the PCA's authority was weakening by the late 1950s. As Vogel predicted, Geoffrey Shurlock of the PCA took exception to the characterisation of Leonard: 'If there is any inference whatsoever in your finished picture that this man is an homosexual, we will be unable to approve it under the requirements of the Production Code.' Shurlock also raised the scenes between Thornhill and Eve on the train which 'should be handled in such a way as not to be offensively sex suggestive'. 'On page 72,' he elaborated, 'the girl's line "I never make love on an empty stomach" is unacceptably sex suggestive and should be omitted.'[24] In a follow-up letter, having seen the remaining script pages, Shurlock recommended the deletion of Thornhill's reference to his ex-wives and cautioned against the concluding scene which showed Thornhill and Eve together in a train compartment: 'We assume, of course, that the couple will be attired in day clothes. Further, the acceptability of this scene will depend upon it not being in any way suggestive of an imminent sex affair.'[25]

The studio's internal correspondence suggests that Vogel saw his role as being to negotiate a middle ground between the film-maker and the censor. In October 1958, with the shooting of the film already well under way, he informed Hitchcock that he had 'convinced [the] Code office not to make issue of this line' – in reference to Eve's 'I never make love on an empty stomach' – but reported that the PCA 'urge us, however, to reconsider it ourselves'.[26] Hitchcock acquiesced and the line was changed to 'I never discuss love on an empty stomach' in the post-synch dubbing. Regarding the suggestion of an 'imminent sex affair' at the end of the film, Vogel told Hitchcock: 'I have emphasized to them that this scene must be played for comedy ... Believe I can "con" them into accepting it even when the couple are not wearing full evening dress.'[27] In fact Thornhill and Eve are in their night clothes in the scene: on this occasion Hitchcock circumvented the censor by dubbing in a line that indicates they have married ('Come along, Mrs Thornhill') and then cut to a shot of the train plunging into a tunnel that he was at pains to tell everyone was a visual metaphor for sexual intercourse.[28] However, while some of Leonard's dialogue was altered, such as calling Thornhill 'sweetie', the clear inference of his homosexuality, including his reference to 'my women's intuition', remained in the film. There is nothing in the production records to indicate why Hitchcock held out on this particular point in the face of opposition from both the studio and the censor. On the one hand it might be seen as evidence of the latent homophobia that some critics have detected in Hitchcock's films.[29] One does not have to be a gay critic to recognise that there is a recurring association between homosexuality and criminality in Hitchcock's films (*Rope, Strangers on a Train, Psycho*). On the other hand the association between homosexuality and political dissidence can be seen as a reflection of the prevailing ideological climate in Cold War America: homosexuality was widely regarded as a threat to national security.[30]

As the script took shape, attention turned to the casting of the film. Hitchcock resisted MGM's attempts to cast its contract artistes Cyd Charisse and Taina Elg (who appeared in the Rank Organisation's remake of *The 39 Steps* in 1959) as Eve.[31] Hollywood gossip columnist Hedda Hopper reported that Hitchcock wanted to cast Elizabeth Taylor.[32] In the event Eva Marie Saint, best known as Marlon Brando's co-star from *On the Waterfront* (1954), was cast as Eve. *North by Northwest* would do for Saint what *The 39 Steps* had for Madeleine Carroll: she had previously been cast in rather serious and even dowdy roles but Hitchcock found a new side to her personality as the cool and sexually confident Eve. Saint's performance certainly impressed the veteran producer Walter Wanger, who wrote admiringly: 'I was delighted to see you all dressed up. I always thought you were a clotheshorse at heart.'[33] James Mason was ideal casting for the suave villain Vandamm, described in the script as 'about forty, slightly professional in manner but definitely sexually attractive (to women)'. Key supporting roles went to Jessie Royce Landis as Thornhill's mother (Landis was in fact the same age, 55, as her screen 'son' Cary Grant) and Hitchcock regular Leo G. Carroll as intelligence chief Professor Lake (known just as 'The Professor' in the film itself). Actors' Studio graduate Martin Landau was a late addition to the cast as henchman Leonard after first choice Herbert Lom was deemed too short.[34]

Robert E. Kapsis has shown how the production discourse of *North by Northwest* set out to condition critical and popular responses to the film. In interviews and press releases during the shooting and post-production, Hitchcock explained how '*North by Northwest* would meet viewer expectations about what constituted the quintessential Hitchcock film'.[35] This strategy might also have been a means of reassuring Hitchcock's public that he was returning to more familiar territory following the mixed reception of his previous two films, *The Wrong Man* and *Vertigo*. One example from many must suffice to illustrate the publicity strategy of *North by Northwest*. In an interview for *Life* magazine, Hitchcock explained how he went about making a thriller 'larger than life':

> I've found the best way to do this is to keep your villains suave and clever – the kind that wouldn't dirty their hands with ordinary vulgar gun play. And your heroes, of course, average men, usually involved, by innocent accident, in a web of dire circumstance. That rules out Supermen of the Sherlock Holmes type, for instance. I think if Holmes were introduced to the public for the first time today he would be more an object of curiosity than someone with whom the reader could identify himself.[36]

The everyman hero, the dire circumstances, the suave villain: these were all key aspects of the Hitchcock formula. Audiences were therefore being conditioned to expect these elements from *North by Northwest* long before they saw the film.

Hitchcock always had the reputation of a master craftsman who prepared every aspect of the production of his films in meticulous detail before shooting: this not only ensured that the finished film bore his imprint but also that it was brought in close to its original budget. As had been the case with *The Man Who Knew Too Much*, however, Hitchcock was obliged to start filming *North by Northwest* before a complete script was ready. This was due entirely to the availability of Cary Grant who was contracted for twelve weeks from 31 July 1958: if the production extended beyond 22 October, Grant would be entitled to additional payments of $25,000 per week.[37] It also meant that the film went into production before certain logistical issues had been sorted out. In particular Hitchcock had hoped to shoot the climax on location at Mount

Rushmore itself. This raised some heckles among the trustees of the monument who were 'concerned that whatever use you make of the Memorial be in keeping with its concept. This Memorial is dedicated to the growth and development of our country; and it has become a symbol of democracy.'[38] MGM's Legal Department advised Ernest Lehman – still working on the final draft of the script – to 'please use adequate language to convey the thought that our leading characters place their lives in jeopardy by pursuing subversive enemy elements and that we felt it to be symbolic in our story that they achieve this against the background of the monuments of the great Presidents of our country'.[39] This may explain why some jokey political references were dropped from the shooting script, such as:

Eve: What do we do now – slide down Lincoln's nose?

Thornhill: Let's make it Jefferson. I'm a Democrat.[40]

In the event the unit was denied permission to shoot on the monument itself and had to make do with a few shots around the cafeteria. The Mount Rushmore sequence would be shot entirely in the studio – which pushed up the cost of sets and extended the shooting schedule.

In fact *North by Northwest* was behind schedule – and consequently over budget – right from the start. The start of principal photography was delayed until 27 August when the cameras rolled in New York. The assistant directors' reports reveal that some of the location shooting was done on the hoof: the first shots were taken outside the United Nations Building from concealed cameras (the United Nations having refused to allow the crew to film inside the building). Hitchcock's cameo as a man missing a bus was shot with a concealed camera at 1.30 pm on 4 September. The unit travelled to Chicago on 8 September, where it shot the exteriors at Union Station and the La Salle art gallery, and then to Mount Rushmore on 15 September for two days. On 17 September the unit returned to MGM's Culver City lot where it remained for three months, with the exception of five days on location at Bakersfield, California, where Hitchcock staged the exteriors for the famous sequence where Thornhill is attacked by a crop-dusting plane on an open prairie (supposedly west of Chicago).[41] It was soon apparent that *North by Northwest* was going to overrun its production schedule and that Grant's overage payments would come into effect. Sol Siegel wrote to Hitchcock:

I know that you are just as concerned as I am at the manner in which the costs are escalating on your picture. Certainly neither of us contemplated this kind of cost at the outset. Do you think there is anything you could do in the remainder of the work that would have the effect of reducing the indicated final cost?[42]

The studio's concern about the increasing cost should be seen in the context of its concurrent investment in *Ben-Hur* – shooting at the Cinecittà Studios in Rome at the same time as *North by Northwest* – which went considerably over budget: in the event it would cost a then-record $15 million. In comparison to *Ben-Hur* – which of course went on to be a huge box-office hit – the overage on *North by Northwest* was relatively modest. It finally came in twenty-two days over schedule and $1 million over budget at a final estimated cost of $4,129,450.[43]

Hitchcock was a meticulous director but he was no spendthrift: the overage on *North by Northwest* arose not from any unnecessary extravagance on his part but rather from having to commence principal photography before the script was complete and without all the logistical issues resolved. Hitchcock's percentage deal which came into effect when the film had grossed twice its negative cost was the studio's safeguard against him going recklessly over budget. That Hitchcock was willing to compromise on costs is demonstrated by the example of the title sequence. Lehman's scripts had always envisaged the opening titles being projected over busy street scenes that 'should capture the tempo of Madison Avenue and Fifth Avenue in the Fifties. Streets swarming with smartly dressed people. Revolving doors of sleek new glass-and-steel office buildings spewing out streams of super-charged New Yorkers, hurrying for cabs and buses and subways and cocktail bars.'[44] Toward the end of production, Hitchcock identified what he felt was 'a script deficiency, which does not allow the character played by Cary Grant to be clearly indicated as an advertising man'. He therefore suggested an entirely new opening sequence that 'would reveal him in his office before we show any titles, and then let the camera roam over the tables … There would be a series of rough layout cards in various stages of completion. These cards would be like proposed advertisements in *Life* or other magazine, but they eventually would be our Main and Credit Titles.'[45] Hitchcock had used a similar mobile camera shot at the beginning of *Rear Window* to establish the James Stewart character's profession as a photo-journalist. However, Siegel pointed out that 'the cost of this will be in the neighbourhood of $20,000 … Personally, I feel that there are so many wonderful things in the picture itself that the addition of an unusual main title is not an utmost necessity.'[46] Hitchcock acquiesced and dropped his idea for an alternative title sequence.

Nevertheless the post-production of *North by Northwest* in the early months of 1959 revealed Hitchcock in characteristically perfectionist mode. He was not satisfied with the sequence where the villains attempt to kill Thornhill by plying him with alcohol before putting him behind the wheel of a car – a sequence that had been shot by a second unit. Hitchcock instructed: 'Take the

Drunk Car Chase apart. Order reprints of Thornhill's Close Ups. The sequence will be reconstructed in terms of Thornhill's Close Ups and the hazards will be put in afterwards.'[47] On 19 February he informed Siegel that 'I have trimmed the picture down to an interim minimum and so far as I can tell, it will take an audience to tell us what else to cut'. He added that 'I do have a number of what I feel are necessary retakes – some of them are photographic flaws, others where I feel that, due to playing the picture way out of continuity, an odd scene or two might be improved'.[48] *North by Northwest* was previewed on 11 June and received an overwhelmingly positive response: it was adjudged 'outstanding' by 98, 'excellent' by 121 and 'very good' by 45 out of 278 members of the test audience. One of the (very few) negative comments was ironic given Hitchcock's next project: 'You overdid Mt Rushmore a bit and we could have done without Mother.'[49]

North by Northwest had the best notices for a Hitchcock film since *Rear Window*: most critics saw it as a superior and polished entertainment that would delight audiences and score at the box office. The views of the trade press were best summed up by *Variety*, which pronounced it 'Alfred Hitchcock at his masterful best. It's the mixture as before, suspense, intrigue, comedy, humour, but seldom has the concoction been served up so delectably or in so glossy a package. It should be top b.o.'[50] The New York critics were similarly enthralled. For A. H. Weiler of the *New York Times* it was 'a suspenseful and delightful Cook's Tour of some of the more photogenic spots in these United States' and 'is all done in brisk, genuinely witty and sophisticated style'.[51] Gene Gleason of the *New York Herald Tribune* called it 'one of the wildest and most entertaining movie marathons of the summer season'.[52] Kate Cameron in the *New York News* felt that Hitchcock 'is back in the groove he created for himself with many top thrillers for the screen before becoming too absorbed in the manner rather than the matter of his presentations'.[53] For Archer Winsten in the *New York Post* it was 'the liveliest Hitchcock film since *Rear Window*, the most entertaining generally, and, specifically, it measures in itself a certain relaxing of the behaviour codes of the movies that has taken place in the past few years.'[54] Hollis Alpert in the *Saturday Review* thought it 'is much the best Hitchcock that has come along in some years', while reserving special mention for Ernest Lehman's contribution: 'Mr Lehman not only provided Hitchcock with exactly the right kind of story to take advantage of his skills, but he has written that rare thing these days – a screen original. It is no wonder, then, that *North by Northwest* is all movie, and a delightful treat as well.'[55] One dissenting voice, however, was Stanley Kauffmann in the *New Republic*: 'The decline of Alfred Hitchcock is no longer news. It is quite clear that the director of *The Lady Vanishes* and *The 39 Steps* is dead and that an obscene ghost is mocking him by superficially imitating him.' Kauffmann preferred Hitchcock's British films and felt that in *North by Northwest* 'the urgent, encompassing reality of his first films is missing, and without it his antics simply look foolish'. He averred that *North by Northwest* 'loses us in cliché and preposterousness' and called the crop-duster sequence – a highlight of the film for many critics – 'probably the low point in Hitchcock's career – pure comic book stuff'.[56]

One feature of the reception discourse of *North by Northwest* that was evident across a number of reviews was that it was understood as a pastiche or even a parody of Hitchcock's previous work. Dick Williams in the *Mirror-News*, for instance, observed that 'Hitchcock has dipped into his cinematic past for the basic ingredients – the spy melodrama and the innocent bystander caught up in menacing events which he does not understand. There are perceptible traces of both his *39 Steps* and *The Lady Vanishes* in *North by Northwest*.'[57] Many reviews commented upon the 'tongue-in-cheek' nature of Hitchcock's direction but the *New Yorker* went further, describing it as 'the brilliant realization of a feat he has unintentionally moved toward for more than a decade – a perfect parody of his own work'.[58] *Variety*'s reviewer also suggested that *North by Northwest* was a spoof or parody, though of the spy genre as a whole rather than specifically of Hitchcock's films: 'Second thoughts on the film will produce the feeling that there are loose ends and stray threads that are never quite bound up or followed through. But the form of the spy melodrama, especially when it is being none too gently spoofed, with counter-espionage and double-agenting rampant, is a loose one and license is permissible.'[59] This view was endorsed by Hitchcock, who told Truffaut that 'I made *North by Northwest* with tongue in cheek; to me it was one big joke.'[60]

The suggestion that *North by Northwest* should be understood as a pastiche or parody rather than as a straight thriller might help to explain why it was not initially regarded as a particularly serious or important film: no doubt it also helps to account for the film's popular success following what some regarded as the artistic pretentions of *Vertigo*. This view has continued to inform later critical assessments. James Naremore, for example, remarks that 'Lehman's screenplay ... was an obvious attempt to draw together themes and situations from at least three of the director's previous films about international espionage, blending them into a spectacular and definitively "Hitchcockian" entertainment'.[61] *North by Northwest* combines aspects of *The 39 Steps* (the innocent protagonist who stumbles by chance upon an international spy ring and who is pursued both by the spies who want to kill him and by the police who suspect him of murder), *Saboteur* (the cross-country pursuit and the climax atop an iconic national monument) and *Notorious* (the compromised heroine obliged by the state to prostitute herself in the service of her country). In particular *North by Northwest* is often seen as an American reworking (remake is perhaps not quite the right term) of *The 39 Steps*: it has even been suggested that '*North by Northwest* is closer to Buchan's novel' than the earlier film.[62] In *North by Northwest*, for example, it is a man who is murdered (as in the Buchan novel) rather than a woman (as in Hitchcock's film), while in the novel Hannay is pursued by an aeroplane as is Thornhill in *North by Northwest*.

In fact it might be argued that the reference points for *North by Northwest* are not so much specific texts as the spy genre as a whole. From John Buchan it borrows the fast-paced narrative of chase and pursuit and the double-hunt motif as the protagonist finds himself on the run from both spies and police: Thornhill follows Richard Hannay in leaving behind his comfortable, sophisticated urban lifestyle and heading in a north-westerly direction where he tracks a master spy to his lair. (It has become a somewhat tiresome pastime among Hitchcock critics to point out that there is no such point on the compass as 'north by northwest': the trajectory of Thornhill's journey from New York to Chicago and then to Rapid City is more westerly than north-westerly, though he does board a plane bearing the logo of Northwest Airlines. To be fair it is a less tiresome pastime than the tortuous attempts to link the title to Hamlet's 'I am but mad north-north-west / When the wind is southerly I know a hawk from a handsaw'.) From Eric Ambler and Graham Greene, *North by Northwest* inherits the character of the reluctant amateur spy ('I got into it by accident – what's your excuse?') whose worldly cynicism sets him apart from the patriotic heroes of the Buchan-Sapper school. From Ian Fleming come the highly visible conspicuous consumption and permissive sexuality – most evident in the sequence on the Twentieth Century Limited train where Thornhill and Eve eat brook trout before making love – that had been absent from pre-war spy fiction but became possible in the 1950s as social mores changed (a point noted in the contemporary review by Archer Winstein). Nor were all the influences fictional: there are a number of allusions to real-life spies in *North by Northwest*. It may be coincidence that Leo G. Carroll's 'Professor' bears a passing resemblance to CIA Director Allen Dulles; but Thornhill's description of the statuette containing the microfilm (the film's 'MacGuffin') as 'the pumpkin' was surely a reference to the Alger Hiss-Whittaker Chambers case in which it was reported that rolls of 35-millimetre film had been hidden inside a hollowed-out pumpkin.[63]

28 A case of mistaken identity and a kidnapping in broad daylight set events
in motion in *North by Northwest* (MGM, 1959).

Until *North by Northwest*, Hitchcock's spy films had all more or less
conformed to either the sensational or the realist lineages of the thriller: *The
Man Who Knew Too Much*, *The 39 Steps*, *The Lady Vanishes*, *Foreign Correspondent*
and *Saboteur* were all sensational melodramas in which action and suspense
took precedence over plot and characterisation, whereas *Secret Agent*, *Saboteur*
and *Notorious* exemplified the realist mode with a greater emphasis on
psychological realism and character motivation. *North by Northwest*, however,
has a foot in both camps: it represents a point of convergence between the two
thriller modes. While its chase-and-pursuit narrative and its outlandish
situations – Thornhill kidnapped at gunpoint in the middle of a crowded hotel
lobby, forcibly plied with alcohol and put behind the wheel of a car, lured to a
remote open prairie and attacked by a crop-dusting plane, and scrambling over
the presidential monuments of Mount Rushmore while clutching a blonde in
one hand and a statuette containing stolen microfilm in the other – locate it
within the sensational lineage, *North by Northwest* also reflects something of
the ideological and moral ambiguity of the existential thriller. This is especially
evident in the film's equivocal attitude towards the politics of the Cold War
and the behaviour of the intelligence services.

North by Northwest may be understood as a satire of the Cold War: it is
cynical in the extreme in its representation of the US intelligence services
('FBI, CIA, ONI ... We're all in the same alphabet soup') who manipulate events

to their own advantage ('We could congratulate ourselves on a marvellous stroke of good fortune. Our non-existent decoy, George Kaplan, created to divert suspicion from our actual agent, has fortuitously become a live decoy') and are willing to leave Thornhill to his own devices in order to preserve the elaborate fiction they have built up around their decoy agent. ('How long do you think he'll stay alive?' 'Well, that's his problem.') Even the apparently avuncular character of the intelligence chief known as 'The Professor' is a cynical pragmatist who has recruited Eve to spy on her lover Vandamm and who manipulates Thornhill into continuing to play the role of Kaplan in order to protect Eve's cover. ('You lied to me!' 'I needed your help.') Thornhill is so outraged that he challenges the moral legitimacy of the security agency's methods:

Professor: War is hell, Mr Thornhill, even when it's a cold one.

Thornhill: If you fellows can't lick the Vandamms of this world without asking girls like her to bed down with them and fly away with them and probably never come back, perhaps you ought to start learning how to lose a few cold wars.

Professor: I'm afraid we're already doing that.

This expression of dissent, even in such a mild form, distances *North by Northwest* from the official ideology of the Cold War: it is a view that could not easily have been expressed only a few years earlier at the height of the McCarthyite-inspired 'red scare' of the 1950s.

The Cold War discourses of *North by Northwest* need to be placed in their historical and ideological contexts. The film was produced during the twilight of the Eisenhower presidency at a time when some political commentators were noting a 'thaw' in US–Soviet relations. This was occasioned in part by the visit of Soviet premier Nikita Khrushchev to the United States in September 1959 – coinciding with the release of *North by Northwest* – and in part by the decision to revoke the Eisenhower Doctrine, which had enabled US intervention to counter Communist expansionism in the Middle East, in the spring of 1959. The 'thaw' might explain why *North by Northwest* is even more vague about the identity of its unnamed foreign power than the remake of *The Man Who Knew Too Much*: only one line ('I needn't tell you how valuable she can be to us over there') hints at the Soviet Union. Vandamm's nationality is uncertain – James Mason plays him as a European sophisticate – and even his strong-arm men are able to pass as Americans. In this sense *North by Northwest* seems the least political of Hitchcock's spy films: it contrasts markedly with *Torn Curtain* and *Topaz*, which followed in the 1960s and were rooted directly in the politics of the Cold War.

29   Thornhill confronts the (apparently) duplicitous Eve Kendall (Eva Marie Saint) in *North by Northwest* (MGM, 1959)

Like Hitchcock's other American spy films, *North by Northwest* displaces the politics of the Cold War onto personal and sexual relationships. It sets up a romantic triangle similar to *Notorious* – Thornhill/Eve/Vandamm in place of Devlin/Alicia/Sebastian – and translates the ideological oppositions of the Cold War into the rivalry between Thornhill and Vandamm for Eve. (The triangle in this instance is complicated by Leonard, who sees through Eve's duplicity more easily than Vandamm, who in turn accuses his 'right arm' of being jealous.) Like Alicia Huberman in *Notorious*, Eve is to all intents and purposes prostituting herself for her country: she has been recruited by the intelligence agency to spy on her lover. Eve seems a less reluctant spy than Thornhill ('Maybe it was the first time anyone ever asked me to do anything worthwhile') and apparently has no qualms either about seducing Thornhill – apparently on instructions from Vandamm – in order to keep him away from the police, or a short while later sending him into what she presumably knows is a trap. Thornhill is bitter at Eve's apparent betrayal and accuses her of being a prostitute ('She's worth every dollar of it, take it from me. She puts her heart into her work – in fact her whole body') until he learns the truth from the Professor. Thereafter Thornhill must rescue Eve from Vandamm but also detach her from the service of the intelligence agency: the film's last scene indicates that he achieves this through marrying her ('Come along ... Mrs Thornhill'). Stanley Cavell argues that '*North by Northwest* derives from the

30   'I know – I look vaguely familiar.' Impersonation and masquerade – here as Thornhill meets Eve on the Twentieth Century Limited – is a recurring motif in *North by Northwest* (MGM, 1959).

genre of remarriage' – he compares it to the Cary Grant-Katharine Hepburn film *The Philadelphia Story* (1940) – 'which means to me that its subject is the legitimizing of marriage, as if the pair's adventures are trials of their suitability for that condition ... It is in any case the only one of Hitchcock's romantic thrillers in which the adventurous pair are actually shown to have married.'[64] (Cavell is mistaken on this point: Ashenden and Elsa are shown to have married at the end of *Secret Agent*. And the original ending of *The 39 Steps* referred to Hannay and Pamela getting married.)

North by Northwest fully mobilises the motif of role-playing and masquerade that is a characteristic of the spy thriller. Cavell, again, makes the point 'that *North by Northwest* is notable, even within the oeuvre of a director pervaded by images and thoughts of the theater and theatricality, for its obsession with the idea of acting'.[65] Most of Vandamm's scenes with Thornhill include references to acting: 'With such expert play acting, you make this very room a theatre', 'Has anyone ever told you that you overplay your various roles rather severely, Mr Kaplan?' and the reference to the Actors' Studio all drive the point home. In the scene immediately before Eve 'shoots' Thornhill at the Mount Rushmore Visitor Centre (the pistol is loaded with blanks) Vandamm even comments on the variety of roles that Thornhill (whom he believes to be Kaplan) has played in the course of the film: 'First you're the outraged Madison Avenue man who claims he's been mistaken for someone else. Then you play the fugitive from justice, supposedly trying to clear his name of a crime he knows he didn't commit. Now you play the peevish lover stung by jealousy and betrayal.' For his part Thornhill is initially insistent that he is not Kaplan but in the course of the film he gradually assumes the identity of the non-existent agent: he gains access to Kaplan's hotel room, tries on his clothers, answers his telephone, and on several occasions even uses his name. In the last act of the film Thornhill becomes Kaplan ('I'm going to have to ask you to go on being him for the next twenty-four hours') in order to see the decoy through to its end.

The casting of Cary Grant is crucial to the film's role-playing motif: this is another reason why it is difficult to imagine *North by Northwest* with James Stewart. Ernest Lehman confirmed in an interview that '*North by Northwest* was written more or less with Cary Grant in mind'.[66] Grant is said to have remarked that 'I play myself to perfection': there is always a sense that, whatever the role, Grant is always performing the part of 'Cary Grant'. Roger Thornhill might be seen as a variation on the comedy roles Grant had played in films such as *Bringing Up Baby* (1938) and *Monkey Business* (1952): the professional man whose familiar world is disrupted by chaotic forces beyond his control. *North by Northwest* takes every opportunity to draw attention to Grant's star presence: there are references to his looks ('I know – I look vaguely familiar. You feel you've seen me somewhere before') and at various points in the film bit-part players perform a double take when they see him: these include the man waiting to use the telephone booth at Grand Central Station and the lady patient in the adjoining room as Thornhill effects his escape from the hospital following his 'death'. The woman, initially fearing an intruder, shouts 'Stop!', then, after putting on her spectacles and seeing him properly, repeats 'Stop?' – this time as an invitation and plea. The self-referential aspects of Grant's performance are another reason why *North by Northwest* is sometimes seen as a parody rather than as a straight thriller.

Like *Saboteur*, the Hitchcock film to which it bears the closest resemblance, *North by Northwest* is defined by its Americanness – though *North by Northwest* is both more subtle and more profound in its representation of American society and politics than the earlier film. Richard H. Millington argues that 'the concept of an American "place" or "space" – America conceived as a particular ideological location or configuration, and exercising a shaping power on what happens within it – drives the action and generates the meanings of the film'.[67] This can be seen on several levels. On the most basic level *North by Northwest* is a travelogue across the United States. Indeed this was an aspect of the promotional discourse of the film: the 'Hitchcock Trailer' – one of two theatrical trailers alongside the more typical 'Thrill Trailer' – featured Hitchcock looking at a map of the United States and asking: 'Have you planned your vacation yet? ... My suggestion is a quiet little tour, say about two thousand miles! I have just made a motion picture, *North by Northwest*, to show you some of these delights, and the ideal place to start our holiday fun-trip is – New York!'[68] The idea that *North by Northwest* was a showcase for some of the most photogenic scenery in America – enhanced of course by its use of colour and VistaVision – featured in contemporary reviews, including Dilys Powell in the *Sunday Times*: 'The crimson-lined hotels, the trains full of lollers in armchairs, the empty, whistling ochre plains – in *North by Northwest* he has taken pleasure in filling the screen with the extravagance of America.'[69]

On another level *North by Northwest* belongs to a lineage of American cinema – other examples include Frank Capra's *It Happened One Night* (1934), Preston Sturges's *Sullivan's Travels* (1941), Dennis Hopper's *Easy Rider* (1969) and Ridley Scott's *Thelma and Louise* (1991) – that might be described as an American picaresque genre. These films are structured around journeys undertaken by their protagonists across parts of the United States that are as much journeys of self-discovery as travelogues. The picaresque genre – in which protagonists find themselves in unfamiliar surroundings where they meet a range of people from diverse social backgrounds – has often been a vehicle for the examination of American society: this ranges from the socially uplifting conclusion of *Sullivan's Travels* to the decidedly pessimistic tone of *Easy Rider* (advertised with the line: 'A man went looking for America and couldn't find it anywhere'). *North by Northwest* may be read as a journey of discovery: Roger Thornhill undergoes a series of trials which bring about his moral and ideological transformation from shallow advertising man (the first minute of the film sees him dictating to his secretary while on the go and stealing another couple's taxi by claiming 'I have a very sick woman here') to a mature and responsible citizen who puts the national interest before his own selfish instincts and in the process rediscovers his capacity for romantic love.[70]

In this reading the locations of *North by Northwest* are far more than just photogenic backgrounds: they are integral to the film's narrative and thematic structures. The first act of *North by Northwest* is set in New York – the bustling crowds and streets of the opening titles evoke the hectic pace of modern city life: tellingly Hitchcock's cameo is as a harassed commuter missing a bus – where Thornhill is fully at home, every inch the confident, self-assured urban professional. However, Thornhill's assurance is undermined when he is mistaken for the elusive George Kaplan by foreign agents and plunged into the 'chaos world' of political intrigue and murder. Robin Wood argues that the

31 Roger Thornhill (Cary Grant) is taken out of his urban comfort zone in *North by Northwest* (MGM, 1959).

purpose of the film's first act is 'a systematic stripping away of all the protective armour of modern city man on which Thornhill relies for his safety. In the midst of crowds, he becomes completely isolated.'[71] This all takes place against the background of New York landmarks such as the Plaza Hotel and the United Nations Building: extraordinary and improbable events occurring in familiar and supposedly safe surroundings is a characteristic Hitchcock motif. For the rest of the film Thornhill is displaced from his comfort zone and is placed in situations of extreme jeopardy: significantly these occur outside the urban milieu on the open prairies of the Midwest and the great stone edifices of Mount Rushmore. For once the set pieces are more than just set pieces but are related thematically to the narrative. The prairie sequence is not just a textbook example of building suspense and using the location to its fullest effect – Thornhill, exposed on the open prairie, has nowhere to hide when the crop-duster attacks – but also symbolises his displacement: the modern urban man, stripped of all protection, is more vulnerable here than at any other point in the film. As for the final act at Mount Rusmore, this may either be understood at face value as a symbol of American democracy or as an ironic comment on the nature of that democracy: 'I don't like the way Teddy Roosevelt's looking at me,' Thornill muses while observing the monument through a telescope. 'I think he's trying to tell me not to go through with this hare-brained scheme.'

North by Northwest is Hitchcock's most spectacular film: and nowhere it its spectacle better demonstrated than in the celebrated crop-duster sequence. This is (arguably) the best set piece in all of Hitchcock's work and one whose influence can be seen in other films, including the James Bond movie *From Russia With Love* (1963), Joseph Losey's *The Damned* (1963) and Alvin Rakoff's sub-Hitchcockian spy caper *Crossplot* (1969). Like the Albert Hall sequence in *The Man Who Knew Too Much*, the crop duster sequence is the focal point – structurally, formally and dramatically – of the film. It is a perfect example of Hitchcock's technique: a slow build-up of tension as Thornhill waits at the roadside for what seems like an eternity wondering if Kaplan will appear (the audience knows at this point that Kaplan does not exist and therefore expect a trap); a red-herring as a farmer dropped off by a truck waits on the other side of the highway: the two men eye each other suspiciusly but it turns out the other man is just waiting for a bus; the farmer's ominous parting comment ('Funny ... that plane's dustin' crops where there ain't no crops'); and the sudden eruption of violence as the plane attacks and Thornhill dodges a series of sweeps until the explosive climax as it crashes into a passing road tanker. The development of the sequence shows that Hitchcock stripped it down to the essentials by removing superfluous dialogue (in early script drafts the farmer explains the chemical composition of the crop spray to Thornhill: 'That dust ain't talcum powder, no siree. DDT, sulphur, benxinehexachloride ...') and privileging Thornhill's point of view. The shooting script includes shots from the pilot's viewpoint but Hitchcock removed these in story-boarding the sequence to stay with Thornhill.[72]

To an even greater extent than the remake of *The Man Who Knew Too Much*, *North by Northwest* exemplifies the process of 'genre upscaling' that occurred in American cinema during the 1950s.[73] Before *North by Northwest* most spy and espionage films were modestly budgeted programmers without major stars. The dominant mode of thriller during the 1950s was *film noir*: the persistence of the *noir* style was exemplified by such films as *The Asphalt Jungle* (1950), *The Big Heat* (1953), *Pickup on South Street* (1953), *The Big Combo* (1955) and *Kiss Me Deadly* (1955), though none of these was a spy film in the usual mould (Samuel Fuller's *Pickup on South Street* is the closest but even so the spy and espionage elements are not the main focus of the narrative). Paul Kerr has argued that *film noir* was the product of a set of industrial and aesthetic conditions in the 1940s and 1950s – including the B-movie and black-and-white cinemato-graphy as standard – and that it declined as a mode of film-making in the late 1950s as the double bill disappeared and colour became the norm.[74] *North by Northwest* was a world away from B-movie *noir* in both its production values and its visual style. Evidence of its influence in the transformation of the genre can be found in the emergence of the spy-adventure film as a major international production trend in the 1960s. As well as the James Bond films, beginning with *Dr No* in 1962, other 'Hitchcockian' films that followed in the wake of *North by Northwest* included a brace of sophisticated comedy-thrillers produced by Stanley Donen, *Charade* (1962) and *Arabesque* (1966), the former also starring Cary Grant, Basil Dearden's *Masquerade* (1965), and Philipe de Broca's *That Man from Rio* (*L'homme de Rio*, 1964), which featured several allusions to *North by Northwest* including the 'MacGuffin' hidden in an Amazon statuette. John Frankenheimer's exemplary conspiracy thriller *The Manchurian Candidate* (1962) – from the novel by Richard Condon – also exemplified genre upscaling even though it was shot in black-and-white: by the early 1960s this was a matter of artistic choice rather than economic necessity.

North by Northwest was a key film – perhaps *the* key film – in the history of spy cinema. It can be enjoyed as a supreme piece of entertainment ('a real *movie movie*') but it is also much more. Hitchcock's return to the spy formula in *North by Northwest* should be seen not just as a pastiche of the director's previous successes but also as using the framework of a genre film as a means of exploring the political and social anxieties of mid-twentieth century America. As James Monaco remarked: '*North by Northwest* ... described with a perspicuity we weren't to realize fully until a decade later, the political landscape against which the anxiety is set.'[75] To this extent it anticipated the paranoid conspiracy thrillers of the 1970s such as *The Parallax View* (1974), *Three Days of the Condor* (1975) and *Coma* (1978). *North by Northwest* had been conceived as 'the Hitchcock picture to end all Hitchcock pictures': in successfully combining the narrative pace and movement of the sensational thriller with the moral and ideological ambiguity of the existential thriller it might also be described as the spy movie to end all spy movies.

13

HITCHCOCK AND JAMES BOND

North by Northwest was a transitional film in the history of spy cinema. In Martin Rubin's history of the thriller in cinema, *North by Northwest* stands on the cusp of what he terms the genre's 'classical period', stretching from the original version of *The Man Who Knew Too Much* and Hitchcock's other British spy films until the late 1950s, and its 'modern period', beginning 'around 1960', when a combination of factors – including the break-up of the studio system, the relaxation of censorship and the increasing visibility of foreign, especially European, films – brought about a revitalisation of popular cinema 'that greatly enhanced the popularity of a genre, whether on a short-term basis (the spy film) or a long-term one (the police film, the horror film)'.[1] For Rubin, *North by Northwest* looks back to the classical period while anticipating certain features of the modern thriller:

> *North by Northwest* is an obvious successor to similarly plotted pre-cold war spy thrillers such as *The 39 Steps* and *Saboteur*. It also anticipates in some ways (such as its apolitical villain and extravagant action scenes) the upcoming series of James Bond films and, in other ways (such as the US intelligence establishment's initially callous disregard for the safety of the hero), the slightly later cycle of pessimistic anti-Bond films.[2]

Kristin Thompson and David Bordwell also link *North by Northwest* and the Bond movies in the context of what they term the 'upscaling' of the spy genre:

> The effect of amplifying B-film material was perhaps most visible in the rise of the big-budget espionage film. Hitchcock's elegant *North by Northwest* (1959) featured an innocent bystander caught up in a spy ring, but the real catalyst for genre upscaling was Ian Fleming's fictional British agent James Bond. After two screen adaptations of the novels, 007 became a proven commodity with the phenomenally profitable *Goldfinger* (1964).[3]

It was during the 1960s that the spy film became a major production trend: in particular this period saw the emergence of the sensational spy action-adventure film for which the catalyst was undoubtedly the success of the James Bond films. Yet the Bond films were themselves influenced to a very considerable extent by *North by Northwest* which – with its glossy visual style, extravagant action set pieces, high-living consumer lifestyle trappings, and its debonair hero, sexually assertive heroine and suave villain – has sometimes been seen as a prototype of the Bonds. James Naremore, for example, contends that *North by Northwest* 'predicts certain features of the sleekly commodified James Bond movies that followed in its wake'.[4]

Hitchcock was involved, albeit briefly and tangentially, in the origin of the Bond film series. Ian Fleming published his first Bond novel, *Casino Royale*, in 1953, and thereafter wrote a further eleven novels and two volumes of short stories until his death in 1964.[5] From the outset Fleming tried to interest film and television producers in the books though without any success other than a live studio dramatisation of *Casino Royale* by the American CBS network in 1954. *Casino Royale* had a connection of sorts to Hitchcock in so far as Charles Bennett was one of two writers credited with adapting it for television (the other was Antony Ellis), while Peter Lorre played the villain Le Chiffre alongside American actor Barry Nelson as Bond and Linda Christian as heroine Valerie Mathis. But Fleming's efforts to sell the film rights to James Bond came to nothing. Alexander Korda read a galley proof of *Live and Let Die* in 1954: 'I really could not put it down until I had finished it,' he told Fleming, though he felt that it would not transfer well to the screen as 'the best stories for films are always the stories that are written specially for films'.[6] The Rank Organisation briefly held an option on *Moonraker*, and American actor John Payne was interested in the same property. In the late 1950s Hitchcock's former Gaumont-British colleague Victor Saville also considered the books. Saville had produced two films of Micky Spillane's Mike Hammer private-eye stories – *I, the Jury* (1953) and *Kiss Me Deadly* (1955) – and saw Bond as a possible successor:

> A few years later, I went to United Artists and proposed buying *Dr No*, the first [sic] James Bond book … [My] proposal was turned down by all except one of the executives, Max Youngstein, who liked the proposition. The fact that the James Bond pictures, a few years later, became a bonanza for United Artists is neither here nor there, for I am sure I would not have made them as well as the producers of the series – indeed, not in the same class.[7]

The British-based American producer Cubby Broccoli was also interested in the books but his then-partner in Warwick Pictures, Irving Allen, was less keen. Richard Maibaum testified that 'Cubby gave me two of the James Bond books to read. I read them and liked them enormously.' Nevertheless Maibaum felt that it would not have been possible to make the Bond films in the 1950s 'because with the censorship of pictures that existed then, you couldn't have even the minimal sex and violence that we eventually put into the pictures'.[8]

The closest that Bond came to the screen before 1962 was a project titled *James Bond of the Secret Service* that producer Kevin McClory announced in the trade press in October 1959.[9] McClory, an Irishman who had worked as foreign location manager for Mike Todd's epic *Around the World in 80 Days* (1956) and had directed one film, a whimsical fable titled *The Boy and the Bridge* (1959), had met Fleming through their mutual friend (and McClory's business partner) Ivar Bryce. McClory persuaded Fleming that the best way to bring Bond to the screen would be through an original screenplay. Fleming therefore collaborated with McClory and British screenwriter Jack Whittingham on a treatment that was to be produced by McClory's Xanadu Productions. It was intended to shoot the film on location in the Bahamas both for the scenic spectacle it offered and to take advantage of the Eady Levy, a subsidy available to the producers of films shot either in Britain or in British territories. Bryce suggested Hitchcock as their director after seeing *North by Northwest* while en route from London to New York on the liner *Queen Mary* in September 1959. He wrote to Fleming: 'It's the most terrific Bond-style thriller – almost plagiarising – and superb. You must manage to see it somehow ... It is exactly the picture we are trying to make.'[10]

Hitchcock and Fleming were acquainted and had a mutual friend in Eric Ambler, who had married Hitchcock's secretary Joan Harrison in 1958. 'I know Hitchcock slightly. And he has always been interested in the Bond saga,' Fleming told Bryce.[11] They shared a favourite hotel – the St Regis in New York – and, as we have seen, the character of Scott ffolliott in *Foreign Correspondent* was originally based on Fleming.[12] Hitchcock expressed an interest in the Bond project, which apparently he saw as a potential vehicle for James Stewart.[13] In the event of course the Hitchcock-directed Bond picture did not happen. There were several reasons for this. Fleming and his colleagues recognised the 'name' value that Hitchcock would have brought but at the same time were wary of handing control of their baby over to him, as Hitchcock would have expected a free hand to develop the film as he liked. And it also soon became apparent that they could not afford Hitchcock's services as producer and director. Xanadu Productions had a budget of only $800,000 in contrast to the $4.3 million that MGM had invested in *North by Northwest*. Hitchcock's fee alone would have accounted for a third of their budget. Fleming's interest in *James Bond of the Secret Service* waned as the financial and logistical problems involved in making the film mounted:

32 The celebrated crop-dusting aeroplane attack set piece in *North by Northwest* (MGM, 1959).

when the project was aborted he used some of the story material, including the criminal organisation known as SPECTRE (Special Executive for Counter-Intelligence, Terrorism, Revenge and Extortion), for his next Bond novel, *Thunderball*. Evidently, however, he had not forgotten Hitchcock, as *Thunderball* includes a reference to *North by Northwest* ('Rather a bind missing *North by North-West* at the Odeon. But one would catch up with it at Southampton.'[14]) McClory and Whittingham subsequently sued Fleming at the High Court in London, claiming that he had failed to acknowledge their contribution to the origin of *Thunderball*: the court found in the plaintiffs' favour and later editions of the novel were obliged to state that it was 'based on a screen treatment by Ian Fleming, Jack Whittingham and Kevin McClory'.[15]

James Bond was eventually brought to the screen by Broccoli and Harry Saltzman who formed Eon Productions to produce a series of films in Britain with financing from United Artists. In July 1961 the British trade press reported that 'Saltzman's project with Albert Broccoli to film the Ian Fleming spy-thriller books is maturing nicely. They have clinched a deal with United Artists for 100 per cent financial backing and distribution of seven stories which will be filmed here and on foreign locations.'[16] The production of the Bond films needs to be seen in the context of the 'Hollywood England' trend of the 1960s. In 1961 United Artists had opened a production office in London under George H. Ornstein: the Bond deal was part of UA's British production strategy that

33   Imitation is the sincerest form of flattery: James Bond (Sean Connery) evades an antagonistic helicopter in *From Russia With Love* (United Artists/Eon Productions, 1963).

also included *Tom Jones* (1963), director Tony Richardson's and writer John Osborne's adaptation of Henry Fielding's novel, and the Beatles films *A Hard Day's Night* (1964) and *Help!* (1965). *Thunderball* was to have been the first Bond film but in the event Broccoli and Saltzman, along with director Terence Young and writer Richard Maibaum, went with *Dr No* instead. *Dr No* was a quite modestly budgeted film at $950,000 (£392,000) but its commercial success ensured the future of what would become the longest-running continuous film series in cinema history.[17]

   The Bond films were the box-office phenomenon of the 1960s. The total worldwide rentals for the first six films were $15.7 million for *Dr No* (1962), $29.4 million for *From Russia With Love* (1963), $49.6 million for *Goldfinger* (1964), $56.4 million for *Thunderball* (1965), $44 million for *You Only Live Twice* (1967) and $24 million for *On Her Majesty's Secret Service* (1969).[18] The budgets of the films increased in ratio to their success: $1.9 million for *From Russia With Love*, $3 million for *Goldfinger*, $5 million for *Thunderball*, reaching a peak of $9 million for *You Only Live Twice*.[19] The Bond series was the example *par excellence* of the upscaling of genre. As Terence Young, who directed *Dr No*, *From Russia With Love* and *Thunderball*, remarked of the first film: 'The original Ian Fleming story was diabolically childish, something straight out of a Grade B thriller ... The only way I thought we could do a Bond film was to heat it up, give it a sense of humour, to make it as cynical as possible.'[20] The production strategy of the Bond films was to broaden the character's appeal by introducing more humour (Bond's witty one-liners after dispatching another villain are not to be found in the books, for example) and by aligning Bond with the emergence of the 'permissive society' of the 1960s (hence Bond's sexual exploits and conquests in the films are more numerous than in the books). The films also sidelined the Cold War background of Fleming's novels with their Soviet antagonists in favour of using the SPECTRE formula of *Thunderball*: SPECTRE becomes Bond's enemy in all but one (*Goldfinger*) of the Bond films of the 1960s. This has been understood as a means of detaching the films from the real geopolitical and ideological context of the Cold War and positioning them even more emphatically than the books as fantasy adventures.[21]

The reception of the early Bond movies reflected the reception discourse of *North by Northwest* in so far as, like Hitchcock's film, they were understood as parodies of the thriller rather than as straight examples of the genre. R. H. 'Josh' Billings of the British trade journal *Kine Weekly* was evidently unsure how to categorise *Dr No*: he settled for 'a bizarre comedy melodrama'.[22] (This recalls the same journal's description of *The 39 Steps* as a 'spectacular espionage comedy melodrama'.) Dilys Powell thought that *Dr No* 'has the air of knowing exactly what it is up to, and that has not been common in British thrillers since the day when Hitchcock took himself off to America. The jokes (one of them, a beauty, has been buzzing round London all the week) are tossed away with exactly the right carelessness.'[23] John Coleman of the *New Statesman* felt that the injection of humour into the snobbery-with-violence world of Ian Fleming was the key to the success of the films:

> These screen doings-over of the Fleming books certainly have their small hints of real nastiness. But the interesting thing is that what has forcibly to become explicit on the screen is a hundred times milder than the horrible imaginings stimulated by Mr Fleming's elliptic pages: better yet it tends to come out funny. Terence Young and his screenwriter, Richard Maibaum, give Bond some nice laconic cracks to round off the surreal events of his working day.[24]

Penelope Houston, the editor of *Sight and Sound*, thought that the third film, *Goldfinger*, 'perfects the formula' and 'assumes a mood of good-humoured complicity with the audience' that was the key to its popular appeal.[25]

Not all critics necessarily 'got' the humour of the Bond movies. Nina Hibbin of the *Daily Worker* – the official mouthpiece of the Communist Party of Great Britain – called *Dr No* 'a brutalised film': 'It doesn't wallow, like horror films do, in blood and torture and slow death. It goes a stage further – by asking you to take such things for granted, playing for a laugh whenever the sardonic

Mr Bond makes a new joke.'[26] The *Monthly Film Bulletin* did not object to the film on ideological grounds but simply thought it was not very good: 'Dr No misses the genuine, sadistic, sybaritic relish attributed to Fleming's novels, and the narrative invention of even second-rate Hitchcock.'[27] However, the most complete dismissal of the Bond movies came from Robin Wood in *Hitchcock's Films*, where he compared them unfavourably with *North by Northwest*: 'If I fail to be entertained by *Goldfinger*, it is because there is nothing there to engage the attention; the result is a nonentity, consequently tedious. The essential triviality of the James Bond films ... sets off perfectly, by contrast, the depth, the charm, the integrity of Hitchcock's film.'[28]

For Wood the difference in quality between *North by Northwest* and the Bond movies was clear: he averred that Hitchcock's film was 'thematically organic' whereas '*Goldfinger* is a collection of bits, carefully calculated with both eyes on the box office, put end to end with no deeper necessity for what happens next than mere plot'.[29] This view rehearses a familiar distinction between the films of an *auteur* director on the one hand, where the form and structure of the film is attributed to the director's overall control, and genre films on the other, which are seen as formulaic, derivative, film-making by numbers. Wood develops this argument through a comparison of the prairie sequence in *North by Northwest* and the similar sequence in *From Russia With Love* where Bond is attacked by a helicopter:

> Compare, first, the crop-dusting sequence in *North by Northwest* with the helicopter attack in *From Russia With Love* (there is a fairly clear relationship between the two) ... From a purely technical viewpoint (if such a thing exists) the Hitchcock sequence is clearly incomparably superior; it is prepared with so much more finesse, shot with so much more care, every shot perfectly judged in relation to the build-up of the sequence ... In comparison, the Bond sequence is messy and unorganised, the *mise-en-scène* purely opportunistic. But there is far more in question here than the ability to construct a 'suspense' sequence: the suspense itself in *North by Northwest* is of a different order. The suspense in the Bond sequence is meaningless: the attack is just an attack, it has no place in any significant development, there is no reason apart from plot – no *thematic* reason – for it to happen to Bond then or to happen in the way it does ... In *North by Northwest* the crop-dusting sequence has essential relevance to the film's development. The complacent, self-confident Cary Grant character is shown here exposed in open country, away from the false security of office and cocktail-bar, exposed to the menacing and the unpredictable. The man who behaved earlier as if nobody mattered except himself, is here reduced to running for his life, scurrying for cover like a terrified rabbit ... The sequence marks a crucial stage in the evolution of the character and his relationships, and through that, of the themes of the whole film.[30]

It would be fair to say that Hitchcock's sequence is superior in technique and execution: in particular the camera in *From Russia With Love* crosses the line so that that the direction of the helicopter is inconsistent whereas in *North by Northwest* Hitchcock carefully maintains continuity in direction on each pass made by the airplane. In addition Hitchcock remains with Thornhill's point of view throughout the sequence: we see the airplane from his perspective but there are no aerial shots of Thornhill from the airplane. In contrast *From Russia With Love* includes point-of-view shots from the pilots' perspective – indeed the sequence opens with an aerial shot from the helicopter – and close-ups of the pilots themselves.[31]

To dismiss the Bond films as entirely derivative and inferior imitations of Hitchcock, however, is limiting and problematic. For one thing the direction and *mise-en-scène* of the Bond films, while not always consistent, are not necessarily as bad as Wood and other critics suggest. *From Russia With Love* is perhaps the most 'Hitchcockian' of all the Bond movies: its highlights include a highly atmospheric pre-title sequence as assassin Red Grant stalks 'Bond' through moonlit formal gardens – Terence Young modelled it on Alain Resnais's *Last Year at Marienbad* (1961) – and a sequence in the San Sofia Mosque in Istanbul that recalls Hitchcock's habit of using famous landmarks as atmospheric background. Other Bond films feature colour motifs and the kind of visual symbolism that Hitchcock also often employed: the gold motif of *Goldfinger* (directed by Guy Hamilton) is fairly obvious, while the motif of carnations than runs throughout *On Her Majesty's Secret Service* (directed by Peter Hunt) is a more discreet example. This sort of symbolism attracts critical plaudits for Hitchcock in *Topaz* but it has passed unnoticed in the Bond film where the carnations map the course of Bond and Tracy's relationship and anticipate her death at the end of the film.[32]

Wood's distinction between the 'organic' nature of *North by Northwest* and the Bond film as 'a collection of bits' also downplays the similarities between the films in terms of their narrative construction. Hitchcock mapped out the structure of his films around a series of stand-out moments or set pieces: in this sense his approach to narrative was never quite as organic as Wood seems to believe. Richard Maibaum, an uncredited contributor to *Foreign Correspondent*, was involved in writing thirteen Bond pictures between *Dr No* and *Licence To Kill* (1989). Maibaum explained how Hitchcock's formula influenced the Bond films:

> Hitchcock once said to me, 'If I have 13 "bumps" I know I have a picture.' By 'bumps', he meant, of course, shocks, highpoints, thrills, whatever you choose to

call them. From the beginning ... Mr Broccoli and Mr Saltzman, the producers, and myself have not been content with 13 'bumps'. We aim for 39. Our objective has been to make every foot of film pay off in terms of exciting entertainment.[33]

It may or may not have been coincidental that Maibaum picked a number associated with one of Hitchcock's spy films: nevertheless the point reinforces the association between Hitchcock and the Bond movies. Hitchcock's films were always notable for their suspense set pieces: the Albert Hall sequence in *The Man Who Knew Too Much*, the assassination in the rain in *Foreign Correspondent*, the Statue of Liberty climax in *Saboteur*, the crop-duster sequence in *North by Northwest* and the same film's climax on Mount Rushmore. Similarly the most memorable moments of the Bond movies tend to be their action set pieces and spectacular stunts: the train-compartment fight in *From Russia With Love*, the car chase in *Goldfinger*, the underwater battle in *Thunderball*, the ski chase in *On Her Majesty's Secret Service* and the breathtaking ski-parachute jump at the beginning of *The Spy Who Loved Me* (1977).

There are moments throughout the Bond series that seem – whether consciously or not – to refer directly to Hitchcock's films. The similarities between the crop-duster in *North by Northwest* and the helicopter attack on Bond in *From Russia With Love* is the most obvious but there are many others. These include the assassin's pistol pointing through the curtains in the British version of *The Man Who Knew Too Much* (repeated in the 'Kiss Kiss' club scene in *Thunderball*), the fake funeral at the beginning of *Secret Agent* (the pre-title sequence of *Thunderball* where Bond attends the funeral of a 'dead' man and again in Bond's own fake death and burial in *You Only Live Twice*), the sudden disappearance of the car in *Foreign Correspondent* (repeated almost shot-for-shot in the car chase in *The Man With the Golden Gun*, 1974), the red flash across the screen as Dr Murchison turns the gun on himself in *Spellbound* (the pre-title sequence of *Casino Royale*, 2006), the safe-cracking sequence in *Marnie* (*You Only Live Twice*), and the fireworks that signify sexual congress in *To Catch A Thief* (*Skyfall*, 2012). *Live and Let Die* (1973) opens with an assassination at the United Nations (*North by Northwest*) and the climax of *A View To A Kill* (1985) takes place on the Golden Gate Bridge in San Francisco (the Statue of Liberty in *Saboteur* and Mount Rushmore in *North by Northwest*). And *Tomorrow Never Dies* (1997) references *The 39 Steps* as Bond is handcuffed to Chinese agent Wai Lin: the difference is that, whereas in Hitchcock's film the situation is used to generate sexual tension (the handcuffed couple have to spend the night together at the inn), in the Bond film it becomes more of a logistical exercise (how to ride a motorcycle while cuffed together).

The popular success of the Bond films was the catalyst for the spy craze of the 1960s. The spy film became a major production trend in American, British, French, Italian and West German cinemas: the peak came between 1965 and 1967 when around two dozen spy movies were released each year. There was, inevitably, a glut of Bond imitations and spoofs. James Coburn starred as an American Bond clone Derek Flint in two films for Twentieth Century-Fox, *Our Man Flint* (1966) and *In Like Flint* (1967), and Dean Martin sleep-walked his way through four films for Columbia Pictures as girl-chasing playboy Matt Helm, *The Silencers* (1966), *Murderer's Row* (1967), *The Ambushers* (1967) and *The Wrecking Crew* (1968), which refashioned Donald Hamilton's noirish thrillers into James Bond-lite. In Britain, the producer-director team of Betty Box and Ralph Thomas offered two modernised Bulldog Drummond thrillers, *Deadlier Than the Male* (1966) and *Some Girls Do* (1969), starring Richard Johnson, while there were also one-off outings for Rod Taylor as John Gardner's Boysie Oakes (*The Liquidator*, 1965) and David Niven as James Leasor's Jason Love (*Where the Spies Are*, 1965). Niven also starred as James Bond himself in Charles K. Feldman's production of *Casino Royale* (1967), an extravagant spoof of the Bond films based on the one Ian Fleming title for which Broccoli and Saltzman did not hold the rights. And these films were just the tip of an iceberg represented by more-or-less forgettable fare including *Licensed to Kill* (1965) *Where the Bullets Fly* (1966), *Agent for H.A.R.M.* (1966), *Assignment K* (1968), *Hammerhead* (1968), *Crossplot* (1969) and *Number One of the Secret Service* (1970). Even a critics' director such as Joseph Losey jumped on the spy bandwagon with *Modesty Blaise* (1966), an exercise in high camp based on the comic-strip by Peter O'Donnell.

The spy-adventure genre also proliferated on television: the small screen was flooded with secret agent series including *Danger Man* (1960–6) and *The Avengers* (1961–9) in Britain – both predated the Bond movies but their content and style changed in response to the success of the films – and *The Man From U.N.C.L.E* (1964–7), *Get Smart* (1965–70), *I Spy* (1965–8) and *Mission: Impossible* (1966–73) in the United States. The publicity material for *The Avengers* acknowledged the series' debts to Hitchcock and Bond: 'The programme was designed as a one-hour thriller series with a tongue-in-cheek slant, combining toughness with humour and sophistication in the style made popular by the films of Alfred Hitchcock and the James Bond novels of Ian Fleming.'[34] Fleming himself was involved in the genesis of *The Man From U.N.C.L.E.*, which starred Robert Vaughan as the Bond-like secret agent Napoleon Solo and David McCallum as his Russian sidekick Ilya Kuryakin, while a link to *North by Northwest* was provided by the presence of Leo G. Carroll who reprised his role as

'The Professor' in all but name as spy chief Mr Waverly.[35] *The Man From U.N.C.L.E.* was popular enough that eight films compiled from two-part television episodes were released as theatrical features in Britain and Europe.[36]

It is an indication of the extent to which the Bond films and their various imitators had become part of the mainstream of popular film culture by the middle of the decade that Hitchcock even considered (briefly) contributing to the cycle. In 1964, following completion of *Marnie*, he spent some time working on a treatment for a film of John Buchan's *The Three Hostages*. Buchan had always been one of Hitchcock's favourite authors but the surviving script materials suggest that he intended to abandon Buchan's story entirely (a page with the heading 'The Three Hostages: Good things in the book to be preserved' is otherwise entirely blank!) and update the story to the present day with Richard Hannay tasked by the President of the United States with rescuing the kidnapped children of three influential men. One scene features a meeting between Hannay and villain Dominic Medina:

> *Hannay:* I say, old boy, what do you know about the three hostages?
>
> *Medina:* Are you talking about the blonde young son of the automobile tycoon, the teenage boy of the shipping magnate, and Senator Harvey Farter's infant boy, all of whom were kidnapped at precisely 7.02 pm yesterday and are being held for the purpose of immobilizing the FBI, Interpol, the Secret Service and the Peace Corps, while a nefarious gang of international thieves – whom we refer to as 'S.W.I.S.H.' – loot the entire world?
>
> *Hannay:* Yes – yes!
>
> *Medina:* Haven't heard a thing about it, old fellow![37]

This is so parodic that it might well have been written in jest: references to Hannay wearing a fur waist band while under the effects of hypnosis would also seem to point in this direction. Other materials suggest that *The Three Hostages* was seen as an international adventure in the style of the Bond films. Alma Hitchcock's notes for the same project include a number of Bond-style set pieces including a spectacular stunt in New York harbour ('A heavy, trying to escape, parachutes from plane and drops onto deck of *Queen Elizabeth* as she sails under New Bridge'), rescuing one of the hostages from an inaccessible mountain lair ('Background of Convent high in mountains on Grecian Island') and a jungle man hunt in the style of *The Most Dangerous Game* ('Tiger Hunt – Men stalking each other – not tiger').[38] It is no doubt entirely coincidental that scenes similar to these later cropped up in the Bond films: May Day parachuting from the Eiffel Tower and landing on a boat on the River Seine in *A View to A Kill*, the villain's hide-out in an abandoned Greek monastery in

For Your Eyes Only (1981), and Kamal Khan stalking Bond through the jungle in *Octopussy* (1983). In the event *The Three Hostages* remained (perhaps fortunately) one of Hitchcock's unrealised projects. Hitchcock explained: 'The reason I dropped the project is that I feel you cannot put hypnotism on the screen and expect it to hold water. It is a condition too remote from the audience's own experiences.'[39] Hitchcock's papers also reveal that there were problems in acquiring the rights from the John Buchan estate, who wanted more than the £5,000 Hitchcock was prepared to offer.[40]

An alternative to the Bond films was represented in the cycle of more realist spy films during the 1960s. These films – sometimes labelled the 'anti-Bond' cycle as they distanced themselves from the sensationalism and parodic excess of the Bond films and their imitators – exemplified the existential lineage of the spy thriller: they were less numerous but tended to fare better with critics for their ideological ambivalence and psychological realism. The emergence of the 'anti-Bond' cycle was represented by two British films of 1965: *The Spy Who Came in from the Cold*, directed by American Martin Ritt from the novel by John le Carré and starring Richard Burton as disillusioned former MI6 agent Alec Leamas, and *The Ipcress File*, directed by Canadian Sidney J. Furie from the novel by Len Deighton and starring Michael Caine as the cynical Cockney spy Harry Palmer (the character is nameless in the novel). *The Ipcress File* prompted two sequels, *Funeral in Berlin* (1966) and *Billion Dollar Brain* (1967), while a further two John le Carré adaptations, *The Deadly Affair* (1966) and *The Looking Glass War* (1969), while not direct sequels, shared the same fictional universe as *The Spy Who Came in from the Cold*. Harry Saltzman, co-producer of the Bond films, also produced the Len Deighton adaptations, while others who crossed over between Bond and the 'anti-Bond' films included director Guy Hamilton (*Goldfinger* and *Funeral in Berlin*) and screenwriter Paul Dehn (*Goldfinger*, *The Spy Who Came in from the Cold* and *The Deadly Affair*). Other examples of the realist spy film included *The Quiller Memorandum* (1966), adapted by Harold Pinter from a novel by Adam Hall and directed by Michael Anderson, and *The Kremlin Letter* (1970), directed by John Huston from the novel by Noel Behn.

Hitchcock saw – and liked – *The Spy Who Came in from the Cold*: he remarked that 'there was a lot of feeling of authenticity in so far as the individual episodes were concerned ... What I liked about it was that on the technical level and in terms of the nature of the characters and what not, they seemed to have more of a ring of truth than [the] James Bond type of thing.' At the same time, though, he felt that the film's plot 'was a most convoluted story ... that part of it was implausible to me and overdone'.[41] Hitchcock's return to the spy film in the 1960s with *Torn Curtain* and *Topaz* saw him attempting to steer a middle ground between the exotic fantasy of James Bond on the one hand and the overly complex plotting and pervading cynicism of *The Spy Who Came in from the Cold* on the other. However, the critical (and in the case of *Topaz* also the commercial) failure of these two films was seen at the time as evidence that Hitchcock, now in his fifth decade as a film-maker, was losing his touch. While it would be fair to say that neither of these films rank among Hitchcock's best – indeed for some critics they are among his worst – they nevertheless demand attention as different, if flawed, variations on the spy formula which Hitchcock had developed over the previous three decades.

14

HITCHCOCK'S COLD WAR: *TORN CURTAIN* (1966)

Hitchcock's decision to return to the spy film with *Torn Cutain* should be understood in two contexts. On one level it was a safe choice of subject following the relative disappointment of *The Birds* (1963) and *Marnie* (1964) – two ambitious films which had both experienced what can at best be described as a mixed reception from critics and public alike. To this extent it can be seen as an instance of Hitchcock – as he often put it – 'running for cover'.[1] And on another level it can be seen as Hitchcock's response to the spy craze of the 1960s and especially the popular success of the James Bond films. Indeed *Torn Curtain* was conceived quite explicitly as a more realist alternative to the excesses of the Bond films. As Hitchcock explained in a letter to François Truffaut:

> I came upon the thought in this way: in realizing that James Bond and the imitators of James Bond were more or less making my wild adventure films, such as *North by Northwest*, wilder than ever, I felt that I should not try and 'go one better'. I thought I would return to the adventure film, which would give us the opportunity for some human emotions in situations that were not too bizarre. In some respects it might have the feeling of *Notorious*, except that I have given it a little more movement than *Notorious* had.[2]

Hitchcock saw *Torn Curtain* as a love story in which the lovers are forced apart by political circumstances – hence the comparison to *Notorious*. There is some anecdotal evidence that he tried to persuade Cary Grant to star in the film – again linking it to *Notorious* – though Grant had decided to retire from the screen following *Walk, Don't Run* (1966).[3]

To some extent the production history of *Torn Curtain* mirrors *North by Northwest* – an original screenplay fleshed out from the germ of an idea, major stars, colourful locations and a carefully orchestrated promotional strategy to prepare the public for a characteristically 'Hitchcockian' piece of entertainment – except that on this occasion the process was less serendipitous and the outcome rather less successful. Hitchcock was now based at Universal Pictures, where he had moved following *Psycho* in a deal again negotiated by his agent Lew Wasserman. Hitchcock's recruitment needs to be understood in the context of the take-over of Universal by the Music Corporation of America (MCA) in the early 1960s. This was the start of a process of institutional and economic restructuring within the US film industry that as the 1960s progressed saw most of the studios being bought by large conglomerates whose primary interests were not in the entertainment business: Paramount by mining giant Gulf & Western (1966), United Artists by insurance and car rental agency Transamerica Corporation (1967), Warner Bros. by Kenney National Services (1969), whose main business was in car rental and parking lots, and MGM by property tycoon Kirk Kerkorian (1969). Wasserman was president of MCA and it was his initiative to acquire Universal and then to sign MCA's clients to the studio.[4] Hitchcock – obviously a prime asset – moved his offices to Universal in 1962 (he had already shot *Psycho* – his last film for Paramount – on the Universal backlot). Hitchcock surrendered some of the autonomy he had known at Paramount – in particular Universal imposed more conditions on budgets and casts – in return for an increased salary ($500,000 per film as producer and director) and a large block of stock that in effect made him a part-owner of the studio.[5]

The origin of *Torn Curtain* is to be found in an 'untitled original story subject' which Hitchcock registered with the Writers Guild of America in November 1964:

This is the problem of the woman who is associated, either by marriage or engagement, to a defector.

In the case of the married woman, there is very little question that she sides with her husband. We have, for example, the case of Burgess and MacLean, where Mrs MacLean eventually followed her husband behind the Iron Curtain, and obviously Mrs MacLean had no other loyalties.

What would be the attitude of a young woman, perhaps in love with, or engaged to, a scientist who could be a defector.[6]

Hitchcock was fascinated by the cases of Guy Burgess and Donald Maclean, the two British Intelligence officers who had defected to the Soviet Union in 1951. Burgess and Maclean were members of the so-called 'Cambridge spy ring', upper-class Communist sympathisers recruited as double agents while at university in the 1930s. Unlike Burgess, an alcoholic homosexual who by all accounts was unhappy in his new life behind the Iron Curtain and longed to return to England, Maclean was joined in Moscow by his wife Melinda and their daughter. Hitchcock's treatment posited that the wife or girlfriend of a defector would follow him behind the Iron Curtain only to discover that he is not a defector at all but a double agent and that by following him she has placed his and her own life in danger: 'This type of story is an emotional, psychological one, expressed in terms of action and movement and, naturally, one that would give me the opportunity to indulge in the customary Hitchcock suspense.'[7]

Hitchcock initially wanted the Russian expatriate Vladimir Nabokov to collaborate in writing the film, but when the author of *Lolita* proved unavailable he turned instead to the Irish-born novelist Brian Moore, whose first novel, *The Lonely Passion of Judith Hearne*, had been much admired. Moore was hired specifically for his ability to write female characters: at this point it was intended that the film, like *Notorious*, would be told largely from the woman's point of view. He also had screenwriting experience, having adapted *The Luck of Ginger Coffey* (1964) from his own novel. Moore's approach, like Hitchcock's, was to block out the structure of the film and to work on characterisation later: the first script materials are not the usual synoptic narrative treatments but a series of typed index cards describing scenes with titles such as 'Bristol Hotel and Bar Ballroom', 'Lost in Warsaw' and 'Theatre Scene'. Moore focused on Julie, the English fiancée of an American scientist called Grant, who defects to Warsaw. Julie's father is an ex-trade unionist who is now a government minister – a Labour government had been elected in Britain in 1964 under Harold Wilson – and Moore uses the character to express some distinctly anti-American sentiments: 'What the bloody hell are you up to my girl? You're all over the front pages here and in the States. You and that Yankee boyfriend of yours. I told you what would happen if you went around with Yanks. You get out of there, do you hear? Bloody traitor that fellow.'[8]

From the outset Hitchcock wanted to include a scene of a messy killing: this was conceived as an antidote to the unrealistically 'clean' deaths in the James Bond films that would see villains dispatched in all sorts of ingenious ways – usually with a humorous quip from Bond. Hence in *Goldfinger* an assailant is electrocuted in a bath ('Shocking – positively shocking!') and in *Thunderball* a heavy is speared through the chest with a harpoon gun ('I think he got the point'). In contrast Hitchcock wanted a scene that not only highlighted the sordid reality of murder but that would also show just how difficult it is to kill someone. One of Moore's cards describes a scene inside a Warsaw farmhouse where Grant comes face to face with a security officer who has followed him to a meeting with a contact in the Polish underground:

Grant knows he must kill Gromek. He picks up a heavy frying pan and bashes him on the head. Gromek falls. The farm woman enters with vodka and glasses ... Gromek, still smiling bizarrely, heaves himself up and makes for the door. Grant fells him. Gromek gets up. The dog jumps around, a nuisance barking. Cut to the taxi driver in the yard. He hears the barks.

Gromek opens his mouth as if to yell. The woman picks up a knife, stabs him in the throat. The blade breaks in his throat. Gurgling, unable to speak because his vocal chords have been cut, the unkillable Gromek moves like Rasputin towards the door. Grant hits him again. He falls, but rises, still living, still struggling.

The old woman suddenly opens the oven door and turns on all the gas taps. With a tremendous effort she and Grant pull Gromek across the floor and hold him in the oven until he expires.[9]

Hence the most famous scene in *Torn Curtain* was present from the outset: this scene would remain more or less unchanged from the initial outline to the finished film except for the omission of the dog and stabbing Gromek in the chest rather than the throat.

Double Agent – as *Torn Curtain* was initially known – took shape through the spring and summer of 1965. There were several changes. The location was changed from Poland to East Germany. The male protagonist became Professor Michael Armstrong ('A head-strong American nuclear scientist'). His fiancée Sarah also became a scientist and daughter of a US Senator rather than a British politician. Moore added significant roles for an East German security chief, Gerhard ('Tall, stout, cigar-smoking. The Chancellor Erhard type of German'), and a Polish countess ('A relic of capitalism, stranded in communist East Germany') who helps Armstrong during his escape.[10] The early drafts of *Double Agent* demonstrate a strong political flavour – and not one that was always necessarily favourable towards America. Armstrong is greeted upon his arrival at Karl Marx University in Leipzig, for example, by demonstrators waving banners declaring 'Remember Hiroshima' and 'Yankee scientist – go home'.[11] These references serve as a reminder that the production of the film coincided with the emergence of student-led protest movements in the West, including the growing support for the Campaign for Nuclear Disarmament (CND) and the early stirrings of opposition to US foreign policy in Southeast Asia. Hitchcock – who had met informally with US Secretary of State Dean Rusk early during preparation of the film – was evidently concerned to tone down the anti-American sentiment: 'Would Michael go so far as to use the phrase in his proposed speech " – our American warmongers – "? ... It seems to me that he talking a bit too much like a communist.'[12]

With the script under way, attention turned to the casting of the film. Paul Newman and Julie Andrews had emerged as front runners from a fairly early stage. Hitchcock was not entirely happy with either but seems to have been persuaded by the studio. He confided in Truffaut: '[After] having had comparatively lesser known stars in the last three pictures' – this presumably did not include Sean Connery who starred in *Marnie* between assignments as James Bond – 'I have now consented to please the whim of the "front office" and use two well known players.' 'But,' he conceded, 'that's the way the business is today. Names are wanted. There is such a shortage that these "cattle" are demanding astronomical figures.'[13] It is an indication of the inflation of star salaries in the 1960s that Newman and Andrews were each guaranteed $750,000, which accounted for nearly three-fifths of the 'above-the-line' cost of *Torn Curtain* ($2,411,6000), which also included story costs and the salaries of Hitchcock and his staff. The overall budget for the film including studio overheads was $5,150,625.[14] Hitchcock had wanted to cast Julie Christie ('Mr Hitchcock saw her in "Billy Liar" and wants to use her' recorded his production assistant Peggy Robertson) but he was overruled by the studio.[15] Andrews was a hot property following the success of *Mary Poppins* (1964) and *The Sound of Music* (1965). The shooting schedule of *Torn Curtain* would be determined by her availability: Hitchcock had to complete principal photography by the end of 1965 as she was due to begin shooting *Hawaii* early in the New Year.

The casting of Newman and Andrews influenced the development of the script in a number of ways. Hitchcock intended that the opening scene – showing the unmarried couple in bed together with their clothes scattered around the floor of their steamship cabin – should challenge Andrews's prim and proper 'Mary Poppins' image. This scene immediately set off alarm bells when the script was submitted to the Production Code office in August 1965: 'The intimacies of lovemaking that are going on between Armstrong and Sarah would seem to be quite unacceptable as written ... The offensiveness of this sequence would be highlighted were it to be suggested that the two are nude in bed together.'[16] (In contrast the 'extremely gruesome' killing of Gromek was not deemed so problematic provided that 'care and discretion should be exercised in the filming of this scene to keep within the limits of good taste'.) As the script was developed further, however, the emphasis shifted away from the original focus on Sarah and more towards Armstrong. The casting of Paul Newman – a terse, introspective performer trained in the 'Method' – signalled a greater emphasis on the characterisation and psychology of the supposed defector. Newman had strong views on the script and (in his view) its many shortcomings. He sent Hitchcock a long list of comments, including his advice on how to direct the set pieces:

34   The censor was concerned about the love scene between Armstrong (Paul Newman) and his wife Sarah (Julie Andrews) at the start of *Torn Curtain* (Universal Pictures, 1966).

1. The main thing that I am concerned with right now is the element of humor. How that is to be injected and how that must necessarily effect the character, I leave to you since you are the eminent craftsman.

2. Since all things start at the beginning, the title 'TORN CURTAIN' should be reconsidered. Frankly, I never disliked it, but the one time I saw it in print it appeared to be a trifle arch, however, what is more worrisome is its lack of mystery which titles like 'NORTH BY NORTHWEST' and 'NOTORIOUS' had.

3. Scene 11 – I wish all of the exposition were out of this scene. It can very comfortably be put into scene 26. Perhaps one reference in the love scene to a nuclear scientist could be affected in order to give the telegram which he receives a certain amount of importance. If we ask ourselves specifically why scene 11 is in the picture, I think the reason should be to attain the highest possible loveability rating so that the audience will care.

4. Scene 76 – Do they really have American correspondents, AP or UPI, in East Berlin?

5. Starting with scene 94, it appears too convenient for Armstrong to wander off to the museum by himself. Even Nureyev, when he defected, was under considerable guard for some time. I doubt very much that a nuclear scientist defecting to East

Berlin on the second or third day after his arrival could move even to the door of his hotel without a guard of some sort intercepting him ...

6. Again, to bring up the other bit, I very strongly believe that the stove becomes a weapon only because of its proximity, and if the peasant woman prepares the oven in advance it will look odd. But, I think if we can avoid making it look like a *deus ex machina*, I do not feel that this will in any way affect the cutting you had planned, nor do I think it will hurt the suspense.

And he continued:

11. Scene 190 – Is it really possible that twenty years after the war there are Russian Army deserters hiding in the woods in East Germany still wearing their Russian uniforms? It would appear to me that the elbows and the seats of their trousers would be so severely abused that they would hardly be wearable.

12. The bus chase is a marvellous chance I think for romance. I am just being funny by using the following examples, but under the humor there lurks a valid suggestion: 'Darling, if they catch us, can they put us in the same cell – so that we can have one last boff before we are shot?'[17]

Brian Moore's scornful response was to dub Newman 'The Deep Thinker of Connecticut', though he provided reassurance regarding the details: that US correspondents in West Berlin were able to attend press conferences in East Berlin and that the Russian Army maintained a large garrison in East Germany ('Desertion from armies is a fact of life, even in the USSR'). Nevertheless he conceded: 'As for his other points – away from the welter of bad taste and nonsense, it's conceivable that he many have some valid ones: viz, more humor, etc.'[18]

In fact Newman was not the only one to express reservations about the script of *Torn Curtain*. Hitchcock showed it to the two Italian writers, Agenore ('Age') Incrocci and Furio Scarpelli, with whom had spent some time working on another (unrealised) project. 'The dialogue needs to be revised. It is flat and has no sparkle,' suggested 'Age' and Scarpelli. 'There was no characterization of the leading roles and no life. Lacks dimension. Armstrong should be characterized more.'[19] In September 1965, with principal photography looming, Hitchcock brought in the two British playwrights Keith Waterhouse and Willis Hall to revise the script. Waterhouse and Hall were best known for *Billy Liar*, a Walter Mitty-ish drama which they had written for the stage and adapted into a film for John Schlesinger in 1963. Their role seems to have been principally to polish the dialogue with a view to introducing more humour. They also responded to some of the concerns raised by Newman, suggesting that such a high-profile defector as Armstrong 'would in fact be given as much freedom as possible. He is a VIP... Just for the record, Burgess and Maclean, the British Foreign Office defectors, were throwing wild parties in Moscow two days after their arrival!'[20] Waterhouse and Hall's 'Polish Script' of 27 September 1965 has the same structure and incident as Brian Moore's 'Final Draft Screenplay' of 2 August but the dialogue is less stilted.[21] Their one important contribution to the characterisation was to turn Sarah into Armstrong's assistant rather than being a scientist in her own right: this was the final stage in the gradual reduction of Sarah's importance in the film and the narrative's shift to Armstrong.

Waterhouse and Hall were still revising script pages as the film went onto the studio floor. Hitchcock kept them on the set partly in order to deflect Paul Newman's attention when the actor wanted to discuss his character's motivation in a particular scene. It was only at a late stage that Hitchcock decided upon his own cameo appearance. This had become so much of a Hitchcock trademark that audiences expected it and were looking out for it: but at the same time it had become increasingly difficult to devise without disrupting the narrative. By this stage of his career Hitchcock preferred to make his appearance as early as possible in the film to prevent audiences becoming distracted. His script notes indicate that his cameo in *Torn Curtain* was intended to contribute to conveying plot information:

> Should we have a brief establishing shot of the lounge of the Hotel d'Angleterre. This could be a spot for Mr Hitchcock's appearance in the film. I made a suggestion the other day that I should be seen sitting in an armchair in the lounge with a nine month old baby on my knee and I'm looking around rather impatiently for the mother to come back. This impatience would be underscored by shifting the baby from one knee to the other, and then with the free hand, surreptitiously wiping the thigh. Having this would enable us to show the sign announcing the presence of the convention members in the hotel. We might even show some of the delegates crowding around the elevator which, of course, would then lead us to the corridor scene on page 10.[22]

Compare this explanation of Hitchcock's cameo in *Torn Curtain* from the production records with the interpretative reading suggested by one Hitchcock scholar: 'The citizen shifting a child parallels the hero's theft of the old East German scientist's brain child. But again this citizen is the god of this film, the maker of everyone and everything there. So he registers embarrassment, even befoulment, by the doings of his creatures, most notably the romantic combination of Mary Poppins and Hud… Hitchcock's god in the lobby reminds us that even the deeds of amoral derring-do in the cold war may be witnessed by a higher judge.'[23]

Torn Curtain was shot entirely in California: a German unit was sent to East Berlin to shoot background plates – under the guise of making a documentary – but the footage it sent back was deemed unusable. The University of

Southern California stood in for the campus of Karl Marx University and the scene on the farm supposedly on the outskirts of Berlin was actually shot at Camarillo. Hitchcock showed his customary attention to detail: for example he insisted 'that all the Extras and Bit players used in this production are to have unfamiliar faces – i.e. not the people who are used over and over again in TV and Features'.[24] One of the extras was Peter Lorre Jr as the taxi driver who takes Armstrong to the fateful rendezvous at the farm. Among the names suggested for the small but important role of German nuclear scientist Professor Lindt were Norman Lloyd (who had played the villain Fry in *Saboteur* and was co-producer of *Alfred Hitchcock Presents*) and film directors William Dierterle and Fritz Lang, though in the event the part went to Austrian émigré Ludwig Donath, a character actor from the 1930s absent from the screen for some time due to the blacklist.

On one level the actual shooting of *Torn Curtain* seems to have gone smoothly: it was completed on schedule and close to budget with few retakes. On another level, however, it had been difficult for Hitchcock who was without three of his key collaborators from the last decade. George Tomasini, who had edited every Hitchcock film since *Rear Window* with the sole exception of *The Trouble With Harry*, had died following *Marnie*. Robert Burks, the cinematographer of every Hitchcock film since *Strangers on a Train* with the sole exception of *Psycho*, was unable to shoot *Torn Curtain* on account of being 'terribly sick with nerves': Jack Warren was a late replacement shortly before the film went into production.[25] And it was over *Torn Curtain* that Hitchcock fell out with Bernard Herrmann, who had scored every one of his films since the *The Trouble With Harry*. Herrmann's highly distinctive, string-dominant scores had been a key element of the mood of *Vertigo*, *North by Northwest*, *Psycho* and *Marnie*, but Hitchcock felt that his style was too dated for the 1960s and wanted a pop-influenced score which Herrmann failed to provide.[26] John Addison, who had won an Academy Award for *Tom Jones* (1963), wrote the unmemorable score for *Torn Curtain*.

Hitchcock made one significant change to *Torn Curtain* in post-production: this was to remove a scene where Armstrong eats in a factory canteen en route to Leipzig where the foreman turns out to be Gromek's brother. Armstrong is disturbed by the similarity between the brothers – actor Wolfgang Kieling played both parts – and is reminded of killing Gromek when his brother uses a similar knife to cut a sausage. Hitchcock told Truffaut:

Aside from the length of the picture, the reason I cut that scene out was also because I remembered the trouble I'd had with *The Secret Agent* [sic]. I made that picture in England thirty years ago and it was a flop. Do you remember the reason why? Because the central figure had to commit a killing he didn't want to do, and the public couldn't identify with a hero who was so reluctant to carry out his mission. So I felt that with *Torn Curtain* I would be falling into this trap again through that factory scene.[27]

Further cuts were imposed by the censors. *Torn Curtain* was initially refused a certificate by the Production Code Administration due to 'an excessively sensual scene of love-making between Paul Newman and Julie Andrews' and the scene in the theatre towards the end of the film where Armstrong effects his escape by shouting 'Fire!' – which the PCA felt might cause panic in cinemas. The studio acquiesced: the film was passed 'with the most glaring intimacies removed from it' and with two of the three cries of 'Fire!' removed.[28]

Torn Curtain was Hitchcock's fiftieth film: the fact that he marked this milestone by returning to the spy thriller might be seen as further evidence of the genre's importance to the shaping of Hitchcock's authorial identity. In fact there are various echoes of Hitchcock's past films (not just his spy films) in *Torn Curtain*. The 'excessively sensual' love-making scene is a link to *Notorious* – though the scene in *Torn Curtain* was neutered by the censors to the extent that it is far less erotic than the older film. The killing of Gromek is a moment of sudden, shocking violence comparable to the murder of Janet Leigh in *Psycho*. The extended suspense sequence on the bus as Armstrong and Sarah make their journey from Leipzig to Berlin might recall *Sabotage* – except that on this occasion there is a happy outcome. There are echoes of Hitchcock's wartime propaganda film *Bon Voyage* in the narrative of escape from enemy territory with the aid of an underground movement. And at the heart of *Torn Curtain* is a web of trust and deception that has broad parallels with *Marnie*. Indeed *Torn Curtain* might be seen as a mirror-image of *Marnie* with the gender roles reversed: here it is the man who is aloof and secretive, while his fiancée is a female Mark Rutland who seeks to correct his transgression. Thus while Mark seeks to 'correct' Marnie sexually, Sarah looks to reposition Armstrong ideologically by bringing him back to the West.

Torn Curtain is more directly rooted in the politics of the Cold War than Hitchcock's previous two spy films *The Man Who Knew Too Much* and *North by Northwest*. In contrast to *North by Northwest* which had focused inwards on the political and social anxieties of 1950s America, *Torn Curtain* looks outwards to the ideological and military rivalries of the Cold War. On this occasion the 'MacGuffin' is an 'anti-missile missile' that could intercept larger ballistic missiles and therefore 'make nuclear weapons obsolete'. This was a topical enough scenario following the Cuban Missiles Crisis of 1962 which had brought the United States and the Soviet Union to the brink of an armed confrontation (the Cuban crisis would provide the background for Hitchcock's next film *Topaz*): Armstrong – a leading American scientist – poses as a defector in order to get close to an East German scientist who has knowledge that could assist the development of the missile system. What differentiates *Torn Curtain* from other films of this type is that Armstrong is acting on his own initiative rather than on behalf of the government and that it is not immediately apparent what his purpose is. Hitchcock explained that 'I wanted to start the story on a note of "misterioso" so as to avoid the beginning I've used in the past and which has now become a cliché; the man who has been given a mission. I just didn't want to repeat that scene again. You have it in every one of the Bond pictures.'[29] In truth Hitchcock had employed such a scene only once, in *Secret Agent*: the device is therefore probably best understood as a means of differentiating *Torn Curtain* from the Bond films rather than as a desire to avoid repeating himself.

In most important respects *Torn Curtain* conforms to what might be described as the official discourses of the Cold War. It asserts the need for the United States to maintain technological ascendancy in the nuclear arms race; it portrays East Germany – a Soviet satellite state – as a police state where suspected dissidents are under constant surveillance (the security chief Gerhard even refers himself to 'the notorious State Security'); and it posits the existence of an underground movement (known as 'Pi') which exists for the purpose of helping dissidents and refugees escape to the West ('We are not a political group. We only help people take a long vacation from this lovely place'). The strong Cold War flavour of *Torn Curtain* begs the question of why Hitchcock turned to this particular subject given his view that 'the public doesn't care for films on politics' and the fact that – as he put it – 'none of them has been really successful': this in reference to Cold War films such as Carol Reed's *The Man Between* (1953), Elia Kazan's *Man on a Tightrope* (1953) and George Seaton's *The Big Lift* (1950).[30] One answer might simply be that Hitchcock was jumping on a bandwagon: *Torn Curtain* was one of group of films in the mid-1960s set against the background of Cold War Berlin that also included *The Spy Who Came in from the Cold* (1965), *Funeral in Berlin* (1966) and *The Quiller Memorandum* (1966). Another answer might be that Hitchcock did not regard *Torn Curtain* as a political film but rather as a romantic suspense story.

Like *Notorious*, *Torn Curtain* blurs the distinction between the public/ political and the private/personal. Armstrong's (apparent) defection is an act of political betrayal but it is also a personal betrayal as it involves deceiving his fiancée Sarah: he has not taken her into his confidence and has led her to believe that he is travelling to Stockholm when in fact he is heading for East Berlin. The motive for Armstrong's defection also collapses the public and the personal. He is piqued because the US government has cancelled funding for his research project: his defection is therefore prompted as much by personal ambition – the alternative to research is to accept a teaching job that he is evidently not interested in – as by ideological commitment. Armstrong's public statement following his defection asserts the importance of research over ideology ('That project is more important than consideration of loyalty to any one country') and suggests that the motive is altruistic ('to produce a defensive weapon that will make all offensive nuclear weapons obsolete and therefore abolish the terror of nuclear warfare'), though of course this could be seen as part of his 'cover story' in order to make his defection appear plausible to the East German authorities. In fact *Torn Curtain* is decidedly ambiguous on this point: it never clear whether Armstrong is a genuinely idealistic scientist committed to the cause of peace or whether he is a patriot playing the role of a misguided idealist in order to procure technological secrets for his government.

Like other Hitchcock spy films, *Torn Curtain* is preoccupied with the motif of role-playing. It is not until a third of the way into the film when he meets a contact at the farm that the truth of Armstrong's defection becomes clear: 'Well, Professor Armstrong, how does it feel to play the part of a dirty defector? I saw you on tv last night – you put on a good act.' Armstrong's 'act' is good enough to fool the East German authorities, the faculty committee at the University of Leipzig, and his own fiancée. Later Armstrong is forced to reveal the truth to Sarah – a moment of romantic reconciliation played out in silent long shot against a highly artificial studio hill-top – in order that she can help his scheme by agreeing to work as his assistant: 'You've got to act as if I've persuaded you to go along with me.' If Armstrong – another one of Hitchcock's amateur spies who finds himself in unaccustomed situations – seems less at ease in playing out his role than other protagonists such as Richard Hannay or Roger Thornhill, this is probably due to a combination of deficiencies in scripting and the different performance style of Paul Newman in comparison to such consummate performers as Robert Donat and Cary Grant: Newman seems to have taken to heart Philip Vandamm's injunction in *North by Northwest* that 'you chaps could stand a little less coaching from J. Edgar Hoover and a little more from the Actors' Studio'.

Torn Curtain has usually been positioned within the 'anti-Bond' cycle of spy films in the mid-1960s that also included *The Spy Who Came in from the Cold* and *The Ipcress File*. While it shares some similarities with those films – its narrative of defection, deception and double agents and its heroine who follows her lover behind the Iron Curtain parallels *The Spy Who Came in the Cold*, for example – *Torn Curtain*, however, lacks the cynicism and moral bleakness of the John le Carré and Len Deighton films. *Torn Curtain* is ultimately a morally optimistic film: it suggests that the individual can make a difference in the wider political struggles of the Cold War as Armstrong succeeds in gaining the intelligence he needs and in escaping back to the West. In contrast the resolution of *The Spy Who Came in from the Cold* is pessimistic in the extreme: the individual is merely a pawn in the secret wars between rival intelligence services. Alec Leamas succeeds in his mission but is morally compromised as a result: the film ends on a downbeat note as he is shot dead at the foot of the Berlin Wall. In this sense *Torn Curtain* is itself a film torn between different modes: Raymond Durgnat suggests that it represents 'a compromise between the spy themes popular in forms as diverse as the Bond films, but with more real a framework and with identification figures who, while more familiar than the Bond-type hero, were also more prosperous than the heroes of Len Deighton – although the latter were better attuned than Hollywood tradition supposed to the public's increasing acceptance of moral seediness as part of espionage and, indeed, life'.[31]

The principal flaw of *Torn Curtain* is that it seems uncertain what kind of spy thriller it wants to be: consequently it hovers between the realist mode on the one hand and the spy-adventure film on the other. The first two-thirds of *Torn Curtain* – focusing on Armstong's defection, the revelation of his real purpose and the suspense arising from whether he will be able to acquire the knowledge he needs before he is exposed – belong to the world of the realist thriller. Here *Torn Curtain* harks back to some of the 'undercover' films of the Second World War such as *13, Rue Madeleine* and *Cloak and Dagger*. In the last third, however, as Armstrong and Sarah effect their escape from East Germany, *Torn Curtain* switches abruptly to a chase-and-pursuit narrative that is markedly lighter in tone than the rest of the film and closer to the style of *North by Northwest*. Yet on this occasion Hitchcock seems to have been unable to reconcile the realistic and sensational modes within the same film: hence *Torn Curtain* satisfies neither as a serious spy drama nor as an adventure film.

The tension between modes within *Torn Curtain* is highlighted through a comparison of its two major set pieces. The killing of Gromek at the farmhouse is by any standards one of Hitchcock's most brilliant sequences. It derives its effect partly from the fact that Gromek has been established as something more than a cardboard heavy – he reminisces fondly about his

35 The killing of Gromek (Wolgang Kieling) in *Torn Curtain* (Universal Pictures, 1966) was intended as an antidote to the 'clean' violence of the James Bond films.

time spent living in New York and there is a running gag about his cigarette lighter never working – and partly from the fact that Armstrong knows he has to kill Gromek or else he will be exposed as a double agent. Hitchcock shoots the killing in a sequence of close-ups without music: the effect is brutal and intense. Gromek simply refuses to die: Armstrong first tries to strangle him to no avail; the farmer's wife stabs him with a butcher's knife but the knife breaks leaving its blade embedded in Gromek's chest; then she hits him with a shovel; until finally she and Armstrong drag Gromek across the floor and hold his head inside the gas stove where he eventually dies from asphyxiation. The sequence has been read both as a corrective to the unrealistic, comic-strip violence of the Bond movies – James Bond never experienced such difficulty in disposing of an enemy – and as an allusion to the Holocaust. Hitchcock apparently endorsed the latter reading when he remarked to film critic Richard Schickel: 'One couldn't hep but think that here we are back at Auschwitz again and the gas ovens.'[32] In contrast the bus sequence – where Armstrong and Sarah make the journey from Leipzig to

36   Armstrong and Sarah's escape on the refugee bus in *Torn Curtain* (Universal Pictures, 1966).

East Berlin on board a decoy bus run by the 'Pi' organisation – is shot as much for comedy as for suspense. It is characterised by its constant sense of movement – entirely the opposite of the claustrophobic interior of the farmhouse – and utilises a light musical score. Much of the suspense arises from the incidental occurrences that delay the bus – including it being held up by a gang of Russian Army deserters hiding in the woods and the comic befuddlement of an old lady with a shopping trolley – while all the time the real bus can be seen through the back window catching up with them. It is a characteristically 'Hitchcockian' suspense sequence that is marred only by some poor back-projection plates (a technical flaw of many of Hitchcock's late films and especially of *Torn Curtain*); but it does not belong in the same film as the scene of the killing of Gromek.

Hitchcock's fiftieth film inevitably attracted much critical interest though its reception was notably less enthusiastic than for *North by Northwest*. The trade press was divided on its merits. The *Motion Picture Herald* averred that '*Torn Curtain* is in the tradition of *To Catch a Thief* and *North by Northwest*, and you can't do better than that in this field'.[33] *Film Daily* called it 'a thriller of thrillers, churning up nerve-pounding excitement in a setting behind the Iron Curtain'.[34] But *Variety* thought it no more than 'an okay Cold War suspenser' in which 'some good general plot ideas are marred by rather routine dialog, and a too relaxed pace contributes to a dull overlength'.[35] *The Hollywood Reporter* concurred that it 'is not top level Alfred Hitchcock. The master has not given this one the customary careful story weaving, and the tension that comes from taut story threads.'[36] The consensus among the New York critics was that it was a lacklustre affair by the director's usual standards. Bosley Crowther found it 'dreary ... a clumsy and creaky spy thriller by the quondam master of the genre at a time when the area of spy movies has been exploded by the likes of James Bond'.[37] Hollis Alpert felt that *Torn Curtain* 'is oddly lethargic (for Hitchcock) and only tepidly suspenseful': he also disliked the murder scene, finding it 'tastelessly gory'.[38] The *New Yorker* felt that the film 'is very bad. The story is preposterous without being at all inventive, and the script, by Brian Moore, is adequate except at pivotal moments, when it flounders in plot exposition.'[39] Richard Schickel in *Life* magazine suggested that '*Torn Curtain* ... more often tends to prove what one has suspected for a long time and been unwilling to admit: that Hitchcock is tired to the point where what once seemed highly personal style is now mere repetition of past triumphs'.[40] And Pauline Kael, then developing a reputation as one of America's most outspoken and ascerbic critics, was scathing: 'Alfred Hitchcock's *Torn Curtain* is a slackly edited, tired rehash of many of his old tricks, and they weren't all that good before.'[41]

Robert E. Kapsis argues that the poor critical reception of *Torn Curtain* was to a large extent a product of changes in popular film culture rather than necessarily a reflection of the quality of the film itself. The contemporary reviews 'illustrate how changing genre conventions can condition the critical vocabulary and frames of reference used by critics in evaluating a film which is perceived as an example of a currently popular genre'. In particular the repeated theme of the reviews that *Torn Curtain* was 'too derivative of Hitchcock's other films ... and not enough like the Bond films revealed the normative nature of the James Bond craze still in force when the film was released'.[42] In this assessment the film failed because it was not like the Bond movies: Hitchcock had sought to differentiate *Torn Curtain* from Bond but in so doing had revealed that he was out of touch with the state of film culture. This point was best expressed in an anonymous review for the magazine *America*:

> I don't think his style and technique have regressed, but rather that they have stood still while movies have in many way progressed. I would, however, consider

the current mammoth cycle of spoofs including James Bond a temporary regression, born of commercial cynicism as well as a genuine inability to confront serious themes in our confusing times. The most financially successful of them are not necessarily better films than Hitchcock's; they are just better attuned to the not very edifying realities of contemporary taste.[43]

Hollis Alpert made much the same point more succinctly when he remarked that 'Hitchcock just hasn't been going to the movies lately. There's a lot he has to catch up on.'

However, this explanation alone is not entirely persuasive. The fact was that Hitchcock was an avid film-viewer: he conscientiously kept up with all the latest releases from Hollywood as well as European films. Therefore to suggest that he was out of touch with popular taste does not tally. A more plausible explanation for the lukewarm reception of *Torn Curtain* was that it was lost among a glut of spy films released in 1966: *Our Man Flint*, *The Silencers*, *Murderer's Row*, *Modesty Blaise*, *Deadlier Than the Male*, *Arabesque*, *The Quiller Memorandum*, *The Deadly Affair*, *Funeral in Berlin*, *The Venetian Affair*, *Where the Bullets Fly* and *The Man From Rio* to name just a dozen of them. Another problem for *Torn Curtain* was that it was caught between different modes: while it was far from being an out-and-out spy adventure fantasy in the mould of the James Bond, Matt Helm, Derek Flint or Bulldog Drummond films, it nevertheless included some adventure elements that made it seem less psychologically plausible than existential spy films such as *The Ipcress File*, *The Spy Who Came in from the Cold*, *The Deadly Affair* and *The Quiller Memorandum*. Whatever the reasons, however, *Torn Curtain* did not turn out to be the popular success that Hitchcock and Universal had hoped. It 'opened' well, grossing $446,532 during its first week in New York, where it was shown in 57 theatres, but faded at the box office thereafter. Its North American rentals amounted to $6.5 million: comparable to other Universal pictures of the time such as *Charade*, *Father Goose* and *The War Wagon*, but representing only a modest success given the cost of production.[44]

It might have been the absence of his regular collaborators, or the hurried production schedule to accomodate Julie Andrews's other commitments that meant Hitchcock was not entirely satisfied with the script, or the complete lack of chemistry between the two stars, or a combination of those factors, but, whatever the reason, *Torn Curtain* is generally regarded as one of Hitchcock's least successful films. Yet, ironically, for once Hitchcock's 'MacGuffin' might not have been quite so far-fetched or irrelevant as in most of his films. One of those who saw *Torn Curtain* at the time of its original release was the Governor of California, an ex-actor by the name of Ronald Reagan, who, elected to the US presidency in the 1980s, and faced with a renewal of Cold War tensions following the Soviet invasion of Afghanistan and the stationing of medium-range Soviet nuclear missiles in Eastern Europe, responded by proposing an anti-missile defence shield, formally known as the Strategic Defence Initiative, popularly dubbed 'Star Wars' by the media, which, in principle at least, was much the same idea as that proposed by Professor Michael Armstrong in *Torn Curtain*.[45]

15

HITCHCOCK'S COLD WAR – TAKE TWO: *TOPAZ* (1969)

The failure of *Torn Curtain* was a profound disappointment for Hitchcock: it would be over three years until the release of his next film. His decision to make yet another spy picture has sometimes been seen as an attempt to 'correct' the mistake of *Torn Curtain*.[1] *Topaz* – a best-selling novel by American author Leon Uris set against the background of the Cuban Missiles Crisis – suggested itself as a ready-made property as Universal already held the screen rights. Hitchcock seems to have seen it as an opportunity to combine topicality and human interest, and again cited *Notorious* as a point of reference: 'We have brought to the screen in *Topaz* the same values that made the novel a best seller for over a year … It remains a story of espionage in high places, and of men and women caught up in the vortex of international tensions. As such it is very close to an earlier film of mine – *Notorious*.'[2]

Leon Uris (1924–2003) is best known as the author of *Exodus*, a best-selling historical novel chronicling the foundation of the state of Israel that was made into an epic film by Otto Preminger in 1960. The son of Polish-Jewish immigrants, Uris had served in the US Marines during the Second World War: he drew upon his experiences for his first novel, *Battle Cry*, also writing the screenplay for the film directed by Raoul Walsh in 1955. He also wrote *The Angry Hills*, filmed by Robert Aldrich in 1959, and the screenplay for *Gunfight at the O.K. Corral* (1957). *Topaz*, published in 1967, resembled *Exodus* in that it was set against the background of recent historical events and featured multiple protagonists. The book spent 52 weeks on the *New York Times* bestseller list and was the number one fiction title in the week of 15 October 1967. Universal bought a two-year option on the book for $50,000, evidently with Hitchcock in mind. *Topaz* was announced as Hitchcock's next film in

May 1968; Uris was paid $125,000 for the rights and another $125,000 to write the screenplay.[3]

Topaz is a labyrinthine novel with a large cast of characters and a range of subplots. It begins with the defection of a high-ranking Soviet intelligence officer, Boris Kuznetov, who reveals that the Soviets have a mole operating at the highest level of the French government ('Boris says anything that Paris knows Moscow will know within twenty-four hours'). *Topaz* was recognised at the time as being based on a real espionage case: the KGB's 'Sapphire' spy ring which had infiltrated the French government and its security service the SEDCE (Service de Documentation Extérieure et de Contreespionnage) in the 1950s. Uris's characters have real-life equivalents: Kuznetov was based on KGB defector Anatoly Golitsyn, while the principal protagonist, French security agent André Devereaux, was a thinly veiled equivalent of Philippe de Vosjoli, an attaché to the French Embassy in Washington who ran a spy ring in Cuba and helped to find evidence of Soviet missile bases in 1962. The publication of *Topaz* sparked a minor diplomatic *contretemps* between France and the United States. It was alleged in France that the CIA had fed Uris with details of the 'Sapphire' case in order to embarrass the French President Charles De Gaulle who had been openly critical of US policy in Vietnam and had withdrawn France from the integrated military command structure of NATO: De Gaulle had refused to believe the intelligence as he suspected it was a CIA plot to undermine him by casting suspicion on his own ministers.[4] Philippe de Vosjoli, however, claimed that he had written the first draft of the book which was rewritten and translated into English by Uris.[5] After the film was announced, Vosjoli filed a lawsuit against Uris and Universal: in 1972 Judge Howard J. Schmidt of the Los Angeles Superior Court ruled in favour of Vosjoli and awarded him $352,000 plus 50 per cent of past and future royalties.[6]

Topaz was a difficult novel to adapt: it is loosely structured with three main episodes – the defection of Kuznetov, Devereaux's mission to Cuba to find evidence of Soviet missiles on behalf of the Americans and his recall to Paris where he exposes the Soviet spy ring – that are all effectively stand-alone stories in their own right. It also has a rather downbeat ending: Devereaux identifies the Soviet spy as his wartime comrade Jacques Granville but Granville is too well-connected and it is Devereaux who is forced into exile with his family. Hitchcock recognised from the outset that the book's complex narrative would need streamlining. His first breakdown of the story omitted whole chapters and entire subplots: he cut out all the flashbacks to Devereaux's wartime experiences in the French Resistance, simplified the romantic life of his daughter Michele and played down the extent of his wife Nicole's affair with Granville.[7] Uris – evidently taking into account Hitchcock's idea of 'pure cinema' which the director expounded over the course of many script conferences – suggested that the opening sequence of Kuznetov's defection in Copenhagen should be played 'in pantomime' without any dialogue. He suggested other sequences in a similar vein: 'At the hideaway, Kuznetov relates something to André in pantomime. Nordstrom observes them walking along the river but cannot hear. The only words we catch at the very end are "Juanita de Cordoba".'[8] Although this particular scene did not make it into the finished film, other 'pantomime' moments did: Devereaux's conversation with his Harlem contact Philippe Dubois in a flower shop and Devereaux watching Philippe's entry into the hotel of the Cuban United Nations delegation. Uris's second treatment included the first of many suggestions for ending the film: a meeting between Granville and his KGB handler Colonel Topov where Granville is shot by an unseen assassin: 'WE FREEZE Granville and Topov, then pull back to see it as a photograph all but filling the front page of France's newspaper *Le Moniteur.*'[9]

Uris delivered an incomplete first draft screenplay in July 1968, including events up to Devereaux leaving Cuba. His script was heavy with political references: it highlighted tensions within the NATO alliance ('Cuba is an American affair. Why should we be drawn into a conflict in which we have no interest?' asks a French brigadier-general in response to an American request for intelligence on Cuba) and included what might be read as a critical reference to US policy in Vietnam ('My country has been drawn into a few conflicts this century in which our interest was questioned', remarks US intelligence officer McKittrick). Uris's script also included unpleasant over-tones of sexual violence as Juanita de Cordoba, a young widow who has been uncovered as part of Devereaux's spy network in Cuba, is last seen having her breasts exposed for carving by a Cuban thug: 'Munoz rips her gown and tears off her brassaire [sic] bearing her breasts ... As the blade touches her breast SCREEN BECOMES WAVY AND ABSTRACT with a splash of red rippling down. O.S. GROAN OF AGONY and SHUDDER from Juanita.'[10] Hitchcock – who had famously murdered Janet Leigh in the shower in *Psycho* and has so often been attacked for his alleged misogyny – balked at this suggestion: 'I think we had better discuss ... how Juanita is treated. We know she has to be killed, but the present climate as you realize is against extreme violence on the screen. It is possible we'll have to shoot alternate scenes for this ...'[11]

In the event this was the end of Uris's contribution as he walked away from the film shortly afterwards and Hitchcock brought in Samuel Taylor, who had written the final draft of *Vertigo*, to complete *Topaz*. Taylor had to work quickly as the location shooting in Europe (Copenhagen and Paris) was scheduled for September 1968. The notes of a story conference at the end of August reveal that Hitchcock had still not worked out how the Soviet mole was to be identified: 'Well, to sum up, gentlemen, we have no ending to our picture. We have to devise some other way to unmask Columbine. It may be that the wife Nicole has to do it in bed ... At least we don't have in the picture a character called R.'[12] Taylor's contribution was to rewrite the Cuba sequence quite extensively and to flesh out the characters of Juanita and Rico Parra – the latter in particular became less of a cardboard heavy than in Uris's treatment. He also found a more elegant solution to the death of Juanita, who is shot by her betrayed lover: 'Parra looks about him then his eyes rest on Juanita. He crosses to her and then with a glance at the rest of the room, puts his arm around her shoulder. He smiles at her and holds her close. We see a slight movement. There is a loud explosion and suddenly Juanita slumps.'[13] Taylor also devised an ending wherein Granville challenges Devereaux to a duel for exposing him as a spy: they meet at dawn at the Roland Garros Stadium where Granville is shot not by Devereaux but by a sniper in the stand. The inference is that Granville has been shot by the Russians as he is no longer of any use to them.

Topaz went into production without a finished screenplay: Taylor was still revising scenes as Hitchcock started shooting the location sequences. As we have seen this situation had occurred several times before – *The Man Who Knew Too Much*, *North by Northwest* and *Torn Curtain* had all started shooting without a finished script in place – but the difference with *Topaz* was that Hitchcock had not had time to finalise his ideas with the writer. A letter from Taylor accompanying revision pages suggests he was still adding new scenes:

> I am sending you herewith a complete sequence of draft screenplay from the moment the plane leaves Wiesbaden through André's first appearance in the picture ... Also, as you will see, I have tried a new scene to add André Devereaux to the picture, a scene we did not discuss. It occurred to me while I was fooling with the first scene, of the three officials at the French Embassy, which I found rather didactic, and I thought I might as well try it. It is certainly less political, which is an advantage. And I think it is a more interesting introduction of your leading character.[14]

Topaz might well have been the most seat-of-the-pants film that Hitchcock ever made: Taylor was still rewriting scenes towards the end of the studio shooting.[15] As late as December 1968 Hitchcock was still evidently dissatisfied with the final act: 'We are in the last quarter of our picture. At the "Safe House" in Virginia, we send André Devereaux off as a man with an urgent mission and 2 or 3 days in which to accomplish it ... This would all indicate that there should be, first and foremost, an urgency about these scenes in which Devereaux must be shown as the instigator.'[16] A final version of the last scene between Devereaux and Granville was not written until 7 April 1969: even then there was evidently continuing uncertainty over the ending as the script pages included alternative dialogue.[17]

Hitchcock was concerned that *Topaz* should be as authentic as possible. Odette Ferry, a Francophone American, was employed 'to work with me on the script so that we don't have our French characters too Americanized in their speech patterns'.[18] The exteriors following the Kusenovs' (as they became in the film) arrival in Washington were shot early on a Sunday morning 'because there'll be fewer 1968 cars around at that time' (the film is set in 1962).[19] An English photographer called Harry Benson was sent to Havana to shoot cine film and stills secretly. Benson's exit from Cuba was a case of life imitating art as he had to be nearly as inventive as Devereaux: 'He got out okay. There were a lot of difficulties but he thinks he's got everything... He sent half his pictures back with a Canadian from the United Nations, so he is now in New York to pick them up.'[20] However, Hitchcock was thwarted on one occasion by an organisation with an even greater regard for authenticity than his own. He had wanted to include a headline from the *New York Times* declaring 'Cuban Missile Crisis Over' for the last shot of the film but the newspaper refused on the grounds of protecting its 'historical record' as it had never used that particular headline. 'While I am in sympathy with their historical record, I do think they are being a shade too meticulous about it,' Hitchcock remarked.[21]

Topaz did not finish shooting until April 1969: it had gone over schedule and over budget by $1,384,375. Its final cost of $6,983,750 made it Hitchcock's most expensive film to date.[22] Ironically, in an effort to avoid what he regarded as the excessive star salaries of *Torn Curtain*, Hitchcock had insisted on using relatively unknown actors. The cast of *Topaz* was headed by Frederick Stafford (star of several Eurospy and war movies) as Devereaux, ex-ballerina Dany Robin as Nicole, John Forsythe as CIA agent Michael Nordstrum, John Vernon as Rico Parra and ex-Bond girl Karin Dor as Juanita de Cordoba. For other roles Hitchcock turned to actors associated with the French new wave including Philippe Noiret, Michel Subor and Michel Piccoli. This strategy may have paid off economically – the total cost of 'talent' on *Topaz* was only $590,800, less than either Paul Newman or Julie Andrews had cost for *Torn Curtain* – but the lack of any star names may have damaged the film's box-office prospects. The higher cost of *Topaz* was accounted for by the addition of another writer (Taylor was paid $100,000), overages on the shooting period ($598,000 over budget) and a large studio overhead of 25 per cent ($1,119,875). The most expensive budget item was Hitchcock himself, who was paid $500,000 for producing and directing.

Topaz continued to be a problematic film into post-production. It was not uncommon for Hitchcock to tinker with films before release but this usually involved little more than the re-editing and tightening of particular scenes. In the case of *Topaz*, however, a test screening in San Francisco persuaded him that the film needed a different ending. He had done this only once before: with *Suspicion* in 1941. *Topaz* had a mixed reception from the preview – most of the 110 completed preview cards considered it only 'fair' or 'good' rather than 'very good' or 'excellent' and a small number added in their own categories of 'poor', 'very poor', 'bad' and 'terrible' – but the duel sequence was described variously as 'anti-climactic', 'unnecessary' and an 'anachronism'. Some of the general comments anticipated the reviews of *Topaz*. One said: 'Mr Hitchcock should be put on a nice pension and allowed to spend the rest of his life watching his great movies from the 30s. Who was the ghost director?' Another said: 'Alfred: Please retire while I hold you in professional esteem for your prior efforts and contributions to American cinema. Signed A Filmmaker of [the] 1970s.'[23]

With the duel evidently seen as a weakness, Hitchcock had to find another ending for *Topaz*. He returned to Paris and shot a short scene at Orly Airport that shows Devereaux and Nicole boarding a plane for Washington when they see Granville boarding another plane – an Aeroflot flight to Moscow – and cheerily wishing them 'Bon voyage'.[24] Additional dialogue was included to reflect the fact that the traitor now got away scot-free:

Nicole: How can they let him get away like this?

Devereaux: I told you, my love, he doesn't miss a trick, they have nothing against him, anyway that's the end of 'Topaz'.[25]

Hitchcock may well have wished that had been the end of *Topaz* but it was not to be. Another version was written for France – where it was feared there might well be a backlash against the suggestion that the government had been penetrated by the KGB – in order to hold out the possibility of Granville being brought to justice in the future:

Nicole: How can they let him get away like this?

Devereaux: I told you, my love, he's clever. There's no evidence against him yet.[26]

Hitchcock felt that allowing Granville to escape was 'the correct ending. In every case, whether it be Philby, Burgess [or] McLean, they've all gotten away with it and they've all gone back to Russia.'[27] However, Samuel Taylor felt that the new ending 'is too light, too comedic, and in essence a betrayal of the very strong story you have told up to this point'.[28]

The uncertainty over the ending was a sure sign that all was not well with the picture: this was demonstrated even further when a third ending was devised by re-editing existing footage of Granville entering his house whereupon a gunshot is heard over a freeze-frame: the implication, clearly, is that Granville has committed suicide. In the afterword to a revised edition of his book-length interview with Hitchcock, François Truffaut described this as 'a purely formal solution which, I suspect, was influenced by a picture that was enjoying a huge success at the time, Costa-Gavras' Z'.[29] The uncertainty over the ending continued right up to the film's release: Hitchcock preferred Orly Airport, Universal preferred the freeze-frame. In the event it was decided that both versions would be offered and that distributors could make up their own minds in different markets – again demonstrating a degree of uncertainty that was uncharacteristic of Hitchcock and suggesting that he might have lost interest in the film. In America and France the freeze-frame was used, while in Britain the freeze-frame was shown to critics but the general release used the airport ending.[30] Hitchcock reluctantly made further cuts for the British market in order to appease the Rank Organisation, whose senior film booker allegedly 'insists on an intermission in order to sell popcorn or potato chips or chocolate bars, ice-cream, or whatever they sell in cinema lobbies'.[31]

Given the travails of its production, it is hardly surprising that *Topaz* turned out to be a less than perfect film. '*Topaz* must surely be one of the most uneven films in the history of the cinema,' writes Robin Wood, 'in which something approaching Hitchcock's best rubs shoulders with his very worst: the relationship of good to bad in the film is very revealing.'[32] On the one hand, *Topaz* includes some bravura set pieces – the defection of Kusenov and the Harlem sequence in which Philippe Dubois enters the Cubans' hotel to copy documents are both classic suspense sequences – and several characteristically 'Hitchcockian' moments. The most famous of these is the overhead shot as Rico Parra shoots Juanita de Cordoba and she falls to the floor with her purple dress spreading out like petals blooming on a flower: it is one of the most beautifully composed and elegant death scenes on film. On the other hand, *Topaz* also features some of the dullest protagonists in Hitchcock's *œuvre* and contains more than its share of narrative *longeurs*. At the heart of the film is a structural flaw in that the best part of the film – Devereaux's mission to Cuba to uncover evidence of Soviet missiles – is a subplot that is relatively tangential to the narrative. In contrast the final act – Devereaux's return to Paris to uncover the mole 'Columbine' and expose the spy ring – is something of an

37   Hitchcock used newspaper inserts to anchor *Topaz* (Universal Pictures, 1969) in a real historical and geopolitical context.

anti-climax: the direction is plodding, the exposition muddled and the ending (in whichever version) unsatisfying in the extreme. To some extent the film's flaws may be related to its source material: *Topaz* is the only one of Hitchcock's American spy films based on a novel rather than being an original screenplay (*Foreign Correspondent* was so far removed from its notional source text as to be an original screenplay in all but name). Uris's novel was always a problematic source: it, too, is unwieldy in structure, but the subject matter does not easily lend itself to a radically different treatment. All that said *Topaz* is not without its points of interest and should not be written off as an outright failure.

Topaz was Hitchcock's first film since the Second World War where the narrative is set against a historically specific background: in this case the Cuban Missiles Crisis. This was precipitated by the discovery not only that the Soviet Union had been supplying arms to Cuba but that Soviet nuclear missiles capable of reaching the American mainland had been or were in the process of being installed in Cuba. On 16 October 1962 President Kennedy demanded the removal of the missiles and instituted a naval blockade of Cuba: in the ensuing stand-off between the two superpowers it was the Soviet Union that backed down. *Topaz* is set against this background of international crisis and the threat of nuclear war. A recurring device of the film is the inclusion of insert shots of newspaper headlines which testify to the mounting hysteria: 'Soviet Bomb, Biggest, Dirtiest, Shocks World', 'Sea Showdown with Reds Near, Soviet Bloc orders Combat Alert', 'Bombing of Missile Bases a Possibility'. In most cases the newspapers are being read by the spies themselves: hence the device links the fictional spies of the film to the 'real' world outside. In this regard it is significant that the final headline indicating the crisis has passed – 'Cuban Missile Crisis Over: Kruschev Agrees to Scrap Bases' – is in a newspaper discarded by an anonymous Parisian.

Even more so than *Torn Curtain*, *Topaz* is a tract of the Cold War: its narrative cannot be separated from the ideological and geopolitical contexts of its production. For some critics its Cold War propaganda is simply too didactic. Raymond Durgnat, for example, avers that *Topaz* 'emphatically reasserts the Cold War in terms of a monolithic polarity which, in 1969, was somewhat archaic'.[33] This is correct to an extent but only to an extent. On the one hand *Topaz* rehearses some familiar iconography of Cold War cinema: the opening title sequence is a montage of newsreel footage of a military parade in Moscow that functions as a display of Soviet power. (The shots of troops, vehicles and missiles are desaturated almost to the point of becoming monochrome except for the flags, banners and warheads which retain their striking bold redness: this effect was part of an experimental use of colour in *Topaz* which demonstrates that Hitchcock, even in his seventieth year, had not lost his penchant for visual and formal experimentation.) Yet in 1969 this reminder of Soviet militarism was still topical: *Topaz* came only a year after the suppression of the 'Prague Spring'. The Cuban sequences of *Topaz* similarly present the Communist regime of Fidel Castro as a brutal military dictatorship that rules by fear and oppression: it tortures its opponents and its minions think nothing of pulling their guns on the streets of Harlem. Rico Parra's heavy black beard and military apparel clearly identify him as a Castro substitute, though the 'real' Castro makes an appearance courtesy of some grainy actuality film cut into a sequence where Devereaux observes a party rally in Havana.

Topaz also conforms to the standard Cold War narrative in its suggestion of dissent and opposition within the Communist bloc. The propagandist demonstration of the strength of the Red Army in the title sequence is undercut by a screen caption which suggests that it does not necessarily reflect the views of everyone in the Soviet Union and sets up Kusenov's defection as a matter of conscience: 'Somewhere in this crowd is a high Russian official who disagrees with his government's display of force and what it threatens.

Very soon his conscience will force him to attempt an escape while apparently on a vacation with his family.' *Topaz* also suggests the existence of an underground resistance in Cuba extending across all classes from the upper echelons of society (Juanita de Cordoba is 'the widow of a hero of the revolution') to the peasantry. *Topaz* was one of the few American films of the 1960s to make direct reference to Cuba and Fidel Castro: the failure of the CIA-backed Bay of Pigs invasion of April 1961 made Cuba a difficult subject for Hollywood. It would be fair to say that *Topaz* significantly exaggerates the extent of internal opposition to the regime: to this extent it possibly reinforces the sort of mindset that had led the CIA into supporting the Bay of Pigs invasion in the belief that the Cubans would rise against Castro.

On the other hand, however, while it is emphatically anti-communist in its politics, *Topaz* tempers its anti-communism with a detached and even cynical perspective towards the role of the United States and its allies in fighting the Cold War. The United States and the Soviet Union might be presented as ideologically opposed but they are not so far removed in their *modus operandi*. That the Soviet authorities do not trust Kusenov is evident at the outset from the degree of surveillance he and his family are under in Copenhagen, but even following his defection Kusenov remains under close observation by the CIA. Kusenov's defection has come at a price ('I made my bargain with the devil') and he is threatened with being returned to the Soviets if he does not cooperate ('The way you're going you may find yourself on the front step of the Russian Embassy tomorrow'). The United States and Soviet Union might represent different political systems and values but *Topaz* suggests there is little difference between them in the methods they employ to fight the Cold War. The moral and ideological ambiguity that had been hinted at in *North by Northwest* emerges much more forcefully in *Topaz*: the CIA are represented not as the avuncular 'Professor' of the former film but as bullies who resort to threats to get what they want.

Topaz also demonstrates its cynicism in its representation of the power plays of the Cold War: Michael Walker argues that *Topaz* suggests 'a much harder view of international politics than Hitchcock had hitherto felt able to present'.[34] The United States is at the top of the hierarchy of power on the Western side and holds the whip hand over its ally France: the Americans reveal the existence of the 'Topaz' spy network only in return for favours from the French. It is André Devereaux who is charged with finding evidence of Soviet missiles in Cuba on behalf of the Americans – much to the chagrin of his wife Nicole ('Darcy, you are French. You are not supposed to be mixed up in this cold war between the Americans and the Russians. You are neutral'). Yet if

38   Juanita de Cordoba (Karin Dor) and Rico Parra (John Vernon) in *Topaz* (Universal Pictures, 1969).

Devereaux is manipulated by the Americans, he too is not averse to manipulating others: he calls upon his friend Philippe Dubois to undertake the dangerous task of gaining access to the Hotel Theresa in Harlem to photograph documents in Rico Parra's briefcase (the Hotel Theresa was where Fidel Castro stayed while attending the United Nations in New York) and recruits his mistress Juanita de Cordoba to spy for him in Cuba. *Topaz* emphasises the consequences of espionage for individuals: Juanita's servants the Mendozas are captured taking photographs and tortured, and Juanita herself pays with her life. In a bitterly ironic twist it is later revealed that the intelligence they gathered was not essential: Nordstrum remarks that it 'confirms our information from other sources – including the U2 plates'. (In reality it was aerial reconnaissance by high-altitude U2 spy planes rather than field intelligence that provided evidence of Soviet missiles in Cuba.)

To this extent *Topaz* reflects the *realpolitik* of the Cold War much more acutely than Hitchcock's previous spy films such as *North by Northwest* or even *Torn Curtain*: the latter film had suggested that individual actions can make a difference to the wider power plays but *Topaz* denies that possibility and presents its various characters – particularly Devereaux and Juanita – as pawns in the game of international espionage. This clearly situates *Topaz* in the existential lineage of the spy thriller: its labyrinthine plotting and moral ambiguity make it a companion piece to the downbeat spy films of the 1960s such as *The Spy Who Came in from the Cold* and *The Quiller Memorandum*. Another similarity to those films is the theme of treachery and betrayal. *Topaz* is preoccupied with the idea of betrayal: most of its characters are guilty of this in one way or another. On one level there is political betrayal: Kusenov reveals Soviet intelligence secrets to the Americans and Granville betrays French secrets to the Soviet Union. The minor Cuban functionary Luis Uribe also sells out his country: literally so in that he accepts money to assist Dubois in gaining access to Rico Parra's briefcase. On another level there is personal betrayal: Devereaux cheats on his wife through his affair with Juanita, while Nicole in turn betrays Devereaux by having an affair with Granville. And in Juanita's case the betrayal is both personal and political: she cheats on one lover (Rico Parra) by sleeping with and spying for another (Devereaux). Ironically the only major character who cannot be accused of betrayal in one form or another is the principal villain: Rico Parra. The complex pattern of betrayal is very much a characteristic of the existential spy thriller: *Topaz* suggests that shifting personal loyalties reflect an uncertain political climate in which no one is ever quite sure who their friends and enemies are.

Like *Notorious* and *North by Northwest*, *Topaz* maps the politics of espionage onto its sexual politics. Devereaux is involved in two romantic/ sexual triangles that bring together the political and the personal: one with Nicole and Granville, the other with Juanita and Parra. 'The combination of sex and spying', Walker suggests, 'enables Hitchcock – and others working in the genre – to link the deceptiveness of sexual relationships to the duplicity of the spy, and to introduce into the bedroom the plotting (the business with the key in *Notorious*) and paraphernalia (André's electronic gifts to Juanita) of the intelligence agent.'[35] In *Topaz* the Devereaux/Juanita/ Parra triangle has echoes of *Notorious* (Devereaux persuades Juanita to dupe Parra just as Devlin calls upon Alicia to dupe Sebastian) and *North by Northwest* (the scene where Devereaux arrives at Juanita's hacienda and Parra emerges with a proprietorial arm around her shoulders resembles the auction scene where Thornhill sees Vandamm with his hand on Eve's neck). However, the outcome is different – tragically so – in *Topaz* in that Juanita is not saved by her 'good' lover from her 'bad' lover but is killed by the latter. The Devereaux/Nicole/Granville triangle is less developed – due in some measure to Hitchcock cutting some of the domestic scenes after the preview though these have since been restored – and lacks both the emotional and the ideological force of the other.

The Hitchcock film that *Topaz* perhaps most resembles is *Secret Agent*: although they were made over thirty years apart there are notable similarities between the two films. *Secret Agent* was also set against a historically specific background and had a problematic ending. The last shot of *Secret Agent* with the superimposed faces of Ashenden and Elsa is mirrored in the short montage of dissolves at the end of *Topaz* recalling the 'good' characters who have died in the course of the film. (This motif also features in other genre films of the 1960s: it seems to have begun with *The Guns of Navarone* (1961). In *Topaz* it serves as a reminder of the human cost of espionage.) *Secret Agent* and *Topaz* are both characterised by an acute sense of moral and ideological ambiguity: it is intriguing that they are also perhaps the two least satisfying of Hitchcock's spy films. In the case of *Topaz* the uneven qualities of the film arise in some measure from attempting to combine some familiar 1960s spy tropes (such as the plethora of spy gadgets including miniaturised and remote-controlled cameras) that might not be out of place in a James Bond film with the more realistic style of the John le Carré and Len Deighton school. *Topaz* clearly does not belong to the fantasy world of James Bond but at the same time it is deficient as an example of the existential school. In particular there is no attempt to explain the reasons why Granville and his fellow spies betray their country for the Soviet Union – a surprising omission given that Hitchcock had always been fascinated by the psychological make-up of traitors like Burgess and Maclean.

Topaz polarised critical opinion: it received some of the worst reviews of Hitchcock's late career but paradoxically also some of the best. The trade press evidently felt that *Topaz* was not up to the master of suspense's highest standards. *The Hollywood Reporter* thought it 'one of the season's major disappointments from a veteran film director'.[36] *Variety* found that 'the picture seems to move predictably and lacks the fun and surprise blood-curdling moments that can lift his thrillers to the skies with breathtaking excitement'.[37] Similarly, *Time* felt that 'Hitchcock seems suddenly to have forgotten his own recipe. *Topaz* contains no chills, no fever – and most disappointing, no entertainment.'[38] Other critics were even less charitable: several suggested that Hitchcock was out touch with popular film culture. Pauline Kael averred that *Topaz* 'is the same damned spy picture he's been making since the thirties, and it's getting longer, slower and duller'.[39] *Cue* magazine echoed Kael: 'The old-fashioned variety of espionage is hopelessly outdated, and this in turn makes old-fashioned spy films an anachronism. Alfred Hitchcock's latest effort at suspense is not only incredible on its face, it is also boring most of the time.'[40]

39   'Well, that's the end of Topaz.' Deveraux (Frederick Stafford) and his wife Nicole (Dany Robin) in one of the three alternative endings for *Topaz* (Universal Pictures, 1969).

For Hollis Alpert in the *Saturday Review*, *Topaz* 'seems a relentless effort to prove that cinematic times have not changed'.[41] And Paul Zimmerman in *Newsweek* compared it to another disappointing late film from a great film-maker: '*Topaz* moves with an arthritic quality reminiscent of Chaplin's *A Countess from Hong Kong* ... And the Hitchcock style, always so fluent and straightforward, seems here oddly old-fashioned.'[42]

While the negative voices were in the majority, however, a significant minority found much to admire in the film. Vincent Canby, who had replaced Bosley Crowther as senior film critic of the *New York Times*, was fulsome in his praise: '*Topaz* is ... quite pure Hitchcock, a movie of beautifully composed sequences, full of surface tensions, ironies, absurdities (some hungry seagulls blow the cover of some Allied agents), as well as odd references to things such as Michelangelo's Pieta.' Canby evidently found it a more profound film than other critics: '*Topaz* is not only most entertaining. It is, like so many Hitchcock films, a cautionary fable by one of the most moral cynics of our time.'[43] Kevin Thomas in the *Los Angeles Times* was slightly less fulsome but nevertheless found much more to like than not: *Topaz* was 'one of those pictures in which the whole is not greater than the sum of its parts, yet some of those parts are indeed pretty great' and included 'bravura displays of the fabled Hitchcock technique, replete with dazzling camera movements and acute imagery'.[44] The most laudatory review came from John Belton, a self-proclaimed 'auteur man', for whom '*Topaz* is Hitchcock's best composed, framed and cut film since *Vertigo*, his classic 50s masterpiece'. Belton admired the film's 'profoundly disturbing ambiguity' and concluded that '*Topaz* is a cinematic parade. The variety of shooting styles, filters, colours, lighting and focal lengths not only illustrate Hitchcock's technical tour de force, but reflect, cinematically, the director's thematic concerns.'[45]

The reception of *Topaz* needs to be understood in the context of the adoption of the *auteur* theory by American film criticism in the late 1960s. Andrew Sarris's polemical *The American Cinema* had been published in 1968: Sarris – who selected Hitchcock as one of his 'pantheon' directors – championed the *auteur* theory as 'a table of values that converts film history into directorial autobiography' and asserted 'that the worst film of a great director may be more interesting though less successful than the best film of a fair to middling director'.[46] *Topaz*, a lesser film by a great director, became a test-case for the *auteur* theory. In general it was the critics who subscribed to the *auteur* theory who liked *Topaz* the best, while those who disliked it were less inclined to endorse the *auteur* idea. Nat Freedland in *Entertainment World*, for example, averred that '*Topaz*, the newest Hitchcock thriller, doesn't succeed at much of anything except in helping disprove the auteur theory and in demonstrating that Alfred Hitchcock's suspense gimmicks are most likely passé'.[47] It is no surprise that one of Hitchcock's most outspoken critics at this time, Pauline Kael, film critic of the *New Yorker*, was also a staunch opponent of the *auteur* theory, which she referred to, in her review of *Topaz*, as uncritical admiration for 'the directors who go on making the same kind of picture in the same way year after year'. A more balanced perspective was offered by Richard Corliss in *Film Quarterly*, who felt that *Topaz* was neither a dud nor a masterpiece but a mixture of the awful and the sublime: '*Topaz*, inept and ineffable, poorly acted and well acted, shoddily shot and exquisitely shot, mediocre and transcendant, should be borne in mind before we send "Hitchcock" to the Pantheon or to critical perdition.' Corliss was one of the few critics to focus on Hitchcock as a genre director rather than just an *auteur*:

> The film is Hitchcock's twenty-eighth in America and his twelfth in the spy
> genre ... Hitchcock's best spy films seem to transcend their maker's intentions –

whether by a witty script (like the one by Charles Bennett, Joan Harrison, James Hilton, and Robert Benchley for *Foreign Correspondent*) or by an actor's extra, usually independent effort (Michael Redgrave) – while, in his worst, Hitchcock's concentration on technique seems empty when there's an absence of dense detail (as in *Notorious*) or involving, living characters (as in *Torn Curtain*).[48]

For Corliss, therefore, Hitchcock's best spy films were enriched by some contribution beyond his direction. Corliss also offered a corrective to the polemical excesses of the *auteur* theory in his assertion that 'any film ... is the result of a number of stimuli, controlled perhaps by the director, but created by actors, writers and technicians. Beneath the mythical Hitchcock who is the author of everything grand in his oeuvre is a partly creative, mostly collaborative craftsman who must rely on the crucial contributions of his co-workers.'

The critical reception of *Topaz* in France – where Hitchcock was made an Officier des Arts et Lettres shortly after completing the film – focused more on the politics of the film than the American reception. In the wake of the Paris riots of May 1968 and the subsequent radicalisation of film culture, French critics had moved on from *la politique des auteurs* and had embraced Marxist theories of ideology in preference to aesthetic and formal criticism. The consensus among the Parisian critics seems to have been that *Topaz* was reactionary Cold War propaganda with few redeeming qualities. *L'Humanité* felt that it 'shares readily in the commonplace and clichés which make up the political mythology most widespread in the United States ... Hitchcock is certainly no political thinker but the material of his film is directly integrated with political propaganda and political conceptions of the United States government.'[49] *L'Express* thought it a throwback to the hawkish Cold War cinema of the 1950s: '[We] see, back in this film, the same anti-red arguments of the cold war period ... if the style is still Hitchcock, the mental level is that of John Wayne.'[50] *Les Nouvelles Littéraires* found it 'out of date both in technique which abuses the "get-that-into-your-heads" process, and in the concept which takes us back to the happily past era of McCarthysme [sic]'.[51] *Le Nouvel Observateur* suggested that Uris's novel 'maintains its ferocious anti-Communism on the screen. Since the master of suspense has renounced all humour, this bias is all the more unpleasant.'[52] In contrast *Les Lettres Françaises* felt that Hitchcock had toned down Uris's 'passionately anti-French' novel and 'is clever enough to make *Topaz* less of a political pamphlet able to arouse passion than a simple spy film in which the master's natural sense of humour carries us through an intrigue with many twists and turns'.[53]

Hitchcock always maintained that the box office was the real test of a film's success rather than the views of critics: in this regard *Topaz* – which after a year had earned domestic rentals of only $3,839,363 – must be regarded as a failure.[54] There are a number of possible explanations for its weak performance at the box office. One is that the spy cycle had run its course by the end of the 1960s: even the James Bond film *On Her Majesty's Secret Service* – released in the same month as *Topaz* (December 1969) – fared less well than previous Bonds (North American rentals of $9.1 million), though that may have been due to the substitution of former male model George Lazenby for Sean Connery as Agent 007. More generally the late 1960s saw profound changes in the nature of film culture in the United States with the emergence of a new wave in American cinema whose films were geared much more directly towards young adults rather than the traditional family audience and took full advantage of the relaxation of censorship following the abolition of the Production Code in 1968 and its replacement by a ratings system. The most successful American movies of the late 1960s reflected changing social mores and were characterised by their anti-establishment outlook. In comparison to films such as *The Graduate* (domestic rentals of $49 million), *Bonnie and Clyde* ($24.1 million), *Midnight Cowboy* ($20.3 million), *Easy Rider* ($19.1 million) and *Bob & Carol & Ted & Alice* ($14.6 million), *Topaz* must have seemed old-fashioned fare indeed.[55] Its lacklustre performance at the box office suggests that Hitchcock had indeed lost touch with popular taste: he was no longer master of the genre he had once owned.

CONCLUSION: HITCHCOCK AND THE SPY FILM

Alfred Hitchcock died on 29 April 1980, four months after receiving an honorary knighthood in the Queen's New Year Honours. By an extraordinary coincidence the third film version of *The 39 Steps* – produced by James Kenelm Clarke and directed by Don Sharp for the Rank Organisation in 1978 – was belatedly released in the United States on the same day.[1] It was unfortunate timing for the film which was inevitably found wanting in comparison with the Hitchcock version. A critic for *New York* magazine, for example, described Sharp's film as 'an obvious bit of routine filmmaking, hardly in a class with Hitchcock's tour de force'.[2] Hitchcock's obituaries duly paid fulsome tribute to the 'master of suspense' and his role in the evolution of the screen thriller. And, while many of the notices reflected the common preference for the director's later American work, it was also acknowledged that 'he set the standard of international intrigue and espionage with such classic thrillers as *The 39 Steps* and *The Lady Vanishes*'.[3]

In fact Hitchcock's last, unrealised project was to have been yet another spy subject. He had been toying with the idea of filming Ronald Kirkbride's novel *The Short Night* since the late 1960s. Like *Topaz*, *The Short Night* was a fictionalised account of a true spy story: it was based on the case of George Blake, an MI6 officer who became a double agent for the KGB in the 1950s. Blake was discovered and tried at the Old Bailey in 1961, but in 1966 he escaped from Wormwood Scrubs prison and succeeded in reaching East Germany and then Moscow where he lived for the rest of his life. In Kirkbride's novel an American whose brother had been one of the agents betrayed by the Blake character (thinly disguised as George Brand) sets out to avenge him: he follows the traitor's wife and children to a rendezvous in Finland where he intends to kill Brand but, arriving before his quarry, finds himself falling in love with the wife. *The Short Night* had clear parallels with *Torn Curtain* and *Topaz*: Hitchcock seems to have seen it as the third of a Cold War triptych. He scouted locations in Finland in August 1968 prior to the location shooting of *Topaz*. In April 1969 Universal included *The Short Night* on its production schedule for 1969–70 and suggested that Hitchcock would start on it as soon as he finished *Topaz*.[4] However, following the disappointing reception of *Topaz* Hitchcock evidently felt the need to change direction. As he told one correspondent: 'For the time, I don't think I will be making *The Short Night*, because it contains political elements; and following *Topz*, I feel that there might be some complaints that I am always making spy pictures.'[5] In the event his next film would be *Frenzy* (1972), a modern 'Jack the Ripper' story based on a novel by Arthur La Bern (*Goodbye Piccadilly, Farewell Leicester Square*). *Frenzy*, modestly budgeted and shot on location in Britain, marked a return to form for Hitchcock: its critical and commercial success surprised the studio, which had expected it to be his last film. Hitchcock followed it with *Family Plot* (1976), a comedy-drama about fake clairvoyants adapted from Victor Canning's *The Rainbird Pattern*. *Family Plot* was also generally well received: critics seem to have regarded it as a more profound and important film than it was intended to be.

Hitchcock never lost his interest in *The Short Night*, however, and returned to it after completing *Family Plot*.[6] James Costigan, an Emmy Award-winning television writer, was the first writer assigned to the project though he never produced a full screenplay. Hitchcock therefore turned to Ernest Lehmann, who had also worked on the early drafts of *Family Plot*. Lehmann completed his first draft of *The Short Night* in March 1978. Hitchcock's friend and colleague Norman Lloyd scouted locations in Finland during the early summer of 1978. However, feeling that the script needed further work, Hitchcock recruited David Freeman, a former magazine journalist. By this time Hitchcock's health was deteriorating – he suffered from heart problems and acute arthritis – and there is some suggestion that the studio never expected the film to be made but allowed Hitchcock to continue working on it in order to maintain the illusion that he was still an active film-maker.[7] Freeman's account of the six months he spent working on *The Short Night* suggests that the evidently ailing director 'moved in and out of senility' and 'seemed in no hurry to finish the work'.[8] In May 1979 Hitchcock finally accepted the inevitable and closed down his production office at Universal.

Freeman's screenplay of *The Short Night* was complete enough for it to be published in the writer's 1984 memoir *The Last Days of Afred Hitchcock*. Quite how it would have turned out as a film is difficult to say: in all likelihood much would have depended on the casting. It is a much better structured script than the unwieldy *Topaz* and has a clearer sense of psychological motivation for its protagonist (finally known as Joe Bailey) than *Torn Curtain*. It also includes its share of what would probably have been critic-pleasing 'Hitchcockian' touches, notably the opening set piece of Brand's escape from prison, which was to have been shot in a single take, rather like the opening of Orson Welles's *Touch of Evil* (1958), and the final climactic confrontation between Bailey and Brand on a train crossing the Russian frontier. At the same time, however, *The Short Night* seems out of touch with developments in the spy film in the 1970s. This was the decade of the paranoid conspiracy thriller, exemplified by *The Conversation* (1974), *The Parallax View* (1974) and *Three Days of the Condor* (1975). These films collectively marked a turn away from external threats such as the Soviet Union and became more inward-looking, with spy conspiracies emanating from within America's own institutions – including its government and intelligence services. In this context the Cold War narrative of *The Short Night* might have seemed somewhat *passé* – a point made by one Universal executive during the preparation of the film: 'My greatest concern, as yours, is "The Russians". Things have changed so since this was first out that one is led to wonder if the audience is really that concerned about secrets getting to the Russians in 1976.'[9]

While it remained unmade, *The Short Night* might be seen as the culmination of Hitchcock's work in the spy genre. As David Freeman observed: '*The Short Night* is about love and spies, a favourite area for Hitchcock. Its antecedents in his films are *The Lady Vanishes*, *The 39 Steps* and *North by Northwest*.'[10] The relationship between the personal and the political had been a recurring theme of Hitchcock's spy films ever since the first version of *The Man Who Knew Too Much*: the politics of international espionage are mapped onto and played out through heterosexual romantic relationships. Most obviously *The Short Night* recalls *Notorious* in dramatising the conflict between love and duty as Joe Bailey falls in love with the wife of the man he intends to kill. And other echoes of previous Hitchcock films in *The Short Night* include *Secret Agent* (the protagonist's mission to assassinate an enemy agent and the climax on board a speeding train) and *Torn Curtain* (the female lead is the wife of a defector).

Hitchcock did not invent the spy film but he played a major role in shaping the genre. Other directors have made important contributions to the history of the spy film of course. Fritz Lang's *Spione* is a foundational film of the genre – an ancestor of the James Bond films with its sensational narrative and megalomaniac master criminal – and it was Walter Forde's *Rome Express* that established the contemporary spy film in the portfolio of the Gaumont-British Picture Corporation a full two years before *The Man Who Knew Too Much*. The style of the Bond films in the 1960s owed much to director Terence Young and screenwriter Richard Maibaum – himself a one-time Hitchcock collaborator on *Foreign Correspondent* – while John Frankenheimer (*The Manchurian Candidate*), Martin Ritt (*The Spy Who Came in from the Cold*), Sidney J. Furie (*The Ipcress File*) and Sydney Pollack (*Three Days of the Condor*) all directed films that were at least the equal of Hitchcock's late spy thrillers. Yet no other film-maker had such a lasting impact on the development of the spy film or produced such a significant body of work in the genre. In particular it was Hitchcock who did more than anyone to legitimate the thriller critically. The low-brow status of the thriller in the dominant critical discourses is one of the reasons why films such as *The 39 Steps* and *North by Northwest* continue to be seen as Hitchcock films rather than as genre films: in this sense Hitchcock's films transcend the genre to which they belong and which they helped to define.

Indeed it may legimately be argued that Hitchcock's spy films represent a paradigm of the genre as a whole. They range in style from the most melodramatic extremities of the sensational or magical thriller – exemplified pre-eminently by the British version of *The Man Who Knew Too Much* – to different variations of the realist or existential thriller represented by *Sabotage*, *Notorious* and *Topaz*. And they include adaptations of major authors within the canon of literary spy fiction – including John Buchan, W. Somerset Maugham and Joseph Conrad – as well as original screen subjects. In this latter regard a gradual transition can be mapped from Hitchcock's British spy pictures to his American films. With the exception of *The Man Who Knew Too Much*, all of Hitchcock's British spy films were based on literary source texts – Buchan (*The 39 Steps*), Maugham (*Secret Agent*), Conrad (*Sabotage*) and Ethel Lina White (*The Lady Vanishes*) – and even *The Man Who Knew Too Much* had started out as a film featuring Sapper's Bulldog Drummond character. In America, however, the original screenplay became dominant among Hitchcock's spy films: *Saboteur*, *North by Northwest* and *Torn Curtain* were all original screenplays, while *Foreign Correspondent* and *Notorious* were both so far removed from their notional source texts as to be original screenplays to all intents and purposes. The odd one out in this pattern is *Topaz*, for which Hitchcock turned to an existing literary property – with somewhat indifferent results.

It is important to consider the relationship between Hitchcock's films and their source texts in any assessment of Hitchcock's contribution to the development of the spy film in popular cinema. That Hitchcock often played fast and loose with his source texts is taken for granted in much Hitchcock scholarship: but at the same time there are some films that on closer inspection turn out to be closer to their literary originals than is often allowed. Among the British films, *Sabotage* is probably the most respectful to its source but – as I hope the case studies have demonstrated – *The 39 Steps* and *The Lady Vanishes* are closer to their source novels than their reputation might suggest. Again this is not to deny the significance of Hitchcock's authorship in transforming the books into screen entertainments – and perhaps in this content 'transform-ation' is a better description of the process than 'adaptation' – but rather to see his spy films in their wider cultural contexts. It seems to me that regardless of their actual sources, Hitchcock's British films of the 1930s all draw to a significant degree upon the themes and motifs of contemporary spy fiction. For example, Hitchcock's preference for reluctant amateur spies rather than professional secret agents aligns his films with the novels of Graham Greene and Eric Ambler. From *The 39 Steps* there is also evidence of an emerging anti-fascist politics in Hitchcock's films which again locates them squarely within the ideological co-ordinates of the decade. And the influence of John Buchan can be seen not only in *The 39 Steps* but also in *The Man Who Knew Too Much* and even to an extent in *Secret Agent*.

In Hitchcock's American spy thrillers, however, a different pattern emerges. It is not just that the original screenplay assumes ascendancy over the literary adaptation but also that the films seem to refer more to other spy films, especially Hitchcock's own, than to literary spy fiction. *North by Northwest* was conceived as 'the Hitchcock picture to end all Hitchcock pictures' but in effect Hitchcock had been remaking his own spy movies ever since *Foreign Correspondent* and *Saboteur*. *Foreign Correspondent* harks back to the British thrillers both in its European setting and as Hitchcock's last collaboration with Charles Bennett. *Saboteur* and *North by Northwest* transpose the basic narrative template of *The 39 Steps* to America. Hitchcock scholars Walter Raubicheck and Walter Srebnick have argued that 'the interesting position of *Saboteur* and *North by Northwest* in the Hitchcock canon as two of the very few films that are not based on outside source material makes them particularly relevant to any study of the director's ideas about narrative construction or of his collaboration with screen- writers'.[11] The most obvious instance of Hitchcock remaking his own work is the American version of *The Man Who Knew Too Much*. It is instructive to study the reception discourses of Hitchcock's later films to understand changes in the contemporary film culture. *North by Northwest*, for example, was widely understood as a sort of Hitchcock 'greatest hits' vehicle as well as a parody of the genre: one critic described it as 'a perfect parody of his own work'. However, by the time of *Torn Curtain* and *Topaz*, there was a sense that Hitchcock's familiar themes and motifs were becoming *passé* – a view summed up in Pauline Kael's description of *Topaz* as 'the same damned spy picture he's been making since the thirties'.

However, perhaps the most compelling evidence for Hitchcock's importance to the history of the spy film is the extent to which his influence continues to permeate the genre. Hitchcock's legacy for the modern film thriller deserves a full study in its own right: a few examples must suffice to make the point. Brian De Palma, to take the most notable example, seems to have built his career as an extended homage to Hitchcock: *Obsession* (1976), *Dressed to Kill* (1980) and *Body Double* (1984) among others. De Palma's *Mission: Impossible* (1996) is his 'Hitchcockian' spy film: it owes more to *North by Northwest* than the television series on which it was supposedly based. One particular shot – the elaborate camera movement featuring a dissolve-through-the-window to the Eurostar express train – is nothing if not a direct homage to Hitchcock's use of a similar effect in *Foreign Correspondent*: De Palma had already used it in *The Untouchables* (1987). John Woo directed the first *Mission: Impossible* sequel, *M:I-2* (2000), which adopts the basic plot of *Notorious* as agent Ethan Hunt (Tom Cruise) recruits Nyah Nordoff-Hall (Thandie Newton) to sleep with and spy on Sean Ambrose (Dougray Scott) who has stolen the formula for the deadly 'chimera' virus. Hitchcock's influence on the James Bond films has already been noted: recent examples include the train sequence in *Casino Royale* (2006) with its echoes of *North by Northwest* and Bond's journey into John Buchan territory in the last act of *Skyfall* (2012). The Jodie Foster vehicle *Flightplan* (2005) is *The Lady Vanishes* on an aeroplane, while *Eagle Eye* (2008) is a techno-thriller variant of *North by Northwest*. The Sherlock Holmes film *Mr Holmes* (2015) includes a Hitchcockian homage in its reference to 'Ambrose Chapel' (*The Man Who Knew Too Much*). And on television the BBC's popular spy series *Spooks* (2002–11) included a number of direct or indirect Hitchcock references, including a spies' rendezvous at the London Zoo aquarium (*Sabotage*), a fake funeral complete with an empty coffin (*Secret Agent*), strangulation by necktie (*Frenzy*) and an agent called Kaplan (*North by Northwest*). Hitchcock's films have become part of the DNA of the spy thriller: his legacy continues to inform the genre long after the master himself has passed.

NOTES

INTRODUCTION

1. Eric Rohmer and Claude Chabrol, *Hitchcock: The First Forty-Four Films*, trans Stanley Hochman (New York, 1988 [1957]), p. 38.
2. Jim Kitses, *Horizons West: Anthony Mann, Budd Boetticher, Sam Peckinpah: Studies of Authorship within the Western* (London, 1969), p. 3.
3. Lindsay Anderson, 'Alfred Hitchcock', *Sequence*, 9 (1949), p. 117.
4. An annotated bibliography published in the 1990s lists over 900 scholarly books and journal articles, and there have been many more since: Jane E. Sloan, *Alfred Hitchcock: A Guide to References and Resources* (Berkeley, CA, 1995), pp. 343–535.
5. Mark Glancy, *The 39 Steps: A British Film Guide* (London, 2003); James Naremore, 'Spies and Lovers', in James Naremore (ed.), *North by Northwest: Alfred Hitchcock, Director* (New Brunswick, NJ, 1993), pp. 3–19.
6. Jean Domarchi and Jean Douchet, 'An Interview with Alfred Hitchcock', trans. Lahcen Hassad and Darlene Sadlier, in Naremore, *North by Northwest*, p. 177.
7. Christopher Cook (ed.), *The Dilys Powell Film Reader* (Manchester, 1991), p. 44.
8. Rohmer and Chabrol, *Hitchcock*, p. ix.
9. Robin Wood, *Hitchcock's Films* (London, 1965), p. 19.
10. Lee Russell, 'Alfred Hitchcock', *New Left Review*, 35 (1966), pp. 89–90.
11. François Truffaut, with Helen G. Scott, *Hitchcock* (London, rev. edn 1986), p. 192.
12. Tom Ryall, *Alfred Hitchcock and the British Cinema* (London, 1986), p. 1.
13. Charles Barr, *English Hitchcock* (Moffat, 1999), p. 185.
14. David Boyd and R. Barton Palmer, 'Introduction: Recontextualizing Hitchcock's Authorship', in David Boyd and R. Barton Palmer (eds), *Hitchcock at the Source: The Auteur as Adaptor* (Albany, NY, 2011), p. 4.
15. Ibid., p. 6.
16. Nigel West, 'Fiction, Faction and Intelligence', *Intelligence and National Security*, 9/2 (2004), pp. 275–89.
17. Michael Denning, *Cover Stories: Narrative and Ideology in the British Spy Thriller* (London, 1987), pp. 1–2.
18. Ibid., p. 2.
19. Ibid., p. 34.

20. Alan R. Booth, 'The Development of the Espionage Film', in Wesley K. Wark (ed.), *Spy Fiction, Spy Films, and Real Intelligence* (London, 1991), p. 138.
21. Peter John Dyer, 'Young and Innocent', *Sight and Sound*, 30/2 (1961), p. 81.
22. Steve Neale, *Genre* (London, 1980), p. 29.
23. Truffaut, *Hitchcock*, p. 89.
24. Ibid., p. 122.
25. John Buchan, *The Power-House* (London, 1984 edn [1913]), p. 92.
26. Wood, *Hitchcock's Films*, p. 29.
27. Robin Wood, *Hitchcock's Films Revisited* (London, 1991), p. 230.
28. Maurice Yacowar, *Hitchcock's British Films* (Hamden, CT, 1977), p. 269.
29. Wood, *Hitchcock's Films Revisited*, p. 275.

1   HITCHCOCK AND BRITISH CINEMA

1. *The Lady Vanishes* was actually produced by Gaumont-British subsidiary Gainsborough Pictures. The complex relationship between Gaumont-British and Gainsborough is best explained in Rachael Low, *The History of the British Film 1929–1939: Film-Making in 1930s Britain* (London, 1985), pp. 126–43, 241–7.
2. Raymond Durgnat, *The Strange Case of Alfred Hitchcock: Or the Plain Man's Hitchcock* (London, 1974), p. 20.
3. David Freeman, *The Last Days of Alfred Hitchcock: A Memoir Featuring the Screenplay of 'Alfred Hitchcock's The Short Night'* (New York, 1984), p. 26.
4. Tom Ryall, *Alfred Hitchcock and the British Cinema* (London, 1986), p. 115.
5. See Philip Kemp, 'Not for Peckham: Michael Balcon and Gainsborough's International Trajectory in the 1920s', in Pam Cook (ed.), *Gainsborough Pictures* (London, 1997), pp. 13–30. On the context of international co-productions at this time, see Andrew Higson and Richard Maltby (eds), *'Film Europe' and 'Film America': Cinema, Commerce and Cultural Exchange 1920–1939* (Exeter, 1999).
6. François Truffaut, with Helen G. Scott, *Hitchcock* (London, rev. edn 1986), p. 73.
7. Ibid., p. 45.
8. Ryall, *Alfred Hitchcock and the British Cinema*, p. 24.
9. Margaret Dickinson and Sarah Street, *Cinema and State: The Film Industry and the British Government, 1927–84* (London, 1984), pp. 5–33.
10. Low, *The History of the British Film 1929–1939* (London, 1985), pp. 116–17.
11. The term 'Elstree blues' originated in a review of *The Man Who Knew Too Much* in the *Daily Express* (4 December 1934): 'After a prolonged spell of Elstree blues and one musical confection at "the Bush" which was not in his line, Alfred Hitchcock leaps once again into the front rank of British film directors.'
12. Truffaut, *Hitchcock*, pp. 67–9.
13. Ibid., p. 84.
14. Ibid., p. 98.
15. Ibid., pp. 102–3.
16. Forsyth Hardy (ed.), *Grierson on the Movies* (London, 1981), p. 108.
17. Ibid., p. 110.
18. Truffaut, *Hitchcock*, p. 135.
19. Michael Balcon, *Michael Balcon Presents … A Lifetime of Films* (London, 1969), p. 27.

20. John Russell Taylor, *Hitch: The Life and Work of Alfred Hitchcock* (London, 1978), p. 118; Donald Spoto, *The Dark Side of Genius: The Life of Alfred Hitchcock* (London, 1983), pp. 136–7; Patrick McGilligan, *Alfred Hitchcock: A Life in Darkness and Light* (Chichester, 2003), pp. 152–3.

21. Truffaut, *Hitchcock*, p. 107.

22. *Motion Picture Daily*, 24 June 1935, p. 22.

23. There are no reliable figures for box-office grosses for British films during this period but according to the statistical methodology devised by John Sedgwick, which calculates a 'popularity index' based on the length of run and the size of cinemas, *Jack's the Boy* was the most popular film released in Britain in 1932, with *Rome Express* fourth and *Love on Wheels* ninth, *The Good Companions* eighth in 1933, *Jew Süss* eighth in 1934, *The Iron Duke* fourth and *The 39 Steps* eighth in 1935. In total 79 Gaumont-British/Gainsborough films were in the annual top hundred between 1932 and 1937. John Sedgwick, *Popular Filmgoing in 1930s Britain: A Choice of Pleasures* (Exeter, 2000), pp. 262–76.

24. 'Interview: Ivor Montagu' (conducted by Peter Wollen, Alan Lovell and Sam Rohdie), *Screen*, 13/3 (1972), p. 88.

25. Low, *The History of the British Film 1929–1939*, p. 136.

26. 'Close Your Eyes and Visualize!', *The Stage*, July 1936, p. 53.

27. Robert E. Kapsis, *Hitchcock: The Making of a Reputation* (Chicago, IL, 1992), p. 22.

28. David Bordwell, Janet Staiger and Kristin Thompson, *The Classical Hollywood Cinema: Film Style and Mode of Production to 1960* (London, 1985), pp. 320–9.

29. Kevin Gough-Yates, 'The British Feature Film as a European Concern: Britain and the Emigré Film-Maker, 1933– 45', in Günter Berghaus (ed.), *Theatre and Film in Exile: German Artists in Britain, 1933–1945* (Oxford, 1989), pp. 135–6. The most comprehensive study of German personnel working in the British film industry is Tobias Hochscherf, *The Contintental Connection: German-Speaking Émigrés and British Cinema, 1927–45* (Manchester, 2011).

30. Balcon, *A Lifetime of Films*, p. 75.

31. Michael Balcon, 'G.B. Goes International', *World Film News*, 1/3 (June 1936), p. 6.

32. BFI Balcon C/64: Michael Balcon to Mark Ostrer, 5 July 1935.

33. 'For '35–36: Sixteen Star-Spangled Specials', *Variety*, 19 June 1935, p. 40.

34. John Sedgwick, 'Michael Balcon's Close Encounter with the American Market, 1934–36', *Historical Journal of Film, Radio and Television*, 16/3 (1996), p. 345.

35. Sarah Street, *Transatlantic Crossings: British Feature Films in the United States* (London, 2002), p. 47.

36. AMPAS MPPA: PCA: *The Lady Vanishes*: undated press clipping, *Time* magazine.

37. The critical literature is extensive, but see in particular Jeffrey Richards, *The Age of the Dream Palace: Cinema and Society in Britain 1930–1939* (London, 1984), *passim*; John Segwick, 'Cinema-Going Preferences in Britain in the 1930s', in Jeffrey Richards (ed.), *The Unknown 1930s: An Alternative History of the British Cinema, 1929–1939* (London, 1998), pp. 1–35; and – for a local perspective – Sue Harper, 'A Lower Middle-Class Taste Community in the 1930s: Admissions Figures at the Regent Cinema, Portsmouth', *Historical Journal of Film, Radio and Television*, 24/4 (2004), pp. 565–87.

38. Russell Ferguson, 'Armaments Rings, Assasins and Political Madmen', *World Film News*, 2/5 (August 1937), p. 4.

39. Hardy (ed.), *Grierson on the Movies*, p. 118.

40. This figure is based on Denis Gifford, *The British Film Catalogue 1895–1970: A Guide to Entertainment Films* (Newton Abbot, 1973), *passim*.
41. I have not been able to see all these films: the list is based on Gifford, *British Film Catalogue*, and, from 1933, on the *Monthly Film Bulletin*.
42. The contexts of quota production are analysed in Steve Chibnall, *Quota Quickies: The Birth of the British 'B' Film* (London, 2007). See also Lawrence Napper, 'A Despicable Tradition? Quota Quickies in the 1930s', and Linda Wood, 'Low-Budget British Films in the 1930s', in Robert Murphy (ed.), *The British Cinema Book* (London, 1997), pp. 37–47, 48–57.
43. Richards, *Age of the Dream Palace*, p. 254.
44. Nicholas Pronay, 'The First Reality: Film Censorship in Liberal England', in K. R. M. Short (ed.), *Feature Films as History* (London, 1981), pp. 113–37; Jeffrey Richards, 'The British Board of Film Censors and Content Control in the 1930s (1): Images of Britain', *Historical Journal of Film, Radio and Television*, 1/2 (1981), pp. 97–116, and 'The British Board of Film Censors and Content Control in the 1930s (2): Foreign Affairs', *Historical Journal of Film, Radio and Television*, 2/1 (1982), pp. 39–48.
45. James C. Robertson, *The British Board of Film Censors: Film Censorship in Britain, 1896–1950* (London, 1985), p. 82.
46. BFI BBFC Scenario Reports 1930–32/94: *When the Gangs Came to London* by Edgar Wallace (book). Black and Till Ltd, 3 November 1932.
47. BFI BBFC Scenario Reports 1935/420: *Soho Racket* (book) by Grierson Dickson. Twickenham Film Studios Ltd, 4 June 1935.
48. BFI BBFC Scenario Reports 1933/216: *The Rumour* (stage play) by C. K. Munro. Gaumont British Picture Corporation Ltd, 14 September 1933.
49. BFI BBFC Scenario Reports 1933/55: *Sabotage* by Michael Hogan (synopsis). Gaumont British Picture Corporation Ltd, 10 May 1933.
50. BFFI BBFC Scenario Reports 1933/140: *Memoirs of a British Agent* (book) by R. H. Bruce Lockhart. Radio Pictures, 13 March 1933.
51. BFI BBFC Scenario Reports 1930–32/64: *Rome Express* (MS and scenario). Gaumont British Picture Corporation Ltd, 9 May 1932.
52. BFI BBFC Scenario Reports 1935/380: *The Thirty-Nine Steps* (scenario). Gaumont British Picture Corporation Ltd, 14 January 1935.
53. BFI BBFC Scenario Reports 1935/460: *The Eunuch of Stamboul* (book) by Dennis Wheatley, J. G. and R. B. Wainwright, 2 September 1935.
54. Jeffrey Richards and Dorothy Sheridan (eds), *Mass-Observation at the Movies* (London, 1987), p. 151.
55. Hochscherf, *The Continental Connection*, p. 90.
56. *Variety*, 21 June 1939.
57. *Motion Picture Herald*, 8 July 1939.
58. Charles Barr, *Ealing Studios* (London, 1977), p. 190.

2 'GOOD, THICK-EAR MELODRAMA OF AN ODDLY ENGLISH TYPE':
THE MAN WHO KNEW TOO MUCH (1934)

1. 'British Film Production: Bulldog Drummond', *The Times*, 1 February 1933, p. 8.
2. François Truffaut, with Helen G. Scott, *Hitchcock* (London, rev. edn 1986), p. 107.

3. Walter C. Mycroft, *The Time of My Life: The Memoirs of a British Film Producer*, ed. Vincent Porter (Lanham, MD, 2006), p. 132.

4. The eight Bulldog Drummond novels were *Bulldog Drummond* (1920), *The Black Gang* (1922), *The Third Round* (1924), *The Final Count* (1926), *The Female of the Species* (1928), *Temple Tower* (1929), *The Return of Bulldog Drummond* (1932) and *Bulldog Drummond at Bay* (1935). In addition Sapper teamed Drummond with another detective hero, Ronald Standish, in *Knock-Out* (1935) and *Challenge* (1937). Following Sapper's death in 1937, Gerald Fairlie wrote several further Bulldog Drummond adventures.

5. Paramount's Bulldog Drummond series comprised *Bulldog Drummond Escapes* (1937), starring Ray Milland, whereafter John Howard assumed the title role for the rest of the series: *Bulldog Drummond Comes Back* (1937), *Bulldog Drummond's Revenge* (1938), *Bulldog Drummond's Peril* (1938), *Bulldog Drummond in Africa* (1938), *Arrest Bulldog Drummond* (1938), *Bulldog Drummond's Secret Police* (1939) and *Bulldog Drummond's Bride* (1939).

6. *Film Weekly*, 12 July 1935.

7. Maurice Yacowar claims to have seen a screenplay of *The Man Who Knew Too Much* held by the British Film Institute Library which 'has a closing scene in a police court, where Uncle Clive is sentenced to twenty shillings or a week for disturbing the peace'. Yacowar, *Hitchcock's British Films* (London, 1977), p. 296. At the time of researching this book (2012–14), the BFI Library's electronic catalogue had no record of a screenplay for *The Man Who Knew Too Much*. The previous card index of the Unpublished Scripts Collection was not available.

8. 'Charles Bennett: First-Class Constructionist', in Pat McGilligan (ed.), *Backstory: Interviews with Screenwriters of Hollywood's Golden Age* (Berkeley, CA, 1986), p. 29.

9. Ibid., p. 25.

10. BFI BBFC Scenario Reports 1934/275: *The Hidden Hand* (scenario). Gaumont British Picture Corporation Ltd, 27 February 1934.

11. BFI Montagu Item 81: Gerald Fairlie to Angus MacPhail, 13 July 1934.

12. BFI BBFC Scenario Reports 1934/295: *The Man Who Knew Too Much* (scenario). Gaumont British Picture Corporation Ltd, 10 May 1934.

13. Ibid.: addendum dated 16 May 1934.

14. Hitchcock's own account of the negotiations with the BBFC can be found in 'The Censor and Sydney Street', *World Film News*, 2/12 (March 1938), pp. 4–5.

15. BFI Montagu Item 81: Gaumont-British Picture Corporation Ltd: 'The Hidden Hand'. Production costs, n.d. The budget includes £750 for the story rights, £500 for the script, £3,583 for direction, £6,600 for set construction, £4,625 for film stock, £900 for wardrobe, £430 for musical direction, £250 for the orchestra and £250 for special effects (listed as 'process and trick shots'). In the same file a Daily Production Cost Return dated 3–4 August 1934 indicates the estimated final direct cost at £48,074. 12s. 8d.

16. Ibid.: undated cross plot titled 'The Hidden Hand'.

17. Ibid.: C. R. Beville to S. C. Balcon, 20 August 1934.

18. John Russell Taylor, *Hitch*, p. 127.

19. 'Interview: Ivor Montagu', p. 76.

20. Michael Balcon, *Michael Balcon Presents... A Lifetime of Films* (London, 1969), p. 62.

21. John Sedgwick, *Popular Filmgoing in 1930s Britain: A Choice of Pleasures* (Exeter, 2000), p. 266.

22. AMPAS MPPA: PCA: *The Man Who Knew Too Much* (Gaumont, 1935): Joseph I. Breen to Vincent G. Hart, 25 January 1935.
23. Ibid.: Breen to Will H. Hays, 26 January 1935.
24. I count six dead policemen in the print of the film currently available on the Region 2 Network DVD in the 'Hitchcock: The British Years' set (VFC26047): the first constable is shot as he approaches the door where the terrorists are hiding, another two fall in the initial charge, a fourth is killed in the bedroom of an adjacent house, a fifth in the second charge and a sixth is shot by Peter Lorre from the window.
25. AMPAS MPPA: PCA: *The Man Who Knew Too Much*: Breen to Hays, 26 January 1935.
26. Ibid.: Breen to Hart, 26 January 1935.
27. Ibid.: Hart to Breen, 4 February 1935.
28. Ibid.: E. Schwengler (GBPC of America) to Hart, 21 June 1935; Breen to Dr James Wingate, 25 April 1935.
29. Peter John Dyer, 'Young and Innocent', *Sight and Sound*, 30/2 (1961), p. 81.
30. The London trade show of *The Return of Bulldog Drummond* was in April 1934; *The Man Who Knew Too Much* was in December 1934.
31. Charles Barr, *English Hitchcock* (Moffat, 1999), p. 148.
32. Kingsley Amis, *The James Bond Dossier* (London, 1966 edn), p. 87.
33. *Yorkshire Post*, 11 December 1934.
34. Chamberlain's comment was made during a BBC radio broadcast on 27 September 1938: <www.bbc.co.uk/archive/ww2outbreak/7904.shtml> (accessed January. 2015).
35. Raymond Durgnat, *The Strange Case of Alfred Hitchcock: Or the Plain Man's Hitchcock* (London, 1974), p. 125.
36. James Chapman, *Past and Present: National Identity and the British Historical Film* (London, 2005), pp. 45–63.
37. *Kinematograph Weekly*, 13 December 1934, p. 21.
38. *Film Weekly*, 14 December 1934.
39. *Monthly Film Bulletin*, 1/12 (January 1935), p. 116.
40. *Cinema Quarterly*, 3/2 (Winter 1934), p. 114.
41. *The Times*, 10 December 1934, p. 12.
42. *The Observer*, 9 December 1934, p. 12.
43. *News Chronicle*, 25 April 1953.
44. *New York Times*, 23 March 1935, p.11.
45. *Washington Post*, 17 September 1935, p. 8.
46. *Independent Exhibitors Film Bulletin*, 3 April 1935, p. 12.
47. *Harrison's Reports*, 9 March 1935, p. 38.
48. Sarah Street, *Transatlantic Crossings: British Feature Films in the United States* (London, 2002), pp. 44–7.
49. *Variety*, 3 April 1935, p. 24.
50. *New York Times*, 7 April 1935, p. X4.
51. Durgnat, *The Strange Case of Alfred Hitchcock*, p. 122.
52. John Pett, 'A Master of Suspense', *Films and Filming*, 6/2 (November 1959), p. 33.
53. Leslie Halliwell, *Halliwell's Hundred: A Nostalgic Choice of Films from the Golden Age* (London, 1982), p. 242.
54. Eric Rohmer and Claude Chabrol, *Hitchcock: The First Forty-Four Films*, trans. Stanley Hochman (New York, 1988 edn), p. 138.

55. Ibid., p. 40.
56. Robin Wood, *Hitchcock's Films Revisited* (London, 1991), pp. 358–9.
57. Ibid., p. 368.

3 HITCHCOCK AND BUCHAN: *THE 39 STEPS* (1935)

1. François Truffaut, with Helen G. Scott, *Hitchcock* (London, rev. edn 1986), p. 122.
2. John Buchan, *The Thirty-Nine Steps*, ed. Christopher Harvie (Oxford, 1993 [1915]), p. 3.
3. Janet Adam Smith, *John Buchan: A Biography* (Oxford, 1965), p. 197.
4. Ibid., p. 178.
5. Buchan, *The Thirty-Nine Steps*, p. 33.
6. Truffaut, *Hitchcock*, p. 130.
7. 'My Screen Memories', *Film Weekly*, 6 May 1936, p. 28.
8. BFI Balcon C/62: 'Copy of Mr M. E. Balcon's notes', 6 November 1934.
9. Truffaut, *Hitchcock*, p. 122.
10. Jeffrey Richards and Jeffrey Hulbert, 'Censorship in Action: The Case of *Lawrence of Arabia*', *Journal of Contemporary History*, 19/1 (1984), pp. 153–69.
11. Charles Barr, *English Hitchcock* (Moffat, 1989), p. 149.
12. 'My Screen Memories', *Film Weekly*, 16 May 1936, p. 28.
13. 'Charles Bennett: First-Class Constructionist', in Pat McGilligan (ed.), *Backstory: Interviews with Screenwriters of Hollywood's Golden Age* (Berkeley, CA, 1986), p. 28.
14. This may be inferred from the music hall sequence at the beginning of the film where one of the audience asks Mr Memory 'Who won the Derby in 1936?' to which Mr Memory replies 'Come back in 1937 and I'll tell you'.
15. BFI Balcon C/62: Michael Balcon to Mark Ostrer, 19 January 1935.
16. H. M. Glancy, 'Warner Bros. Film Grosses, 1921–1951: The William Schaefer Ledger', *Historical Journal of Film, Radio and Television*, 15/1 (1995), pp. 127–44.
17. 'For 35–36: Sixteen Star Spangled Specials', *Variety*, 19 June 1935, p. 40.
18. BFI Balcon C/2: 'Mr M.E. Balcon's Notes on "Thirty Nine Steps"', 26 November 1934.
19. BFI BBFC Scenario Reports 1935/380 and 380a: *The Thirty-Nine Steps* (scenario), Gaumont British Picture Corporation Ltd, 14 January 1935.
20. 'Hitchcock Finishes Gaumont-British Spy Melodrama', *Kinematograph Weekly*, 14 March 1935, p. 55.
21. Molly Haskell, *From Reverence to Rape: The Treatment of Women in the Movies* (Chicago, IL, 2nd edn 1987), p. 349.
22. 'The Man Who Made *The 39 Steps*', *Film Pictorial*, 23 November 1935.
23. *Kinematograph Weekly*, 13 June 1935, p. 3.
24. AMPAS Hitchcock f. 1381: Hitchcock to Janet Smith, 16 January 1964.
25. Stuart McDougal, 'Mirth, Sexuality and Suspense: Alfred Hitchcock's Adaptation of *The 39 Steps*', *Literature/Film Quarterly*, 3/3 (1975), p. 232.
26. Eric Rohmer and Claude Chabrol, *Hitchcock: The First Forty-Four Films*, trans. Stanley Hochman (New York, 1988 edn), p. 42.
27. Buchan, *The Thirty-Nine Steps*, p. 27.
28. Barr, *English Hitchcock*, p. 154.
29. Robin Wood, *Hitchcock's Films Revisited* (London, 1991), p. 275.
30. Truffaut, *Hitchcock*, p. 122.

31. Michael Denning, *Cover Stories: Narrative and Ideology in the British Spy Thriller* (Manchester, 1987), p. 49.
32. Wood, *Hitchcock's Films Revisited*, p. 276.
33. Buchan, *The Thirty-Nine Steps*, p. 38.
34. David Bordwell, Janet Staiger and Kristin Thompson, *The Classical Hollywood Cinema: Film Style and Mode of Production to 1960* (London, 1985), p. 79.
35. *Cinema Progress*, 1 (December 1935), p. 24.
36. Barr, *English Hitchcock*, p. 153.
37. Bordwell et al., *Classical Hollywood Cinema*, p. 79.
38. Mark Glancy, *The 39 Steps: A British Film Guide* (London, 2003), p. 27.
39. Stephen Constantine, *Unemployment in Britain between the Wars* (Harlow, 1980), p. 3.
40. Buchan, *The Thirty-Nine Steps*, p. 42.
41. *Kinematograph Weekly*, 13 June 1935.
42. *Monthly Film Bulletin*, 2/17 (June 1935), p. 72.
43. *Motion Picture Daily*, 24 June 1935, p. 22.
44. *The Hollywood Reporter*, 29 June 1935.
45. *The Times*, 6 June 1935, p. 14.
46. *Manchester Guardian*, 8 June 1935, p. 9.
47. *Daily Telegraph*, 10 June 1935.
48. *Sunday Times*, 9 June 1936.
49. *New Statesman*, 22 July 1935.
50. David Parkinson (ed.), *The Graham Greene Film Reader: Reviews, Essays, Interviews and Film Stories* (Manchester, 1993), p. 399.
51. *Variety*, 26 June 1935, p. 9.
52. *Kinematograph Weekly*, 17 June 1935, p. 54.
53. John Sedgwick's 'POPSTAT' methodology calculates that it was the eighth most popular release of 1935 behind *Lives of a Bengal Lancer*, *Top Hat*, *The Scarlet Pimpernel*, *The Iron Duke*, *On Wings of Song*, *Sanders of the River* and *Dark Angel*. Sedgwick, *Popular Filmgoing in 1930s Britain: A Choice of Pleaures* (Exeter, 2000), p. 269.
54. *Variety*, 6 November 1935, p. 11.
55. *Variety*, 8 January 1936, p. 19.
56. AMPAS MPPA: PCA: *The 39 Steps* (Gaumont-British, 1935): Vincent G. Hart to Arthur Lee, 9 July 1935.
57. Ibid.: Hart to Lee, 2 July 1935.
58. Ibid.: C. E. Schwengeler to Hart, 5 July 1935.
59. *Time*, 23 September 1935.
60. *Los Angeles Times*, 15 September 1935, p. A2.
61. *New York Times*, 14 September 1935.
62. *Variety*, 25 September 1935, p. 9.
63. BFI Balcon C/48: Arthur Lee to Mark Ostrer, 19 September 1935.
64. *Motion Picture Daily*, 2 January 1936, p. 1.
65. Glancy, *The 39 Steps*, p. 89.
66. AMPAS Hitchcock f. 1057: MacPhail to Hitchcock, 8 September 1957.
67. Ibid: MacPhail to Hitchcock, 7 September 1957.
68. AMPAS Hitchcock f. 660: Sidney Bernstein to Hitchcock, 25 February 1958.

69. Leslie Halliwell, *Halliwell's Film Guide* (London, 6th edn 1987), p.1039.
70. Truffaut, *Hitchcock*, p.129.
71. There are specific echoes of the clock-hanging climaxes of Harold Lloyd's *Safety Last* (1923) and Will Hay's *My Learned Friend* (1943).
72. 'Former *Spooks* star Rupert Penty-Jones returns to action in new version of *39 Steps*', *Daily Record*, 27 December 2008: <www.dailyrecord.co.uk/showbiz/celebrity-intervi ew/2008/12/27/86908-2097823> (accessed October 2015).
73. 'The 39 Steps to Close After Nine Years in the West End', *The Stage*, 17 June 2015: <www.thestage.co.uk/news/2015/39-steps-closes-nine-years-west-end> (accessed October 2015).

4   HITCHCOCK AND MAUGHAM: *SECRET AGENT* (1936)

1. W. Somerset Maugham, *Ashenden* (London, 2000 [1928]), pp. v–vii.
2. François Truffaut, with Helen G. Scott, *Hitchcock* (London, rev. edn 1986), pp. 131–5.
3. Maugham, *Ashenden*, pp. viii–ix.
4. Ibid., p. ix.
5. Julian Symons, *Bloody Murder: From the Detective Story to the Crime Novel: A History* (Harmondsworth, rev. edn 1985), p. 219.
6. Anthony Curtis, *The Pattern of Maugham: A Critical Portrait* (London, 1974), p. 111.
7. 'My Screen Memories', *Film Weekly*, 30 May 1936, p. 26.
8. 'Charles Bennett: First-Class Constructionist', in Pat McGilligan (ed.), *Backstory: Interviews with Screenwriters of Hollywood's Golden Age* (Berkeley, CA, 1986), p. 28.
9. BFI Balcon C/62: Michael Balcon to Jack Warner, 28 August 1935.
10. Ibid.: Warner to Balcon, 17 August 1935.
11. Patrick McGilligan, *Alfred Hitchcock: A Life in Darkness and Light* (Chichester, 2003), pp. 182–3.
12. BFI BBFC Scenario Reports 1935/441: *Ashenden* (book) by Somerset Maugham. Gaumont British Picture Corporation Ltd, 23 July 1935.
13. BFI BBFC Scenario Reports 1935/486: *Secret Agent* (Scenario). Gaumont British Picture Corporation Limited, 4 November 1935.
14. BFI BBFC Scenario Reports 1935/486a.
15. BFI Balcon C/79: 'Mr M. E. Balcon's Comments on "The Secret Agent" [sic]', 28 October 1935.
16. AMPAS MPPA: PCA: *Secret Agent*: Vincent G. Hart to Joseph Breen, 14 November 1935.
17. Ibid.: Hart to Arthur Lee, 13 November 1935.
18. C. A. Lejeune, 'The Mystery of The Secret Agent', *Observer*, 10 May 1936, p. 16.
19. Maugham, *Ashenden*, p. 56.
20. BFI Montagu 57: Ivor Montagu to Michael Balcon, 4 May 1936.
21. AMPAS Hitchcock f. 679: *Topaz*: 'August 27th Story Conference in Mr Hitchcock's Office', transcript of tape recording [1968].
22. Raymond Durgnat, *The Strange Case of Alfred Hitchcock: Or the Plain Man's Hitchcock* (London, 1974), p. 131.
23. Truffaut, *Hitchcock*, p. 139.
24. *Time*, 15 June 1936.
25. Charles Barr, *English Hitchcock* (Moffat, 1999), p. 163.
26. Truffaut, *Hitchcock*, p. 142.

27. Michael Denning, *Cover Stories: Narrative and Ideology in the British Spy Thriller* (London, 1987), p. 34.

28. R. Barton Palmer, '*Secret Agent*: Coming in from the Cold, Maugham Style', in R. Barton Palmer and David Boyd (eds), *Hitchcock at the Source: The Auteur as Adaptor* (Albany, NY, 2011), p. 95.

29. Tom Ryall, *Alfred Hitchcock and the British Cinema* (London, 1986), p. 131.

30. Lesley Brill, *The Hitchcock Romance: Love and Irony in Hitchcock's Films* (Princeton, NJ, 1988), p. 185.

31. Alain Kerzoncuf and Charles Barr, *Hitchcock Lost and Found: The Forgotten Films* (Lexington, KY, 2015), p. 119.

32. *The Times*, 11 May 1936, p. 10.

33. *Kinematograph Weekly*, 14 May 1936, p. 21.

34. *Monthly Film Bulletin*, 3/29 (May 1936), p. 83.

35. *The Hollywood Reporter*, 24 June 1936, p. 2.

36. *Independent Exhibitors' Film Bulletin*, 17 June 1936, p. 10.

37. *The Spectator*, 15 May 1936, p. 102.

38. Ibid.

39. David Parkinson (ed.), *The Graham Greene Film Reader: Reviews, Essays, Interviews and Film Stories* (Manchester, 1993), p. 708.

5 HITCHCOCK AND CONRAD: *SABOTAGE* (1936)

1. Alfred Hitchcock, 'My Screen Memories', *Film Weekly*, 23 May 1936, p. 28.

2. Alfred Hitchcock, 'Direction', in Charles Davy (ed.), *Footnotes to the Film* (London, 1937), p. 12.

3. Paula Marantz Cohen, *Alfred Hitchcock: The Legacy of Victorianism* (Lexington, KY, 1995), p. 30.

4. François Truffaut, with Helen G. Scott, *Hitchcock* (London, 1986 edn), pp. 85–6.

5. Matthew Paul Carlson, 'Conrad's *The Secret Agent*, Hitchcock's *Sabotage*, and the Inspiration of "Public Uneasiness"', in Mark Osteen (ed.), *Hitchcock and Adaptation: On the Page and Screen* (Lanham, MD, 2014), pp. 79–94.

6. Frederick R. Karl and Laurence Davies (eds), *The Collected Letters of Joseph Conrad,* vol. 3 (New York, 1988), p. 439.

7. Tom Ryall, *Alfred Hitchcock and the British Cinema* (London, 1986), pp. 23–31.

8. Sylvia Hardy, 'H. G. Wells and British Silent Cinema: The War of the Worlds', in Andrew Higson (ed.), *Young and Innocent? The Cinema in Britain 1896–1930* (Exeter, 2002), pp. 242–55.

9. Carlson, 'Conrad's *The Secret Agent*, Hitchcock's *Sabotage*', p. 80.

10. Joseph Conrad, *The Secret Agent: A Simple Tale* (Oxford, 1983 [1907]), p. xxix.

11. F. R. Leavis, *The Great Tradition* (London, 1948), p. 220.

12. For critical discussion of *The Secret Agent*, see Ian Watt (ed.), *Conrad: The Secret Agent: A Casebook* (London, 1973); Jacques Berthoud, '*The Secret Agent*', in J. H. Stape (ed.), *The Cambridge Companion to Joseph Conrad* (Cambridge, 1996), pp. 100–21; and John G. Peters (ed.), *Joseph Conrad: Contemporary Reviews*, vol. 2. '*Typhoon*' to '*Under Western Eyes*' (Cambridge, 2012), pp. 334–45.

13. Conrad, *The Secret Agent*, pp. xxxi, xxxix.

14. Donald Spoto, *The Dark Side of Genius: The Life of Alfred Hitchcock* (London, 1983), p. 156.

15. Eric Rohmer and Claude Chabrol, *Hitchcock: The First Forty-Four Films*, trans. Stanley Hochmann (New York, 1988 [1957]), p. 47.
16. Ibid., p. 48.
17. Patrick McGilligan, *Alfred Hitchcock: A Life in Darkness and Light* (Chichester, 2003), pp. 201–3.
18. *Motion Picture Herald*, 6 June 1936, p. 66.
19. *Film Daily*, 24 February 1936, p. 12.
20. *The Times*, 3 September 1935, p. 10.
21. 'A Talk with Mr Conrad', *Manchester Guardian*, 3 November 1922, p. 10.
22. Marantz Cohen, *Alfred Hitchcock: The Legacy of Victorianism*, p. 173.
23. Charles Barr, *English Hitchcock* (Moffat, 1999), p. 237.
24. While there are several article-length studies of the adaptation of *The Secret Agent* into *Sabotage*, none of these seem to have consulted the script materials held by the British Film Institute Library which include a 'full treatment' dated 17 April 1936 (BFI Scripts S230) and an undated shooting script (BFI Scripts S231). In addition to Carlson's chapter and the chapter of Marantz Cohen's book cited above, see also Michael A. Anderegg, 'Conrad and Hitchcock: *The Secret Agent* inspires *Sabotage*', *Literature/Film Quarterly*, 3/3 (1975), pp. 215–25, and Mark Osteen, '"It Doesn't Pay to Antagonize the Public": *Sabotage* and Hitchcock's Audience', *Literature/Film Quarterly*, 28/4 (2000), pp. 259–68.
25. BFI BBFC Scenario Reports 1933/155: *Sabotage* by Michael Hogan (synopsis). Gaumont British Picture Corporation Ltd, 10 May 1933.
26. BFI Scripts Collection S231: *Sabotage*. Shooting Script, n.d.
27. Barr, *English Hitchcock*, p. 170.
28. Truffaut, *Hitchcock*, p. 144.
29. Ibid.
30. BFI BBFC Scenario Reports 1936/88: *Sabotage* (scenario), Gaumont British Picture Corporation Ltd, 15 June 1936.
31. BFI BBFC Scenario Reports 1936/109: *Sabotage* (portion of scenario), Gaumont British Picture Corporation Ltd, 18 July 1936.
32. *The Times*, 15 May 1936, p.14.
33. Truffaut, *Hitchcock*, pp. 144–5.
34. Ibid., p. 153.
35. Conrad, *The Secret Agent*, p. 7.
36. Rachael Low, *The History of the British Film 1929–1939: Film Making in 1930s Britain* (London, 1985), p. 143.
37. Michael Balcon, *Michael Balcon Presents ... A Lifetime of Films* (London, 1969), pp. 95–6.
38. McGilligan, *Alfred Hitchcock*, p. 190.
39. Conrad, *The Secret Agent*, p. xxxvi.
40. Osteen, '"It Doesn't Pay to Antagonize the Public"', p. 261.
41. The National Archives, Kew, London: WORK 19/215: 'W.H.S.' to Mr Heasman, 6 February 1939. My thanks to Llewella Chapman, who found this document in the course of her own research into official attitudes towards filming at the royal palaces.
42. Simon Shaw, '"Not Forgotten": The 1939 IRA Bomb Attack', *Historic Coventry*: <*www.historiccoventry.co.uk/articles/s-shaw.php*> (accessed March 2016).

43. Tony Shaw, *Cinematic Terror: A Global History of Terrorism on Film* (New York, 2015), p. 40.

44. AMPAS MPPA: PCA: *The Woman Alone* (1937): Note in the censors' file, 27 February 1937.

45. 'Brazil Bans "Sabotage" and "The Road Back"', *New York Times*, 30 October 1937, p. 3.

46. Christopher Andrew, *The Defence of the Realm: The Authorized History of MI5* (London, 2009), pp. 160–213.

47. Curiously the blurb-writer for the DVD of *Sabotage* released by Delta Entertainment in 2001 identifies Nazi Germany as the instigator of the conspiracy: 'As German saboteurs infiltrate England with plans to blow up key industrial and civilian locations, the British spare no effort to trap the Nazis before they can complete their mission.'

48. Forsyth Hardy (ed.), *Grierson on the Movies* (London, 1981), p. 110.

49. A. J. P. Taylor, *English History 1914–1945* (Oxford, 1965), p. 313.

50. Jeffrey Richards, *The Age of the Dream Palace: Cinema and Society in Britain 1930–1939* (London, 1984), pp. 11–12.

51. The postcode can be seen on the address label on one of the film cans.

52. Truffaut, *Hitchcock*, p. 22.

53. McGilligan, *Alfred Hitchcock*, p. 13.

54. Marantz Cohen, *Alfred Hitchcock: The Legacy of Victorianism*, p. 41.

55. David Parkinson (ed.), *The Graham Greene Film Reader: Mornings in the Dark* (Manchester, 1993), pp. 163–4.

56. Anthony Lejeune (ed.), *The C. A. Lejeune Film Reader* (Manchester, 1991), pp. 106–7.

57. Truffaut, *Hitchcock*, p. 145.

58. *The Times*, 7 December 1936, p. 12.

59. *Monthly Film Bulletin*, 3/36 (December 1936), p. 213.

60. *Manchester Guardian*, 3 December 1936, p. 7.

61. John Sedgwick, *Popular Filmgoing in 1930s Britain: A Choice of Pleasures* (Exeter, 2000), pp. 272–3.

62. Leslie Halliwell, *Seats in All Parts: Half a Lifetime at the Movies* (London, 1985), pp. 22–3.

63. *New York Times*, 27 February 1937, p. 167.

64. *Los Angeles Times*, 7 March 1937, p. C-3.

65. Ezra Goodman, 'Mysterious Mr Hitchcock', *Cinema Progress*, 3/2 (1938), p. 9.

66. *Motion Picture Herald*, 2 January 1937, p. 68.

67. *Harrison's Reports*, 30 January 1937, p. 19.

68. William Rothman, *Hitchcock: The Murderous Gaze* (Cambridge, MA, 1982), p. 175.

69. Charles Barr, *English Hitchcock* (Moffat, 1999), p. 175.

70. Raymond Durgnat, *The Strange Case of Alfred Hitchcock: Or the Plain Man's Hitchcock* (London, 1974), p. 137.

71. Neil Sinyard, *The Films of Alfred Hitchcock* (London, 1986), p. 35.

6   AGE OF APPEASEMENT: *THE LADY VANISHES* (1938)

1. The opening credits of *The Lady Vanishes* declare: 'G-B Pictures presents … A "Gainsborough" picture.'

2. Rachael Low, *The History of the British Film 1929–1939: Film Making in 1930s Britain* (London, 1985), pp. 241–7. See also Sue Harper, '"Nothing to Beat the Hay Diet":

Comedy and Gaumont and Gainsborough', in Pam Cook (ed.), *Gainsborough Pictures* (London, 1997), pp. 80–98.

3. Eric Rohmer and Claude Chabrol, *Hitchcock: The First Forty-Four Films*, trans. Stanley Hochman (New York, 1988 edn), p. 54.

4. Geoff Brown, *Launder and Gilliat* (London, 1977), pp. 89–90; Bruce Babington, *Launder and Gilliat* (Manchester, 2002), p. 6; Patrick McGilligan, *Alfred Hitchcock: A Life in Darkness and Light* (Chichester, 2003), p. 206.

5. AMPAS Hitchcock f. 1381: Hitchcock to Adrian House, 14 February 1967.

6. François Truffaut, with Helen G. Scott, *Hitchcock* (London, rev. edn 1986), p. 167.

7. Hitchcock's extended negotiations with Selznick throughout 1937–8 are documented in Leonard J. Leff, *Hitchcock and Selznick: The Rich and Strange Collaboration of Alfred Hitchcock and David O. Selznick in Hollywood* (London, 1988).

8. Ethel Lina White, *The Lady Vanishes* (London, 1997 [1936]), p. 16.

9. Ibid., p. 57.

10. Ibid., pp. 53, 57.

11. Ibid., pp. 159–60.

12. Ibid., p. 59.

13. Ibid., p. 83.

14. Ibid., pp. 160–1, 164.

15. Basil Radford and Naunton Wayne reprised their roles as Charters and Caldicott in *Night Train to Munich* (1940), *Crooks' Tour* (1941) and *Millions Like Us* (1943), all written and the last also directed by Frank Launder and Sidney Gilliat, and played similar parts under different names in other films including *Dead of Night* (1945), *Girl in a Million* (1946), *It's Not Cricket* (1949) and *Passport to Pimlico* (1949).

16. According to Frank Launder: 'He [Hitchcock] told us he did not care for the opening and thought the last reel could be made more exciting. Sidney worked on the revisions at his home in Cromwell Road. The difference between the new opening we then wrote and the one in the original script was that the pace was faster. And the last reel was certainly more exciting, with more twists and turns, after we had worked on it.' Quoted in Brown, *Launder and Gilliat*, p. 89.

17. 'Anglo-American Film Agreement', *The Times*, 11 July 1938, p. 12.

18. 'Cinema Sights in London', *New York Times*, 20 November 1938, p. 106.

19. AMPAS MPPA: PCA: *The Lady Vanishes* (1938): f. S. Harman to Arthur Lee, 5 October 1938.

20. Truffaut, *Hitchcock*, p. 161.

21. Ibid., p. 159.

22. Charles Barr, *English Hitchcock* (Moffat, 1999), p. 191.

23. Ibid., p. 202.

24. Sue Harper, *Women in British Cinema: Mad, Bad and Dangerous to Know* (London, 2000), p. 34.

25. AMPAS Hitchcock f. 350: *The Lady Vanishes* ['The Wheel Spins' inside the cover], 166 pages, undated screenplay.

26. On 30 September 1938, Chamberlain landed at Heston aerodrome and declared to the waiting press: 'My good friends, this is the second time there has come back from Germany to Downing Street peace with honour. I believe it is peace in our time.'

< https://eudocs.lib.byu.edu/Neville_Chamberlain's_Peace_For_Our_Time > (accessed February 2015).

27. *New Statesman*, 15 October 1938.
28. Andrew Sinclair, 'Introduction', *Masterworks of the British Cinema: The Lady Vanishes, Brief Encounter, Henry V* (London, 1990), p. 8.
29. Matthew Sweet, 'Mustard and Cress', *Guardian Review*, 29 December 2007, p. 10.
30. A. J. P. Taylor, *The Origins of the Second World War* (London, 1961), p. 189.
31. See David Hucker, *Public Opinion and the End of Appeasement in Britain and France* (Farnham, 2011), *passim*.
32. On *Sixty Glorious Years*, see James Chapman, *Past and Present: National Identity and the British Historical Film* (London, 2005), pp. 78–87.
33. AMPAS Hitchcock f. 350: *The Lady Vanishes*: insert page headed 'Lost Lady'.
34. *Monthly Film Bulletin*, 5/56 (August 1938), p. 196.
35. *The Times*, 10 October 1938, p. 12.
36. *Observer*, 19 October 1938, p. 18.
37. *World Film News*, 3/7 (November 1938), p. 314.
38. *World Film News*, 3/7 (November 1938), p. 311.
39. *New York Times*, 26 December 1938, p. 29.
40. Transcript of the radio programme *Mainly about Manhattan* for the British Broadcasting Corporation, 19 January 1939: <http://the.hitchcock.zone/wiki/Mainly_About_Manhattan> (accessed March 2015).
41. *The Hollywood Reporter*, 22 March 1939.
42. *Variety*, 22 March 1939.
43. Philip French, 'The Lady Vanishes', *Observer Magazine*, 28 September 1980, p. 97.
44. Brown, *Launder and Gilliat*, pp. 95–6.
45. Graham Fuller, 'Mystery Train', *Sight and Sound*, NS 18/1 (January 2008), p. 40.
46. Peter William Evans, *Carol Reed* (Manchester, 2005), p. 40.
47. BFI BBFC Scenario Reports 1939/64: *Report on a Fugitive* (treatment), Gainsborough Pictures Ltd, 10 November 1939.
48. *Manchester Guardian*, 25 July 1940, p. 4.
49. 'The Lucrative Case for Believing in Yesterday', *Guardian*, 18 December 1978, p. 11.
50. 'The Lady Vanishes: Can you Improve on Hitchcock?', *Daily Telegraph*, 17 March 2013: www.telegraph.co.uk/culture/tvand radio/9927079/The-Lady-Vanishes-can-you-improve- on-Hitchcock.html (accessed May 2016).
51. 'One Disappears, Another Delivers', *New York Times*, 16 Aug. 2013, p. C-1.

7   HITCHCOCK AND AMERICAN CINEMA

1. Anthony Lejeune (ed.), *The C. A. Lejeune Film Reader* (Manchester, 1991), p. 171.
2. Lindsay Anderson, 'Alfred Hitchcock', *Sequence*, 9 (1949), p. 119.
3. The phrase 'Gone With the Wind Up' is attributed to the veteran actor Sir Seymour Hicks though I have been unable to identify the original source.
4. Quoted in Charles Barr, 'Deserter or Honored Exile? Views of Hitchcock from Wartime Britain', *Hitchcock Annual*, 13 (2004–5), p. 5.
5. Patrick McGilligan, *Alfred Hitchcock: A Life in Darkness and Light* (Chichester, 2003), pp. 219–21.

6. Quoted in Nicholas John Cull, *Selling War: The British Propaganda Campaign Against American 'Neutrality' in World War II* (Oxford, 1995), p. 50.

7. H. Mark Glancy, *When Hollywood loved Britain: The Hollywood 'British' Film 1939–45* (Manchester, 1999), pp. 1–4.

8. Alain Kerzoncuf and Charles Barr, *Hitchcock Lost and Found: The Forgotten Hitchcock* (Lexington, KY, 2015), pp. 121–92.

9. Leonard J. Leff, *Hitchcock and Selznick: The Rich and Strange Collaboration of Alfred Hitchcock and David O. Selznick in Hollywood* (London, 1988), pp. 31–4.

10. The seven features were *Foreign Correspondent* (Walter Wanger, 1940), *Mr and Mrs Smith* (RKO Radio Pictures, 1941), *Suspicion* (RKO Radio Pictures), *Saboteur* (Universal 1942), *Shadow of a Doubt* (Universal, 1943), *Lifeboat* (Twentieth Century-Fox, 1944) and *Notorious* (RKO Radio Pictures, 1946).

11. Larry Swindell, '1939: A Very Good Year', *American Film*, 1/3 (1975), p. 28.

12. Thomas Schatz, *Boom and Bust: American Cinema in the 1940s* (Berkeley, CA, 1997), p. 172.

13. Ibid., p. 170.

14. David O. Selznick to Hitchcock, 19 September 1939, marked 'not sent': Rudy Behlmer (ed.), *Memo from David O. Selznick* (New York, 1972), pp. 276–9.

15. François Truffaut, with Helen G. Scott, *Hitchcock* (London, rev. edn 1986), p. 176.

16. Ibid., p. 186.

17. The 'Mr Moto' series was produced by Twentieth Century-Fox – it ran in parallel to the popular 'Charlie Chan' series of detective films – and comprised eight films: *Think Fast, Mr Moto* (1937), *Thank You, Mr Moto* (1937), *Mr Moto's Gamble* (1938), *Mr Moto Takes a Chance* (1938), *Mysterious Mr Moto* (1938), *Mr Moto's Last Warning* (1939), *Mr Moto in Danger Island* (1939) and *Mr Moto Takes a Vacation* (1939). It is generally held that the series was killed off by the outbreak of the Second World War, though the last film was made over two years before the Japanese attack on Pearl Harbor.

18. Tino Balio, *Grand Design: Hollywood as a Modern Business Enterprise, 1930–1939* (Berkeley, CA, 1993), p. 290.

19. Francis MacDonnell, *Insidious Foes: The Axis Fifth Column and the American Home Front* (New York, 1995), p. 1.

20. Hadley Cantril, with Hazel Gaudet and Herta Herzog, *The War of the Worlds: A Study in the Psychology of Panic* (Princeton, NJ, 1940), *passim*.

21. Nick Roddick, *A New Deal in Entertainment: Warner Brothers in the 1930s* (London, 1983), pp. 161–4.

22. AMPAS MPPA: PCA: *Confessions of a Nazi Spy* (1939): 'K.L.' to Joseph I. Breen, n.d.

23. Ibid.: Breen to Jack Warner, 30 December 1938. The letter is marked as unsent.

24. Clayton R. Koppes and Gregory D. Black, *Hollywood Goes to War: How Politics, Profits and Propaganda Shaped World War II Movies* (London, 1987), p. 30.

25. H. Mark Glancy, 'Warner Bros. Film Grosses, 1921–51: The William Schaefer Ledger', *Historical Journal of Film, Radio and Television*, 15/1 (1995), pp. 62–3.

26. In 1940 the British Treasury imposed currency restrictions on the amount of revenue that US distributors could remit back to the United States from the distribution of their films in Britain. These funds were 'frozen' but could be invested in the British production sector. MGM (*The Adventures of Tartu*) and RKO (*Squadron Leader X*, *Yellow Canary*, *Escape to Danger*) were among the studios who produced films in Britain during the war.

27. Patrick McGilligan, *Alfred Hitchcock*, p. 267.
28. Quentin Falk, *Travels in Greeneland: The Cinema of Graham Greene* (London, 1984), p. 27.
29. Brian McFarlane, *Lance Comfort* (Manchester, 1999), pp. 44–5.
30. 'Guardian Film Lecture', National Film Theatre (3 September 1984), in David Parkinson (ed.), *Mornings in the Dark: The Graham Greene Film Reader* (Manchester, 1993), p. 559.
31. James Naremore, *More than Night: Film Noir in its Contexts* (Berkeley, CA, rev. edn 2008), p. 15.
32. Raymond Borde and Étienne Chaumeton, *Panorama du Film Noir Américain 1941–1953*, trans. Paul Hammond (San Francisco, CA, 2002 [1955]), p. 161.
33. Naremore, *More than Night*, p. 72.
34. Borde and Chuameton, *Panorama du Film Noir Américain*, p. 96.
35. James Naremore, 'Hitchcock at the Margins of *Noir*', in Richard Allen and S. Ishii Gonzalès (eds), *Alfred Hitchcock: Centenary Essays* (London, 1999), pp. 263–77.
36. Martin Rubin, *Thrillers* (Cambridge, 1999), p. 60.
37. Quoted in Falk, *Travels in Greeneland*, pp. 36–7.
38. Koppes and Black, *Hollywood Goes to War*, p. 35.
39. Quoted in Patrick McGilligan, *Fritz Lang: The Nature of the Beast* (London: Faber & Faber, 1997), p. 281.
40. Thomas Elsaesser, 'Too Big and Too Close: Alfred Hitchcock and Fritz Lang', *Hitchcock Annual*, 12 (2003–4), p. 8.
41. Similar films in Britain were the RAF Film Unit's *Now It Can be Told* (1946) and Ealing's *Against the Wind* (1947).
42. Andrew Sarris, *The American Cinema: Directors and Directions 1929–1968* (New York, 1996 [1968]), p. 64.

8 'A MASTERPIECE OF PROPAGANDA': *FOREIGN CORRESPONDENT* (1940)

1. Vincent Sheean, *Personal History* (New York, 1935), p. 49.
2. Matthew Bernstein, *Walter Wanger: Hollywood Independent* (Berkeley, CA, 1994), p. 158.
3. *Variety*, 17 January 1940.
4. AMPAS Wong Howe f. 54: *Personal History* – script changes, 24 June 1938. The presence of this script in the James Wong Howe Collection at the Margaret Herrick Library would seem to indicate that the ace cinematographer was to have shot the film.
5. AMPAS MPPA: PCA: *Personal History* (1938): Joseph I. Breen to Walter Wanger, 21 June 1938.
6. Ibid.: Breen to Will H. Hays, 21 June 1938.
7. Quoted in Colin Shindler, *Hollywood Goes to War: Films and American Society 1939–52* (London, 1979), p. 5.
8. Bernstein, *Walter Wanger*, p. 158.
9. Patrick McGilligan, *Alfred Hitchcock: A Life in Darkness and Light* (Chichester, 2003), p. 248.
10. Bernstein, *Walter Wanger*, p. 440.

11. AMPAS Hitchcock f. 238: 'Personal History: Original Story by Alfred Hitchcock and Joan Harrison Suggested by Vincent Sheean's Book of the Same Name', 1st complete line, 20 November 1939, p. 1.

12. Ibid., p. 4.

13. 'Getting Too "Personal"', *Variety*, 13 Mar. 1940, p. 5.

14. 'Charles Bennett: First-Class Constructionist', in Pat McGilligan (ed.), *Backstory: Interviews with Screenwriters of Hollywood's Golden Age* (Berkeley, CA, 1986), p. 37.

15. François Truffaut, with Helen G. Scott, *Hitchcock* (London, rev. edn 1986), p. 176.

16. 'Richard Maibaum: A Pretense of Seriousness', in McGilligan, *Backstory*, p. 276.

17. McGilligan, *Alfred Hitchcock*, p. XX.

18. AMPAS Hitchcock f. 239: *Personal History*, shooting script, undated but including revisions dated 3 March, 18 March, 26 March, 30 March, 23 April and 24 May 1940.

19. Ibid.

20. Quoted in Susan A. Brewer, *To Win the Peace: British Propaganda in the United States during World War II* (Ithaca, NY, 1997), p. 80.

21. Douglas W. Churchill, 'Much Ado about Hollywood', *New York Times*, 14 April 1940, p. 129.

22. AMPAS MPPA: PCA: *Foreign Correspondent* (1940): Joseph I. Breen to Will H. Hays, 18 March 1940.

23. 'Personal History of a Foreign Correspondent', *Hollywood Magazine*, 29/8 (August 1940), p. 63.

24. Michael Todd Bennett, 'Anglophilia on Film: Creating an Atmosphere for Alliance, 1935–41', *Film and History*, 27/1–4 (1997), pp. 4–21.

25. H. Mark Glancy, *When Hollywood Loved Britain: The Hollywood 'British' Film 1939–45* (Manchester, 1999), p. 20.

26. Ibid., p. 15.

27. Ibid., pp. 30, 32.

28. See Marianne Hicks, '"No War This Year": Selkirk Porter and the Editorial Policy of the *Daily Express*, 1938–39', *Media History*, 14/2 (2008), pp. 167–83.

29. David Bordwell, Janet Staiger and Kristin Thompson, *The Classical Hollywood Cinema: Film Style and Mode of Production to 1960* (London, 1985), pp. 72–4.

30. Steve Neale, 'Propaganda', *Screen*, 18/3 (1977), pp. 9–40.

31. Glancy, *When Hollywood Loved Britain*, p. 116.

32. On the reporting of the Blitz to America, see Nicholas John Cull, *Selling War: The British Propaganda Campaign Against American 'Neutrality' in World War II* (New York, 1995), pp. 97–125.

33. *Washington Post*, 26 September 1940, p. 8.

34. *Los Angeles Times*, 28 August 1940, p. 11.

35. *Harrison's Reports*, 24 August 1940, p. 134.

36. *Variety*, 28 August 1940, p. 3.

37. *New York Times*, 1 September 1940, p. X3.

38. Anthony Lejeune (ed.), *The C. A. Lejeune Film Reader* (Manchester, 1991), pp. 171–2.

39. Christopher Cook (ed.), *The Dilys Powell Film Reader* (Manchester, 1991), pp. 43–4.

40. *Documentary News Letter*, 1/11 (November 1940), p. 6.

41. *Documentary News Letter*, 1/12 (December 1940), p. 6.

42. *Kinematograph Weekly*, 10 January 1940, p. 34.

43. Quoted in Shindler, *Hollywood Goes to War*, p. 8.

9 THE ENEMY WITHIN: *SABOTEUR* (1942)

1. François Truffaut, with Helen G. Scott, *Hitchcock* (London, rev. edn 1986), p. 214.
2. Ibid., p. 205.
3. Thomas Schatz, *The Genius of the System: Hollywood Filmmaking in the Studio Era* (New York, 1988), p. 326.
4. AMPAS Hitchcock f. 635: M. R. Davis to Hitchcock, 19 December 1946.
5. AMPAS Hitchcock f. 631: Untitled Original Treatment by Alfred Hitchcock and Joan Harrison, 20 August 1941 (including later pages dated 22 September 1941).
6. Patrick McGilligan, *Alfred Hitchcock: A Life in Darkness and Light* (Chichester, 2003), p. 295.
7. AMPAS Hitchcock f. 632: 'Alfred Hitchcock: Untitled Original', 30 October 1941.
8. AMPAS Hitchcock f. 633: 'Untitled Hitchcock Original. Screen Play by Dorothy Parker, Joan Harrison & Peter Viertel', 12 December 1941.
9. Clayton R. Koppes and Gregory D. Black, *Hollywood Goes to War: How Politics, Profits and Propaganda Shaped World War II Movies* (London, 1987), pp. 56–60.
10. AMPAS MPPA: PCA: *Saboteur*. Production Code Administration to Jack H. Skirball, 16 December 1941.
11. AMPAS Hitchcock f. 633: 'Untitled Hitchcock Original': 'Blue – Changes 1/8/42'.
12. Ibid.
13. AMPAS MPPA: PCA: *Saboteur*. PCA to Maurice Pivar (Universal), 5 January 1942.
14. Ibid.: PCA to Pivar, 26 January 1942.
15. Ibid.: PCA to Pivar, 12 February 1942.
16. Lindsay Anderson, 'Alfred Hitchcock', *Sequence*, 9 (August 1949), p. 120.
17. Eric Rohmer and Claude Chabrol, *Hitchcock: The First Forty-Four Films*, trans. Stanley Hochman (New York, 1988), p. 68.
18. Robin Wood, *Hitchcock's Films Revisited* (London, 1991), p. 240.
19. Truffaut, *Hitchcock*, p. 209.
20. Thomas Schatz, *Boom and Bust: American Cinema in the 1940s* (Berkeley, CA, 1997), p. 240.
21. Ibid., p. 242.
22. Francis MacDonnell, *Insidious Foes: The Axis Fifth Column and the American Home Front* (New York, 1995), p. 159.
23. Norman Polmar and Thomas B. Allen, *Spy Book: The Encyclopedia of Espionage* (London, 1997), pp. 179–80.
24. MacDonnell, *Insidious Foes*, p. 157.
25. Polmar and Allen, *Spy Book*, p. 268.
26. Truffaut, *Hitchcock*, p. 205.
27. This is probably a reference to the Smith Act – the principal anti-sedition law enacted by the Roosevelt Administration – which had in fact been passed before Pearl Harbor. It proscribed certain named groups and allowed for internment without trial. See Jeffrey Rogers Hummel, 'Not Just Japanese Americans: The Untold Story of US Repression during "the Good War"', *Institute for Historical Review*, <www.ihr.org/jhr/v07/v07p285_Hummel.html>; (accessed April 2015).
28. Robin Wood, 'Hitchcock and Fascism', *Hitchcock Annual*, 13 (2004–5), p. 48.
29. Truffaut, *Hitchcock*, p. 209.
30. *New York Times*, 8 May 1942, p. 27.
31. *Harrison's Reports*, 2 May 1942, p. 70.

32. *Washington Post*, 23 April 1942, p. 12.
33. *Sunday Times*, 31 May 1942.
34. *New Statesman*, 6 June 1942.

10 THE WOMAN WHO KNEW TOO MUCH: *NOTORIOUS* (1946)

1. Quoted in Leonard J. Leff, *Hitchcock and Selznick: The Rich and Strange Collaboration of Alfred Hitchcock and David O. Selznick in Hollywood* (London, 1988), p. 175.
2. Matthew H. Bernstein, 'Unrecognizable Origins: "The Song of the Dragon" and *Notorious*', in R. Barton Palmer and David Boyd (eds), *Hitchcock at the Source: The Auteur as Adaptor* (Albany, NY, 2011), p. 139.
3. Thomas Schatz, *The Genius of the System: Hollywood Filmmaking in the Studio Era* (New York, 1988), p. 393.
4. AMPAS Hitchcock f. 522: *Notorious*: Budget report dated 31 August 1946. This records a figure of $126,484.75 for 'screenplay' against a budget of $121,997. An additional 'story' cost of $44,052 presumably refers to the rights to original story by John Taintor Foote.
5. Alain Kerzoncuf and Charles Barr, *Hitchcock Lost and Found: The Forgotten Films* (Lexington, KY, 2015), pp. 175–82.
6. Kerry Segrave, *American Films Abroad: Hollywood's Domination of the World's Movie Screens from the 1890s to the Present* (Jefferson, NC, 1997), p. 123.
7. AMPAS Hitchcock f. 551: 'Notorious': 46-page treatment by Ben Hecht, no date.
8. Ibid.
9. Norman Polmar and Thomas B. Allen, *Spy Book: The Encyclopedia of Espionage* (London, 1997), p. 504.
10. Leff, *Hitchcock and Selznick*, p. 180.
11. Ibid., pp. 182–4.
12. Ibid., p. 185.
13. Schatz, *Genius of the System*, p. 395.
14. AMPAS Hitchcock f. 551: 'Notorious': 46-page treatment by Ben Hecht, no date.
15. AMPAS Hitchcock f. 552: David O. Selznick to Hitchcock, 9 May 1945: memorandum accompanying Selznick's annotations on the 'Temporary Incomplete Script', no date.
16. François Truffaut, with Helen G. Scott, *Hitchcock* (London, rev. edn 1986), p. 240.
17. Polmar and Allen, *Spy Book*, pp. 223–4.
18. Truffaut, *Hitchcock*, p. 241.
19. AMPAS MPPA: PCA: *Notorious*: Joseph I. Breen to David O. Selznick, 25 May 1945.
20. Ibid.: 'Notorious', 15 June 1945.
21. Ibid.: Breen to Selznick, 25 May 1945.
22. Quoted in Schatz, *Genius of the System*, p. 397.
23. Ibid., p. 398.
24. AMPAS MPPA: PCA: *Notorious*: Breen to William Gordon, 21 September 1945.
25. Ibid.: Breen to Gordon, 22 October 1945.
26. Ibid.: Breen to Gordon, 29 November 1945.
27. Truffaut, *Hitchcock*, p. 400.
28. McGilligan, *Alfred Hitchcock*, p. 380.
29. Schatz, *Genius of the System*, p. 403.

30. AMPAS MPPA: PCA: *Notorious*: Memo headed 'Notorious – Deletions Requested', 26 June 1946.
31. Ibid.: William Gordon to Joseph I. Breen, 28 June 1946.
32. William Rothman, *Hitchcock: The Murderous Gaze* (Cambridge, MA, 1982), p. 246.
33. Donald Spoto, *The Dark Side of Genius: The Life of Alfred Hitchcock* (London, 1983), p. 289.
34. Lindsay Anderson, 'Alfred Hitchcock', *Sequence*, 9 (1949), p. 122.
35. Thomas Leitch, '*Notorious*: Hitchcock's Pivotal Film', *Hitchcock Annual*, 17 (2011), p. 2.
36. Ibid., pp. 7–13.
37. Ibid., p. 2.
38. David Bordwell, Janet Staiger and Kristin Thompson, *The Classical Hollywood Cinema: Film Style and Mode of Production to 1960* (London, 1985), pp. 70–84.
39. 'Introduction', to E. Ann Kaplan (ed.), *Women in Film Noir* (London, 1978). p. 2.
40. See Nora Gilbert, '"She Makes Love for the Papers": Love, Sex and Exploitation in Hitchcock's Mata Hari Films', *Film and History*, 41/2 (2011), pp. 6–18.
41. Tania Modleski, *The Women Who Knew Too Much: Hitchcock and Feminist Theory* (London, 1988), p. 58.
42. Ibid., pp. 57–71; Robin Wood, *Hitchcock's Films Revisited* (London, 1991), pp. 303–10, 321–6.
43. Schatz, *Genius of the System*, p. 399.
44. *New York Times*, 16 August 1946, p. 29.
45. *Los Angeles Times*, 23 August 1946, p. A7.
46. *Washington Post*, 26 August 1946, p. 10.
47. *Variety*, 24 July 1946, p. 14.
48. *Harrison's Reports*, 27 July 1946, p. 119.
49. *Film Bulletin*, 5 August 1946, p. 9.
50. Thomas Schatz, *History of the American Cinema*, vol. 6. *Boom and Bust: American Cinema in the 1940s* (Berkeley, CA, 1997), p. 467.

11 UPSCALING THE GENRE: *THE MAN WHO KNEW TOO MUCH* (1956)

1. John Pett, 'Improving on the Formula', *Films and Filming*, 6/3 (December 1959), p. 32.
2. Eric Rohmer and Claude Chabrol, *Hitchcock: The First Forty-Four Films*, trans. Stanley Hochman (New York, 1988), p. 138.
3. François Truffaut, with Helen G. Scott, *Hitchcock* (London, rev. edn 1986), p. 120.
4. Kristin Thompson and David Bordwell, *Film History: An Introduction* (New York, 1994), p. 391.
5. Russell Malony, 'Alfred Joseph Hitchcock', *New Yorker*, 10 September 1938, pp. 28–32.
6. Donald Spoto, *The Dark Side of Genius: The Life of Alfred Hitchcock* (London, 1983), p. 359.
7. AMPAS Hitchcock f. 379: Sidney Bernstein to Hitchcock, 10 February 1955.
8. Patrick McGilligan, *Alfred Hitchcock: A Life in Darkness and Light* (Chichester, 2003), p. 479.
9. The anti-trust ruling was known as the 'Paramount Decree' because Paramount had been the test case US Supreme Court ruling in the case of the *Department of Justice v. Paramount Pictures Corporation* (3 May 1948).

10. Thomas Schatz, *The Genius of the System: Hollywood Filmmaking in the Studio Era* (New York, 1988), pp. 482–3.
11. Ephraim Katz, *The Macmillan International Film Encyclopedia* (London, 1996), p. 631.
12. Truffaut, *Hitchcock*, p. 333.
13. AMPAS Paramount Box 133 f. 4: A. A. Grosser to Frank Coffey, 8 April 1955.
14. AMPAS Paramount Box 133 f. 12: Hugh B. Brown to Coffey, 21 February 1955.
15. AMPAS Paramount Box 133 f. 7: 'Detailed Production Cost: "The Man Who Knew Too Much"', 24 January 1957.
16. AMPAS Hitchcock f. 20: Mary Dorfman (SWG) to John Monck, 1 November 1955.
17. McGilligan, *Alfred Hitchcock*, p. 508.
18. AMPAS Hitchcock f. 359: '"The Man Who Knew Too Much": Notes', 31 January 1955.
19. Ibid.
20. Ibid.: '"The Man Who Knew Too Much": Notes', 1 February 1955.
21. Ibid.: '"The Man Who Knew Too Much" Skeleton', 7 February 1955.
22. Ibid.: 'The Man Who Knew Too Much', 17 February 1955.
23. AMPAS Hitchcock f. 363: *The Man Who Knew Too Much*. Screenplay by John Michael Hayes. First Draft Screenplay, 25 March 1955.
24. AMPAS Hitchcock f. 368: '"The Man Who Knew Too Much": Notes by Angus MacPhail', 25 April 1955.
25. Ibid.: Hitchcock to John Michael Hayes, 27 April 1955.
26. McGilligan, *Alfred Hitchcock*, p. 511.
27. AMPAS MPPA: PCA: *The Man Who Knew Too Much* (1955): Geoffrey M. Shurlock to Luigi Luraschi, 29 April 1955.
28. AMPAS Hitchcock f. 391: Luigi Luraschi to Hitchcock, 15 June 1955.
29. Ibid.
30. AMPAS Paramount Box 133 f. 12: C. O. Erickson to Frank Caffey, 19 May 1955.
31. Ibid.: Erickson to Caffey, 21 May 1955.
32. Ibid.: S. W. Sawyer to f. N. Bush, 25 February 1955.
33. Ibid.: Erickson to Caffey, 7 June 1955.
34. Ibid.: Notes by Hugh Brown following telephone conversation with Erickson, 7 June 1955.
35. AMPAS Hitchcock f. 392: Don Hartman to Russell Holman, 11 October 1955.
36. AMPAS Hitchcock f. 389: *The Man Who Knew Too Much*, 1st preview – Crown, Pasadena, 29 November 1955.
37. Leslie Halliwell, *Halliwell's Film Guide* (London, 6th edn 1987), p. 654.
38. Raymond Durgnat, *The Strange Case of Alfred Hitchcock: Or the Plain Man's Hitchcock* (London, 1974), pp. 269–70.
39. Robin Wood, *Hitchcock's Films Revisited* (London, 1991), p. 368.
40. AMPAS Paramount Scripts: *The Man Who Knew Too Much*. Screenplay by John Michael Hayes and Angus MacPhail. Final draft screenplay, 7 May 1955.
41. Ina Rae Hark, 'Revalidating Patriarchy: Why Hitchcock Remade *The Man Who Knew Too Much*', in Walter Raubicheck and Walter Srebnick (eds), *Hitchcock's Rereleased Films: From 'Rope' to 'Vertigo'* (Detroit, MI, 1991), p. 216.
42. Ibid., p. 218.
43. Wood, *Hitchcock's Films Revisited*, p. 364.
44. Truffaut, *Hitchcock*, p. 379.

45. AMPAS Hitchcock f. 359: 'The Man Who Knew Too Much', 17 February 1955.
46. James Smith, 'The MacDonald Discussion Group: A Communist Conspiracy in Britain's Cold War Film and Theatre Industry – or MI5's Honey-Pot?', *Historical Journal of Film, Radio and Television*, 35/3 (2015), pp. 454–72.
47. *Los Angeles Mirror-News*, 23 May 1956.
48. *New York Times*, 17 May 1956, p. 37.
49. *Saturday Review*, 26 May 1956.
50. *Los Angeles Times*, 29 April 1956, p. D1.
51. *Monthly Film Bulletin*, 25/269 (June 1956), p. 73.
52. *Manchester Guardian*, 23 June 1956, p. 5.
53. *Observer*, 24 June 1956, p. 9.
54. Jean-Luc Godard, *Godard on Godard*, ed. and trans. Tom Milne (London, 1972), pp. 37–8.
55. Robert E. Kapsis, *Hitchcock: The Making of a Reputation* (Chicago, IL, 1992), p. 119.
56. Andrew Sarris, 'Hitchcock's Les Parents Terribles', *Village Voice*, 12 September 1984, p. 45.

12 'THE HITCHCOCK PICTURE TO END ALL HITCHCOCK PICTURES': *NORTH BY NORTHWEST* (1959)

1. Jean Domarchi and Jean Douchet, 'An Interview with Alfred Hitchcock', trans. Lahcen Hassan and Darlene Sadlier, *Cahiers du Cinéma*, 102 (December 1959), p. 17.
2. Ernest Lehman, 'Introduction', *North by Northwest* (London, 1989), p. vii.
3. François Truffaut, with Helen G. Scott, *Hitchcock* (London, rev. edn 1986), p. 380.
4. Lesley Brill, *The Hitchcock Romance: Love and Irony in Hitchcock's Films* (Princeton, NJ, 1988), p. 4.
5. Quoted in Leonard J. Leff, 'Hitchcock at Metro', in Marshall Deutelbaum and Leland Poague (eds), *A Hitchcock Reader* (Ames, IA, 1986), p. 43.
6. Peter Lev, *History of the American Cinema, vol. 7. Transforming the Screen 1950–1959* (Berkeley, CA, 2003), p. 198.
7. Thomas Schatz, *The Genius of the System: Hollywood Filmmaking in the Studio Era* (New York, 1988), p. 483.
8. Patrick McGilligan, *Alfred Hitchcock: A Life in Darkness and Light* (Chichester, 2003), p. 542.
9. Ibid., p. 575.
10. Truffaut, *Hitchcock*, p. 378.
11. AMPAS Hitchcock f. 536: Kenneth McKenna to Rudi Manta, 26 September 1957.
12. Ibid.: Otis L. Guernsey Jr to Hitchcock, n.d.
13. Ibid.: Guernsey to Hitchcock, 14 October 1957. The letter elaborates: 'At that time, a couple of secretaries in a British embassy invented – for the fun of it and to relieve the boredom of an inactive post – a fake master spy. They gave him a name and a record and planted information around to lure the Nazis on his trail. To their delight and astonishment, the enemy gobbled the bait and spent some valuable time and energy trying to hunt down the non-existent operative.'
14. Lehman, 'Introduction', p. ix.
15. Truffaut, *Hitchcock*, pp. 392–3.
16. Ibid., p. 393.

17. Lehman, 'Introduction', p. x.
18. AMPAS Hitchcock f. 506: *North by Northwest* [the title has been crossed out and replaced with 'Breathless!'] by Ernest Lehman, 22 November 1957, including revision pages dated up to 8 May 1958.
19. AMPAS Turner/MGM Scripts Box 2323 N-739: *North by Northwest*. Shooting script, 12 August 1958.
20. AMPAS Hitchcock f. 537: Allen Henderson to Hitchcock, 23 July 1959.
21. AMPAS Hitchcock f. 509: *North by Northwest*. Temporary complete script, 12 August 1958.
22. AMPAS Hitchcock f. 542: Robert Vogel to Hitchcock, 14 August 1958.
23. Ibid.: Vogel to Hitchcock, 2 September 1958.
24. AMPAS MPAA: PCA: *North by Northwest*: Geoffrey M. Shurlock to Robert Vogel, 21 August 1958.
25. Ibid.: Shurlock to Vogel, 16 October 1958.
26. AMPAS Hitchcock f. 542: Vogel to Hitchcock, 13 October 1958.
27. Ibid.: Vogel to Hitchcock, 17 October 1958.
28. Truffaut, *Hitchcock*, p. 212.
29. Robin Wood, *Hitchcock's Films Revisited* (London, 1991), pp. 336–57.
30. Robert J. Corber, *In the Name of National Security: Hitchcock, Homophobia and the Political Construction of Gender in Postwar America* (Durham, NC, 1993), pp. 61–9.
31. AMPAS Hitchcock f. 527: MGM: 'Stock Actors Monthly Bulletin', December 1958.
32. 'Hitchcock Would Costar Liz, Cary', *Los Angeles Times*, 17 June 1958, p. C-8.
33. AMPAS Saint Box 5 f. 37: Walter Wanger to Eva Marie Saint, 16 July 1959.
34. A cable to London requests: 'Please advise actual height Herbert Lom.' AMPAS Hitchcock f. 527: Cohn to Raymond, 11 August 1958.
35. Robert E. Kapsis, *Hitchcock: The Making of a Reputation* (Chicago, IL, 1992), p. 55.
36. AMPAS Hitchcock f. 544: Manuscript draft of an article by Herbert Brean for *Life*, n.d.
37. AMPAS Hitchcock f. 526: S. N. Rittenberg to Hitchcock, 17 October 1958.
38. AMPAS Hitchcock f. 537: Lincoln Borghum to Hitchcock, 27 August 1958.
39. AMPAS Hitchcock f. 536: R. Morton to Ernest Lehman, 4 August 1958.
40. AMPAS Hitchcock f. 510: *The Man on Lincoln's Nose*. Temporary incomplete script, 21 July 1958, including revision pages dated 8 August 1958.
41. AMPAS Hitchcock f. 522: Assistant Director's Reports 25 August–18 December 1958.
42. AMPAS Hitchcock f. 542: Sol Siegel to Hitchcock, 6 November 1958.
43. AMPAS Hitchcock f. 530: Daily Progress Report: *North by Northwest*, 9 February 1959.
44. AMPAS Hitchcock f. 506: *North by Northwest* by Ernest Lehman, 22 November 1957.
45. AMPAS Hitchcock f. 542: Hitchcock to Sol Siegel, 16 December 1958.
46. Ibid.: Siegel to Hitchcock. 19 December 1958.
47. AMPAS Hitchcock f. 532: 'Mr Hitchcock's Cutting Notes', 29 January 1959.
48. AMPAS Hitchcock f. 540: Hitchcock to Siegel, 17 February 1959.
49. AMPAS Hitchcock f. 541: '*North by Northwest*: First Preview: First Report', Howard Strickling, 11 June 1959.
50. *Variety*, 30 June 1959.
51. *New York Times*, 7 August 1959, p. 28.
52. *New York Herald Tribune*, 7 August 1959.

53. *New York News*, 7 August 1959.
54. *New York Post*, 7 August 1959.
55. *Saturday Review*, 18 July 1959.
56. *New Republic*, 10 August 1959.
57. *Mirror-News*, 24 July 1959.
58. *New Yorker*, 8 August 1959.
59. *Variety*, 30 June 1959.
60. Truffaut, *Hitchcock*, p. 134.
61. James Naremore, 'Spies and Lovers', in James Naremore (ed.), *North by Northwest: Alfred Hitchcock, Director* (New Brunswick, NJ, 1993), p. 4.
62. Jocelyn Camp, 'John Buchan and Alfred Hitchcock', *Literature/Film Quarterly*, 6/3 (1978), pp. 230–1.
63. Lisa Gitelman and Jonathan Auerbach, 'Microfilm, Containment and the Cold War', *American Literary History*, 19/3 (2007), p. 745.
64. Stanley Cavell, '*North by Northwest*', in Marshall Deutelbaum and Leland Poague (eds), *A Hitchcock Reader* (Ames, IA, 1986), p. 250.
65. Ibid., p. 252.
66. 'Dialogue on Film: Ernest Lehman', *American Film*, 1/11 (1976), p. 33.
67. Richard H. Millington, 'Hitchcock and American Character: The Comedy of Self-Construction in *North by Northwest*', in Jonathan Freedman and Richard Millington (eds), *Hitchcock's America* (New York, 1999), p. 136.
68. AMPAS Turner/MGM Scripts Box 2323 N-743: *North by Northwest*: 'Hitchcock Trailer', script, n.d.
69. Christopher Cook (ed.), *The Dilys Powell Film Reader* (Manchester, 1992), p. 48.
70. Christopher D. Morris, 'The Direction of *North by Northwest*', *Cinema Journal*, 36/4 (1997), pp. 43–56.
71. Robin Wood, *Hitchcock's Films* (London, 1965), p. 103.
72. AMPAS Turner/MGM Scripts Box 2323 N-739: *North by Northwest*. Shooting script, 12 August 1958.
73. Kristin Thompson and David Bordwell, *Film History: An Introduction* (New York, 1994), pp. 391–5.
74. Paul Kerr, 'Out of What Past?: Notes on the B *Film Noir*', in Paul Kerr (ed.), *The Hollywood Film Industry* (London, 1986), pp. 220–45.
75. University of Texas at Austin, Cinema Texas Program Notes, 8/3, 15 January 1975: copy on the microfilm for *North by Northwest*, Margaret Herrick Library, Los Angeles.

13 HITCHCOCK AND JAMES BOND

1. Martin Rubin, *Thrillers* (Cambridge, 1999), p. 119.
2. Ibid., p. 118.
3. Kristin Thompson and David Bordwell, *Film History: An Introduction* (New York, 1994), p. 394.
4. James Naremore, 'Spies and Lovers', in James Naremore (ed.), *North by Northwest: Alfred Hitchcock, Director* (New Brunswick, NJ, 1993), p. 6.
5. The James Bond books – all originally published by Jonathan Cape – were: *Casino Royale* (1953), *Live and Let Die* (1954), *Moonraker* (1955), *Diamonds Are Forever* (1956), *From Russia, With Love* (1957), *Dr No* (1958), *Goldfinger* (1959), *For Your Eyes Only*

(1960 – short story collection), *Thunderball* (1961), *The Spy Who Loved Me* (1962), *On Her Majesty's Secret Service* (1963), *You Only Live Twice* (1964), *The Man With the Golden Gun* (1965) and *Octopussy and the Living Daylights* (1966 – short stories).

6. Quoted in Andrew Lycett, *Ian Fleming* (London, 1995), p. 250.

7. Roy Moseley, *Evergreen: Victor Saville in his own Words* (Carbondale, IL, 2000), p. 197. The manuscript copy of Saville's memoir held by the British Film Institute is slightly different: 'I made four [*sic*] films and said "I've got the successor now to the Spillanes. There's a man named Fleming who's written a book called "Dr No". I'm sure it's the best there is and I have an option on the rest of his work." I went to United Artists who turned me down. I was foolish. I'd become too rich to care ... I don't regret not making them. They are rather poor really and I don't know that I would necessarily have been good at them. They're so unreal.' BFI Saville 1: 'Shadows in a Screen', November 1974.

8. 'Richard Maibaum: A Pretence of Seriousness', in Pat McGilligan (ed.), *Backstory: Interviews with Screenwriters of Hollywood's Golden Age* (Berkeley, CA, 1986), p. 284.

9. *Kinematograph Weekly*, 1 October 1959, p. 21.

10. Quoted in Robert Sellers, *The Battle for Bond* (Sheffield, 2007), p. 34.

11. Ibid., p. 35.

12. Hitchcock had intended to film the kidnapping of Thornhill at the beginning of *North by Northwest* in the King Creole Room at the St Regis, though in the event the location was changed to the Oak Bar of the Plaza Hotel and shot in the studio. In *Live and Let Die*, Bond stays at 'the best hotel in New York, the St Regis, at the corner of Fifth Avenue and 5th Street'. Ian Fleming, *Live and Let Die* (London, 2004 edn [1954]), p. 5.

13. Sellers, *Battle for Bond*, p. 44.

14. Ian Fleming, *Thunderball* (London, 2004 edn [1961]), p. 88.

15. Lycett, *Ian Fleming*, p. 432.

16. *Kinematograph Weekly*, 20 July 1961, p. 17.

17. On the history of the Bond films, see John Brosnan, *James Bond in the Cinema* (London, 2nd edn 1981); James Chapman, *Licence To Thrill: A Cultural History of the James Bond Films* (London, 2nd edn 2007); Matthew Field and Ajay Chowdhury, *Some Kind of Hero: The Remarkable Story of the James Bond Films* (London, 2015); and Steven Jay Rubin, *The James Bond Films: A Behind the Scenes History* (London, 1981).

18. 'James Bond's 25th Anniversary', *The Hollywood Reporter*, 14 July 1987, p. S-26.

19. Ibid.

20. Richard Schenkman, 'The Terence Young Interview', *Bondage*, 10 (1981), p. 7.

21. Tony Bennett and Janet Wollacott, *Bond and Beyond: The Political Career of a Popular Hero* (London, 1987), p. 37.

22. *Kinematograph Weekly*, 13 December 1962, p. 5.

23. *Sunday Times*, 7 October 1962.

24. *New Statesman*, 11 October 1963.

25. Penelope Houston, '007', *Sight and Sound*, 34/1 (Winter 1964–5), p. 16.

26. *Daily Worker*, 6 October 1962.

27. *Monthly Film Bulletin*, 29/345 (October 1962), p. 136.

28. Robin Wood, *Hitchcock's Films* (London, 1965), p. 100.

29. Ibid.

30. Ibid., pp. 22–3.

31. In fact the draft screenplays of *North by Northwest* reveal that it was originally planned to include an aerial shot of Thornhill running away and close-ups of the pilot, who is revealed to be Licht, one of the heavies involved in Thornhill's kidnapping at the start of the film. These were dropped at the story-boarding stage. As a consequence there is no explanation in the film for Licht's absence from the last act at Mount Rushmore.

32. I am grateful to Llewella Chapman for drawing my attention to the significance of this motif in *On Her Majesty's Secret Service*.

33. 'James Bond's 39 Bumps', *New York Times*, 13 December 1964, p. 22.

34. 'A History of *The Avengers*: With a Guide to the Characters of John Steed and Emma Peel', publicity notes by press officer Marie Donaldson on the BFI Library microfiche for *The Avengers*: undated but prepared for the fourth season in 1965.

35. Cynthia W. Walker, '*The Man From U.N.C.L.E.*: Ian Fleming's Other Spy', in Robert G. Weiner, B. Lynn Whitfield and Jack Becker (eds), *James Bond in World and Popular Culture: The Films are Not Enough* (Newcastle upon Tyne, 2010), pp. 235–51.

36. The eight *Man From U.N.C.L.E.* films were *To Trap a Spy* (1965), *The Spy With My Face* (1965), *One of Our Spies is Missing* (1966), *The Spy in the Green Hat* (1966), *One Spy Too Many* (1966), *The Helicopter Spies* (1967), *The Karate Killers* (1967) and *How To Steal the World* (1968).

37. AMPAS Hitchcock f. 1245: 'The Three Hostages', 7 July 1964.

38. AMPAS Hitchcock f. 1243: '"The Three Hostages": Mrs Hitchcock's Ideas for Above', 1 March 1964.

39. François Truffaut, with Helen G. Scott, *Hitchcock* (London, rev. edn 1986), p. 473.

40. AMPAS Hitchcock f. 1244: '"The Three Hostages" by John Buchan', 28 January 1964.

41. AMPAS Hitchcock f. 679: *Topaz*: Transcript of story conference, 27 August 1968.

14 HITCHCOCK'S COLD WAR: *TORN CURTAIN* (1966)

1. Hitchcock used this phrase several times in the Truffaut interview: 'Whenever you feel yourself entering an area of doubt or vagueness, whether it be in respect to the writer, the subject matter, or whatever it is, you've got to run for cover.' François Truffaut, with Helen G. Scott, *Hitchcock* (London, rev. edn 1984), p. 269.

2. AMPAS Hitchcock f. 1482: Hitchcock to François Truffaut, 22 October 1965.

3. Patrick McGilligan, *Alfred Hitchcock: A Life in Darkness and Light* (Chichester, 2003), p. 663.

4. Paul Monaco, *The Sixties: 1960–1969* (Berkeley, CA, 2001), p. 32.

5. McGilligan, *Alfred Hitchcock*, p. 653.

6. AMPAS Hitchcock f. 944: 'Untitled Original Story Subject by Alfred J. Hitchcock, 19 November 1964.

7. Ibid.

8. AMPAS Hitchcock f. 822: 'Labour Minister's Home – London': Scene 29B.

9. Ibid: 'Interior of Warsaw Farmhouse': Scenes 35 and 35a.

10. AMPAS f. 823: *Double Agent*. Script outline, 19 May 1965.

11. AMPAS f. 825: *Double Agent*. Additional script pages, undated.

12. AMPAS Hitchcock f. 833: 'Mr Hitchcock's Notes on Second Draft', 7 July 1965.

13. AMPAS Hitchcock f. 1482: Hitchcock to Truffaut, 22 October 1965.

14. AMPAS Hitchcock f. 876: Budget Estimate: *Torn Curtain*: Project No. 1973.

15. AMPAS Hitchcock f. 880: Undated note headed 'Julie Christie', appended to a memo by Peggy Robertson dated 25 June 1965. Other suggestions for the female lead included Suzanne Pleshette (who had appeared for Hitchcock in *The Birds*), Lee Remick, Natalie Wood, Jean Seberg and Samantha Eggar.

16. AMPAS MPPA: PCA: *Torn Curtain*: Geoffrey M. Shurlock to Alfred Hitchcock, 13 August 1965.

17. AMPAS Hitchcock f. 839: Paul Newman to Hitchcock, 30 August 1965.

18. Ibid.: Brian Moore to Hitchcock, 2 September 1965.

19. Ibid. f.: '"Torn Curtain": Script Notes – Age & Scarpelli's Comments', 24 August 1965.

20. AMPAS Hitchcock f. 840: Keith Waterhouse and Willis Hall to Hitchcock, n.d.

21. AMPAS Hitchcock f. 843: *Torn Curtain*. Screenplay, 27 September 1965 ('Polish Script' bearing the names Keith Waterhouse & Willis Hall).

22. AMPAS Hitchcock f. 851: 'Mr Hitchcock's Notes on Screenplay Dated Sept 27, 1965', 12 October 1965.

23. Maurice Yacowar, *Hitchcock's British Films* (New York, 1977), p. 276.

24. AMPAS Hitchcock f. 880: Peggy Robertson to Don Baer, 20 August 1965.

25. AMPAS Hitchcock f. 884: Note headed 'Bob Burks' by Peggy Robertson, 16 September 1965.

26. McGilligan, *Alfred Hitchcock*, pp. 673–4.

27. Truffaut, *Hitchcock*, pp. 482–3.

28. AMPAS MPPA: PCA: *Torn Curtain*: File note by J. A. Vizzard, 30 March 1966.

29. Truffaut, *Hitchcock*, p. 477.

30. Ibid., p. 379.

31. Raymond Durgnat, *The Strange Case of Alfred Hitchcock: Or the Plain Man's Hitchcock* (London, 1974), p. 369.

32. McGilligan, *Alfred Hitchcock*, p. 675.

33. *Motion Picture Herald*, 27 July 1966.

34. *Film Daily*, 25 July 1966

35. *Variety*, 16 July 1966.

36. *The Hollywood Reporter*, 14 July 1966.

37. *New York Times*, 31 July 1966.

38. *Saturday Review*, 13 August 1966.

39. *New Yorker*, 6 August 1966.

40. *Life*, 26 August 1966.

41. *New Republic*, 8 October 1966.

42. Robert E. Kapsis, *Hitchcock: The Making of a Reputation* (Chicago, IL, 1992), p. 99.

43. *America*, 20 August 1966.

44. Joel W. Finler, *The Hollywood Story* (London, 2003), p. 269.

45. McGilligan, *Alfred Hitchcock*, p. 675.

15 HITCHCOCK'S COLD WAR – TAKE TWO: *TOPAZ* (1969)

1. Patrick McGilligan, *Alfred Hitchcock: A Life in Darkness and Light* (Chichester, 2003), p. 683.

2. AMPAS Hitchcock f. 738: 'Mr Hitchcock's Teleprompter Speech for Universal International Sales Conference', 10 Mar. 1969.

3. 'Hitchcock Returns with "Topaz"', *Motion Picture Exhibitor*, 15 May 1968, p. 5.

4. John Scali, 'The Spies around De Gaulle', *Look*, 14 May 1968, pp. 45–7.

5. 'French Writer Sues Uris, Universal for Cut of Filmization of "Topaz"', *Variety*, 6 February 1968, p. 4.

6. '"Topaz" Decision to Cost Uris and MCA $352,350 Plus 50%', *The Hollywood Reporter*, 10 February 1972. In fact the decision was against Uris only.

7. AMPAS Hitchcock f. 665: 'Mr Hitchcock's Chapter Breakdown', 2 February 1968.

8. AMPAS Hitchcock f. 667: 'Topaz: Outline by Leon Uris from Consultations with Mr Hitchcock', 9 April 1968.

9. AMPAS Hitchcock f. 668: 'Topaz: Narrative Outline by Leon Uris', 15 June 1968.

10. AMPAS Hitchcock f. 675: *Topaz* by Leon Uris. First draft screenplay. An attached note indicates pages 1–51 received 16 July 1968, pages 52–85 received 31 July 1968.

11. AMPAS Hitchcock f. 669: 'Mr Hitchcock's Notes on "Narrative Outline"', 18 June 1968.

12. AMPAS Hitchcock f. 679: 'August 27th Story Conference in Mr Hitchcock's Office', transcript of tape recording.

13. AMPAS Hitchcock f. 681: 'Topaz: New Outline as Dictated by Mr Hitchcock with Mr Taylor', 4 September 1968.

14. AMPAS Hitchcock f. 690: Sam Taylor to Hitchcock, 3 Oct. 1968.

15. AMPAS Hitchcock f. 688 includes revision pages for the studio scenes set in Paris dated between 22 November 1968 and 14 January 1969, while AMPAS Hitchcock f. 689 has the same for the Cuba section dated between 17 January and 4 February 1969.

16. AMPAS Hitchcock f. 695: Hitchcock to Taylor, 11 December 1968.

17. AMPAS Hitchcock f. 708: 'Final Duel Sequence – Revised', 7 April 1969.

18. AMPAS Hitchcock f. 742: Hitchcock to Odette Ferry, 14 October 1968.

19. AMPAS Hitchcock f. 679: 'August 27th Story Conference in Mr Hitchcock's Office'.

20. AMPAS Hitchcock f. 724: 'Jean' to Herb Coleman, 10 February 1969.

21. Ibid.: Hitchcock to Adele Franz, 24 April 1969.

22. AMPAS Hitchcock f. 715: Universal Pictures Production Cost Report: *Topaz*, 18 January 1969.

23. AMPAS Hitchcock f. 775: Preview cards for *Topaz*. Other comments included: 'The duel seemed an unnecessary anachronism – therefore the conclusion was lame'; 'You ruined a fabulous book'; 'I can't believe this is Hitchcock'; 'This is not a "Hitchcock" film, no matter who directed it'.

24. AMPAS Hitchcock f. 710: 'Topaz – Revised Ending', 26 August 1969.

25. Ibid.: 'Topaz – Revised Dialogue for New Ending', 18 September 1969.

26. Ibid.: 'Topaz – Revised Ending. Alternative Version for France'.

27. Dan Auiler, *Hitchcock's Secret Notebooks* (London, 1999), p. 538.

28. AMPAS Hitchcock f. 739: 'Topaz – Suggested Trims and Changes', 18 October 1969.

29. François Truffaut, with Helen G. Scott, *Hitchcock* (London, rev. edn 1986), p. 510.

30. 'Hitchcock's "Topaz" Shuffles Endings', *Variety*, 4 February 1970.

31. AMPAS Hitchcock f. 739: Hitchcock to Peggy Robertson, 23 October 1969.

32. Robin Wood, *Hitchcock's Films Revisited* (London, 1991), p. 222.

33. Raymond Durgnat, *The Strange Case of Alfred Hitchcock: Or the Plain Man's Hitchcock* (London, 1974), p. 380.

34. Michael Walker, '*Topaz* and Cold War Politics', *Hitchcock Annual*, 13 (2004–5), p. 152.
35. Ibid., pp. 143–4.
36. *The Hollywood Reporter*, 9 December 1969, p. 3.
37. *Variety*, 11 November 1969, p. 3.
38. *Time*, 19 January 1970.
39. *New Yorker*, 27 December 1969.
40. *Cue*, 3 December 1969.
41. *Saturday Review*, 27 December 1969.
42. *Newsweek*, 29 December 1969.
43. *New York Times*, 20 December 1969.
44. *Los Angeles Times*, 19 December 1969.
45. '"Topaz" Revisited: An Auteur-Man Looks at Hitchcock', *BAD*, 4 February 1970, p. 31.
46. Andrew Sarris, *The American Cinema: Directors and Directions 1969–1968* (New York, 1996 edn), pp. 30, 17.
47. *Entertainment World*, 12 December 1969, p. 18.
48. *Film Quarterly*, 23/3 (Spring 1970), pp. 41–4.
49. AMPAS Hitchcock f. 797: *L'Humanité*, 14 March 1970 (trans.).
50. Ibid.: *L'Express*, 12 March 1970 (trans.).
51. Ibid.: *Les Nouvelles Littéraires*, 19 March 1970 (trans.).
52. Ibid.: *Le Nouvel Observateur*, 16 March 1970 (trans.).
53. Ibid.: *Les Lettres Françaises*, 17 March 1970 (trans.).
54. 'Big Rental Films of 1970', *Variety*, 6 January 1971, p. 9.
55. David A. Cook, *Lost Illusions: American Cinema in the Shadow of Watergate and Vietnam, 1970–1979* (Berkeley, CA, 2000), p. 497.

CONCLUSION

1. 'A New Film Version of "The 39 Steps" Opening this Week', *New York Times*, 27 April 1980, p. D8.
2. William Wolf, 'The Thrill is Gone', *New York*, 26 May 1980, p. 20.
3. 'Alfred Hitchcock, Master of Suspense and Celebrated Film Director, Dies at 80', *New York Times*, 30 April 1980, A-1.
4. 'Universal Sets Product, Release Schedule for 1969–70', *Independent Film Journal*, 15 April 1969, p. 34.
5. AMPAS Hitchcock f. 1216: Hitchcock to Ilmo Makela, 26 May 1970. Makela had been Hitchcock's guide on his scouting trip to Finland in 1968.
6. *Variety*, 23 February 1977, p. 28.
7. Donald Spoto, *The Dark Side of Genius: The Life of Alfred Hitchcock* (London, 1983), p. 540.
8. David Freeman, *The Last Days of Alfred Hitchcock: A Memoir Featuring the Screenplay of 'Alfred Hitchcock's The Short Night'* (Woodstock, NY, 1984), p. 36.
9. AMPAS Hitchcock f. 1216: Ned Tanen to Hitchcock, 8 November 1976.
10. Freeman, *Last Days of Hitchcock*, p. 5.
11. Walter Raubicheck and Walter Srebnick, 'Wrong Men on the Run: *The 39 Steps* as Hitchcock's Espionage Paradigm', in Mark Osteen (ed.), *Hitchcock and Adaptation: On the Page and Screen* (Lanham, MD, 2014), p. 38.

BIBLIOGRAPHY

ARCHIVAL SOURCES

British Film Institute, London:
  BBFC Scenario Reports 1930–1939 (BFI BBFC)
  BFI Scripts Collection (BFI Scripts)
  Michael and Aileen Balcon Collection (BFI Balcon)
  Ivor Montagu Collection (BFI Montagu)
  Victor Saville Collection (BFI Saville)

Margaret Herrick Library, Academy of Motion Picture Arts and Sciences, Los Angeles:
  Cary Grant Collection (AMPAS Grant)
  Alfred Hitchcock Collection (AMPAS Hitchcock)
  MGM/Turner Scripts Collection (AMPAS MGM/Turner Scripts)
  Motion Picture Producers Association: Production Code Administration files
    (AMPAS MPPA: PCA)
  Paramount Pictures Production Records (AMPAS Paramount)
  Paramount Pictures Scripts Collection (AMPAS Paramount Scripts)
  Eva Marie Saint Collection (AMPAS Saint)

FILM JOURNALS AND TRADE PAPERS

I have drawn upon a range of film journals and trade papers to supplement archival sources; specific references are identified in the endnotes. For Britain I have used *Cinema Quarterly, Documentary News Letter, Film Weekly, Films and Filming, Kinematograph Weekly, Monthly Film Bulletin, Sight and Sound* and *World Film News.* For the United States I have consulted *American Cinematographer,*

Cinema Progress, Film Daily, Harrison's Reports, The Hollywood Reporter, Independent Exhibitors' Film Bulletin, Independent Film Journal, Motion Picture Daily, Motion Picture Exhibitor, Motion Picture Herald and *Variety*.

NEWSPAPERS AND PERIODICALS

Again specific references can be traced through the endnotes: where film reviews are quoted without a page number these have been taken from either the British Film Institute Library's digitised microfiche or the clippings files in the Margaret Herrick Library Core Collection. British sources include the *Daily Express, Daily Record, Daily Telegraph, Daily Worker, Manchester Guardian, New Statesman, News Chronicle, Observer, Spectator, Sunday Times* and *The Times*. For the United States I have used *America, Cue, Life, Look, Los Angeles Mirror-News, Los Angeles Times, New Republic, New York, New York Herald Tribune, New York Post, New York Times, New Yorker, Newsweek, Saturday Review, Time, Village Voice* and the *Washington Post*.

SOURCE TEXTS

Buchan, John, *The Power-House* (London: J.M. Dent & Sons, 1984 [1913]).
Buchan, John, *The 39 Steps*, ed. Christopher Harvie (Oxford: Oxford University Press, 1993 [1915]).
Conrad, Joseph, *The Secret Agent: A Simple Tale*, ed. Roger Tennant (Oxford: Oxford University Press, 1983 [1907]).
Fleming, Ian, *Thunderball* (London: Penguin Classics, 2004 [1960]).
Household, Geoffrey, *Rogue Male* (London: Orion, 2002 [1939]).
Maugham, W. Somerset, *Ashenden* (London: Vintage, 2000 [1928]).
Sheean, Vincent, *Personal History* (New York: Garden City Publishing, 1937).
Uris, Leon, *Topaz* (London: William Kimber, 1968 [1967]).
White, Ethel Lina, *The Lady Vanishes* (London: Bloomsbury, 1997 [1936, first published as *The Wheel Spins*]).

PUBLISHED SCREENPLAYS

Masterworks of the British Cinema: Brief Encounter, Henry V, The Lady Vanishes, ed. Andrew Sinclair (London: Faber & Faber, 1990).
North by Northwest (London: British Film Institute, 1989).

PUBLISHED FILM AND LITERARY CRITICISM

Davy, Charles (ed.), *Footnotes to the Film* (London: Lovat Dickson, 1937).
Godard, Jean-Luc, *Godard on Godard*, ed. and trans. Tom Milne (London: Faber & Faber, 1972).

Greene, Graham, *The Pleasure-Dome: The Collected Film Criticism 1935–40*, ed. John Russell Taylor (London: Secker & Warburg, 1972).

Greene, Graham, *The Graham Greene Film Reader: Mornings in the Dark*, ed. David Parkinson (Manchester: Carcanet Press, 1993).

Grierson, John, *Grierson on the Movies*, ed. Forsyth Hardy (London: Faber & Faber, 1981).

Halliwell, Leslie, *Halliwell's Hundred: A Nostalgic Choice of Films from the Golden Age* (London: Granada, 1982).

Halliwell, Leslie, *Halliwell's Film Guide* (London: Grafton, 6th edn, 1987).

Hitchcock, Alfred, *Hitchcock on Hitchcock*, ed. Sidney Gottlieb (London: Faber & Faber, 1995).

Lejeune, C.A., *The C.A. Lejeune Film Reader*, ed. Anthony Lejeune (Manchester: Carcanet Press, 1991).

Peters, John G. (ed.), *Joseph Conrad: Contemporary Reviews*, vol. 2, *'Typhoon' to 'Under Western Eyes'* (Cambridge: Cambridge University Press, 2012).

Powell, Dilys, *The Dilys Powell Film Reader*, ed. Christopher Cook (Manchester: Carcanet Press, 1991).

AUTOBIOGRAPHIES AND PUBLISHED INTERVIEWS

Balcon, Michael, *Michael Balcon Presents … A Lifetime of Films* (London: Hutchinson, 1969).

Buchan, John, *Memory Hold-the-Door* (London: Hodder & Stoughton, 1940).

Freeman, David, *The Last Days of Alfred Hitchcock: A Memoir Featuring the Screenplay of 'Alfred Hitchcock's The Short Night'* (Woodstock, NY: Overlook Press, 1984).

Halliwell, Leslie, *Seats in All Parts: Half a Lifetime at the Movies* (London: Granada, 1985).

'Ivor Montagu' (interview conducted by Peter Wollen, Alan Lovell and Sam Rohdie), *Screen*, 13: 3 (1972), pp.

McGilligan, Pat (ed.), *Backstory: Interviews with Screenwriters of Hollywood's Golden Age* (Berkeley, CA: University of California Press, 1986).

Mycroft, Walter, *The Time of my Life: The Memoirs of a British Film Producer*, ed. Vincent Porter (Lanham, MA: Scarecrow Press, 2006).

Saville, Victor, *Evergreen: Victor Saville in his own Words*, ed. Roy Moseley (Carbondale, IL: Southern Illinois University Press, 2002).

Schenkman, Richard, 'The Terence Young Interview', *Bondage*, 10 (1981), pp. 7–11.

Schickel, Richard (ed.), *The Men Who Made the Movies: Interviews* (New York: Atheneum, 1976).

Truffaut, François, with Helen G. Scott, *Hitchcock* (London: Paladin, rev. edn 1986 [1968]).

BIOGRAPHIES

Adam Smith, Janet, *John Buchan: A Biography* (Oxford: Hart-Davis, 1965).

Barrow, Kenneth, *Mister Chips: The Life of Robert Donat* (London: Methuen, 1985).

Bernstein, Matthew, *Walter Wanger: Hollywood Independent* (Berkeley, CA: University of California Press, 1994).

Croall, Jonathan, *John Gielgud: Matinee Idol to Movie Star* (London: Methuen Drama, 2011).

Lownie, *John Buchan: The Presbyterian Cavalier* (London: Canongate, 1995).

Lycett, Andrew, *Ian Fleming* (London: Weidenfeld & Nicolson, 1995).

McGilligan, Patrick, *Alfred Hitchcock: A Life in Darkness and Light* (Chichester: John Wiley & Sons, 2003).

Moorehead, Caroline, *Sidney Bernstein: A Biography* (London: Jonathan Cape, 1985).

Spoto, Donald, *The Dark Side of Genius: The Life of Alfred Hitchcock* (London: William Collins, 1983).

Taylor, John Russell, *Hitch: The Life and Work of Alfred Hitchcock* (London: Faber & Faber, 1978).

Thomson, David, *Showman: The Life of David O. Selznick* (New York: Alfred A. Knopf, 1992).

BOOKS AND EDITED COLLECTIONS

Adamson, Judith, *Graham Greene and Cinema* (Norman, OK: Pilgrim Books, 1984).

Allen, Richard and S. Ishii Gonzalès (eds), *Alfred Hitchcock: Centenary Essays* (London: British Film Institute, 1999).

Allen, Richard and S. Ishii Gonzalès (eds), *Hitchcock: Past and Future* (London: Routledge, 2004).

Amis, Kingsley, *The James Bond Dossier* (London: Jonathan Cape, 1965).

Andrew, Christopher, *The Defence of the Realm: The Authorized History of MI5* (London: Allen Lane, 2009).

Babington, Bruce, *Launder and Gilliat* (Manchester: Manchester University Press, 2002).

Balio, Tino, *History of the American Cinema*, vol. 5, *Grand Design: Hollywood as a Modern Business Enterprise, 1930–1939* (Berkeley, CA: University of California Press, 1993).

Barr, Charles, *Ealing Studios* (London: Cameron & Tayleur/David & Charles, 1977).

Barr, Charles, *English Hitchcock* (Moffat: Cameron & Hollis, 1999).

Behlmer, Rudy (ed.), *Memo from David O. Selznick* (New York: Viking Press, 1972).

Bennett, Tony, and Janet Woollacott, *Bond and Beyond: The Political Career of a Popular Hero* (London: Macmillan, 1987).

Bernstein, Matthew, *Walter Wanger: Hollywood Independent* (Berkeley, CA: University of California Press, 1994).

Bloom, Clive (ed.), *Twentieth-Century Suspense: The Thriller Comes of Age* (London: Macmillan, 1990).

Bordwell, David, Janet Staiger and Kristin Thompson, *The Classical Hollywood Cinema: Film Style and Mode of Production to 1960* (London: Routledge, 1985).

Borde, Raymond and Étienne Chaumeton, *Panorama du Film Noir Américain 1941–1953*, trans. Paul Hammond (San Francisco, CA: City Lights Books, 2002 [1955]).

Boyd, David and R. Barton Palmer (eds), *Hitchcock at the Source: The Auteur as Adaptor* (Albany, NY: SUNY Press, 2011).

Brewer, Susan A., *To Win the Peace: British Propaganda in the United States during World War II* (Ithaca, NY: Cornell University Press, 1997).

Brill, Lesley, *The Hitchcock Romance: Love and Irony in Hitchcock's Films* (Princeton, NJ: Princeton University Press, 1988).

Brosnan, John, *James Bond in the Cinema* (London: Tantivy Press, 2nd edn, 1981).

Brown, Geoff, *Launder and Gilliat* (London: British Film Institute, 1977).

Cantril, Hadley, with Hazel Gaudet and Herta Herzog, *The War of the Worlds: A Study in the Psychology of Panic* (Princeton, NJ: Princeton University Press, 1940).

Chapman, James, *Licence to Thrill: A Cultural History of the James Bond Films* (London: I.B.Tauris, 1999).

Chapman, James, *Past and Present: National Identity and the British Historical Film* (London: I.B.Tauris, 2005).

Chibnall, Steve, *Quota Quickies: The Birth of the British 'B' Film* (London: British Film Institute, 2007).

Chowdhury, Ajay, and Matthew Field, *Some Kind of Hero: The Remarkable Story of the James Bond Films* (London: History Press, 2015).

Conrad, Peter, *The Hitchcock Murders* (London: Faber & Faber, 2000).

Constantine, Stephen, *Unemployment in Britain between the Wars* (Harlow: Longman, 1980).

Cook, David A., *History of the American Cinema*, vol. 9, *Lost Illusions: American Cinema in the Shadow of Watergate and Vietnam, 1970–1979* (Berkeley, CA: University of California Press, 2000).

Cook, Pam (ed.), *Gainsborough Pictures* (London: Cassell, 1997).

Corber, Rober J., *In the Name of National Security: Hitchcock, Homophobia, and the Political Construction of Gender in Postwar America* (Durham, NC: Duke University Press, 1993).

Cull, Nicholas John, *Selling War: The British Propaganda Campaign Against American 'Neutrality' in World War II* (New York: Oxford University Press, 1995).

Curtis, Anthony, *The Pattern of Maugham: A Critical Portrait* (London: Taplinger, 1974).

Davis, Brian, *The Thriller* (London: Studio Vista, 1973).

Denning, Michael, *Cover Stories: Narrative and Ideology in the British Spy Thriller* (London: Routledge & Kegan Paul, 1987).

Deutelbaum, Marshall and Leland Poague (eds), *A Hitchcock Reader* (Ames, IA: Iowa State University Press, 1986).

Dickinson, Margaret and Sarah Street, *Cinema and State: The Film Industry and the British Government, 1927–84* (London: British Film Institute, 1985).

Durgnat, Raymond, *The Strange Case of Alfred Hitchcock: Or The Plain Man's Hitchcock* (London: Faber & Faber, 1974).

Evans, Peter William, *Carol Reed* (Manchester: Manchester University Press, 2005).

Falk, Quentin, *Travels in Greeneland: The Cinema of Graham Greene* (London: Quartet Books, 1984).

Finler, Joel W., *The Hollywood Story* (London: Wallflower Press, 2003).

Freedman, Jonathan and Richard Millington (eds), *Hitchcock's America* (New York: Oxford University Press, 1999).

Glancy, Mark, *When Hollywood Loved Britain: The Hollywood 'British' Film, 1939–45* (Manchester: Manchester University Press, 1999).

Glancy, Mark, *The 39 Steps: A British Film Guide* (London: I.B.Tauris, 2003).

Gifford, Denis, *The British Film Catalogue*, vol. 1, *Fiction Film, 1895–1994* (London: Fitzroy Dearborn, 3rd edn, 2000).

Gottlieb, Sidney (ed.), *Hitchcock on Hitchcock* (London: Faber & Faber, 1995).

Harper, Sue, *Women in British Cinema: Mad, Bad and Dangerous to Know* (London: Continuum, 2000).

Haskell, Molly, *From Reverence to Rape: The Treatment of Women in the Movies* (Chicago, IL: University of Chicago Press, 2nd edn, 1987).

Higson, Andrew and Richard Maltby (eds), *'Film Europe' and 'Film America': Cinema, Commerce and Cultural Exchange 1920–1939* (Exeter: University of Exeter Press, 1999).

Hochscherf, Tobias, *The Continental Connection: German-Speaking Émigrés and British Cinema, 1927–45* (Manchester: Manchester University Press, 2011).

Hucker, David, *Public Opinion and the End of Appeasement in Britain and France* (Farnham: Ashgate, 2011).

Kapsis, Robert E., *Hitchcock: The Making of a Reputation* (Chicago, IL: University of Chicago Press, 1992).

Karl, Frederick R. and Laurence Davies (eds), *The Collected Letters of Joseph Conrad*, vol. 3 (Cambridge: Cambridge University Press, 1988).

Katz, Ephraim, *The Macmillan International Film Encyclopedia* (London: Macmillan, 1996).

Kerzoncuf, Alain and Charles Barr, *Hitchcock Lost and Found: The Forgotten Films* (Lexington, KY: University Press of Kentucky, 2015).

Kitses, Jim, *Horizons West: Anthony Mann, Budd Boetticher, Sam Peckinpah: Studies of Authorship within the Western* (London: British Film Institute, 1969).

Koppes, Clayton R. and Gregory D. Black, *Hollywood Goes to War: How Politics, Profits and Propaganda Shaped World War II Movies* (London: I.B.Tauris, 1987).

Leavis, F.R., *The Great Tradition* (London: Chatto & Windus, 1948).

Leff, Leonard J., *Hitchcock and Selznick: The Rich and Strange Collaboration of Alfred Hitchcock and David O. Selznick in Hollywood* (London: Weidenfeld & Nicolson, 1988).

Lev, Peter, *History of the American Cinema*, vol. 7. *Transforming the Screen 1950–1959* (Berkeley, BA: University of California Press, 2003).

Low, Rachael, *The History of the British Film 1929–1939: Film Making in 1930s Britain* (London: George Allen & Unwin, 1985).

MacDonell, Francis, *Insidious Foes: The Axis Fifth Column and the American Home Front* (New York: Oxford University Press, 1995).

McFarlane, Brian, *Lance Comfort* (Manchester: Manchester University Press, 1999).

Marantz Cohen, Paula, *Alfred Hitchcock: The Legacy of Victorianism* (Lexington, KY: University Press of Kentucky, 1995).

Modleski, Tania, *The Women Who Knew Too Much: Hitchcock and Feminist Theory* (London: Methuen, 1988).

Monaco, Paul, *History of the American Cinema*, vol. 8, *The Sixties 1960–1969* (Berkeley, CA: University of California Press, 2001).

Murphy, Robert (ed.), *The British Cinema Book* (London: British Film Institute, 1997).

Naremore, James (ed.), *North by Northwest: Alfred Hitchcock, Director* (New Brunswick, NJ: Rutgers University Press, 1993).

Naremore, James, *More than Night: Film Noir in its Contexts* (Berkeley, CA: University of California Press, rev. edn 2008).

Neale, Steve, *Genre* (London: British Film Institute, 1980).

Osteen, Mark (ed.), *Hitchcock and Adaptation: On the Page and Screen* (Lanham, MD: Rowman & Littlefield, 2014).

Palmer, R. Barton, *Hollywood's Dark Cinema: The American Film Noir* (New York: Twaye, 1994?).

Palmer, R. Barton, and David Boyd (eds), *Hitchcock at the Source: The Auteur as Adaptor* (Albany, NY: State University of New York Press, 2011).

Polmar, Norman and Thomas B. Allen, *Spy Book: The Encyclopedia of Espionage* (London: Greenhill Books, 1987).

Raubicheck, Walter and Walter Srebnick (eds), *Hitchcock's Rereleased Films* (Detroit, MI: Wayne State University Press, 1991).

Ray, Robert B., *A Certain Tendency of the Hollywood Cinema, 1930–1980* (Princeton, NJ: Princeton University Press, 1985).

Richards, Jeffrey, *The Age of the Dream Palace: Cinema and Society in Britain 1930–1939* (London: Routledge & Kegan Paul, 1984).

Richards, Jeffrey and Dorothy Sheridan (eds), *Mass-Observation at the Movies* (London: Routledge & Kegan Paul, 1987).

Robertson, James, *The British Board of Film Censors: Film Censorship in Britain, 1896–1950* (London: Croom Helm, 1985).

Rohmer, Eric and Claude Chabrol, *Hitchcock: The First Forty-Four Films*, trans. Stanley Hochman (New York: Ungar, 1988).

Rothman, William, *Hitchcock: The Murderous Gaze* (Cambridge, MA: Harvard University Press, 1982).

Ryall, Tom, *Alfred Hitchcock and the British Cinema* (London: Croom Helm, 1986).

Rubin, Martin, *Thrillers* (Cambridge: Cambridge University Press, 1999).

Rubin, Steven Jay, *The James Bond Films: A Behind the Scenes History* (London: Talisman Books, 1981).

Sarris, Andrew, *The American Cinema: Directors and Directions 1929–1968* (New York: Da Capa Press, 1996 [1968]).

Schatz, Thomas, *The Genius of the System: Hollywood Filmmaking in the Studio Era* (New York: Pantheon, 1988).

Schatz, Thomas, *History of the American Cinema*, vol. 6, *Boom and Bust: American Cinema in the 1940s* (Berkeley, CA: University of California Press, 1997).

Sedgwick, John, *Popular Filmgoing in 1930s Britain: A Choice of Pleasures* (Exeter: University of Exeter Press, 2000).

Segrave, Kerry, *American Films Abroad: Hollywood's Domination of the World's Movie Screens from the 1890s to the Present* (Jefferson, NC: McFarland, 1997).

Sellers, Robert, *The Battle for Bond: The Genesis of Cinema's Greatest Hero* (Sheffield: Tomahawk Press, 2007).

Shaw, Tony, *British Cinema and the Cold War: The State, Propaganda and Consensus* (London: I.B.Tauris, 2001).

Shaw, Tony, *Hollywood's Cold War* (Edinburgh: Edinburgh University Press, 2007).

Shaw, Tony, *Cinematic Terror: A Global History of Terrorism on Film* (New York: Bloomsbury, 2015).

Shindler, Colin, *Hollywood Goes to War: Films and American Society 1939–52* (London: Routledge & Kegan Paul, 1979).

Sinyard, Neil, *The Films of Alfred Hitchcock* (London: Admiral Books, 1986).

Sloan, Jane E., *Alfred Hitchcock: A Filmography and Bibliography* (Berkeley, CA: University of California Press, 1993).

Spicer, Andrew, *Film Noir* (Harlow: Pearson Education, 2002).

Spoto, Donald, *The Art of Alfred Hitchcock: Fifty Years of his Motion Pictures* (New York: Doubleday, 1976).

Stape, J.H. (ed.), *The Cambridge Companion to Joseph Conrad* (Cambridge: Cambridge University Press, 1996).

Street, Sarah, *Transatlantic Crossings: British Feature Films in the United States* (London: Continuum, 2002).

Symons, Julian, *Bloody Murder: From the Detective Story to the Crime Novel: A History* (Harmondsworth: Allen Lane, rev. edn 1985).

Taylor, A.J.P., *English History 1914–1945* (Oxford: Oxford University Press, 1965).

Thompson, Kristin and David Bordwell, *Film History: An Introduction* (New York: McGraw Hill, 1994).

Wark, Wesley K. (ed.), *Spy Fiction, Spy Films, and Real Intelligence* (London: Frank Cass, 1991).

Watt, Ian (ed.), *Conrad: The Secret Agent – A Casebook* (London: Macmillan, 1973).

Wood, Robin, *Hitchcock's Films* (London: Zwemmer, 1965).

Wood, Robin, *Hitchcock's Films Revisited* (London: Faber & Faber, 1991).

Yacowar, Maurice, *Hitchcock's British Films* (New York: Archon Books, 1977).

ARTICLES AND CHAPTERS

Abrast, Merritt, 'Hitchcock's Terrorists: Sources and Significance', *Literature/Film Quarterly*, 39/3 (2011), pp. 165–73.

Anderegg, Michael A., 'Conrad and Hitchcock: *The Secret Agent* Inspires *Sabotage*', *Literature/Film Quarterly*, 3/3 (1975), pp. 214–25.

Anderson, Lindsay, 'Alfred Hitchcock', *Sequence*, 9 (1949), pp. 113–24.

Barr, Charles, 'Deserter or Honored Exile? Views of Hitchcock from Wartime Britain', *Hitchcock Annual*, 13 (2004–5), pp. 1–24.

Bennett, Michael Todd, 'Anglophilia on Film: Creating an Alliance, 1935–41', *Film and History*, 24/1–4 (1997), pp. 4–21.

Bertens, Hans, 'A Society of Murderers Run on Sound Conservative Lines: The Life and Times of Sapper's Bulldog Drummond', in Clive Bloom (ed.), *Twentieth-Century Suspense: The Thriller Comes of Age* (London: Macmillan, 1990), pp. 51–68.

Camp, Jocelyn, 'John Buchan and Alfred Hitchcock', *Literature/Film Quarterly*, 6/3 (1978), pp. 230–40.

Cavell, Stanley, '*North by Northwest*', *Critical Enquiry*, 7/4 (1981), pp. 761–76.

Chapman, James, 'Celluloid Shockers', in Jeffrey Richards (ed.), *The Unknown 1930s: An Alternative History of the British Cinema, 1929–1939* (London: I.B.Tauris, 1998), pp. 75–97.

Chapman, James, 'Hitchcock and Bond', *Hitchcock Annual*, 19 (2014), pp. 153–80.

Detelbaum, Marshall, 'Seeing in *Saboteur*', *Literature/Film Quarterly*, 12/1 (1984), pp. 58–64.

Dickstein, Morris, 'Beyond Good and Evil: The Morality of Thrillers', *American Film*, 6/9 (1981), pp. 49–52.

Dyer, Peter John, 'Young and Innocent', *Sight and Sound*, 30/2 (Spring 1961), pp. 80–3.

Elsaesser, Thomas, 'Too Big and Too Close: Alfred Hitchcock and Fritz Lang', *Hitchcock Annual*, 12 (2003–4), pp. 1–41.

Frayne, John P., '*North by Northwest*', *Journal of Aesthetic Education*, 9/2 (1975), pp. 77–95.

Friedman, Seth, 'Misdirection in Fits and Starts: Alfred Hitchcock's Popular Reputation and the Reception of his Films', *Quarterly Review of Film and Video*, 29 (2012), pp. 76–94.

Fuller, Graham, 'Mystery Train', *Sight and Sound*, NS 18/1 (Dec. 2008), pp. 36–40.

Gilbert, Nora, '"She Makes Love for the Papers": Love, Sex and Exploitation in Hitchcock's Mata Hari films', *Film and History*, 41/2 (2011), pp. 6–18.

Gitelman, Lisa, and Jonathan Auerbach, 'Microfilm, Containment and the Cold War', *American Literary History*, 19/3 (2007), pp. 745–68.

Glancy, H.M., 'Warner Bros. Film Grosses, 1921–1951: The William Schaefer Ledger', *Historical Journal of Film, Radio and Television*, 15/1 (1995), pp. 127–44.

Gough-Yates, Kevin, 'The British Feature Film as a European Concern: Britain and the Emigré Film-Maker, 1933–45', in Günter Berghaus (ed.), *Theatre and Film in Exile: German Artists in Britain, 1933–1945* (Oxford: Berg, 1989), pp. 125–46.

Hardy, Sylvia, 'H. G. Wells and British Silent Cinema: The War of the Worlds', in Andrew Higson (ed.), *Young and Innocent? The Cinema in Britain 1896–1930* (Exeter: University of Exeter Press, 2002), pp. 242–55.

Harper, Sue, 'A Lower Middle-Class Taste Community in the 1930s: Admissions Figures at the Regent Cinema, Portsmouth', *Historical Journal of Film, Radio and Television*, 24/4 (2004), pp. 565–87.

Hartman, Geoffrey H., 'Plenty of Nothing: Hitchcock's *North by Northwest*', *Yale Review*, 71/1 (1981), pp. 13–27.

Hicks, Marianne, '"No War This Year": Selkirk Porter and the Editorial Policy of the *Daily Express*, 1938–39', *Media History*, 14/2 (2008), pp. 167–83.

Homberger, Eric, 'English Spy Thrillers in the Age of Appeasement', *Intelligence and National Security*, 5/1 (1990), pp. 80–91.

Houston, Penelope, '007', *Sight and Sound*, 34 (Winter 1964–5), pp. 16–18.

Keane, Marian, 'The Design of Authorship', *Wide Angle*, 4 (1980), pp. 43–56.

Kerr, Paul, 'Out of What Past? Notes on the B *Film Noir*', in Paul Kerr (ed.), *The Hollywood Film Industry* (London: Routledge & Kegan Paul/British Film Institute, 1986), pp. 220–45.

Leff, Leonard J., 'Hitchcock at Metro', *Western Humanities Review*, 37/2 (1983), pp. 97–124.

Leitch, Thomas M., 'Murderous Victims in *The Secret Agent* and *Sabotage*', *Literature/Film Quarterly*, 14/1 (1986), pp. 64–8.

Leitch, Thomas M., 'It's the Cold War, Stupid: An Obvious History of the Political in Hitchcock', *Literature/Film Quarterly*, 27/1 (1999), pp. 3–15.

Leitch, Thomas M., '*Notorious*: Hitchcock's Pivotal Film', *Hitchcock Annual*, 17 (2011), pp. 1–42.

McDougal, Stuart, 'Mirth, Sexuality and Suspense: Alfred Hitchcock's Adaptation of *The 39 Steps*', *Literature/Film Quarterly*, 3/3 (1975), pp. 232–9.

Marantz Cohen, Paula, 'The Ideological Transformation of Conrad's *The Secret Agent* into Hitchcock's *Sabotage*', *Literature/Film Quarterly*, 22/3 (1994), pp. 199–220.

Morris, Christopher D., 'The Direction of *North by Northwest*', *Cinema Journal*, 36/4 (1997), pp. 43–56.

Neale, Steve, 'Propaganda', *Screen*, 18/3 (1977), pp. 9–40.

Osteen, Mark, '"It Doesn't Pay to Antagonize the Public": *Sabotage* and Hitchcock's Audience', *Literature/Film Quarterly*, 28/4 (2000), pp. 259–68.

Pett, John, 'A Master of Suspense', *Films and Filming*, 6/2 (1959), pp. 33–4.

Pett, John, 'Improving on the Formula', *Films and Filming*, 6/3 (1959), pp. 9–10.

Phillips, Louis, 'Wherein the Truth Lies: Honesty and Deception in Hitchcock's *North by Northwest*', *Armchair Detective*, 20/3 (1987), p. 254.

Pronay, Nicholas, 'The First Reality: Film Censorship in Liberal England', in K.R.M. Short (ed.), *Feature Films as History* (London: Croom Helm, 1981), pp. 113–37.

Renov, Michael, 'From Identification to Ideology: The Male System of Hitchcock's *Notorious*', *Wide Angle*, 4 (1980), pp. 30–7.

Richards, Jeffrey, 'The British Board of Film Censors and Content Control in the 1930s (1): Images of Britain', *Historical Journal of Film, Radio and Television*, 1/2 (1981), pp. 97–116.

Richards, Jeffrey, 'The British Board of Film Censors and Content Control in the 1930s (2): Foreign Affairs', *Historical Journal of Film, Radio and Television*, 2/1 (1982), pp. 39–48.

Richards, Jeffrey, and Jeffrey Hulbert, 'Censorship in Action: The Case of *Lawrence of Arabia*', *Journal of Contemporary History*, 19/1 (1984), pp. 153–69.

Rossi, John, 'Hitchcock's *Foreign Correspondent*', *Film and History*, 12/2 (1982), pp. 24–34.

Rothman, William, 'Alfred Hitchcock's *Notorious*', *Georgia Review*, 29/4 (1975), pp. 884–927.

Russell, Lee [Peter Wollen], 'Alfred Hitchcock', *New Left Review*, 35 (1966), pp. 89–92.

Schenkman, Richard, 'The Terence Young Interview', *Bondage*, 10 (1981), pp. 7–11.

Sedgwick, John, 'Michael Balcon's Close Encounter with the American Market, 1934–36', *Historical Journal of Film, Radio and Television*, 16/3 (1996), pp. 333–48.

Shaw, Simon, '"Not Forgotten": The 1939 IRA Bomb Attack', *Historic Coventry*, <www.historiccoventry.co.uk/articles/s-shaw.php> (accessed March 2016).

Smith, Gregory O., 'Jolly Old Sports: English Character, Comedy, and Cricket in *The Lady Vanishes*', *Film and History*, 42/2 (2012), pp. 55–70.

Smith, James, 'The MacDonald Discussion Group: A Communist Conspiracy in Britain's Cold War Film and Theatre Industry – or MI5's Honey-Pot?', *Historical Journal of Film, Radio and Television*, 35/3 (2015), pp. 454–72.

Smith, John M., 'Conservative Individualism: A Selection of English Hitchcock', *Screen*, 13/3 (1973), pp. 51–69.

Swindell, Larry, '1939: A Very Good Year', *American Film*, 1/3 (1975), p. 28.

Walker, Cynthia W., '*The Man From U.N.C.L.E.* Ian Fleming's Other Spy', in Robert G. Weiner, B. Lynn Whitfield and Jack Becker (eds), *James Bond in World and Popular Culture: The Films are Not Enough* (Newcastle upon Tyne: Cambridge Scholars Publishing, 2010), pp. 235–51.

Walker, Michael, '"A Hitchcock Compendium": Narrative Strategies in *Torn Curtain*', *Hitchcock Annual*, 14 (2006), pp. 95–120.

Walker, Michael, '*Topaz* and Cold War Politics', *Hitchcock Annual*, 13 (2004–5), pp. 127–53.

West, Nigel, 'Fiction, Faction and Intelligence', *Intelligence and National Security*, 9/2 (2004), pp. 275–89.

Wierzbicki, James, 'Grand Illusion: The "Storm Cloud" Music in Hitchcock's *The Man Who Knew Too Much*', *Journal of Film Music*, 1/2–3 (2003), pp. 217–38.

Wollen, Peter, '*North by Northwest*: A Morphological Analysis', *Film Form*, 1 (1976), pp. 9–34.

Wood, Robin, 'Hitchcock and Fascism', *Hitchcock Annual*, 13 (2004–5), pp. 25–63.

FILMOGRAPHY

THE MAN WHO KNEW TOO MUCH

GB. Gaumont-British Picture Corporation. 1934.

Director: Alfred Hitchcock. *Producer:* Michael Balcon. *Associate producer:* Ivor Montagu. *Screenplay:* Charles Bennett and D. B. Wyndham Lewis. *Scenario:* Edwin Greenwood and A. R. Rawlinson. *Additional dialogue:* Emlyn Williams. *Photography:* Curt Courant. *Art direction:* Alfred Junge. *Editor:* H. St C. Stewart. *Unit production manager:* Richard Beville. *Music:* Arthur Benjamin. *Musical director:* Louis Levy. *Running time:* 75 minutes.

Cast: Leslie Banks (Bob Lawrence), Edna Best (Jill Lawrence), Peter Lorre (Abbott), Frank Vosper (Ramon), Hugh Wakefield (Clive), Nova Pilbeam (Betty), Pierre Fresnay (Louis Bernard), Cicely Oates (Nurse Agnes), D. A. Clarke Smith (Inspector Binstead), George Curzon (Gibson). Uncredited actors include Clare Greet (Mrs Sprocket), Henry Oscar (Barbor), Charles Paton (Shop proprietor), and Frederick Piper and a young George Sanders as uniformed policemen. I have not been able to identify a cameo appearance by Hitchcock in the film: although he had appeared in several previous films – including *The Lodger, Blackmail* and *Murder!* – the director's cameo had not yet become a custom. Some sources suggest that Hitchcock's are the hands holding the cymbals in close up during the Albert Hall sequence.

THE 39 STEPS

GB. Gaumont-British Picture Corporation. 1935.

Director: Alfred Hitchcock. *Producer:* Michael Balcon. *Associate producer:* Ivor Montagu. *Adaptation:* Charles Bennett. From the novel by John Buchan. *Continuity:* Alma Reville. *Dialogue:* Ian Hay. *Photography:* Bernard Knowles.

Editor: Derek Twist. *Art direction:* O. Werndorff. *Dresses:* J. Strassner. *Wardrobe:* Marianne. *Musical director:* Louis Levy. *Running time:* 81 minutes.

Cast: Robert Donat (Richard Hannay), Madeleine Carroll (Pamela), Lucie Mannheim (Miss Smith), Godfrey Tearle (Professor Jordan), Peggy Ashcroft (Crofter's wife), John Laurie (Crofter), Helen Haye (Mrs Jordan), Frank Cellier (Sheriff), Wylie Watson (Mr Memory), Jerry Verno, Gus MacNaughton (Commercial travellers), Peggy Simpson (Maid). Uncredited actors include Frederick Piper (Milkman) and Miles Malleson (London Palladium manager). Hitchcock makes his cameo appearance as a passer-by dropping litter outside the music hall as Hannay boards the bus with Annabella Smith.

SECRET AGENT

GB. Gaumont-British Picture Corporation. 1936.

Director: Alfred Hitchcock. *Producer:* Michael Balcon. *Associate producer:* Ivor Montagu. *Screenplay:* Charles Bennett. From the play by Campbell Dixon based on the novel *Ashenden* by W. Somerset Maugham. *Dialogue:* Ian Hay. *Continuity:* Alma Reville. *Additional dialogue:* Jesse Lasky Jr. *Photography:* Bernard Knowles. *Editor:* Charles Frend. *Art direction:* O. Werndorff. *Dresses:* J. Strassner. *Musical director:* Louis Levy. *Running time:* 83 minutes.

Cast: John Gielgud (Ashenden/Brodie), Madeleine Carroll (Elsa Carrington), Peter Lorre (The General), Robert Young (Marvin), Percy Marmont (Caypor), Florence Kahn (Mrs Caypor), Charles Carson ('R'), Lilli Palmer (Lilli). Uncredited actors include Howard Marion Crawford as Carl. No Hitchcock cameo identified.

SABOTAGE

GB. Gaumont-British Picture Corporation. 1936.

Director: Alfred Hitchcock. *Producer:* Michael Balcon. *Associate producer:* Ivor Montagu. *Screenplay:* Charles Bennett. From the novel *The Secret Agent* by Joseph Conrad. *Dialogue:* Ian Hay, Helen Simpson. *Continuity:* Alma Reville. *Additional dialogue:* E. V. H. Emmett. *Photography:* Bernard Knowles. *Editor:* Charles Frend. *Art direction:* O. Werndorff. *Dresses:* J. Strassner. *Wardrobe:* Marianne. *Musical director:* Louis Levy. Cartoon sequence by arrangement with Walt Disney. *Running time:* 75 minutes.

Cast: Sylvia Sidney (Mrs Verloc), Oscar Homolka (Verloc), John Loder (Ted), Desmond Tester (Stevie), Joyce Barbour (Renee), Matthew Boulton (Superintendent Talbot), William Dewhurst (The Professor), S. J. Warmington

(Hollingshead). Uncredited actors include Torin Thatcher (Yunct), Aubrey Mather (Greengrocer), Martita Hunt (The Professor's daughter), Frederick Piper (Bus conductor) and a young Charles Hawtrey as a visitor to the London Aquarium. No Hitchcock cameo identified.

THE LADY VANISHES

GB. Gainsborough Pictures. 1938.

Director: Alfred Hitchcock. *Producer:* Edward Black. *Screenplay:* Sidney Gilliat and Frank Launder. Based upon the novel *The Wheel Spins* by Ethel Lina White. *Continuity:* Alma Reville. *Photography:* Jack Cox. *Editing:* R. E. Dearing. *Cutter:* Alfred Roome. *Settings (art direction):* [Alexander] Vetchinsky. *Musical director:* Louis Levy. *Running time:* 97 minutes.

Cast: Margaret Lockwood (Iris Henderson), Michael Redgrave (Gilbert), Paul Lukas (Dr Hartz), Dame May Whitty (Miss Froy), Cecil Parker (Mr Todhunter), Linden Travers ('Mrs' Todhunter), Naunton Wayne (Caldicott), Basil Radford (Charters), Mary Clare (Baroness), Emile Boreo (Hotel manager), Googie Withers (Blanche), Sally Stewart (Julie), Philip Leaver (Signor Doppo), Zelma Van Dias (Signora Doppo), Catherine Lacey (Nun), Josephine Wilson (Madame Kumar), Charles Oliver (Officer), Kathleen Tremaine (Anna). Hitchcock appears near the end of the film as a passer-by shrugging his shoulders at Victoria Station.

FOREIGN CORRESPONDENT

USA. Walter Wanger Productions/United Artists. 1940.

Director: Alfred Hitchcock. *Producer:* Walter Wanger. *Screenplay:* Charles Bennett, Joan Harrison. *Dialogue:* James Hilton, Robert Benchley. *Director of photography:* Rudolph Maté. *Associate:* Richard Irvine. *Special photographic effects:* Paul Eagler. *Art direction:* Alexander Golitzen. *Interior decoration:* Julia Heron. *Supervising editor:* Otto Lovering. *Editor:* Dorothy Spencer. *Costumes:* I. Magnin & Co. *Special production effects:* William Cameron Menzies. *Music:* Alfred Newman. *Running time:* 120 minutes.

Cast: Joel McCrea (Johnny Jones), Laraine Day (Carol Fisher), Herbert Marshall (Stephen Fisher), George Sanders (Scott ffolliott), Albert Bassermann (Van Meer), Robert Benchley (Stebbins), Edmund Gwenn (Rowley), Eduardo Ciannelli (Krug), Harry Davenport (Powers), Martin Kosleck (Tramp), Frances Carson (Mrs Sprague), Ian Wolfe (Stiles), Edward Conrad (Latvian gentleman), Charles Wagenheim (Assassin), Charles Halton (Bradley), Barbara Pepper

(Dorine), Emory Powell (Captain of USS *Mohican*), Roy Gordon (Mr Brood), Gertrude Hoffman (Mrs Benson), Martin Lamont (Captain of aircraft), Barry Bernard (Steward), Holmes Herbert (Assistant Commissioner), Leonard Mudie (McKenna), John Burton (English announcer). Hitchcock makes his cameo appearance as a man reading a newspaper on the street when Johnny hears someone call Van Meer's name.

SABOTEUR

USA. Frank Lloyd Productions/Universal Pictures. 1942.

Director: Alfred Hitchcock. *Producer:* Frank Lloyd. *Associate producer:* Jack H. Skirball. *Original screenplay:* Peter Viertel, Joan Harrison, Dorothy Parker. *Director of photography:* Joseph Valentine. *Art direction:* Jack Otterson. *Associate:* Robert Boyle. *Set decorations:* R. A. Gausman. *Editor:* Otto Ludwig. *Musical director:* Charles Previn. *Musical score:* Frank Skinner. *Running time:* 109 minutes.

Cast: Robert Cummings (Barry Kane), Priscilla Lane (Patricia Martin), Otto Kruger (Tobin), Alan Baxter (Freeman), Norman Lloyd (Fry), Alma Kruger (Mrs Sutton), Clem Bevans (Neilson), Vaughan Glazer (Mr Miller), Dorothy Peterson (Mrs Mason), Ian Wolfe (Robert), Frances Carson (Society woman), Murray Alper (Truck driver), Kathryn Adams (Young mother), Pedro de Cordoba (Bones), Billy Curtis ('The Major'), Marie Le Deaux (Fat woman), Anita Bolster (Lorelei), Jeanne Romer and Lynn Romer (Siamese Twins). Hitchcock makes his cameo appearance standing outside a drugstore in New York.

NOTORIOUS

USA. A Selznick Release for RKO Radio Pictures. 1946.

Producer and director: Alfred Hitchcock. *Screenplay:* Ben Hecht. *Production assistant:* Barbara Kean. *Director of photography:* Ted Tetzlaff. *Special effects:* Vernon L. Walker, Paul Eagler. *Art directors:* Albert S. D'Agostino, Carroll Clark. *Set decorations:* Darrell Silvera, Claude Carpenter. *Editor:* Theron Warth. *Costumes:* Edith Head. *Musical director:* C. Bakaleinikoff. *Orchestral arrangement:* Gil Grau. *Running time:* 100 minutes.

Cast: Cary Grant (Devlin), Ingrid Bergman (Alicia Huberman), Claude Rains (Alexander Sebastian), Louis Calhern (Paul Prescott), Madame Konstantin (Madame Sebastian), Reinhold Schunzel (Dr Anderson), Moroni Olsen (Beardsley), Ivan Triesault (Eric Mathis), Alex Minotis (Joseph), Wally Brown (Hopkins), Sir Charles Mendl (Commodore), Ricardo Costa (Dr Barbosa),

Edward Krumschmidt (Hupka), Fay Baker (Ethel). Hitchcock makes his cameo appearance as a guest drinking champagne at Sebastian's reception.

THE MAN WHO KNEW TOO MUCH

USA. Paramount Pictures. 1956.

Producer and director: Alfred Hitchcock. *Associate producer:* Herbert Coleman. *Screenplay:* John Michael Hayes. Based on a story by Charles Bennett and D. B. Wyndham Lewis. *Director of photography:* Robert Burks. Technicolor. Vista-Vision. *Technicolor consultant:* Richard Mueller. *Art direction:* Hal Pereira and Henry Bumstead. *Set decoration:* Sam Komen and Arthur Kramer. *Editor:* George Tomasini. *Special photographic effects:* John P. Fulton. *Costumes:* Edith Head. *Music:* Bernard Herrmann. *'Storm Cloud Cantata' by:* Arthur Benjamin and D. B. Wyndham Lewis. *Songs:* 'Whatever Will Be' and 'We'll Love Again' by Jay Livingston and Ray Evans. *Running time:* 120 minutes.

Cast: James Stewart (Dr Ben McKenna), Doris Day (Jo McKenna), Brenda de Banzie (Mrs Drayton), Bernard Miles (Drayton), Ralph Truman (Inspector Buchanan), Daniel Galin (Louis Bernard), Mogens Wieth (Ambassador), Alan Mowbray (Val Parnell), Hillary Brooke (Jan Peterson), Christopher Olsen (Hank McKenna), Reggie Nalder (Rien), Richard Wattis (Assistant manager), Noel William (Woburn), Alix Talton (Helen Parnell), Caroline Jones (Cindy Fontaine), George Howe (Ambrose Chappell), Richard Wordsworth (Ambrose Chappel Jr). Hitchcock makes his cameo appearance as one of the crowd watching the acrobats in Marrakesh.

NORTH BY NORTHWEST

USA. Metro-Goldwyn-Mayer. 1959.

Producer and director: Alfred Hitchcock. *Associate producer:* Herbert Coleman. *Screenplay:* Ernest Lehman. *Director of photography:* Robert Burks. Technicolor. VistaVision. *Colour consultant:* Charles K. Hagedon. *Production designer:* Robert Boyle. *Art directors:* William A. Horning & Merrill Pye. *Set decorators:* Henry Grace & Frank McKelvey. *Editor:* George Tomasini. *Special effects:* A. Arnold Gillespie & Lee LeBlanc. *Titles:* Saul Bass. *Music:* Bernard Herrmann. *Running time:* 136 mins.

Cast: Cary Grant (Roger Thornhill), Eva Marie Saint (Eve Kendall), James Mason (Phillip Vandamm), Jessie Royce Landis (Mrs Thornhill), Leo G. Carroll (The Professor), Josephine Hutchinson ('Mrs Townsend'), Philip Ober (Lester Townsend), Martin Laundau (Leonard), Adam Williams (Valerian), Robert

Ellenstein (Licht), Edward Platt (Victor Larrabee), Les Tremayne (Auctioneer), Philip Coolidge (Dr Cross), Edward Binns (Captain Junkett), Patrick McVey (Sergeant Flamm), Ken Lynch (Charlie), John Beradino (Sergeant Emil Klinger), Nora Marlowe (Anna), Doreen Lang (Maggie), Anderson Lockwood (Judge). Hitchcock makes his cameo at the end of the opening titles as a man missing a bus.

TORN CURTAIN

USA. Universal Pictures. 1966.

Producer and director: Alfred Hitchcock. *Associate producer:* Herbert Coleman. *Screenplay:* Brian Moore. *Director of photography:* John F. Warren. Technicolor. *Production designer:* Hein Hockrith. *Art director:* Frank Arrigo. *Set decoration:* George Milo. *Editor:* Bud Hoffman. *Special effects:* Albert Whitlock. *Costume supervisor:* Grady Hunt. *Miss Andrews's costumes:* Edith Head. *Music:* John Addison. *Running time:* 120 minutes.

Cast: Paul Newman (Professor Michael Armstrong), Julie Andrews (Sarah Sherman), Lila Kedrova (Countess Kuchinska), Hansjoerg Felmy (Gerhard), Wolfgang Kieling (Gromek), Tamara Toumanova (Ballerina), Ludwig Donath (Professor Gustav Lindt), Günter Strack (Professor Karl Manfred), David Opatoshu (Jacobi), Gisela Fischer (Dr Koska), Mort Mills (Farmer), Carolyn Conwell (Farmer's wife), Arthur Gould-Porter (Freddy), Gloria Gorvin (Fraulein Mann), Robert Boon (Professor Winkelmann), Peter Bourne (Professor Henstrom), Rico Cattani (Heinrich). Peter Lorre Jr appears uncredited as the taxi driver who takes Armstrong to the farm. Hitchcock's cameo is as a man sitting with a baby on his lap in the hotel lobby.

TOPAZ

USA. Universal Pictures. 1969.

Producer and director: Alfred Hitchcock. *Associate producer:* Herbert Coleman. *Screenplay:* Samuel Taylor. From the novel by Leon Uris. *Director of photography:* Jack Hildyard. Technicolor. *Special photographic effects:* Albert Whitlock. *Production designer:* Henry Bumstead. *Set decorations:* Joh Austin. *Editor:* William H. Ziegler. *Costumes:* Edith Head. *Men's costume supervisor:* Peter Saldutti. *Music:* Maurice Jarre. *Cuban technical adviser:* J. P. Mathieu. *French technical adviser:* Odette Ferry. *Running time:* 126 minutes.

Cast: Frederick Stafford (André Devereaux), John Forsythe (Michael Nordstrom), Dany Robin (Nicole Devereaux), John Vernon (Rico Parra),

Karin Dor (Juanita de Cordoba), Michel Piccoli (Jacques Granville), Philippe Noiret (Henri Jarre), Claude Jade (Michele Picard), Michel Subor (François Picard), Roscoe Lee Browne (Philippe DuBois), Per-Axel Arosenius (Boris Kusenov), Edmon Ryan (McKittreck), Sonya Kolthoff (Mrs Kusenov), Tina Hedstrom (Tamara Kusenov), John Van Dreelen (Claude Martin), Don Randolph (Luis Uribe), Roberto Contreras (Muñoz), Carlos Rivas (Hernandez), Roger Til (Jean Chabrier), Lewis Charles (Mendoza), Anna Navarro (Carlotta Mendoza), Sandor Szabo (Emile Redon), Lew Brown (American official), John Roper (Thomas), George Skaff (René d'Arcy). Hitchcock makes his cameo appearance as a man in a wheelchair at the airport as Devereaux and Nicole meet their daughter Michele and her fiancé François.

INDEX